**Advances
in
Genetics**

Volume 40
Cumulative Subject Index
Volumes 20–39

Advances
in
Genetics

Volume 40
Cumulative Subject Index
Volumes 20–39

QH
431
.A1
A3
v. 40

Edited by

Jeffery C. Hall
Department of Biology
Brandeis University
Waltham, Massachusetts

Jay C. Dunlap
Department of Biochemistry
Dartmouth Medical School
Hanover, New Hampshire

Theodore Friedmann
Department of Pediatrics
Center for Molecular Genetics
  School of Medicine
University of California, San Diego
  La Jolla, California

Francesco Giannelli
Division of Medical & Molecular
  Genetics
United Medical & Dental Schools of
  Guy's and St. Thomas' Hospitals
London Bridge London,
  United Kingdom

Academic Press
San Diego   New York   Boston   London   Sydney   Tokyo   Toronto

This book is printed on acid-free paper. ∞

Academic Press
a division of Harcourt Brace & Company
525 B Street, Suite 1900, San Diego, California 92101-4495, USA
http://www.apnet.com

Academic Press
24-28 Oval Road, London NW1 7DX, UK
http://www.hbuk.co.uk/ap/

International Standard Book Number: 0-12-017640-8

PRINTED IN THE UNITED STATES OF AMERICA
98 99 00 01 02 03 EB 9 8 7 6 5 4 3 2 1

Contents

Contents of Volumes 20–39

VOLUME 20

Influenza Virus Genetics   1
Christoph Scholtissek

Genetics of Applied Microbiology   38
Vedpal Singh Malik

Plant Tissue Cultures in Genetics and Plant Breeding   127
Indra K. Vasil, Mulkh R. Ahuja, and Vimla Vasil

Mechanisms of Genetic Sex Determination, Gonadal
Sex Differentiation, and Germ-Cell Development
in Animals   217
John R. McCarrey and Ursula K. Abbott

Recent Advances in Histocompatibility
Immunogenetics   291
George D. Snell

Hereditary Anemias of the Mouse: A Review
for Geneticists   358
Elizabeth S. Russell

VOLUME 21

The *Ah* Locus, A Multigene Family Necessary for Survival
in a Chemically Adverse Environment: Comparison with
the Immune System   2
Daniel W. Nebert, Masahiko Negishi, Matti A. Lang,
Leonard M. Hjelmeland, and Howard J. Eisen

Expression of Ribosomal Genes in Bacteria   53
Lasse Lindahl and Janice M. Zengel

The Genetics of Transfer RNA in *Drosophila*   123
Eric Kubli

Mutagenesis in *Saccharomyces cerevisiae*   173
Christopher W. Lawrence

Triticale: Present Status and Future Prospects   256
P. K. Gupta and P. M. Priyadarshan

Regulatory Gene Variation in Higher Plants   347
John G. Scandalios and James A. Baum

VOLUME 22

Structural Variation in Mitochondrial DNA   2
Ronald R. Sederoff

**The Structure and Expression of Nuclear Genes
in Higher Plants**   109
John C. Sorenson

**Chromatin Structure and Gene Regulation
in Higher Plants**   145
Steven Spiker

**The Molecular Genetics of Crown Gall
Tumorigenesis**   210
P. J. J. Hooykaas and R. A. Schilperoort

VOLUME 23

Recovery, Repair, and Mutagenesis in *Schizosaccharomyces pombe*   1
J. Phipps, A. Nasim, and D. R. Miller

Gene Transfer in Fungi   74
N. C. Mishra

Y Chromosome Function and Spermatogenesis in *Drosophila hydei*   179
Wolfgang Hennig

Recent Developments in Population Genetics   235
Michael T. Clegg and Bryan K. Epperson

Genetics, Cytology, and Evolution of Gossypium   272
J. E. Endrizzi, E. L. Turcotte, and R. J. Kohel

VOLUME 24

Heat-Shock Proteins and Development   1
Ursula Bond and Milton J. Schlesinger

Mechanisms of Heat-Shock Gene Activation in Higher Eukaryotes   31
Mariann Bienz and Hugh R. B. Pelham

Regulatory Gene Action during Eukaryotic Development   73
Joel M. Chandlee and John G. Scandalios

The Genetics of Biogenic Amine Metabolism, Sclerotization, and Melanization in *Drosophila melanogaster*   127
Theodore R. F. Wright

Developmental Control and Evolution in the Chorion Gene Families of Insects   223
F. C. Kafatos, N. Spoerel, S. A. Mitsialis, H. T. Nguyen, C. Romano, J. R. Lingappa, B. D. Mariani, G. C. Rodakis, R. Lecanidou, and S. G. Tsitilou

The Significance of Split Genes to Developmental Genetics   243
Antoine Danchin

Gene Transfer into Mice   285
George Scangos and Charles Bieberich

The Molecular Basis of the Evolution of Sex   323
H. Bernstein, F. A. Hopf, and R. E. Michod

Gene Dosage Compensation in *Drosophila melanogaster*   371
John C. Lucchesi and Jerry E. Manning

Developmental Morphogenesis and Genetic Manipulation in Tissue and Cell Cultures of the Gramineae   431
Fionnuala Morrish, Vimla Vasil, and Indra K. Vasil

VOLUME 25

Transferrin: Evolution and Genetic Regulation of Expression   1
Barbara H. Bowman, Funmei Yang, and Gwendolyn S. Adrian

The *Drosophila* Alcohol Dehydrogenase
Gene–Enzyme System 40
Geoffrey K. Chambers

Genetics Research on Braconid Wasps 110
Daniel S. Grosch

The Variable Mitochondrial Genome of Ascomycetes:
Organization, Mutational Alterations, and Expression 186
Klaus Wolf and Luigi Del Giudice

VOLUME 26

Genetics of Angiosperm Pollen 1
Ercole Ottaviano and David L. Mulcahy

Microbial Superoxide Dismutases 65
Hosni M. Hassan

Bacterial Genes Involved in Response to Near-Ultraviolet
Radiation 100
A. Eisenstark

Meiosis in Maize: *mei* Genes and Conception of Genetic
Control of Meiosis 149
Inna N. Golubovskaya

VOLUME 27

Genetic Regulatory Hierarchy in *Caulobacter* Development 1
Ruth Bryan, David Glaser, and Lucille Shapiro

Combinatorial Associations of Regulatory Proteins and the Control of Cell Type in Yeast   33

George F. Sprague, Jr.

Genetic Control of Cell Type and Pattern Formation in *Caenorhabditis elegans*   63

Paul W. Sternberg

The Regulatory Hierarchy Controlling Sex Determination and Dosage Compensation in *Caenorhabditis elegans*   118

Anne M. Villeneuve and Barbara J. Meyer

Genetic Control of Sex Determination in *Drosophila*   189

Monica Steinmann-Zwicky, Hubert Amrein, and Rolf Nöthiger

Role of Gap Genes in Early *Drosophila* Development   239

Ulrike Gaul and Herbert Jäckle

Role of the *zerknüllt* Gene in Dorsal–Ventral Pattern Formation in *Drosophila*   277

Christine Rushlow and Michael Levine

Molecular and Genetic Organization of the Antennapedia Gene Complex of *Drosophila melanogaster*   309

Thomas C. Kaufman, Mark A. Seeger, and Gary Olsen

Establishment and Maintenance of Position-Specific Expression of the *Drosophila* Homeotic Selector Gene *Deformed*   363

William McGinnis, Thomas Jack, Robin Chadwick, Michael Regulski, Clare Bergson, Nadine McGinnis, and Michael A. Kuziora

Mechanisms of a Cellular Decision during Embryonic Development of *Drosophila melanogaster*: Epidermogenesis or Neurogenesis   403
José A. Campos-Ortega

VOLUME 28

Response of Plant Antioxidant Defense Genes to Environmental Stress   2
John G. Scandalios

Genetic Analysis of Oxygen Defense Mechanisms in *Drosophila melanogaster*   43
John P. Phillips and Arthur J. Hilliker

DNA Rearrangements in Response to Environmental Stress   73
Christopher A. Cullis

Molecular Genetics of Cold Acclimation in Higher Plants   99
Michael F. Thomashow

Influence of Environmental Factors on Photosynthetic Genes   133
Luis Herrera-Estrella and June Simpson

Activation, Structure, and Organization of Genes Involved in Microbial Defense in Plants   165
Richard A. Dixon and Maria J. Harrison

Molecular and Cellular Biology of the Heat-Shock Response   235
Ronald T. Nagao, Janice A. Kimpel, and Joe L. Key

Effects of Heat and Chemical Stress on Development   275

Nancy S. Petersen

VOLUME 29

Genetics and Molecular Biology of *Neurospora crassa*   2

N. C. Mishra

The Structure and Biogenesis of Yeast Ribosomes   63

John L. Woolford, Jr.

Evolutionary Genetics of Fish   120

Dennis A. Powers

***Drosophila* Transposable Elements: Mechanisms of Mutagenesis and Interactions with the Host Genome**   229

Patricia A. Smith and Victor G. Corces

The Genetics and Molecular Biology of *zeste* in *Drosophila melanogaster*   302

Vincenzo Pirrotta

VOLUME 30

Molecular Genetics of Nitrate Reductase in Higher Plants   1

Frédérique Pelsy and Michel Caboche

Genetic Implications of Somaclonal Variation in Plants   41

Virginia M. Peschke and Ronald L. Phillips

The *Mu* Elements of *Zea mays*   77
Vicki L. Chandler and Kristine J. Hardeman

Molecular Perspectives on the Genetics of Mosquitoes   123
Nora J. Besansky, Victoria G. Finnerty, and Frank H. Collins

Genetics and Molecular Biology of Telomeres   185
Harald Biessmann and James M. Mason

Molecular Genetics of Superoxide Dismutases in Yeasts and Related Fungi   252
Edith Butler Gralla and Daniel J. Kosman

Genetics of the Mammalian Carbonic Anhydrases   321
Richard E. Tashian

VOLUME 31

Sex, Segments, and the Central Nervous System: Common Genetic Mechanisms of Cell Fate Determination   1
Joseph B. Duffy and J. Peter Gergen

Neurogenesis in *Xenopus*: A Molecular Genetic Perspective   29
Beatriz Ferreiro and William A. Harris

Cell Cycle Genes of *Drosophila*   79
Cayetano Gonzalez, Luke Alphey, and David Glover

Genetic and Molecular Analysis of *Drosophila* Behavior   139
C. P. Kyriacou and Jeffrey C. Hall

Genetics and Molecular Genetics of Sulfur Assimilation in the Fungi   187
George A. Marzluf

Genetic and Biochemical Analysis of Alternative RNA Splicing   208
Dianne Hodges and Sanford I. Bernstein

VOLUME 32

After Gene Therapy: Issues in Long-Term Clinical Follow-Up and Care   1
Fred D. Ledley

Gaucher Disease   17
Ernest Beutler

The Genetics of Non-insulin-Dependent Diabetes Mellitus   51
T. S. Pillay, W. J. Langlois, and J. M. Olefsky

The Hemophilias   99
P. M. Green, J. A. Naylor, and F. Giannelli

The Influence of Molecular Biology on Our Understanding of Lipoprotein Metabolism and the Pathobiology of Atheosclerosis   141
Thomas P. Knecht and Christopher K. Glass

Molecular Genetics of Phenylketonuria: From Molecular Anthropology to Gene Therapy   199
Randy C. Eisensmith and Savio L. C. Woo

Sex Determination and its Pathology in Man   275
Alan J. Schafer

VOLUME 34

Morphology and Structure of Polytene Chromosomes   1
I. F. Zhimulev

VOLUME 35

Phototransduction and Circadian Clock Pathways Regulating Gene Transcription in Higher Plants   1
Shawn L. Anderson and Steve A. Kay

Apoptosis   35
Brian V. Harmon and David J. Allan

Molecular Basis for X-Linked Immunodeficiencies   57
C. I. Edvard Smith and Luigi D. Notarangelo

Gene Therapy of Duchenne Muscular Dystrophy   117
Ariberto Fassati, Stephen Murphy, and George Dickson

The Contribution of the Mouse to Advances in Human Genetics   155
Elizabeth M. C. Fisher

prune/Killer of prune: A Conditional Dominant Lethal Interaction in Drosophila   207
Lisa Timmons and Allen Shearn

Chiasmata, Crossovers, and Meiotic Chromosome Segregation   253
Carol A. Bascom-Slack, Lyle O. Ross, and Dean S. Dawson

Molecular Genetics of Familial Cardiomyopathies   285
Aman S. Coonar and William J. McKenna

VOLUME 36

The Peripheral Neuropathies and Their Molecular Genetics   1
C. Bell and N. Haites

Tumor Suppressor Genes and Human Cancer   45
Melissa A. Brown

Genetic Redundancy   137
John F. Y. Brookfield

Genetics of Hybrid Inviability in *Drosophila*   157
Pierre Hutter

Regulation of Bacterial Gene Expression by Metals   187
David J. Westenberg and Mary Lou Guerinot

Chromosome Rearrangements in *Neurospora* and Other Filamentous Fungi   239
David D. Perkins

VOLUME 37

Polytene Chromosomes, Heterochromatin, and Position Effect Variegation   1
I. F. Zhimulev

VOLUME 38

Body Plan Genes and Human Malformation   1
Edoardo Boncinelli, Antonio Mallamaci, and Vania Broccoli

Molecular Genetics of the Hereditary Ataxias   31
Massimo Pandolfo and Laura Montermini

The *Minute* Genes in *Drosophila* and Their Molecular Functions   69
Andrew Lambertsson

Genetics of Biological Rhythms in *Drosophila*   135
Jeffrey C. Hall

DNA Breakage and Repair   185
P. A. Jeggo

VOLUME 39

Genetic Organization of Polytene Chromosomes   1
I. F. Zhimulev

Subject Index

A1, *Mu* elements of *Zea mays* and, 30:92, 30:109, 30:113
Abf1p, yeast ribosomes and, 29:70–29:77, 29:84, 29:103
ABF1, yeast ribosomes and, 29:77
abnormal chemosensory jump mutant *Drosophila melanogaster*, 31:147–148
Abnormalities
  chromosomal, 33:101–130
  aneuploidy
    45,X, 33:109–110
    47,XXX, 33:110–113
    47,XXY, 33:110–113
    47,XYY, 33:113–114
  cell division origin, 33:107–109
  disomic gamete frequencies, 33:125–129
  monosomy
    etiology, 33:105–106
    frequency, 33:102–105
    overview, 33:101–102
  parental origin, 33:106–107
  sex chromosome polysomy, 33:114–115
  trisomy
    13, 33:122–123
    14, 33:122–123
    15, 33:122–123
    16, 33:121–122
    18, 33:120–121
    21, 33:115–120
    22, 33:122–123
  etiology, 33:105–106
  frequency, 33:102–105
  mechanisms, 33:123–125
  sex determination, 33:300–313
    familial agonadism, 33:313
    hermaphrodites, 33:311–313
    XX males, 33:308–313
    XY females, 33:301–308
abo gene, X chromosome, 37:59–60
Abscisic acid
  cor gene expression regulation
    alfalfa, 28:118–28:119
    Arabidopsis, 28:119

frost tolerance increase by, 28:117–28:118
Gramineae
  in developing embryo, wheat, 24:446
  in embryogenic callus after long-term culture, 24:452
  in young and mature leaves, *Pennisetum purpureum*, 24:448
  embryogenic callus production and, 24:449
  nitrate reductase and, 30:20
Ac, *Mu* elements of *Zea mays* and, 30:81, 30:111, 30:115
  properties of transposition, 30:105, 30:108
  structure, 30:91, 30:96
Accessory chromosomes, *see* B chromosomes
ACE1, superoxide dismutases and, 30:276–30:277, 30:277, 30:304
Ace gene, oligogene bands, 39:136
Acetate, superoxide dismutases and, 30:280, 30:285, 30:290, 30:296
Acetylcholine receptor, evolutionary genetics of fish and, 29:178
Acetylcholinesterase, mosquitoes and, 30:149–30:150
N-Acetyldopamine
  Drosophila
    developmental profile, 24:151–24:153
    glucosides in hemolymph, 24:143–24:145
N-Acetyltransferase, *Drosophila*, high activity in nervous tissue, 24:142
achaete gene, *Drosophila* transposable elements and, 29:245–29:246
achaete (T5) gene
  Drosophila melanogaster
    in neurogenesis, 31:16
    in sex determination, 31:8
Achlya, organization of mtDNA in, 22:46
Acid β-glucosidase
  Gaucher disease treatment, 32:29–30, 32:32, 32:35
Acid phosphatase, sex differences in braconid wasps, 25:141

1

Acinetobacter calcoaceticus, mercury resistance protein of, **36**:206

Acridine orange stain, intercalary heterochromatin identification, **37**:143–145

Acriflavine-nitrate, intercalary heterochromatin identification, **37**:146–149

ACTH, evolutionary genetics of fish and, **29**:197–**29**:198

Actin
genes coding for, **22**:128
mosquitoes and, **30**:144
Mu elements of *Zea mays* and, **30**:112

Actin-binding proteins
genes for *Drosophila melanogaster*, **31**:107
actin 5C gene, band–loop relations, **39**:156

Actin gene family, *Drosophila melanogaster*, **31**:106–107

α-Actinin
cis-acting mutations
effects on alternative splicing, **31**:258–259

Actinomycin D, transcription inhibition, **39**:68–71, 76

Activated protein C, *see* Protein C

Activator, somaclonal variation and, **30**:52–**30**:54, **30**:56

Activin gene
Xenopus laevis, **31**:41–43

Acute myeloid leukemia, p21 abnormalities in, **36**:63

Acute-phase reaction, TF synthesis and, **25**:27, **25**:28

N-Acylcysteinamide, in peptide, NUR absorption, **26**:108–**26**:109

Adaptation
evolutionary background of, **36**:138–**36**:139
evolutionary genetics of fish and, **29**:158–**29**:161, **29**:163–**29**:164, **29**:202

Adenosine, RNA synthesis inhibition, **39**:70

Adenosine deaminase deficiency disorder, gene therapy, **35**:87–89

Adenoviral vectors, Duchenne muscular dystrophy gene therapy, **35**:129–134

Adenovirus, *see also* Viral vectors
E1A transcripts
production by alternative splice sites, **31**:229–231

Adenovirus, E1A protein of, *See* E1A oncoprotein

ADH, *see* Alcohol dehydrogenase

Adh gene
band organization, **39**:149, 153
chromomere–gene–loop relations, **39**:157
dosage compensation, **39**:78

Drosophila species
developmental program of expression, **25**:52–**25**:53
ecology, natural populations in
hibiscus flowers, **25**:71–**25**:72
succulent cacti, decaying, **25**:70–**25**:71
wineries, **25**:69–**25**:70
evolutionary genetics, **25**:72–**25**:76
D. melanogaster group, **25**:73–**25**:74
D. mulleri group, **25**:74–**25**:75
transposable elements and, **29**:249–**29**:250, **29**:254
puff development, **39**:209, 211, 303

Adh locus
Drosophila melanogaster
alleles
Adh^F and *Adh^S*, comparison
ADH expression variation, **25**:54–**25**:55, **25**:57–**25**:58
behavioral response to alcohol, **25**:68–**25**:69
coding sequences, **25**:47, **25**:84–**25**:86
Adh^null, **25**:44, **25**:48, **25**:51, **25**:72, **25**:78, **25**:86
polymorphism, **25**:43–**25**:44, **25**:45, **25**:47–**25**:48, **25**:73, **25**:81
cloning, **25**:46
DNA sequencing
Adh variants, **25**:47–**25**:48
flanking regions, **25**:48–**25**:49
genetic map, **25**:41–**25**:43
molecular structure, **25**:46–**25**:47
comparison with
D. mulleri duplicated locus, **25**:52–**25**:53, **25**:70–**25**:71, **25**:74
Hawaiian *Drosophila* gene, **25**:53, **25**:74
intron location, ADH structure and, **25**:62
population genetics, **25**:76–**25**:86, *see also* Population genetics
transcription, control by two promoters, **25**:46–**25**:47, **25**:51–**25**:52
developmental program, **25**:50–**25**:51

ADRI, superoxide dismutases and, 30:280,
30:285
Adverse therapeutic experiences
clinical identification, 32:5–8
ongoing therapy, 32:8–12
AEC, see S-(2-Aminoethyl)-L-cysteine
Aedes, see Mosquitoes
Aerobiosis
nitrate reductase and, 30:3
superoxide dismutases and, 30:270,
30:275–30:276
physiology of mutants, 30:289,
30:293–30:295, 30:305
Aflatoxin B$_1$, effect on braconid wasp
hatchability, 25:170
Agammaglobulinemia
cloning studies, 35:67–73
animal models, 35:73
Bruton's agammaglobulinemia tyrosine
kinase role, 35:69–71
gene map, 35:67–69
mutation analysis, 35:71–72
future research directions, 35:89–90
historical perspective, 35:58–59
overview, 35:57–58
phenotypes, 35:65–67, 35:72–73
Agar plate method, screening by, 20:40–20:41
Agglutinins, in yeast mating, 27:36
Aggregation, zeste in Drosophila melanogaster
and, 29:332–29:336, 29:339
Aging
antioxidant physiology and, Drosophila,
28:61–28:62
braconid wasp life-span
diet and, 25:136
egg production and, 25:137
rearing temperature and, 25:136–25:137
starvation effects, sex differences,
25:135–25:136
X-ray dose-dependent effects
hatchability and, 25:148–25:149
polyploidy and, 25:146–25:148
recessive gene mutations and, 25:148
DNA damage accumulation during asexual
phase, Paramecium tetraurelia,
24:359–24:360
mt genome during culture senescence
Neurospora intermedia, 25:244
Podospora anserina, 25:241–25:244
Neurospora crassa poky mutants, cytochrome

aa$_3$ and b synthesis, 25:239
nuclear envelope role, 24:267–24:268
oxygen radicals and, 28:43, 28:46
TF gene expression and, 25:23–25:24
Agonadism
familial, 33:313
Agrobacterium
detection and isolation of plasmids in,
22:218–22:219
nitrate reductase and, 30:28
relationship between Ti-, Ri- and other
plasmids
DNA homology studies, 22:242–22:244
genetic analysis and complementation
studies of virulence functions,
22:244–22:246
incompatibility studies, 22:239–22:242
Agrobacterium tumefaciens
dicot plant species
genetic transformation by infection,
24:463–24:464
genetic systems for, 22:225–22:226
chromosomal linkage maps of,
22:230–22:231
introduction of plasmids from other
bacterial species and their expression,
22:227–22:230
mutagenesis and isolation of mutants,
22:226
transformation, transduction, and
conjugation in, 22:226–22:227
Ah complex
comparison with immunoglobulin system
clinical disease, 21:33–21:34
initiation of programming in control
animal, 21:32–21:33
overlapping specificities, 21:34–21:39
phylogenetic expression, 21:33
reciprocal relationship between P-450 and
immune system, 21:34
early studies, 21:8–21:11
evidence for multiple structural gene
products, 21:16–21:26
linkage, 21:11
pleiotypic response of Ah locus,
21:11–21:13
regulation by Ah cytosolic receptor,
21:13–21:16
suggestive evidence for temporal genes,
21:26–21:27

aj42 mutant
Drosophila melanogaster, **31**:171
β-Alanine, *Drosophila*
metabolism, genetics, **24**:197–**24**:198
synthesis pathway in black mutations,
24:200–**24**:202
Alanosine, effects on braconid wasp females
egg production and, **25**:165
egg size and, **25**:167
oogonium sensitivity to, **25**:171
N-β-Alanyldopamine
developmental profile, **24**:151–**24**:153
glucosides in hemolymph, **24**:143–**24**:144
β-Alanyldopamine hydrolase
in *ebony* and *tan* mutations, *Drosophila*, **24**:199
β-Alanyldopamine synthetase
in *ebony* and *tan* mutations, *Drosophila*,
24:198–**24**:199
Albula, evolutionary genetics of fish and, **29**:124
Alcaligenes eutrophus, metal detoxification in,
36:223–**36**:226
Alcaligenes xylosoxidans, metal detoxification in,
36:223–**36**:226
Alcohol dehydrogenase
in developing pollen, maize, **26**:21, **26**:24
isozyme analysis, **26**:25
developmental control by regulatory genes
Drosophila, **24**:89–**24**:90
maize, **24**:103–**24**:105
mouse, **24**:86–**24**:87
Drosophila melanogaster
activity
during development, **25**:50
diet and, **25**:56
genotype and, **25**:54–**25**:55
induction in tissue culture, **25**:56
selection and, **25**:57–**25**:58
allozymes ADH-F and ADH-S
Adh allele distribution and,
25:80–**25**:81
kinetics, **25**:60
structure, **25**:61–**25**:63
intron location in *Adh* gene and,
25:62
substrate specificity, **25**:59–**25**:60
thermal stability, **25**:60–**25**:61
behavioral response to ethanol and,
25:66–**25**:68
dietary alcohol detoxification
distinction from ALDH function, **25**:64

products, **25**:63–**25**:64
role in ethanol tolerance, hypotheses,
25:64–**25**:65
evolutionary origin, **25**:75–**25**:76
isozymes, **25**:61
comparison with proteins in *D. mulleri*
group, **25**:71
mRNA coding for, *Drosophila*,
24:380–**24**:381
Mu elements of *Zea mays* and, **30**:79–**30**:80,
30:92, **30**:95, **30**:109–**30**:112
somaclonal variation and, **30**:58
Alcohols
Drosophila reactions to
dietary, detoxification by ADH,
25:63–**25**:65
environmental, behavior adaptation,
25:65–**25**:68, **25**:79
in tissue culture, ADH induction, **25**:56
puff activity effects, **39**:253
Aldehyde dehydrogenase, *Drosophila*, distinction
from alcohol dehydrogenase function, **25**:64
Aldehyde oxidase, *Drosophila*
developmental control by regulatory genes,
24:94–**24**:95
male/female activity, autosomal fragment in X
chromosome and, **24**:407, **24**:408
Alder, nitrate reductase and, **30**:5
Alfalfa
cold acclimation
cor gene expression
ABA effects, **28**:118–**28**:119
freezing tolerance and, **28**:117
mRNA populations and, **28**:115
polypeptide profiles and, **28**:111
somaclonal variation and, **30**:53, **30**:55
Algae, carbonic anhydrases and, **30**:323,
30:343
Alglucerase
Gaucher disease treatment, **32**:30–33,
32:39–41
Alkaline phosphatase, *Drosophila*
distinction from alkaline phosphatase-1,
24:156
pupal, yellow-body-derived, **24**:156
Alkaline phosphatase-1, *Drosophila*
Aph-1 alleles and, **24**:154–**24**:156
larval and pupal variants, **24**:156
properties, **24**:154
tyrosine-O-phosphate hydrolysis, **24**:154

Alleles
  carbonic anhydrases and, 30:337–30:338,
    30:343, 30:346–30:348
  Drosophila transposable elements and, 29:230
    foldback elements, 29:286–29:288
    hobo, 29:274
    mariner, 29:278–29:280
    P elements, 29:260, 29:262–29:264,
      29:268–29:269, 29:271–29:273
    retrotransposons, 29:241–29:258, 29:260
  evolutionary genetics of fish and
    detection of variation, 29:123–29:126,
      29:128
    development, 29:174–29:175
    environmental change, 29:164–29:166,
      29:171
    immune system, 29:188
    nomenclature, 29:131, 29:134
  mosquitoes and, 30:149, 30:157, 30:160
  Mu elements of *Zea mays* and, 30:78–30:79
    applications, 30:114–30:115
    assay for monitoring, 30:81, 30:83
    characteristics, 30:87–30:90
    gene expression, 30:108–30:111
    properties of transposition, 30:100
    regulation, 30:98
  Neurospora crassa and, 29:2, 29:19, 29:41,
    29:43
    gene transfer, 29:6–29:7, 29:9
    nitrate reductase and, 30:17–30:18, 30:21,
      30:23, 30:27–30:28
    somaclonal variation and, 30:47, 30:53,
      30:55, 30:64–30:65
    superoxide dismutases and, 30:262, 30:297
      molecular genetics, 30:282–30:283
      physiology of mutants, 30:299,
        30:301–30:302, 30:305–30:306
    yeast ribosomes and, 29:98, 29:104
      nucleolus, 29:89, 29:91
      ribosomal protein genes, 29:72, 29:74
      ribosomal proteins, 29:70–29:71
  zeste in *Drosophila melanogaster* and chromatin
    packaging, 29:339, 29:342
    discovery, 29:303, 29:305
    function, 29:326–29:329
    transvection, 29:306, 29:311–29:312
Alloantigens
  demonstrated by methods other than grafting,
    20:296–20:297, 20:341–20:342
  antigens of skin and liver, 20:305–20:306

  Ly antigens of B cells, 20:303–20:304
  Ly antigens of T cells, 20:300–20:303
  Ly-M-1 antigen, 20:297–20:300
  miscellaneous antigens of lymphocytes,
    20:304–20:305
  recombinant inbred strains, 20:297
  Thy-1 antigen, 20:300
Allopatry, definition of, 36:158
Allopurinol, heterochromatin gene expression
  modification, 37:344
Allotetraploids
  Gossypium spp.
    diploidization, 23:347–23:349
    homologous pairing suppression,
      23:349–23:352
    origin
      genomic, 23:327–23:331
      mono- vs polyphyletic, 23:335–23:339
      new evidence, 23:339–23:347
      time and place of, 23:332–23:335
Alu
  carbonic anhydrases and, 30:334
  telomeres and, 30:195
Aluminum lactate, puff activity effects, 39:253
Amalgam gene
  Drosophila
    mRNA, distribution during embryogenesis,
      27:327–27:329
    protein product
      association with cell membrane, 27:325
      localization during embryogenesis,
        27:330–27:332
      organization in five domains, 27:326
      sequences similar to members of
        immunoglobulin family,
        27:326–27:327
      structure, position in ANT-C, 27:316,
        27:325–27:326
α-Amanitin, RNA synthesis inhibition,
  39:71–72
Amantadine, resistance, of influenza virus,
  20:25
amd gene, 37C1-2 band, 39:139
Amia calva, evolutionary genetics of fish and,
  29:127
Amines, biogenic, *Drosophila*, *see also*
  Catecholamines
    N-acetylation by NAT, 24:142
    conjugates in hemolymph
      NAD, 24:143–24:145

Anchor cell, C. *elegans*
  generation, *lin-12* role, 27:79, 27:81,
    27:88–27:89, 27:92
  interactions with
    VPCs, 27:75–27:78
    VU cells, 27:66, 27:81
Anchusa officinalis, MGS, experimental, 26:17
Andante mutant
  Drosophila melanogaster, 31:169–170
Androgenesis
  nutritional requirements for, 20:145–20:146
  physiology of, 20:146–20:148
Androgenetic plants
  origin of, 20:139–20:145
  uses of, 20:148–20:151
Anemias
  macrocytic
    erythroid homeostatic mechanisms,
      20:390–20:393
    genetic structure of *W*, *Sl* and *an* loci,
      20:380–20:386
    hypochromic, general comments,
      20:440–20:442
    macrocytic, 20:379–20:380
      abnormal fetal erythropoiesis,
        20:386–20:387
      attempt to put it all together,
        20:408–20:411
      implantation therapy, 20:395–20:401
      nonerythroid aspects of hemopoiesis in
        W/W, *Sl/Sl* and *an/an* mice,
        20:393–20:395
      pertinent genetic stocks for physiological
        studies, 20:387–20:390
      radiosensitivity of anemic mice,
        20:404–20:406
      studies *in vitro*, 20:406–20:408
      therapy of *W*-anemias, 20:401–20:404
    microcytic, 20:420–20:424
    secondary to genetic defects in other
      systems, 20:442
      cribriform degeneration, 20:445
      diminutive mice, 20:444–20:445
      newborn Strong's luxoid mice, 20:444
      tail-short heterozygotes,
        20:443–20:444
    sex-linked, 20:417–20:420
    spontaneous hereditary hemolytic
      absence of hemoglobinopathy and
        enzyme defect, 20:427–20:428

autoimmune hemolytic anemia of
    NZB/B mice, 20:431–20:436
  descriptions of single-locus hemolytic
    syndromes, 20:426–20:427
  evidence of red cell membrane defects,
    20:428–20:430
  genetic information, 20:424–20:426
  identification of heterozygous carriers,
    20:430
  transitory siderocytic of flexed mice,
    20:412–20:417
Aneuploid genotypes, viability, *Drosophila*,
    27:213–27:215
Aneuploids
  frequency in *Gossypium hirsutum* seeds,
    monosomic lines, 23:315–23:316
  production by translocations in *Gossypium*
    spp., 23:305–23:306
Aneuploidy
  chromosome numerical abnormalities
    45,X, 33:109–110
    47,XXX, 33:110–113
    47,XXY, 33:110–113
    47,XYY, 33:113–114
  puff activity effects, 39:253
  somaclonal variation and, 30:44,
    30:48–30:49, 30:61
Angiogenesis, thrombospondin gene inhibition
  of, 36:59
Animal breeding, chromosome rearrangements
  in, 36:241
Animal models, *see specific model*
Aniridia, Wilms' tumor with, 36:69
Anisomycin, RNA synthesis inhibition, 39:72
Ankyrin repeats, in INK4 protein family, 36:64
Anopheles, *see also* Mosquitoes
  chromosomal rearrangement localization,
    37:29
  late replication study, 37:32
Anoxia
  effect on SOD, *Iris pseudacorus*, 28:30
  heat-shock puff induction, 39:345,
    39:350–351
  heterochromatin compaction, 37:13
Anquilla, evolutionary genetics of fish and,
    29:127
Antennapedia
  gene
    band organization, 39:144
    distribution estimation, 39:118

Antennapedia (continued)
  homeotic, Drosophila
    dominant gain-of-function mutations,
      27:313, 27:336, 27:338–27:339
    expression during embryogenesis,
      27:338
    promoters P1 and P2, distinct functions,
      27:335, 27:337
    activation by gap genes, 27:267,
      27:268
    protein product, homeotic sequences,
      27:370, 27:371
    structure, 27:335–27:337
  mosquitoes and, 30:171
  zeste, in Drosophila melanogaster and,
    29:321–29:322, 29:340
Antennapedia complex
  distinction from BX-C genes, 27:355
  genetic map, 27:311–27:312
  homeotic loci, head-specifying,
    27:335–27:350, see also Antennapedia
  exon/intron structures, 27:351, 27:352
  expression pattern, comparison with trunk-
    specifying, 27:348–27:349
  homeobox and opa repeat positions,
    27:351, 27:353
  origin and evolution
    duplication-divergence events and,
      27:350–27:351
    similarity to mouse homeotic genes,
      27:350
  protein products, comparison with BX-C
    genes, 27:349
  nonhomeotic loci, 27:315–27:335, see also
    Amalgam gene; Bicoid gene; Fushi tarazu,
    pair-rule gene; Zerknüllt gene
  relatedness of nine homeoboxes,
    27:353–27:354
Anterior–posterior axis
  formation
    in Drosophila melanogaster
      gap to pair-rule gene patterns,
        31:11–12
      pair-rule interactions, 31:12–14
      periodicity gradients, 31:10–11
    in Xenopus laevis
      Hox gene role, 31:56–57
      patterns
        induction, 31:54–55
        lability, 31:53–54
        posterior dominance, 31:55–56

prepattern, 31:53–54
Anterior pituitary, evolutionary genetics of fish
  and, 29:190–29:196
Anterior-posterior axis, Drosophila
  homeotic gene functional domains,
    27:372–27:374
  maternal-effect gene roles, 27:246–27:249
  postitional information genes, hierarchy,
    27:374–27:376
ANT gene (Drosophila), 36:178–36:179
Antheraea polyphemus
  chorion proteins, 24:225–24:226, 24:228
  genes, chorion protein-encoding, 24:226,
    24:233
Anthocyanin, Mu elements of Zea mays and,
  30:81, 30:83
Anthracnose disease, see Colletotrichum
  lindemuthianum, bean infection
Antibiotics
  resistance, mosquitoes and, 30:168–30:169
  synthesis
    genetic control, 20:89–20:93
    multivalent induction of secondary
      metabolite formation,
      20:98–20:101
    plasmids and, 20:93–20:98
  yeast ribosomes and, 29:65, 29:70,
    29:73–29:74, 29:99–29:100
Antibodies
  active chromosome transcription region
    localization, 39:47–52
  Drosophila transposable elements and, 29:266,
    29:285
  evolutionary genetics of fish and,
    29:167–29:168, 29:181,
    29:183–29:184, 29:200
  isolated chromosome studies, localization,
    34:329
  Neurospora crassa and, 29:24
  nitrate reductase and, 30:6, 30:8, 30:10,
    30:20, 30:22–30:23
  nonhistone nuclear protein isolation,
    34:228–229, 34:238
  positional effect, gene expression
    inactivation, 37:329
  yeast ribosomes and, 29:72, 29:89–29:90
  zeste in Drosophila melanogaster and, 29:316
Antifreeze genes, evolutionary genetics of fish
  and, 29:162–29:163
Antigenic variability, of influenza virus, genetic
  basis for, 20:13–20:21

Antigens
  evolutionary genetics of fish and, **29**:181,
    29:183, **29**:188–**29**:189
  mouse
    H-2, developmental control by regulatory
      genes, **24**:84–**24**:85
    MHC (major histocompatibility complex),
      induction by class I and II genes in
      transgenics, **24**:312–**24**:313
  surface of human hepatitis B virus, expression
    in yeast, **23**:137–**23**:138
  telomeres and, **30**:195–**30**:196, **30**:205,
    30:224
  yeast ribosomes and, **29**:86, **29**:95–**29**:96
Antimony
  bacterial detoxification of, **36**:216–**36**:220
  biological toxicity of, **36**:188
Antimycin A, heat-shock puff induction, **39**:345
Antirrhinum majus, transposons, temperature
  effects, **28**:78
Antisense
  mRNA, protein synthesis theory, **38**:91
  regulation, of bacterial iron-regulation genes,
    36:198
  transcripts, of tumor suppressor genes, **36**:103
Antithrombin III, **33**:135–136
Antp gene, *Drosophila* transposable elements
  and, **29**:250
APC protein
  attenuated type (AAPC), **36**:75
  regulation of, **36**:75
  structure of, **36**:74
  as tumor suppressor gene product, **36**:49,
    36:99
APC tumor suppressor gene
  characteristics of, **36**:49, **36**:72–**36**:76, **36**:106
  implication in familial adenomatous coli,
    36:73, **36**:95
  mutations on, **36**:77, **36**:96
Apholate, effects on braconid wasps
  egg production and, **25**:165
  hatchability and, **25**:169
  sperm inactivation, **25**:172–**25**:173
Apocytochrome *c*, *Neurospora crassa* and,
  29:35–**29**:36, **29**:38
Apodystrophins, Duchenne muscular dystrophy
  role, **35**:121
Apoenzyme, nitrate reductase and, **30**:4, **30**:6,
  30:17, **30**:20–**30**:27
Apolipoprotein B, **32**:156–164
  gene polymorphisms, **32**:161–164

post-transcriptional mRNA editing,
    32:159–161
  triglyceride-rich lipoprotein clearance,
    32:156–159
Apolipoprotein E, lipoprotein remnant
  metabolism, **32**:164–175
Apoptosis
  bax gene mediation of, **36**:59
  function of, **36**:60
  historical perspective, **35**:35–53
    acceptance, **35**:49–53
    applications, **35**:50–52
    concept development, **35**:46–49
    definition, **35**:40–41
    morphology, **35**:41–46
    overview, **35**:35–36
    shrinkage necrosis, **35**:36–40
  pRb role in, **36**:55
  p53 role in, **36**:59
  WT1 regulation of, **36**:71
Apple, self-incompatibility overcoming
  mentor pollen, **26**:46
  pioneer pollen effect, **26**:31
Apterygotan insects, *see also specific species*
  intercalary α-heterochromatin, **37**:138–141
  polyteny occurrence, **34**:64–72
Arabidopsis nidulans, nitrate reductase and,
  30:17, **30**:26–**30**:27
Arabidopsis thaliana
  cab3 gene, photoregulation, **28**:146
  cold acclimation
    mRNA populations
      Northern blot analysis, **28**:115–**28**:116
      in vitro translation, **28**:114
      polypeptide profile, **28**:110–**28**:111, **28**:112
    cor gene express
      ABA effects, comparison with cold, **28**:119
      boiling-stable polypeptides, **28**:120–**28**:121
      drought stress and, **28**:120
  HMGR mRNA, elicitor-induced, **28**:201
  HSP70 genes, organization, **28**:238–**28**:239
  nitrate reductase and, **30**:2, **30**:30
    apoenzyme mutants, **30**:21–**30**:22
    gene expression, **30**:9, **30**:11
    genetics, **30**:13–**30**:15, **30**:17–**30**:18,
      30:27
  pollen
    lethal embryo mutant expression, **26**:13
    MGS, experimental, **26**:17
  transformation by *Agrobacterium tumefaciens*,
    28:174

Arboviruses, mosquitoes and, 30:123–30:124, 30:155, 30:171
AreA, nitrate reductase and, 30:26
ARF1 tumor suppressor gene
  characteristics of, 36:48, 36:52
  complex structure of, 36:67, 36:68
Aristapediod zeste in Drosophila melanogaster, 29:340
Aromatic sulfates
  as sulfur source
    Neurospora crassa, 31:192–194
Arrhythmogenic right ventricular cardiomyopathy, 35:310–312
ArsA, ArsC, ArsD, and ArsR proteins, as bacterial metal-responsive proteins, 36:217–36:223, 36:226
Arsenate, heat-shock puff induction, 39:345
Arsenic
  effects of bacteria, 36:190
  detoxification, 36:216–36:220
ars gene
  role in bacterial arsenic detoxification, 36:216
  in sulfur circuit
    Neurospora crassa, 31:191–192
Aryl sulfatase
  in sulfur circuit, Neurospora crassa, 31:192–194
Arylsulfatase B, mouse
  developmental control by regulatory genes, 24:84
Ascarid worms, polytene chromosome occurrence, 34:97
Ascaris megalocephala, chromatin diminution, 37:78–81
Ascaris, telomeres and, 30:209, 30:227–30:228
AS-C, see Subdivision 1B of X chromosome
AS-C gene complex, oligogene bands, 39:137
Asci, of N. crassa, translocation effects on, 36:242–36:244, 36:253, 36:265
Ascomycetes, see Saccharomyces cerevisiae
Ascospores, Neurospora crassa and, 29:2, 29:15, 29:42–29:43, 29:45
ASF-SF2, in alternative splicing, 31:220–225
Ashkenazi Jews, BRCA1 and BRCA2 gene mutations in, 36:86
Aspartate aminotransferase, isozymes in pollen during development, maize, 26:25
Aspergillus, amplified mtDNAs in, 22:54–22:56
Aspergillus, Neurospora crassa and, 29:27, 29:43, 29:47–29:48

Aspergillus amstelodami, mtDNA in ragged mutation, 25:241
Aspergillus nidulans
  avirulence genes, 28:171
  benA33 mutant, meiotic spindle disassembly delay, 26:168
  chromosome rearrangements in, 36:244, 36:264, 36:277–36:280
  mitochondrial genome
    genes
      atp8, continuous, 25:214
      cob, mosaic, 25:222
      cox1, mosaic, 25:212, 25:217–25:218
    rRNA
      rnl, interrupted by intron and miniinsert, 25:208
      rns, continuous, 25:209
    tRNA
      clustering, 25:199
      structure and code, 25:210, 25:211
    introns, 25:198
    mutants and maps, 25:202–25:203
    sequence duplications, 25:192
    unassigned orfs, 25:196–25:197
    homology with human counterparts, 25:196
  transformation
    applications, 23:153
    genomic library, 23:154
    methods, 23:152–23:153
Astrason pink, RNA synthesis inhibition, 39:72
Astyanax fasciatus, evolutionary genetics of fish and, 29:177
Asynapsis
  homologous chromosomes
    causes, 34:173–174
    occurrence, 34:157–163
Ataxias, see Hereditary ataxias
Ataxia telangiectasia
  chromosomal linkage of, 36:95
  tumor suppressor gene role in, 36:49, 36:90–36:91, 36:95
Atherosclerosis, 32:141–191
  apolipoprotein E, 32:164–175
  atherogenesis, 32:185–186
  high-density lipoprotein metabolism, 32:175–183
  cholesterol ester transfer protein, 32:180–183
  transgenic mouse genetics, 32:178–180

historical perspective, 32:142–147
lipoprotein (a) metabolism, 32:183–185
lipoprotein remnant metabolism, 32:164–175
low-density lipoprotein receptor pathway, 32:147–164
apolipoprotein B, 32:156–164
defect therapy, 32:153–156
transgenic mouse genetics, 32:152–153
macrophage scavenger receptors, 32:186–190
ATM, as tumor suppressor gene product, 36:49
ATM gene, DNA repair mechanisms, 38:207–208
ATP
binding to HSP70, 24:3, 24:58
Neurospora crassa and, 29:38
nitrate reductase and, 30:30
yeast ribosomes and, 29:102
ATPase-9 Neurospora crassa and, 29:27, 29:38
ATPases
Neurospora crassa and, 29:40
in RNA splicing, 31:226–228
subunits, ascomycetes
mitochondrial genes coding for, 25:213–25:214, 25:216
Atractyloside, heat-shock puff induction, 39:345, 39:350
Attacins, mosquitoes and, 30:155, 30:171
AT tumor suppressor gene, characteristics of, 36:49, 36:95
Aurantine, puff activity effects, 39:253
Aureolaria spp. pollen competition in natural populations, 26:35, 26:48
aurora mutant
Drosophila melanogaster, 31:102–103
Autonomous elements
Mu elements of Zea mays and, 30:81, 30:83, 30:91
somaclonal variation and, 30:53, 30:55
Autonomous replicating sequences
telomeres and, 30:221–30:222
yeast ribosomes and, 29:77–29:78
Autoradiography
[3H]uridine labeling method, 39:41–47
interband detection, 39:87
Autosomal dominant progressive ataxias, 38:34–49
classification, 38:35
clones, 38:40–47
SCA1 gene, 38:40–43

SCA2 gene, 38:43–44
SCA3 gene, 38:44–46
SCA6 gene, 38:46–47
epidemiology, 38:49
Machado–Joseph disease, 38:44–46
mapped genes, 38:47–49
SCA4 gene, 38:47–48
SCA5 gene, 38:48
SCA7 gene, 38:48–49
polyglutamine proteins, 38:39–40
triplet repeat expansions, 38:35–39
Autosomes
dosage compensation, 39:76–79, 39:83
during Drosophila hydei spermatocyte stage, 23:208–23:209
heterochromatin gene expression modification, 37:339–341
mitotic heterochromatin genetic content, 37:60–65
mosquitoes and, 30:144
telomeres and, 30:193, 30:195–30:196
Autp gene, band organization, 39:144
Auxotrophy
nitrate reductase and, 30:15, 30:31
superoxide dismutases and, 30:261, 30:289, 30:293–30:295, 30:305
Avena sativa, pollen and sporophytic response to Helminthosporium victoriae, 26:19
awd Gene, prune/Killer of prune interaction, 35:209–221
awd^{Kpn} mutation analysis, 35:218–221
early studies, 35:209
Killer of prune allele, 35:209–210
neomorphic character, 35:219–221
nm23 gene comparison, 35:214–216
nucleoside diphosphate kinase activity, 35:216–218
phenotypes, 35:211–214
Axons
demyelination of, in CMT1 and CMT2 diseases, 36:3, 36:6, 36:8
function of, 36:21–36:22
5-Azacytidine, somaclonal variation and, 30:58, 30:64
Azide
heat-shock puff induction, 39:345
inhibition of SODs, 26:69, 26:72
Azotobacter vinelandii, molybdenum-regulated gene in, 36:201, 36:202
Azure B stain, RNA staining, 39:40–41

B23, yeast ribosomes and, 29:88–29:89
Bacillus cereus, mercury resistance gene of,
    36:205, 36:206
Bacillus firmus, CadC protein from, 36:220
Bacillus spp., mercury resistance gene of,
    36:205, 36:206–36:207, 36:214
Bacillus stearothermophilus
    MnSOD, 26:70
    superoxide dismutases and, 30:266, 30:306
Bacillus subtilis
    flagellar genes, regulation, 27:14,
        27:25–27:27
    iron-regulated gene in, 36:191, 36:193
    mercury resistance gene of, 36:205, 36:206
    Neurospora crassa, and, 29:35
    sporulation
        environmental stress-induced,
            27:23–27:24
        genetic control, 27:18, 27:24–27:25
        stages, 27:24
Backcrossing
    carbonic anhydrases and, 30:335
    superoxide dismutases and, 30:295
Bacteria
    antimony detoxification in, 36:216–36:220
    arsenic detoxification in, 36:216–36:220
    carbonic anhydrases and, 30:323, 30:345
    evolutionary genetics of fish and,
        29:129–29:130
    iron as essential metal for, 36:190–36:199
    mercury detoxification in, 36:205–36:216
    metal regulation of gene expression in,
        36:187–36:238
    molybdenum as essential metal for,
        36:199–36:205
    mosquitoes and, 30:151, 30:155, 30:158
    Mu elements of Zea mays and, 30:106
    nitrate reductase and, 30:2–30:3, 30:7
    plant pathogen, avirulence genes,
        28:170–28:171, 28:172–28:173
    superoxide dismutases and, 30:253, 30:255,
        30:269
    taxonomy, crown galls and, 22:210–22:213
    use in environmental contamination
        detection, 36:189
    yeast ribosomes and, 29:65, 29:73,
        29:93–29:95, 29:99, 29:101
Bacteriophages
    HSP gene activation in E. coli, 24:17–24:18
    molecular cloning, 23:84

T7
    NUV absorption by peptide,
        26:108–26:109
    oxygen-inactivated 3' to 5' exonuclease,
        SOD effects, 26:112
    UV-irradiated
        prophage reactivation, 24:333
    T4, recombinational repair
        multiplicity reactivation, 24:331–24:333
        postreplication, 24:333
Bacteroides fragilis, metal substitution in
    Fe-MnSODs, 26:71
BAH, see β-alanyldopamine hydrolase
Balancer chromosomes, of Drosophila, 36:140
Balbiani nuclei, historical perspective, 34:5,
    34:15–16
Balbiani rings
    historical perspective, 34:14–15
    [³H]uridine labeling method, 39:41–47
    interband organization, 39:90
    isolated nuclei, 34:324–326
    molecular organization, 39:397–407
    morphology, 39:387–397
    puffing involvement, 39:203–204, 39:212
    ribonucleoprotein granules, 39:56–67
    springtail chromosomes, 34:69, 34:71
Bands, see also Chromomeres
    chromomere pattern
        map building basis, 34:187–190
        mapping procedures
            artificial bands, 34:212–213
            band sizes, 34:207–212
            chromosome morphology relation,
                34:198–202
            cytological repeats, 34:213–215
            interbands, 34:207–213
            methods, 34:202–207
            pattern fixation, 34:190–197
            seasonal changes, 34:300–304
        chromosome structure, 34:215–219
        DNA content, 34:210–212
        infusoria chromosomes, 34:82–83
        number estimation, historical perspective,
            34:12–14
Barley
    dehydrins, boiling-stable, 28:121
    frost hardiness, gene control, 28:107
    genes coding for seed storage proteins of,
        22:125
    isolated plastids, psbA photoregulation, 28:137

nitrate reductase and
biochemistry, 30:4, 30:7
gene expression, 30:9–30:10
genetics, 30:13–30:14, 30:17, 30:20–30:21
somaclonal variation and, 30:45
BAS, see β-alanyldopamine synthetase
bax gene
p53
transactivation of, 36:59
upregulation of, 36:60
B cells
evolutionary genetics of fish and, 29:181
Ly antigens of, 20:303–20:304,
20:341–20:342
B chromosomes
characteristics, 37:282–304
fitness association, 37:302–303
heterochromatin association, 37:300–301
number, 37:295–297
occurrence, 37:288–294
pairing, 37:299–300
properties, 37:436
supernumerary effects, 37:301–304
designation symbols, 37:282
heterochromatin detection, 37:6
bcl-2 gene, as p53 target, 36:59, 36:60
Bean
anthracnose disease
cytology, 28:167
HRGP gene induction, 28:198
localization of PAL and CHS, 28:192
race specificity, 28:168–28:169
CHS gene15 promoter, 28:207,
28:210–28:213
PAL gene family, structures, 28:193–28:194
Pseudomonas syringae infection, GUS
induction, 28:193
Becker muscular dystrophy, 35:118, 120, 124
Beckwith-Weidemann syndrome (BWS)
p57 protein role in, 36:47, 36:48, 36:50,
36:64
Wilms' tumor with, 36:69, 36:92
Belgovskaya–Prokofyeva, heterochromatization
theory, 37:395–399
Benzamide
heat-shock puff induction, 39:345–346
puff activity effects, 39:254
RNA synthesis inhibition, 39:72
Berberine
puff activity effects, 39:254

RNA synthesis inhibition, 39:72–73
Ber-1 gene, puff development, 39:302
Besleria triflora, pollen competition, 26:33
Beta cells, function in non-insulin-dependent
diabetes mellitus gene, 32:52–53, 32:55
Beta vulgaris, ethofumerase tolerance in pollen
and sporophyte, 26:15
Bicoid gene
Drosophila melanogaster, 31:11–12
maternal, Drosophila
as anterior pattern organizer,
27:246–27:248, 27:376
effects on other gene expression
Dfd and, 27:380–27:381
hb and, 27:250–27:251, 27:255,
27:321–27:323, 27:375, 27:386
in mutant embryos stau exu and vas
exu, 27:257–27:260
Kr and, 27:251–27:254
in mutant embryos stau exu and vas
exu, 27:257–27:260
mRNA spatial distribution
during embryogenesis, 27:322–27:325
in oocyte, 27:278
mutant phenotypes, 27:320–27:321
protein product
localization in embryo, 27:249, 27:321,
27:323
organization in four domains, 27:322
structure, position in ANT-C, 27:316,
27:321–27:322
Bilobella aurantiaca, intercalary α-
heterochromatin, 37:141
Biochemical markers
apoptosis detection, 35:48–49
expressed sequence tags, mouse libraries,
35:166–168, 35:191–194
Biological clock, Neurospora crassa and, 29:46
Biological rhythms, see also Chronogenetics
Drosophila melanogaster
aj42 mutant, 31:171
Andante mutant, 31:169–170
Clock mutant, 31:169
disconnected mutant, 31:170–171
ebony mutant, 31:169–170
period gene
behavioral effects, 31:161–162
molecular biology, 31:162–166
sequence similarities with arnt, Ahr, and
sim, 31:167–169

Biological rhythms (continued)
   threonine–glycine repeats, 31:162–166
   transcript localization, 31:164–166
   PER protein
      circadian cycling, 31:166–167
      expression, 31:164–166
      transcript localization, 31:164–166
Biological species concept, formulation of,
   36:158, 36:159
Biotechnology
   fungal transformation and, 23:125
   Neurospora crassa and, 29:47
Birds, sex determination in, 20:221–20:223
Bismuth, bacterial detoxification of, 36:216
bithorax
   Drosophila
      bithorax complex
         distinction from ANT-C genes,
            27:310–27:311, 27:355
         expression pattern, 27:267
         genetic and molecular analyses, 27:311
         Ubx, see Ultrabithorax
         zeste in, 29:302–29:303, 29:305
         transposable elements and, 29:247
            alleles, 29:244–29:245
      locus, zeste in Drosophila melanogaster and,
         29:303, 29:340
BK virus, human
   early region, in transgenic mouse, 24:306
   in immunocompromised patients, symptoms,
      24:307
Bladder cancer, pRb aberrations in, 36:54
Blastomeres
   trophoblast cells
      mammalian polytene chromosome
         occurrence, 34:98–105
Blood, BRCA1 mutation studies on, 36:86
Blue-light photoreceptors
   in photosynthetic gene regulation, 28:140
   plant transcription regulation, 35:9–11
Bobbed
   gene, rDNA gene mutations, 38:83–84
   mutations, in D. melanogaster, 36:144
Body plan genes, human malformation
   body axes establishment, 38:3–16
   domains, 38:3
   dorsoventral patterning, 38:14–16
   floor plate role, 38:14–15
   forebrain region, 38:3–7
   Hox gene cluster, 38:8–14

   isthmic region, 38:7–8
   midbrain region, 38:3–7
   notochord role, 38:14–15
   rhombospinal region, 38:8–14
   rostrocaudal patterning, 38:3–14
   sonic hedgehog gene, 38:15–16
   limb patterning, 38:16–21
      homeobox genes, 38:18–21
      limb development, 38:16
      secreted molecules, 38:16–18
   ocular anlage patterning
      eye formation, 38:21
      homeobox genes, 38:21–22
   overview, 38:1–3
   tooth anlage patterning
      homeobox genes, 38:23
      tooth development, 38:22–23
Bombyx mori
   chorion
      protein-encoding, 24:229–24:234
         expression in Drosophila, 24:235–24:238
      proteins, 24:225–24:226
      structure, 24:224
Bone cancer, tumor suppressor gene mutations
   in, 36:96
Bone disease, treatment with
   aminohydroxypropylidine biphosphonate,
   32:28
Bone marrow transplantation, Gaucher disease
   treatment, 32:34–35
Bortedella bronchiseptica, iron-regulated gene in,
   36:191, 36:196
Bovine papilloma virus, in transgenic mouse,
   24:307
Brachydanio rerio, evolutionary genetics of fish
   and, 29:175
Braconid wasps
   behavior
      female response to host caterpillar, 25:126,
         25:130
      flight, 25:131
      grooming, 25:129–25:130
      gynandromorph, 25:118–25:119
      immobility response to stress,
         25:131–25:132
      male sexual response, 25:129
      genetic relatedness and,
         25:132–25:134
      pheromone-mediated, 25:117–25:118
      rotation effects, 25:132–25:133

chemical mutagen effects
  egg production and, **25**:164–**25**:167
  egg size and, **25**:167–**25**:168
  hatchability and
    oocyte sensitivity, **25**:168–**25**:171
    oogonium sensitivity, **25**:171–**25**:172
  lethal postembryonic mutations in sperm,
    25:173–**25**:174
  sperm inactivation, **25**:172–**25**:173
embryogenesis
  early stages, **25**:112
  oogenesis, cytology, **25**:111–**25**:112
enzymatic activities, **25**:140–**25**:142
eye color mutants, biochemistry,
  25:138–**25**:140
fatty acid composition, **25**:143
genetic mosaicism, **25**:112–**25**:117
  appendage striping, **25**:113
  body segments, **25**:114
  eyes, **25**:113, **25**:115–**25**:116
  sexual dimorphism and, **25**:114–**25**:115
  spontaneous production, *ebony* mutant and,
    25:116–**25**:117
life-span
  diet and, **25**:136
  egg production and, **25**:137
  rearing temperature and, **25**:136–**25**:137
  starvation and, **25**:135–**25**:136
  X-ray dose-dependent effects,
    25:146–**25**:149
morphogenetic fate mapping, **25**:119–**25**:120
population genetics, **25**:143–**25**:146
postembryonic development, **25**:120–**25**:126
  DNA in nuclei during metamorphosis,
    25:124
  larval
    central nervous system, **25**:121–**25**:122
    midgut, **25**:122, **25**:123
    multinuclear cells, **25**:122–**25**:124
    ovarioles, **25**:125–**25**:126
radiation effects
  body weight genetic variability and, **25**:149
  hatchability decline, **25**:151–**25**:153
  infecundity, **25**:153–**25**:155
  life-span reduction, **25**:146–**25**:149
  modification by
    chemical agents, **25**:155–**25**:157
    flight simulation, **25**:158–**25**:160
    orbital flight, **25**:157–**25**:158
  sperm damage, **25**:150–**25**:151

radioisotope digestion effects,
  25:161–**25**:162
sex determination
  alleles at sex locus, **25**:110, **25**:112
  male development from unfertilized eggs,
    25:134–**25**:135
sex differences
  enzymatic activities, **25**:141
  life-span under starvation, **25**:135–**25**:136
  ultraviolet ray effects, **25**:163–**25**:164
urates in fat body
  genetic constitution and diet effects,
    25:136, **25**:142
  oocyte growth and, **25**:143
  X-ray effects, **25**:148
venom
  injection apparatus, **25**:127–**25**:128
  paralyzing action, **25**:127, **25**:128–**25**:129
Bradyrhizobium elkanii, mercury resistance
  protein of, **36**:206
Bradyrhizobium japonicum
  iron-regulated gene in, **36**:198
  mercury resistance protein of, **36**:206
Brain
  behavior, biological rhythm studies,
    38:163–167
  cancer
    in neurofibromatosis type, **36**:2, **36**:81
    p21 suppression of, **36**:62
  patterning, homeobox genes, rostrocaudal
    axis, **38**:3–7
  TF synthesis, rat
    aging and, **25**:23–**25**:24
    development and, **25**:14, **25**:16
    localization, **25**:14, **25**:23
Brassica campestris
  leaves, FeSOD, **26**:67
  pollen, β-galacotosidase, **26**:24
Brassica napus, cold acclimation
  cor gene expression, ABA effect, **28**:119
  cycloheximide effect, **28**:100
  mRNA populations and, **28**:114
  plasma membrane behavior and, **28**:102
  polypeptide profiles and, **28**:111, **28**:112
Brassica oleracea, pollen, distorted segregation
  for *gal* locus, **26**:12
BRCA1 protein
  aberrant subcellular locallization of, **36**:104,
    36:105
  as tumor suppressor gene products, **36**:49

BRCA2 protein, as tumor suppressor gene
product, 36:49
BRCA1 tumor suppressor gene
antisense transcripts of, 36:103
characteristics of, 36:49, 36:52, 36:85–36:90,
36:106
complex structure of, 36:67
implications in breast cancer, 36:85, 36:95
mutations on, 36:88, 36:96, 36:98, 36:99,
36:106
BRCA2 tumor suppressor gene
characteristics of, 36:49, 36:85–36:90
implications in breast cancer, 36:85, 36:95,
36:106
mutational analysis of, 36:89–36:90, 36:106
BR-C genes
band organization, 39:142–143
DNA–RNA hybrid antibodies, 39:51–52
ecdysterone-induced puffs, 39:291–299
Break-fuion-bridge cycle, somaclonal variation
and, 30:206, 30:229
Breaks, see Chromosomes, breaks
Breast cancer
BRCA1 and BRCA2 role in, 36:85, 36:95,
36:104
chromosomal linkages of, 36:95
DCC gene implication in, 36:78
in AT heterozygotes, 36:90
p53 aberrations in, 36:58
pRb aberrations in, 36:54
tumor suppressor gene mutations in, 36:96
tumor suppressor gene role in, 36:49, 36:95
14B region genes, chromomere–gene–loop
relations, 39:159–160
15B region genes, chromomere–gene–loop
relations, 39:159–160
Brevibacterium lactofermentum, dtxR homolog of,
36:197
Brevooritia, evolutionary genetics of fish and,
29:129
br gene
band organization, 39:142
puff development, 39:299
Bridge-breakage-fusion cycles, role in genome
studies, 36:240
Bristle-forming cells
polyteny occurrence, 34:43–46
5-Bromodeoxyuridine
heterochromatin gene expression
modification, 37:342–343

puff activity effects, 39:254, 39:266
bronze, Mu elements of Zea mays and, 30:79,
30:98
brown loci, zeste in Drosophila melanogaster and,
29:305, 29:309
Brugia, 30:123
physiology, 30:158–30:159
Brugia pahangi, mosquitoes and, 30:155
Bruton's agammaglobulinemia tyrosine kinase,
x-linked cloning studies, 35:69–72
Bubble ascus phenomenon, in N. crassa
chromosome rearrangements, 36:274
bw+ gene, position effects, 37:371–376
BX-C gene complex, oligogene bands, 39:136
Bz1, Mu elements of Zea mays and,
30:92–30:93, 30:100, 30:103
bz1, Mu elements of Zea mays and, 30:89,
30:106, 30:115
Bz2, Mu elements of Zea mays and, 30:94,
30:102
bz2, Mu elements of Zea mays and, 30:98,
30:113

C46P medium, puff activity effects, 39:259
C50 medium, puff activity effects, 39:259
Cabbage, cold acclimation, Rubisco isozymes
and, 28:109
CAB gene, plant transcription regulation,
circadian clock pathways, 35:1–28
cis- and trans-acting element requirements,
35:20–25
cyanobacteria model, 35:17–20
future research directions, 35:25–28
gene characteristics, 35:2–6
overview, 35:1–2
photoreceptors, 35:6–11
blue-light receptors, 35:9–11
phytochrome, 35:6–9
phototransduction pathway analysis,
35:15–17
signal transduction intermediates,
identification, 35:11–14
c-abl transcription factor, pRb regulation of,
36:55
cacophony mutant
Drosophila melanogaster, 31:152–154
Cacti, succulent, Drosophila spp. in decaying
parts, 25:70–25:71

CAD, *see* Coniferyl alcohol dehydrogenase
CadC and CadF proteins, role in bacterial
cadmium detoxification, 36:220, 36:221,
36:222–36:223, 36:226
Cadherins, neural plate, *Xenopus laevis*,
31:66–67
Cadmium
bacterial detoxification of, 36:220, 36:221,
36:222–36:226
bacterial resistance to, 36:221,
36:223–36:226
biological toxicity of, 36:188
metallothionein gene transcription and,
25:25, 25:26
neural tube defects induction, 28:277–28:278
prevention by low-dose pretreatment,
28:280
Cadmium chloride
heat-shock puff induction, 39:346–347
puff activity effects, 39:254
Caenorhabditis elegans
bipotent cells AC/VU, 27:66–27:67
cell-cell interaction, 27:65–27:66
cell lineage, 27:63–27:64, 27:65
AC, *see* Anchor cell
neuroblast QL, homeobox gene actions,
27:101–27:103
VPC, *see* Vulval precursor cells
cell-type specification, genetic control
cell death program, 27:99
glp-1 locus, 27:100
heterochronic genes, 27:79, 27:98–27:99
homeobox-containing genes,
27:100–27:103, 27:110
mab-5 role, 27:99–27:100, 27:104
vulval, 27:74–27:98, *see also* Vulva,
development
coordinate control of sex determination and
dosage compensation, 27:152–27:162
number of genes involved, 27:163–27:165
sdc genes, 27:153–27:158
comparison with *dpy-29*, 27:161–27:162
xol-1 gene, 27:158–27:161
developmental control genes, 27:104–27:105
interactions, complexity, 27:109–27:110
order of action, 27:105–27:107
subprograms for sublineages,
27:107–27:109
dosage compensation
demonstration, 27:145–27:146

dumpy genes, requirement for,
27:147–27:150
mechanism, 27:151–27:152
timing during embryogenesis,
27:150–27:151
genetic analysis, methods
epistasis, 27:71–27:72
extragenic suppression, 27:72
mosaics, 27:72–27:73
mutant isolation, 27:68–27:70
null phenotypes, 27:70–27:71
terminology, 27:68
germ line sex determination
spermatogenesis, hermaphrodite-specific,
27:143, 27:178
sperm/oocyte decision, 27:142–27:143
molecular genetics, methods, 27:73–27:74
sex-controlling genes, 27:103–27:104
epistasis, 27:138–27:141
feminization *(fem)*, 27:132–27:137,
27:142–27:143
hermaphroditization *(her)*, 27:131–27:132,
27:137–27:138
temperature-sensitive periods, 27:129,
27:140, 27:150–27:151, 27:156,
27:157
transformer *(tra)*, 27:126–27:131,
27:143–27:145
sex determination
mutant phenotypes, 27:124–27:125
primary signal (X/A ratio), 27:122–27:125
sexual differentiation, 27:172–27:174
irreversibility *versus* plasticity,
27:177–27:179
sexual dimorphism, anatomy, 27:118–27:122
X/A ratio, 27:122–27:125, 27:166–27:169,
27:176–27:177
dosage compensation and, 27:152–27:154
yolk protein gene, expression in
hermaphrodite intestine, 27:174,
27:178–27:179
Caenorhabditis, telomeres and, 30:199
Café-au-lait skin spots, in neurofibromatosis type
1, 36:79, 36:104
Caffeine
effects on radiation injuries in
Schizosaccharomyces pombe,
23:27–23:33, 23:35, 23:38–23:40,
23:50–23:51
heat-shock puff induction, 39:347

CAG triplet repeat expansions, autosomal
dominant progressive ataxias, 38:35–39
Cairnsian mutations, Neurospora crassa and,
29:25
Calcium
defense response gene activation and, 28:204,
28:205
evolutionary genetics of fish and, 29:179
Neurospora crassa and, 29:10, 29:23
role in cellular integrity, 36:188
telomeres and, 30:195
Calcium-54, braconid wasp feeding effects,
25:162
Callase, see β-26:1,3-Glucanase
Calliphora
erythrocephala, zeste in Drosophila melanogaster
and, 29:329
zeste in Drosophila melanogaster and, 29:330
Callose, microspore isolation, 26:7
Callus, Gramineae
embryogenic, producing somatic embryo,
24:436, 24:438
embryo development from single cells,
24:440–24:441
from embryo tissues, 24:445–24:447
from leaf tissues, 24:447–24:449
regenerant phenotypic uniformity,
24:441–24:442
type I, compact, nodular, maize,
24:439–24:440
type II, soft, friable, maize, 24:439–24:440
nonmorphogenic, 24:436, 24:442, 24:444
organogenic, producing adventitious shoots,
24:436, 24:438
unsuitable for clonal propagation,
24:438–24:439
protoplast yield from, 24:457, 24:460
rooty, 24:436–24:437
shooty, 24:436–24:437
Calmodulin, plant transcription regulation, 27,
35:12–14
Campylobacter jejuni, iron-regulated gene in,
36:191
CaMV, nitrate reductase and, 30:28, 30:30
Cancer
apoptosis, 35:50–52
chromosome rearrangements in, 36:241
development, 33:255–270
future research directions, 33:269–270
homeobox genes

cancer role, 33:267
developmental processes, 33:265–266
expression
cancers, 33:268–269
leukemia, 33:267–268
tumorigenesis, in vivo model, 33:267
paired-box genes
embryonic development role,
33:256–259
expression
brain cancers, 33:260–263
primary human tumors, 33:260
rhabdomyosarcoma, 33:264–265
Wilms' tumor, 33:263–264
oncogene classification, 33:259
tumorigenesis, in vivo model,
33:259–260
mammalian tumor cells, polytene
chromosome occurrence, 34:105
melanotic pseudotumors, morphology change
induction, 34:306–307, 34:311
ovarian tumors, Drosophila, 34:58–59
shrinkage necrosis, 35:38–39
telomere role, 32:298–300
tumor suppressor gene role in,
36:45–36:136
Candida glabrata, superoxide dismutases and,
30:261
CAP20 tumor suppressor gene, characteristics
of, 36:47
Carbamate, mosquitoes and, 30:149
Carbamyl phosphate synthetase, Neurospora
crassa and, 29:40–29:41
Carbon
Neurospora crassa and, 29:38
superoxide dismutases and, 30:260–30:261,
30:271
molecular genetics, 30:279–30:281,
30:283–30:286
physiology of mutants, 30:294–30:296,
30:304
yeast ribosomes and, 29:84
Carbon dioxide
carbonic anhydrases and, 30:321–30:323,
30:333, 30:336, 30:345
nitrate reductase and, 30:30
Carbonic anhydrase-related protein, 30:321
chromosomal localization, 30:335
genes, 30:322, 30:332
Carbonic anhydrases, 30:321–30:322

CA I, 30:321, 30:325–30:329,
30:332–30:334
chromosomal localization, 30:334–30:335
evolutionary origins, 30:322–30:324
future directions, 30:349
genetic variations, 30:336–30:344,
30:346–30:347
CA II, 30:321–30:322, 30:325,
30:329–30:334
chromosomal localization,
30:334–30:335
evolutionary origins, 30:322–30:324
future directions, 30:349
genetic variations, 30:336,
30:339–30:341, 30:343–30:348
CA III, 30:321, 30:325, 30:329–30:334
chromosomal localization, 30:334
evolutionary origins, 30:322–30:324
genetic variation, 30:336–30:337, 30:341,
30:348
CA IV, 30:321–30:322, 30:332,
30:334–30:335
β-carbonic anhydrases, 30:323, 30:325
CA V, 30:321–30:322, 30:335
CA VI, 30:321–30:322, 30:334–30:335
CA VII, 30:321–30:322, 30:324–30:325,
30:334–30:335
chromosomal localization, 30:334–30:336
evolutionary origins, 30:322–30:325
future directions, 30:348–30:349
genetic variations, 30:336, 30:338–30:341
activity mutation, 30:336–30:337
allelic polymorphisms, 30:346–30:348
deficiency mutations, 30:337,
30:342–30:346
Carboxypeptidases, mosquitoes and, 30:154
Carcinogenesis, nuclear envelope role,
24:267–24:268
Carcinogens, evolutionary genetics of fish and,
29:171–29:172
Cardiac muscle, pathology in muscular
dystrophy, 33:181–182
β-Cardiac myosin, hypertrophic cardiomyopathy
role, 35:290–292, 35:302
Cardiac myosin-binding protein C, hypertrophic
cardiomyopathy role, 35:295–296
Cardiomyopathy, see Familial cardiomyopathies
CARP, see Carbonic anhydrase-related protein
Carrier tests, hemophilia, 32:110–113,
32:129–130

Casbene synthase, *Rhizopus stolonifer*-induced,
castor bean, 28:201
Cassia fasciculata, MGS, excess pollination and,
26:16
CAT, see Chloramphenicol acetyltransferase
Catalase
deficiency in mutants not sensitive to NUV,
E. coli, 26:102, 26:112–26:113, 26:119,
26:121–26:122
detoxification of NUV-induced H_2O_2,
26:111, 26:122
developmental control by regulatory genes
maize, 24:100–24:103
mouse, 24:86
in *Drosophila*
activity during development, 28:55
biological role, 28:56
genes, tissue specific expression of,
21:362–21:363
inactivation by NUV *in vitro* and *in vivo*,
26:107
isozymes, in pollen during development,
maize, 26:25
in maize, isozymes
characteristics, 28:13, 28:14
developmental expression, 28:15–28:16
CAT-2 in scutellum, 28:16–28:17
genetics, 28:13–28:14
responses to
hydrogen peroxide, 28:28–28:29
light, 28:21–28:23
paraquat, 28:23–28:25
temperature chronic elevation,
28:28–28:29
subcellular localization, 28:15
superoxide dismutases and
molecular genetics, 30:276,
30:279–30:280, 30:287
physiology, 30:256, 30:260
physiology of mutants, 30:296,
30:301–30:302, 30:307
structure, 30:269
Catalysis, superoxide dismutases and,
30:267–30:268, 30:271–30:272
Catecholamine-O-methyltransferase (COMT),
Drosophila, 24:142
Catecholamines, insects
developmental analysis, *Drosophila*,
24:151–24:154
metabolism

Catecholamines, insects (continued)
in Drosophila, Ddc gene cluster and,
24:177–24:178
during melanization, 24:145–24:147
during sclerotization, 24:146–24:150
synthesis and metabolism pathways,
24:128–24:129, 24:135
Catecholamine X, formation from DOPA,
Drosophila
amd gene and, 24:169
pathway of, 24:170
Catenins, association with APC gene, 36:73
Cathespin D, mosquitoes and, 30:154
Cation diffusion facilitators, role in bacterial
metal resistance, 36:224
Catostomus commersoni, evolutionary genetics of
fish and, 29:197–29:198
CAT1, superoxide dismutases and, 30:280,
30:297
Caulobacter crescentus
CuZnSOD, 26:67
flagellar genes
cluster location, 27:5–27:6
comparison with
B. subtilis spo genes, 27:24
E. coli flagellar genes, 27:20
consensus sequences, 27:12–27:15,
27:17
positive control hierarchy, 27:8–27:13
regulation strategies, 27:15–27:17
timing of expression, 27:6–27:7,
27:17–27:18
flagellum, structure, 27:4–27:6
life cycle, 27:2–27:4
C4b-binding protein
interactions with protein S in thrombophilia,
33:144–147
CCAAT-binding transcription factor, in HSP
gene induction
by adenovirus protein E1A, 24:51
by heat, 24:44, 24:46, 24:52
CCP1, superoxide dismutases and, 30:287
CDC17, telomeres and, 30:219
cdc2 gene family in Drosophila melanogaster,
31:81–83
cdc17, telomeres and, 30:219
CDK-cyclin complexes
negative regulators of, 36:61, 36:74
tumor suppressor gene effects on, 36:47,
36:48, 36:51, 36:64, 36:66

CDKN1s, as protein partners of CDK
molecules, 36:105
CDKN2 tumor suppressor genes, characteristics
of, 36:48
cDNA
Drosophila transposable elements and, 29:252,
29:278
evolutionary genetics of fish and, 29:131,
29:146, 29:201
endocrine system, 29:192, 29:195,
29:197–29:200
environmental change, 29:162, 29:168,
29:170
mosquitoes and, 30:125, 30:148–30:149,
30:151, 30:153–30:154, 30:159–30:160
Mu elements of Zea mays and, 30:98, 30:111,
30:116
Neurospora crassa and, 29:10, 29:13, 29:19,
29:45
nitrate reductase and, 30:6–30:10, 30:23,
30:27–30:28
use in gene studies, 36:139
yeast ribosomes and, 29:69
zeste in Drosophila melanogaster and, 29:313
Cecropins, mosquitoes and, 30:155–30:156,
30:171
Cell adhesion molecules
neural plate
Xenopus laevis, 31:66
Cell adhesion proteins, Ig-like motif in, 36:22
Cell cycle
dividing cell heterochromatin morphology,
37:5–43
chromosomal rearrangement localization,
37:29–30
compaction degree, 37:5–14
anoxia effects, 37:13
distamycin A effects, 37:11
genetic control, 37:13
Hoechst 33258 effects, 37:9–11
mechanisms, 37:13–14
overview, 37:5–6
permanence, 37:6–9
radiation effects, 37:12–13
temperature effects, 37:11–13
developing animal heterochromatin
formation, 37:35–43, 37:440–443
differential staining, 37:14–24
C-staining, 37:14–15
enzymatic chromosome digestion, 37:24

heterochromatin heterogeneity, 37:24
H-staining, 37:15–21
N-staining, 37:21–23
Q-staining, 37:15–21
heterochromatin quantity variation,
   37:33–35
late replication, 37:30–33
pairing, 37:24–28
interphase chromocenter formation,
   37:8, 37:24–25
meiosis, 37:28
mitosis, 37:26–28
historical perspective, 34:9
negative regulators of, 36:51, 36:59, 36:60
p53 as negative regulator of, 36:59, 36:60
of *Schizosaccharomyces pombe*
growth
   DNA synthesis, 23:6–23:7
   mitochondrial functions, 23:7–23:8
   protein synthesis, 23:6–23:7
   RNA synthesis, 23:6–23:7
meiotic, 23:9–23:18
   mating types, 23:11–23:13
   morphology, 23:9–23:11
   mutants of, 23:10–23:14
   physiology, 23:9–23:11
   recombinations, 23:14–23:18
phases G_1 and G_2, 23:4
radiation resistance during, 23:19–23:22
regulation system, 23:5–23:6
vegetative mitotic, 23:4–23:6
somaclonal variation and, 30:61–30:62
telomeres and, 30:202
Cell cycle genes
Drosophila melanogaster
cdc2 gene family, 31:81–83
cyclins, 31:83–88
kinesin family motor proteins, 31:103–106
   kinease heavy chain (khc), 31:104
   no distributive disjunction (nod),
      31:105–106
   nonclaret disjunctional (ncd), 31:104–105
microtubule-associated proteins,
   31:99–101
   exuperantia (exu), 31:100–101
   haywire (hay), 31:100
   whirlgig (wrl), 31:100
microtubule organizing center, 31:101–103
   aurora mutant, 31:102–103
   DMAP-190, 31:102

DMAP60, 31:102
   merry-go-round mutant, 31:102–103
   microtubule interacting protein A (mipA),
      31:101–102
   p34^{cdc2} activity, 31:89–93
   polo kinase, 31:93–94
   protein phosphatase 1, 31:96
   protein phosphatase 2A, 31:96–97
   tubulin gene family, 31:97–99
Cell fusion, in fungal gene transfer,
   23:79–23:80
Cell hybrids, intertypic, rodents
   TF gene expression extinction, 25:28–25:29
   karyotypic analysis and, 25:29
Cellia, mosquitoes and, 30:129
Cell incubation
   morphology change induction
      in vitro incubation, 34:297–299
      in vivo incubation, 34:291–297
Cell synchronization
   in *Schizosaccharomyces pombe*
      induction methods, 23:19
      selection techniques, 23:18–23:19
Cell-type-controlling genes, *C. elegans*
   anchor cell-specifying *lin-12*, 27:79, 27:81
   cell death-programming, 27:99
   glp-1 locus, 27:100
   heterochronic, 27:79, 27:98–27:99
   homeobox-containing, hierarchy,
      27:100–27:103, 27:110
   mab-5 role, 27:99–27:100, 27:104
   VPC generation, *lin-24, lin-26, lin-33,*
      unc-83, unc-84, 27:79
   VPC specification
      lin-12
         2° cell-specifying, 27:82, 27:84, 27:95
         mutations, 27:88–27:89
         pathway, 27:91–27:92, 27:96, 27:98,
            27:105–27:107
      lin-1, lin-25, lin-31, 27:94–27:95
      Muv class, 27:82, 27:92–27:94
      lin-15, mutations, 27:82, 27:91
      secondary lineage execution
         lin-17, 27:85–27:87, 27:105–27:107
         lin-11, lin-18, 27:85–27:86
      Vul class, 27:81–27:82, 27:92–27:94
         B. subt lus spo genes
         let-23, 27:81–27:82, 27:90–27:91
         lin-3, 27:81–27:82, 27:89–27:90
         lin-2, lin-7, lin-10, 27:81–27:82, 27:90

Cell-type-specific genes, yeast
α-specific
activation by MATα1 protein,
27:37–27:38
UAS binding to PRTF and,
27:42–27:46
UAS detection analysis, 27:43–27:45
a-specific
repression by MATα2
in α and a cells, 27:37–27:38,
27:47–27:48
in a/α cells, 27:40, 27:48
UAS, binding to PRTF, 27:46–27:48
Cellular growth, possible role of peripheral
myelin protein 22 in, 36:28
Cellularization, genes in *Drosophila melanogaster*,
31:107–109
Cellular senescence, telomeres and,
30:206–30:208
CE1, mosquitoes and, 30:148
CE2, mosquitoes and, 30:148
Central nervous system
connexin32 in, 36:29
in *Ddc* mutants, *Drosophila*, 24:161–24:162
postembryonic development, braconid wasps,
25:121–25:122
TF synthesis during development and aging,
rat, 25:14, 25:16, 25:18, 25:23–25:24
Centromeres
carbonic anhydrases and, 30:334
evolutionary genetics of fish and, 29:137,
29:144
fungal, isolation and characterization,
23:112–23:114
heterochromatin gene expression
modification, 37:339–341
mosquitoes and, 30:150–30:151
Neurospora crassa and, 29:12, 29:14–29:16,
29:41, 29:43, 29:45
pericentromeric heterochromatin
inactivation, 37:378–391
heterochromatin amount effects,
37:381–382
inactivation strength, 37:383–385
rearrangement breaks, 37:385–390
revertant strain cytological analysis,
37:379–381, 37:389–390
polytene chromosome heterochromatin,
37:89–133
cytogenetics, 37:124–133
morphology, 37:89–98

quantity variations, 37:36–39, 37:109–124
structural components, 37:98–109
DNA, 37:98–105
proteins, 37:105–106
structural changes, 37:106–109
somaclonal variation and, 30:49, 30:52
telomeres and, 30:193, 30:225–30:226
Cercosporin, CAT stimulation, maize,
28:29–28:30
Cerpis, somaclonal variation and, 30:49
Ceruloplasmin, copper-binding, gene linkage to
TF on chromosome 3, human, 25:11
Cervical cancer, p53 implication in, 36:57
Cesium-137, *see* Gamma rays
c-fos gene
as p53 target, 36:59
regulation of, 36:85
cGMP, plant transcription regulation, 27,
35:12–14
Chagasia bathana, mosquitoes and, 30:126
Chalcone synthase
induction by infection/elicitor, 28:189
timing, 28:190–28:191
isozymes, 28:177
in phytoalexin biosynthesis, 28:176
Channa, evolutionary genetics of fish and,
29:138
Charcot-Marie-Tooth disease, *See* CMT disease
Chelating agents, effects of irradiated braconid
wasps, 25:157
Chemostat, screening and, 20:43
Chemotropism, pollen tubes *in vitro* and *in vivo*,
26:32
Chiasmata
function, 32:276–277
Chicken embryo, heart defects induction,
28:278, 28:279
Chironomus
Cla-element identification, 37:105,
37:219–220
heterochromatin puff induction,
37:106–109
intercalary α-heterochromatin, 37:138
telomeres and, 30:196
Chitinase, pathogen-induced, plants
purification and localization, 28:178–28:179
structure, from cDNA, 28:198–28:199
homologies, 28:199–28:200
in transgenic tobacco, 28:215
Chlamydomonas
linear mitochondrial genome of, 22:28

plastid genes
  cab expression, nitrogen deficiency and,
    28:151
  in transformed chloroplasts, 28:138
Chlamydomonas reinhardtii
  carbonic anhydrases and, 30:343
  nitrate reductase and, 30:9, 30:23, 30:27
Chloral hydrate, heat-shock puff induction,
    39:346, 39:350
Chloramphenicol, heat-shock puff induction,
    39:346–347
Chloramphenicol acetyltransferase
  gene, *zeste* in *Drosophila melanogaster* and,
    29:322
  induction in transgenic mouse by
    αA-crystallin-CAT fusion gene,
      24:303–24:304
    α2 type I collagen-CAT gene, 24:304
  mosquitoes and, 30:169–30:170
Chlorate, nitrate reductase and, 30:28
  hypersensitivity, 30:15, 30:18
  resistance, 30:14, 30:21–30:22
Chlorate resistance, in bacteria, molybdate role
    in, 36:200
Chlorella, nitrate reductase and, 30:4, 30:8
Chloroform, puff activity effects, 39:253
Chlorophyll *a/b*-binding proteins
  circadian rhythm, 28:148–28:150
  iron deficiency and, 28:151–28:152
  nitrogen deficiency and, 28:157
  photoregulation, 28:11, 28:139,
    28:144–28:146
  plastid factors and, 28:146–28:147
Chloroplasts, *see also* Plastids
  carbonic anhydrases and, 30:323, 30:325
  genome polymorphism, 23:244–23:245
  Neurospora crassa and, 29:30
  nitrate reductase and, 30:8–30:9, 30:30
  somaclonal variation and, 30:41
  superoxide dismutases and, 30:256, 30:268,
    30:271
Chlorosis, nitrate reductase and, 30:16
Cholesterol ester transfer protein
  high-density lipoprotein metabolism,
    32:180–183
Cholinesterase, mosquitoes and, 30:157
Choline-O-sulfate, utilization by *Neurospora
  crassa*, 31:195–196
Chorion
  genes
    in *Drosophila*, 24:227, 24:228–24:229

amplification during development,
    24:231–24:232
  chromosomal organization, 24:231
  coded by *s15-1*, 27:225–27:227
  proteins encoded by, 24:229
  regulatory intergenic elements
    5′-flanking DNA, 24:233, 24:239
    localization, 24:235, 24:237
    sex-specific gene expression, 27:224
  in silk moths
    architectural, E family, 24:228
    chromosomal organization,
      24:229–24:231
    expression
      during development, 24:230
      in transgenic *Drosophila*,
        24:235–24:238
    regulatory intergenic elements
      5′-flanking DNA, 24:232–24:234,
        24:239
      function, 24:237–24:238
      localization, 24:235, 24:237
    structural, α and β groups,
      24:225–24:227
  α/β super family
    conversion-like events, 24:228
    nomenclature and sequence
      homologies, 24:226
    structure, fruit flies and silk moths,
      24:223–24:225
Chromatids, *see also* Sister chromatid exchange
  mosquitoes and, 30:145
  Mu elements of *Zea mays* and, 30:107
  position effect, pompon formation, 37:421–422
  structure
    nonpolytene chromosomes, 34:243–247
    polytene chromosomes, 34:247–260
    trophoblast cells, 34:104–105
  synapsis
    chromosome variation, 34:150–157
    polyteny morphology, 34:125–129
  telomeres and, 30:229
Chromatin
  conformation in *Drosophila*
    cis-acting regulator effects, 24:415–24:418
  diminution, 37:78–89
    Ascaris megalocephala, 37:78–81
    Cyclops, 37:81–84
    dipteran insects, 37:84–86
    infusoria, 37:86–88
    physiological significance, 37:89

Chromatin (continued)
  Drosophila transposable elements and,
    29:270
  evolutionary genetics of fish and, 29:143
  general features in higher plants
    histones, 22:157–22:164
    nonhistone chromatin proteins,
      22:164–22:170
    nucleosomes and higher order structure,
      22:154–22:157
  position effect
    compaction, 37:400–413, 37:428–429
    characteristics, 37:402–404
    discontinuous compaction, 37:406–407,
      37:410
    formation, 37:404–406, 37:410
    historical perspectives, 37:400–401
    late-replication, 37:410
    occurrence frequencies, 37:411–413
    parental effects, 37:408–409
    temperature effects, 37:407–408
    state changes, 37:422–428
  somaclonal variation and, 30:50
  structure, gene regulation and,
    22:145–22:154
  telomeres and, 30:199, 30:215, 30:222
  transcriptionally active
    DNA modification and, 22:190–22:192
    fractionation and nuclease sensitivity,
      22:171–22:174
    nonhistone chromosomal proteins and,
      22:186–22:190
    role of histones in determining structure,
      22:174–22:186
    visualization by electron microscopy,
      22:170–22:171
  yeast ribosomes and, 29:78, 29:87, 29:89
  zeste in Drosophila melanogaster and, 29:302,
    29:318, 29:334
  packaging, 29:338–29:343
  transvection, 29:308–29:309
Chromatography, mosquitoes and, 30:140
Chromium, bacterial gene induction by, 36:221
Chromium chloride, puff activity effects, 39:254
Chromocenter
  centromeric heterochromatin DNA
    hybridization, 37:99–105
  formation
    interphase heterochromatin pairing, 37:8,
      37:24–25

  meiotic pairing, 37:28
  mitotic pairing, 37:26–28
  polytene sets, 37:95, 37:98
  morphological analysis, heterochromatin
    cytogenetics, 37:129–132
Chromomeres
  band–gene
    number relations, 39:94–118
    gene distribution, 39:115–118
  band–gene–loop relations, 39:156–160
    Adh gene, 39:157
    14B region genes, 39:159–160
    15B region genes, 39:159–160
    87DE region genes, 39:157–158
    ftz gene, 39:157
    histone genes, 39:157
    Sgs-4 gene, 39:157
  band–gene number relations
    gene number calculation, 39:94–113
    region genetic analysis, 39:113–115
  banding pattern variability, 39:20–40
    P-element role, 39:28–32, 39:90–94
    temperature induced variation, 39:33–34
  DNA replication unit correlation,
    39:436–442
  historical perspectives, 39:3–9, 39:9–20
  individual band organization, 39:118–156
    artificial bands, 39:148–150
    37C1-2 band, 39:139–145
    multiband genes, 39:153–156
    oligogene bands, 39:129–139
    overlapping gene bands, 39:150–153
    polygene bands, 39:126–129
    simple bands, 39:145–147
  interchromomeres, organization
    genetic organization, 39:87–94
    molecular organization, 39:87–94
    overview, 39:84–87
  pattern
    band mapping
      artificial bands, 34:212–213
      band sizes, 34:207–212
      chromosome morphology relation,
        34:198–202
      cytological repeats, 34:213–215
      interbands, 34:207–213
      methods, 34:202–207
      pattern fixation, 34:190–197
      historical perspective, 34:13–14
      map building basis, 34:187–190

seasonal changes, **34:**300–304
stability, **39:**2
transcription, *see* Transcription
type variation, **39:**6–9
Chromosomal syndromes, mouse models,
35:175–177
Chromosome 1
CMT2A disease linkage to, **36:**21
CMT1B disease linkage to, **36:**19, **36:**21
CMT1 disease linkage to, **36:**4–**36:**5
CMT2 disease linkage to, **36:**5–**36:**6
(*N. crassa*), rearrangements in, **36:**255
tumor suppressor genes on, **36:**47, **36:**68
Chromosome 2
(*Drosophila*)
Lhr mutation on, **36:**168
mhr mutation on, **36:**170
(*N. crassa*), rearrangements in, **36:**255,
36:256
tumor suppressor genes on, **36:**50, **36:**76,
36:93, **36:**95
Chromosome 3
CMT2B disease linkage to, **36:**21
CMT2 disease linkage to, **36:**6
human
TF gene family location, **25:**9–**25:**11
rearrangement during primate evolution,
25:11
(*N. crassa*), rearrangement in, **36:**255
tumor suppressor genes on, **36:**49, **36:**50,
36:76, **36:**84, **36:**95
Chromosome 5
(*N. crassa*), rearrangements in, **36:**255
tumor suppressor gene on, **36:**49, **36:**95
Chromosome 6
(*N. crassa*), rearrangement in, **36:**255
tumor suppressor genes on, **36:**47
Chromosome 7
(*N. crassa*), rearrangements in, **36:**255
peripheral myelin protein zero linkage to,
36:22–**36:**23
tumor suppressor gene on, **36:**50, **36:**95
Chromosome 9
cytogenetic abnormalities in, **36:**65
(*Drosophila*), *Lhr* mutation on, **36:**168
as site of common deletion in cancer, **36:**65
tumor suppressor genes on, **36:**47, **36:**48,
36:65, **36:**95
Chromosome 11
CMT1A disease gene on, **36:**10

p57 gene on, **36:**64
tumor suppressor genes on, **36:**47, **36:**48,
36:49, **36:**50, **36:**69, **36:**90, **36:**92,
36:95, **36:**102, **36:**104
Chromosome 12
p27 gene on, **36:**63
tumor suppressor gene on, **36:**47
Chromosome 13
breast cancer susceptibility gene on, **36:**86
retinoblastoma linkage to, **36:**53
tumor suppressor gene on, **36:**49, **36:**53,
36:95
Chromosome 16
translocation on, **36:**69
tumor suppressor gene on, **36:**95
Chromosome 17
breast cancer susceptibility gene on, **36:**86
CMTA1A disease linkage to, **36:**8, **36:**21
CMT1 disease linkage to, **36:**5
Déjerine-Sottas disease linkage to, **36:**21
duplication and deletion testing on, **36:**35
HNPP linkage to, **36:**13, **36:**21
neurofibromatosis type 1 linkage to, **36:**79
TP53 tumor suppressor gene on, **36:**47
trisomy of, **36:**9
tumor suppressor genes on, **36:**47, **36:**49,
36:71, **36:**95
Chromosome 22
tumor supressor genes on, **36:**47, **36:**49,
36:83, **36:**95
Chromosome 8, CMT4A disease linkage to,
36:6–**36:**7, **36:**21
Chromosome 10, tumor suppressor gene on,
36:95
Chromosome 19, tumor suppressor gene on,
36:68
Chromosome 18, tumor suppressor genes on,
36:50, **36:**78
Chromosome capping, telomeres and,
30:201–**30:**203, **30:**222–**30:**223
Chromosome fields
spatial organization, **34:**340–344
Chromosome III (*Saccharomyces cerevisiae*),
36:140
Chromosome 4 (*N. crassa*), rearrangements in,
36:255
Chromosome pairing
Drosophila melanogaster
homologs in male meiosis, **31:**117–118
mei-S332 mutant, **31:**120

Chromosome pairing (*continued*)
  orientation disruptor (ord) mutant,
    31:120–121
  parallel sister chromatids (pasc) function,
    31:121
  sister chromatids, 31:118–120
Chromosomes
  abnormalities in plant tissue cultures,
    28:82–28:83
  B chromosomes, 37:282–304
    designation symbols, 37:282
    fitness association, 37:302–303
    heterochromatin association, 37:300–301
    heterochromatin detection, 37:6
    number, 37:295–297
    occurrence, 37:288–294
    pairing, 37:299–300
    properties, 37:436
    recombinational repair enhancement,
      maize, 24:339
    supernumerary effects, 37:301–304
  3B nullisomics, desynaptic effect in meiosis,
    wheat, 26:184, 26:186
  breaks, intercalary heterochromatin
    identification, 37:150–165
    constrictions, 37:150, 158
    fissures, 37:158–159
    frequency, 37:161–165
    shift, 37:159–160
  carbonic anhydrases and, 30:232,
    30:333–30:336
  circular, meiotic recombination, sister
    chromatid exchange, 33:48
  Drosophila transposable elements and
    foldback elements, 29:285–29:288
    hobo, 29:275–29:278
    mariner, 29:279–29:281
    P elements, 29:262–29:264,
      29:269–29:270
    retrotransposons, 29:236–29:237, 29:244,
      29:257–29:258
  elimination, dipteran insects, 37:84–86
  eukaryotic
    ars (autonomously replicating sequences)
      characterization, 23:106–23:108
      isolation, 23:104–23:106
      significance in transformation,
        23:108–23:109
  evolutionary genetics of fish and, 29:147,
    29:187

  linkage groups, 29:144, 29:146–29:147
  nuclear genomic structures,
    29:135–29:143
  frost hardiness-effecting, wheat, 28:106,
    28:107
  fungal
    artificial, construction, 23:115–23:116
    mapping by
      chimeric plasmid insertion,
        23:120–23:121
      gene location, 23:121
      overlap hybridization, 23:119–23:120
      physical distances in terms of nucleotide
        base pairs, 23:120
      resident gene replacement,
        23:121–23:122
  germline cell heterochromatin, 37:304–306
  Gossypium spp.
    alien additions, 23:326–23:327
    homologous pairing, suppression in
      allotetraploids, 23:349–23:352
    size in genomic groups, 23:291, 23:293
    substitution using monosomes,
      23:322–23:323
    translocation, 23:296–23:307, *see also*
      Translocation
  libraries
    human genes, *see* Human Genome Project
    mouse genomics, 35:165–168
    yeast artificial chromosome libraries,
      35:166, 168
  mapping, *see* Genome mapping
  in *mei* mutants
    pairing impairment, maize,
      26:164–26:167
    segregation abnormalities, maize,
      26:167–26:168
    stickiness, plants, 26:164
  meiotic recombination, sister chromatid
    exchange
    circular chromosomes, 33:48
    nonhomologous chromosome repeats,
      33:50
  mosquitoes and
    genetic differentiation, 30:126–30:127,
      30:133, 30:135–30:136
    genetic transformation, 30:164, 30:166,
      30:169
    genome characterization, 30:139,
      30:141–30:142, 30:144–30:147

mt in ascomycetes, organization and
replication, **25**:227–**25**:228
Mu elements of *Zea mays* and, **30**:83, **30**:97,
30:106–**30**:108
Neurospora crassa and, **29**:2–**29**:5, **29**:43,
29:46–**29**:48
DNA transaction, **29**:19, **29**:24–**29**:25
genetic material, **29**:12–**29**:16, **29**:18
gene transfer, **29**:5–**29**:6, **29**:10–**29**:11
membrane, **29**:38
metabolism, **29**:41
mitochondria, **29**:26–**29**:27, **29**:32, **29**:34
nitrate reductase and, **30**:17–**30**:18,
30:21–**30**:22
numerical abnormalities, **33**:101–130
aneuploidy
45,X, **33**:109–110
47,XXX, **33**:110–113
47,XXY, **33**:110–113
47,XYY, **33**:113–114
cell division origin, **33**:107–109
disomic gamete frequencies, **33**:125–129
monosomy
etiology, **33**:105–106
frequency, **33**:102–105
overview, **33**:101–102
parental origin, **33**:106–107
sex chromosome polysomy, **33**:114–115
trisomy
13, **33**:122–123
14, **33**:122–123
15, **33**:122–123
16, **33**:121–122
18, **33**:120–121
21, **33**:115–120
22, **33**:122–123
etiology, **33**:105–106
frequency, **33**:102–105
origin mechanisms, **33**:123–125
physiology, **30**:147, **30**:149–**30**:151
position effect, inactivation spreading,
37:311, **37**:329–330
proterminal regions, **32**:273–306
chromosome ends from primates,
32:295–296
function, **32**:275–278
in genetic disease, **32**:296–305
cancer, **32**:298–300
chromosome healing *in vivo*,
32:301–303

contiguous gene syndromes, **32**:303–305
cryptic translocations, **32**:303–305
telomere repeat loss, **32**:296–301
structure, **32**:281–294
associated sequences, **32**:282–283
chromosome end sequence, **32**:289–294
minisatellites, **32**:284–285
properties, **32**:281–282
subterminal repeat sequences,
32:287–289
subterminal sequence isolation,
32:285–287
rearrangement
effect on tumor suppressor genes, **36**:93
gene expression inactivation
initiation, **37**:429–433
position effect, **37**:310–311,
37:329–330
vital genes, **37**:316–318
intercalary heterochromatin identification,
37:198–206
in *Neurospora crassa*, see *Neurospora crassa*
parental genotype effects, **37**:339,
37:341–342
role in human pathology, **36**:241
studies on, **36**:241–**36**:242
in *Schizosaccharomyces pombe*, number of,
23:3
segregation, telomeres and, **30**:195, **30**:206,
30:208, **30**:217, **30**:220
segregation fidelity, meiotic reciprocal
recombination, **35**:253–278
chiasma formation, **35**:273–276
chromosome segregation studies,
35:276–277
disjunction enhancement, **35**:265–271
bivalents, **35**:268–269
chiasma binder, **35**:271–273
pairing, **35**:265–268
partner recognition, **35**:265–268
spindle attachment, **35**:269–271
exchange contributions, **35**:255–265
crossover cytology, **35**:259–261
recombination mutant use, **35**:256–257
spontaneous nondisjunctions,
35:257–259
yeast chromosome model, **35**:261–265
overview, **35**:253–255
recombination intermediates, **35**:273–276
sex-determining factors, **37**:306

Chromosomes (continued)
 size
  bands, chromomere pattern analysis,
   34:207–212
  historical perspective, 34:9
  nuclei, 34:260–280
  somaclonal variation and, 30:43, 30:65
   genetic consequences, 30:48–30:52,
    30:56, 30:59, 30:61–30:62
   unusual genetic behavior, 30:64–30:65
  stretching, isolated chromosome studies,
   34:330–332
 superoxide dismutases and, 30:273, 30:277,
  30:281, 30:283, 30:298, 30:303
 telomeres, 32:273–306
  binding proteins, 32:280–281
  in cancer, 32:298–300
  chromosome ends from other primates,
   32:295–296
  chromosome healing in vivo, 32:301–303
  telomerase activity, 32:301–302
  telomerase inactivity in somatic tissues,
   32:302–303
  telomere capture, 32:303
  contiguous gene syndromes, 32:303–305
  cryptic translocation, 32:303–305
  function, 32:273–275
  isolation, 32:279–281
  reintroduction into mammalian cells,
   32:300–301
  repeat loss, 32:296–301
  structure, 32:279–281
   4p telomere, 32:290–291
   16p telomere, 32:291–293
   7q telomere, 32:291
   21q telomere, 32:293–294
   Xp/Yp pseudoautosomal region,
    32:289–290
 telomeres and, 30:185–30:186,
  30:232–30:233
  formation, 30:226–30:232
  function, 30:201–30:209, 30:211,
   30:213–30:222
  gene expression, 30:222–30:224
  nuclear organization, 30:224–30:226
  structure, 30:186–30:187, 30:190–30:198,
   30:200–30:201
 X and Y in pollen tubes, role in growth rate,
  Silene alba, 26:3
 Y chromosome

 deletion mapping, 33:284–287
 structure, 33:283–284
 yeast ribosomes and, 29:70, 29:73,
  29:86–29:87, 29:99
 zeste in Drosophila melanogaster and, 29:302
 chromatin packaging, 29:337–29:342
 discovery, 29:303–29:305
 DNA binding, 29:319
 function, 29:326–29:327, 29:329
 molecular biology, 29:313
 polytene, 29:316–29:318
 protein, 29:334
 transvection, 29:306, 29:311–29:312
Chromosome walking, Neurospora crassa and,
 29:16
Chromosome X
 in Drosophila
  autosomal cloned gene relocation to,
   24:407–24:410
  autosomal fragment translocation to,
   24:407
  cloned gene relocation to autosome,
   24:411–24:413
  early cytological observations,
   24:377–24:378
  elements lethal in single dose in females
   and duplicated in males,
   24:418–24:420
  in female soma, both chromosome active,
   24:376–24:377
  fragment translocation to autosome,
   24:406
  RNA synthesis equal in males and females,
   24:378–24:380
  segment addition to genome
   RNA synthesis over all regions,
    24:387–24:388
  x-linked gene activities,
   24:386–24:387
  in Drosophila hydei primary spermatogenesis,
   23:185, 23:208–23:210
 in transgenic mouse
  inactivation, chicken TF gene expression
   unaffected by, 25:18
Chromosome Y
 Drosophila, lack of effect on X-linked genes,
  24:391
 during spermatogenesis of
  Drosophila hydei, 23:179–23:228
  DNA sequences, 23:223–23:226

lampbrush loops, *see* Lampbrush loops
mutations, 23:217–23:221
protein expression, 23:215–23:217
Drosophila hydei x *D. neohydei* hybrid,
23:204–23:205
Chronogenetics
arrhythmic phenotypes, 38:149–157
brain-behavioral studies, 38:163–167
clock-resetting signals, 38:171–172
courtship song cycle, 38:159–160
egg-to-adult development, 38:161
environmental synchronization, 38:142–145
fundamentals, 38:135–142
long-period phenotypes, 38:146–148
non-temporal phenotypes, 38:161–163
ovarian diapause, 38:158–159
overview, 38:135–136, 38:173
period gene expression, 38:163–168,
38:172–173
short-period phenotypes, 38:148–149
visual rhythms, 38:157–158
CHS, *see* Chalcone synthase
chy2, yeast ribosomes and, 29:72–29:73
ci^+ gene
Dubunin effect, 37:357–362
position effects, 37:371
Cinnamic acid, phenylpropanoid pathway
regulation, 28:189
CIPI tumor suppressor gene, 36:61
characteristics of, 36:47
CIP/KIP gene family, tumor suppression by,
36:61–36:64
Circadian cycling, *see also* Biological rhythms
PER protein, *Drosophila melanogaster*,
31:166–167
Circadian rhythm, *see also* Chronogenetics
Cat3 mRNA, maize leaves, 28:22–28:23
mosquitoes and, 30:171
Neurospora crassa and, 29:42
nitrate reductase and, 30:10–30:11, 30:28,
30:31
photosynthetic gene expression,
28:147–28:150
plant transcription regulation, 35:1–28
CAB gene characteristics, 35:2–6
cis- and *trans*-acting element requirements,
35:20–25
cyanobacteria model, 35:17–20
future research directions, 35:25–28
overview, 35:1–2

photoreceptors, 35:6–11
blue-light receptors, 35:9–11
phytochrome, 35:6–9
phototransduction pathway analysis,
35:15–17
signal transduction intermediate
identification, 35:11–14
Cirri, *Drosophila*
development from maxillary segment, 27:365
in *hsDfd* larvae, 27:391, 27:393, 27:394
missing in *Dfd*_mutants, 27:366–27:367
cis-acting elements
for bacterial molybdate repression, 36:202
carbonic anhydrases and, 30:334
Drosophila, 29:240–29:257, 29:264
ftz gene and, 27:334–27:335
zen gene and, 27:302–27:303
Mu elements of *Zea mays* and, 30:116
superoxide dismutases and, 30:271, 30:276,
30:285–30:286
Citrullus vulgaria, superoxide dismutases and,
30:268
Citrus clementina, somaclonal variation and,
30:47
Citrus sinensis, somaclonal variation and, 30:44
c-jun gene, as p53 target, 36:59
c-ki-ras, revolutionary genetics of fish and,
29:172–29:173
4CL, *see* 4-Coumarate:CoA lipase
Cla-element, identification, 37:105,
37:219–220
ClaI, mosquitoes and, 30:135
Clarkia dudleyana, pollen,
phosphoglucoisomerase-encoding genes,
26:22
Claviceps purpurea, *Neurospora crassa* and,
29:35
Clines, evolutionary genetics of fish and,
29:164–29:165
Clinical care
long-term, 32:1–15
adverse experiences
clinical identification, 32:5–8
ongoing, 32:8–12
benefit, 32:12–13
gene therapy risks, 32:3–5, 32:9,
32:13–14
informed consent, 32:9, 32:13–14
Clock (Clk) mutant
Drosophila melanogaster, 31:169

Clones
  Drosophila transposable elements and, 29:241,
      29:252
  evolutionary genetics of fish and, 29:129,
      29:146, 29:201
  endocrine system, 29:192, 29:195, 29:198,
      29:200
  environmental change, 29:168, 29:171
  nervous system, 29:177–29:179
  mosquitoes and, 30:125, 30:162,
      30:169–30:171
  genetic differentiation, 30:129–30:130,
      30:134–30:135
  genome characterization, 30:141–30:143,
      30:145–30:146
  physiology, 30:148–30:154, 30:157,
      30:159–30:160
  Mu elements of Zea mays and, 30:80
  applications, 30:113–30:114
  gene expression, 30:111
  properties of transposition, 30:100
  regulation, 30:97–30:98
  structure, 30:93, 30:95
  Neurospora crassa and, 29:4, 29:42–29:47
  DNA transaction, 29:19, 29:22
  genetic material, 29:13–29:18
  gene transfer, 29:5, 29:9–29:12
  membrane, 29:38–29:39
  nitrate reductase and, 30:6, 30:9–30:10,
      30:13, 30:27–30:28
  somaclonal variation and, 30:57–30:58
  superoxide dismutases and, 30:262–30:263,
      30:266, 30:269
  molecular genetics, 30:272–30:273,
      30:280, 30:287–30:288
  physiology of mutants, 30:302, 30:307
  telomeres and
  formation, 30:227, 30:232
  function, 30:217–30:218
  structure, 30:193, 30:195, 30:197, 30:199
  yeast ribosomes and, 29:86, 29:96, 29:103
  genetic analysis, 29:99–29:100, 29:103
  ribosomal protein genes, 29:71–29:73,
      29:75, 29:77, 29:80–29:81, 29:83
  zeste in Drosophila melanogaster and, 29:313,
      29:319, 29:321
Cloning, see also Autosomal dominant progressive
      ataxias, clones; Molecular cloning
  diabetes-susceptibility gene identification,
      32:57, 32:60, 32:61–62

historical perspective, 34:20
  isolated chromosome studies, 34:329
  phenylalanine hydroxylation cDNA,
      32:204–205
Clostridium pasteurianum, molybdenum-
      regulated gene in, 36:203
CLP8, yeast ribosomes and, 29:101, 29:103
Clupea harengus, evolutionary genetics of fish
      and, 29:125, 29:128
CMT1A disease
  CMT1A-REP sequence in chromosome for,
      36:19
  crossover region on chromosome for,
      36:14–36:16
  duplications in, 36:8–36:9, 36:34
  fine mapping for, 36:8
  gene duplication in, 36:26, 36:33
  genetic locus of, 36:19
  (HMSNIa), linkage to chromosome 17p,
      36:5
  HNPP disease comparison to, 36:14–36:16,
      36:33
  molecular mechanisms in, 36:8–36:19
  molecular testing for, 36:34–36:35
  monomer unit of, 36:11–36:12
  mutation role in, 36:28
  overexpression of peripheral myelin protein 22
      gene in, 36:28
  peripheral myelin protein 22 gene mutation in,
      36:28, 36:29
  peripheral myelin protein 22 gene role in,
      36:9–36:10, 36:19, 36:20
  phenotype of, 36:9, 36:10, 36:11
  role of peripheral myelin protein 22 in, 36:27
  schematic map of markers for, 36:12
  severity of, 36:33
  transgenic rat models of, 36:27
CMT2A disease
  genetic locus of, 36:19
  linkage to chromosome 1, 36:6
CMT4A disease, genetic locus of, 36:19
CMT1B disease
  chromosome 1 linkage of, 36:19–36:21
  gene substitution in, 36:25
  genetic locus of, 36:19
  (HMSNIb), linkage to chromosome 1, 36:5
  molecular mechanisms for, 36:19–36:21
CMT2B disease
  genetic locus of, 36:19
  linkage to chromosome 3, 36:6

CMT2C disease
  genetics of, **36:**6
  symptoms of, **36:**6
CMT1C disease, linkage to chromosome 1,
    36:5
CMT1 disease
  age of onset, **36:**3
  autosomal dominant inheritance of,
    36:4–**36:**6
  chromosome linkages of, **36:**4–**36:**5
  clinical variants of, **36:**4
  differential diagnosis of, **36:**3
  as hypertrophic form of CMT disease, **36:**3
  molecular testing for, **36:**34–**36:**36
  neural "onion bulbs" in, **36:**3
  X-linked inheritance of, **36:**7–**36:**8
CMT2 disease, **36:**3
  age of onset, **36:**3
  autosomal dominant inheritance of,
    36:4–**36:**6
  differential diagnosis of, **36:**3
  mutation screening on, **36:**36
  as neuronal form of CMT disease, **36:**3
CMT4 disease
  clinical symptoms of, **36:**6
  subtypes (CMT4A, CMT4B, and CMT4C)
    of, **36:**6–**36:**7
CMT diseases
  age of onset, **36:**3, **36:**4
  autosomal recessive inheritance of, **36:**6–**36:**7
  clinical classification of, **36:**2–**36:**4
  discovery of, **36:**2
  electrodiagnostics of, **36:**2, **36:**3–**36:**4
  genetic classification of, **36:**4–**36:**6
  in inherited muscular disorders, **36:**2
  molecular testing for, **36:**34–**36:**36
  nerve pathology in, **36:**3–**36:**4
  nerve protein role in, **36:**21
  X-linked inheritance of, **36:**6–**36:**7
CMTX1 disease, genetic locus of, **36:**19
CMTX2 disease, genetic locus of, **36:**19
CMTX disease, genetics of, **36:**7
CMTX3 disease, gentic locus of, **36:**19
c-myb, pRb role in induction of, **36:**55
c-myc
  evolutionary genetics of fish and,
    29:171–**29:**172
  regulation of, **36:**85
cnr/ncc system, role in bacterial metal resistance,
    36:224–**36:**225, **36:**226

CNS, *see* Central nervous system
cnx mutants, nitrate reductase and, **30:**17,
    30:19–**30:**20, **30:**26
Cobalt
  bacterial resistance to, **36:**221,
    36:223–**36:**226
  in proteins, **36:**188
Cobalt-58, braconid wasp feeding effects,
    25:161
Cobalt chloride, puff activity effects, **39:**255
Cochliobolus heterostrophus, chromosome
    rearrangements in, **36:**264, **36:**280
Coding region mutations, of tumor suppressor
    genes, **36:**95–**36:**99
Cofactors, nitrate reductase and, **30:**4–**30:**6
  mutants, **30:**17–**30:**20
Coiling
  Istanbul hypothesis, **34:**14
  longitudinal orientation, **34:**344
Colchicine
  heat-shock puff induction, **39:**347
  heterochromatin gene expression
    modification, **37:**343
  puff activity effects, **39:**255
Cold acclimation, plants
  comparison with heat-shock response,
    28:121–**28:**122, **28:**124
  freezing tolerance, woody perennials, **28:**99
  gene expression and, **28:**106–**28:**116,
    28:123–**28:**124
  inheritance, **28:**105–**28:**108
  isozyme profiles and, **28:**108–**28:**109
  lipid composition and, **28:**99–**28:**100
  OCR polypeptides and, **28:**116–**28:**123
  plasma membrane injury, **28:**101–**28:**104
    lipid composition and, **28:**103–**28:**104
Cold-regulated polypeptides, plants
  boiling-stable property, **28:**120–**28:**121
  composition, **28:**110–**28:**113
  function, hypothesis, **28:**124
  physical location, **28:**122–**28:**123
  potential conservation, **28:**123
Cold shock, heat-shock puff induction, **39:**347
Collembolan order, apterygotan insects,
    polyteny occurrence, **34:**64–72
Colletotrichum lindemuthianum, bean infection
  cytology, **28:**167
  enzyme induction, **28:**192
  HRGP gene induction, **28:**198
  race specificity, **28:**168–**28:**169

Collinsia tinctoria, sticky mutants, meiosis
  blockage, **26:**164
Colon cancer
  DCC gene role in, **36:**78–**36:**79
  dietary fat role in, **36:**76
  disruption of DNA repair in, **36:**77
  methylation if *INK4A* gene in, **36:**68
  NF1 implication in, **36:**80, **36:**81
  p21 suppression of, **36:**62, **36:**63
  tumor suppressor gene mutations in, **36:**96
  tumor suppressor role in, **36:**49
  Wit-1 gene role in, **36:**73
Colony color, screening and, **20:**42–**20:**43
Colony hybridization
  fungal transformation detection by, **23:**89,
    23:94–**23:**95
Colony morphology, screening and, **20:**41–**20:**42
Compaction
  dividing cell heterochromatin
    anoxia effects, **37:**13
    distamycin A effects, **37:**11
    genetic control, **37:**13
    Hoechst 33258 effects, **37:**9–11
    mechanisms, **37:**13–14
    overview, **37:**5–6
    permanence, **37:**6–9
    radiation effects, **37:**12–13
    supercompaction, **37:**440–443
    temperature effects, **37:**11–13
  position effect, **37:**400–413, **37:**428–429
    characteristics, **37:**402–404
    discontinuous compaction, **37:**406–407,
      37:410
    formation, **37:**404–406, **37:**410
    historical perspectives, **37:**400–401
    late-replication, **37:**410
    occurrence frequencies, **37:**411–413
    parental effects, **37:**408–409
    temperature effects, **37:**407–408
Competence
  ectodermal
    in *Xenopus laevis*
      protein kinase C function, **31:**51
      spatial aspects, **31:**49–50
      temporal aspects, **31:**48–49
      Xotch function, **31:**51–53
Complementarity-determining regions,
  evolutionary genetics of fish and, **29:**187
Complementation
  fungal transformation detection by,
    23:87–**23:**88, **23:**90–**23:**93

groups
  nitrate reductase and, **30:**15–**30:**17, **30:**19,
    30:21–**30:**23, **30:**26
  superoxide dismutases and, **30:**305
COMT, *see* Catecholamine-O-methyltransferase
Conditional dominant lethality, *see prune/Killer
  of prune* Interaction
Conidia, *Neurospora crassa* and, **29:**42–**29:**43,
  29:45
Coniferyl alcohol dehydrogenase
  induction by infection/elicitor, **28:**189–**28:**190
  in lignin biosynthesis, **28:**176, **28:**197
Conjugation, homologous chromosomes,
  synapsis relation, **34:**172–173
Connexin32
  distribution and structure of, **36:**29–**36:**30
  gene encoding, **36:**30
  as major myelin protein, **36:**22, **36:**31
  mutation effects on, **36:**30, **36:**32
  in noneural tissue, **36:**30
  role in peripheral neuropathies, **36:**33–**36:**34
Connexin32 gene, **36:**20
  implication in CMTX disease, **36:**22
  mutations in, **36:**20
  mutation testing on, **36:**35, **36:**36
Connexins, functions of, **36:**29, **36:**30
Contiguous gene syndromes, **32:**303–305
Coordinate genes, positional function
  along AP axis, *Drosophila*, **27:**375, **27:**376,
    see also Bicoid gene
Copia element, *Drosophila* transposable elements
  and, **29:**232, **29:**234, **29:**239,
    29:250–**29:**257
Copper
  bacterial resistance to, **36:**221, **36:**223
  induction of CuZnSOD, **26:**82
  in proteins, **36:**188
  superoxide dismutases and, *see* Superoxide
    dismutases
  tolerance in plants
    MGS and, **26:**19–**26:**20
    in pollen and sporophyte, **26:**15
Copper homeostasis, **33:**233–248
  characteristics, **33:**233–235
  Menkes disease
    clinical findings, **33:**235–237
    future research directions, **33:**247–248
    molecular genetics, **33:**238–242
    mottled mouse model, **33:**245–246
  Wilson disease
    clinical findings, **33:**235, **33:**237–238

future research directions, **33**:247–248
Long–Evans Cinnamin rat model,
  33:246–247
molecular genetics, **33**:242–245
Coprinus cinereus, chromosome rearrangements
  in, **36**:281
Coprinus radiatus, chromosome rearrangements
  in, **36**:281
Corn, nitrate reductase and, **30**:4
COR polypeptides, *see* Cold-regulated
  polypeptides
Corticotropin-releasing factor, evolutionary
  genetics of fish and, **29**:197–**29**:198
Cortisone, cleft plate induction, mouse, **28**:278
  prevention by low-dose pretreatment, **28**:280
Corynebacterium diphtheriae, DtxR of, **36**:196
Cosmids, molecular cloning, **23**:84
Cosmos, pollen ontogeny, **26**:6
Costus allenii, MGS, experimental, **26**:17–**26**:18
Cotton (*Gossipium* spp.), **23**:271–**23**:354
  alien chromosome addition, **23**:326–**23**:327
  classical genetical studies, **23**:352–**23**:357
  cultivated, improvement by new technology,
    23:352–**23**:354
  genomes, morphology, **23**:290–**23**:296
  monoisodisomic, **23**:325–**23**:326
  monotelodisomic, **23**:323–**23**:325
  mutants
    Asiatic diploid, **23**:274, **23**:276–**23**:281
    New World allotetraploid, **23**:274–**23**:275,
      23:281–**23**:290
  tetrasomic, **23**:326
  translocations, **23**:296–**23**:307
  trisomic, **23**:326
4-Coumarate:CoA lipase, induction by
  infection/elicitor, **28**:189
Counterselection, nitrate reductase and, **30**:31
Courtship behavior
  Drosophila melanogaster
    characterization, **31**:151–152
    experience effects on mating, **31**:159–160
    and female receptivity, **31**:158–159
    neurogenic control, **31**:160–161
  song cycle, *Drosophila* rhythm genetics,
    38:159–160
Coyne model, of *Drosophila* hybrid viability,
  36:178
cpc-1, Neurospora crassa and, **29**:40, **29**:49
CpG islands, hypermethylation of, in cancer,
  36:56, **36**:68, **36**:102
Crocus, pollen ontogeny, **26**:5–**26**:6

Cross-hybridization
  mosquitoes and, **30**:153, **30**:166
  Mu elements of *Zea mays* and, **30**:97
  telomeres and, **30**:214
Crossing over, frequency, **37**:76–77
Crossovers, *see* Chromosomes, segregation
  fidelity
Cross-reactivity, telomeres and, **30**:199
Crown gall cells, suppression of tumorous
  character of
  fate of T-DNA in plants regenerated from
    tumor cells, **22**:258–**22**:263
  T-DNA mutations, **22**:252–**22**:257
Crown gall tumorigenesis
  bacterial taxonomy and, **22**:210–**22**:213
  T-DNA and
    expression of, **22**:250–**22**:252
    structure of, **22**:246–**22**:250
  tumor induction, **22**:213–**22**:218
CRY genes, yeast ribosomes and, **29**:65, **29**:70,
  29:79, **29**:83, **29**:103
CRY1 genes, yeast ribosomes and, **29**:85
  ribosomal protein genes, **29**:75,
    29:78–**29**:79, **29**:83
  ribosomal proteins, **29**:65, **29**:70, **29**:72
Crystal cells, *Drosophila* larvae
  abnormalities in mutations
    Bc (*Black cells*), **24**:192
    lz (*lozenge*), **24**:192–**24**:193
  phenol oxidase-containing in hemolymph,
    24:191–**24**:192
Cs gene, 37C1-2 band, **39**:139
c-src, evolutionary genetics of fish and, **29**:171
C-staining
  differential heterochromatin staining,
    37:14–15
  intercalary heterochromatin identification,
    37:141
CTA1, superoxide dismutases and, **30**:285,
  30:287, **30**:296–**30**:297, **30**:306
CTF, *see* CCAAT-binding transcription factor
CTT1, superoxide dismutases and, **30**:279,
  30:282, **30**:286–**30**:287, **30**:297, **30**:306
Cucurbita pepo, MGS, excess pollination and,
  26:16
Cucurbita spp., pollen, acid phosphatase-
  encoding genes, **26**:21
Culex, **30**:123–**30**:125, **30**:172–**30**:173
  genome characterization, **30**:137–**30**:138,
    30:140, **30**:143, **30**:145
  physiology, **30**:147–**30**:148

Cultures
  age, somaclonal variation and, 30:45–30:46
  hemopoiesis in, 20:376–20:378
  type, somaclonal variation and,
    30:43–30:45
CUP1, superoxide dismutases and,
    30:276–30:277, 30:279, 30:304
CUP2, superoxide dismutases and, 30:277
Currie, Alistair, apoptosis concept development,
    35:35–53
  acceptance, 35:49–53
  applications, 35:50–52
  definition, 35:40–41
  morphology, 35:41–46
  overview, 35:35–36
  shrinkage necrosis, 35:36–39
  studies, 35:46–49
Cy, Mu elements of Zea mays and, 30:79,
    30:93, 30:98–30:99
Cyanide
  heat-shock puff induction, 39:347
  irreversible inhibition of CuZnSOD, 26:69
  resistance in Fe-MnSODs, 26:72
Cyanobacteria
  carbonic anhydrases and, 30:325
  ferredoxin regulation in, 36:198
  plant transcription regulation, circadian
    regulation pathways, 35:17–20
CYC1, yeast ribosomes and, 29:75
Cyclic AMP
  protein kinase dependence on, inactivation
    in meiosis initiation, yeast,
    26:157–26:158
  puff activity effects, 39:254
  superoxide dismutases and, 30:279,
    30:285–30:286, 30:303
  TF mRNA reduction, rat liver, 25:27
Cyclic GMP
  hsp protein regulation, 39:382, 39:386
  superoxide dismutases and, 30:302–30:303
  transcription–dosage compensation
    overview, 39:76–79
  sex chromosome activity, 39:79–83
Cyclin A
  genetic studies, 31:85–86
  mitotic behavior during development,
    31:83–88
Cyclin B
  genetic studies, 31:85–86
  maternal transcripts, 31:86–88

mitotic behavior during development,
    31:83–88
  and pole cell development, 31:86–88
Cyclin C, 31:88–89
Cyclin D, 31:88–89
Cyclin-dependent kinases
  complexes of, p57 protein inhibition of, 36:64
  effect on tumor-suppressor genes, 36:46,
    36:47, 36:48, 36:55
  p21 inhibition of, 36:60
Cyclin E, 31:88–89
Cyclin E-CDK2, p27 binding of, 36:63
Cycloheximide
  effect on frost tolerance, 28:100
  heat-shock puff induction, 39:347
  puff activity effects, 39:255
  RNA synthesis inhibition, 39:73
Cyclops, chromatin diminution, 37:81–84
cyc-1 Neurospora crassa and, 29:36
CYC1, superoxide dismutases and,
    30:282–30:284
CYH2, yeast ribosomes and, 29:69–29:70,
    29:75, 29:98
CYLD1 gene, implication in cylindromatosis,
    36:95
Cylindromatosis, chromosomal linkage of,
    36:94, 36:95
cys-3 gene
  Neurospora crassa
    control of, 31:201
    positive sulfur regulation by, 31:197–199
    regulation of sulfate permeases,
      31:194–195
    in sulfur circuit, 31:190–192
cys-14 gene
  Neurospora crassa
    proteins encoded by, 31:195
    in sulfur circuit, 31:191–192
CYS3 protein
  autogenous regulation of, 31:201
  DNA binding, 31:199–200
  as DNA-binding nuclear protein,
    31:201–202
  molecular characterization, 31:202–203
  mutation studies, 31:200–201
Cysteine, dietary, female braconid wasp
  radioprotection, 25:157
Cystosol, nitrate reductase and, 30:30
Cytochrome
  mosquitoes and, 30:150

nitrate reductase and, 30:6, 30:8, 30:23
superoxide dismutases and, 30:259
Cytochrome aa_3, ascomycetes
Neurospora crassa, absence in mutants
poky, 25:238
synthesis during aging, 25:239
stopper, 25:240
Podospora anserina, decrease during
senescence, 25:242
Cytochrome b, ascomycetes
absence in N. crassa mutants
poky, 25:238
synthesis during aging, 25:239
stopper, 25:240
cob-encoded, S. cerevisiae
absence in intron 4 mutants, 25:222
variations in exon mutants, 25:219–25:220
Cytochrome c
hemelyase, Neurospora crassa and,
29:35–29:36, 29:38
Neurospora crassa and, 29:36–29:37
oxidase, ascomycetes
mitochondrial genes coding for,
25:212–25:213
peroxidase, superoxide dismutases and,
30:287, 30:302
reductase, nitrate reductase and,
30:19–30:20, 30:22–30:23
superoxide dismutases and
molecular genetics, 30:280,
30:282–30:284
physiology, 30:257, 30:260, 30:262
structure, 30:267, 30:269
Cytochrome P-450
genes, evolutionary genetics of fish and,
29:167–29:168
immune system and, 21:34
multiple forms of, 21:7–21:8
nature of, 21:3–21:4
number of forms of, 21:40
Cytogenetic maps, see Genetic mapping
Cytokine receptor, signaling properties, severe
combined immunodeficiency cloning
studies, 35:76–77
Cytokines, as possible tumor suppressors, 36:93
Cytokinesis, genes involved in Drosophila
melanogaster, 31:109–110
Cytokinins
photosynthetic gene expression and,
28:152–28:153

PR protein induction in shoots, 28:190,
28:192
Cytological repeats, intercalary heterochromatin
identification, 37:225
Cytoplasm
carbonic anhydrases and, 30:331
evolutionary genetics of fish and, 29:166
mosquitoes and, 30:172
nitrate reductase and, 30:3, 30:8, 30:30
superoxide dismutases and, 30:268–30:269,
30:287, 30:294, 30:296, 30:306
yeast ribosomes and, 29:69, 29:82, 29:93,
29:101
assembly, 29:94–29:95, 29:98
nucleolus, 29:88–29:89
Cytotype, Drosophila transposable elements and,
29:276, 29:282
P elements, 29:262–29:263, 29:267–29:269,
29:272–29:273
czc system, role in bacterial metal resistance,
36:223–36:226

Dactylium dendroides
SOD, 30:269, 30:278
biosynthesis, copper-induced, 26:82
Dactylorchis fuchsii, pollen ontogeny, 26:4
Dark repair
Schizosaccharomyces pombe after uv
irradiation, 23:26–23:35
dimer excision, 23:27–23:28
inhibitors, 23:38–23:40
main pathway, 23:33–23:35
recombinational, 23:28–23:31
second prereplicative, 23:31–23:33
Darwin, Charles, 36:138, 36:181
DAT, see Dopamine acetyltransferase
Datura innoxia, nitrate reductase and,
30:13–30:14
Datura stramonium, meiosis, dyad gene and,
26:183
Daucus, somaclonal variation and, 30:4
daughterless-abolike mutant
Drosophila melanogaster, 31:108
Daughterless gene
Drosophila
interaction with AS-C and neurogenic
genes, 27:440
molecular organization, 27:207, 27:440

Daughterless gene (*continued*)
  requirement for neural development,
    27:165, 27:440
  neuralizing signal in PNS,
    27:445–27:446
  sex-controlling function, 27:165, 27:439
  Sxl gene activation, 27:206
Drosophila melanogaster
  role in neurogenesis, 31:16
  role in somatic sexual fate determination,
    31:5–6
DCC
  tumor suppressor gene
  characteristics of, 36:50
  implication in colon cancer, 36:78
  mutations in, 36:78
  as tumor suppressor gene product, 36:50,
    36:52
DDC, *see* DOPA decarboxylase
Ddc gene
  37C1-2 band, 39:139
  dosage compensation, 39:78
deadpan gene
  Drosophila melanogaster
  denominator role, 31:6
  sequence identities with *h*, 31:7–8
Deafness, maternally inherited, 32:78–80
Debaromyces hansonii, superoxide dismutases
  and, 30:259
decapentaplegic gene, *zeste* in *Drosophila*
  melanogaster and, 29:312, 29:320–29:323,
  29:327
Defective elements, *Mu* elements of *Zea mays*
  and, 30:91
Defects, *see* Abnormalities
Defense response genes, plants
  activation by fungal elicitors, 28:202–28:204
  potential signaling pathways,
    28:204–28:205
  casbein synthase-encoding, 28:201
  CHI family, structures, 28:196–28:197
  chitinase-encoding, bean, 28:198–28:199
  CHS family
    expression in transgenic plants, 28:215
    115 promoter protein binding sites, bean,
      28:207, 28:210–28:213
    homology to PAL, 28:210–28:213
    structures, 28:195–28:196
  4CL family, structures, 28:195
  clones, characteristics, 28:182–28:187

glucanase-encoding, 28:199
Hyp, HRGP-encoding, 28:197–28:198
PAL family
  expression in transgenic plants, 28:215
  structures, 28:193–28:195
PR-1 family, 28:200
thionin-encoding, 28:201
in transgenic plants
  expression, 28:214–28:215
  prospects, 28:216
wound-inducible, potato
  promoters, 28:206, 28:209, 28:213
  structures, 28:199
Deformation genetics, *see* Human malformation
  genes
Deformed gene, homeotic, *Drosophila*
  autoregulation of transcription unit,
    27:389–27:398
  engrailed gene role, 27:395–397
  heat-shock-inducible fusion gene (*hsDfd*)
    effect
    Dfd protein ectopic expression and,
      27:389–27:393
    homeotic transformations in *hsDfd*
      embryos, 27:391–395
    mechanism of, 27:396–27:398
  expression pattern during embryogenesis
    ftz gene coexpression, 27:377–27:378,
    27:380
  initiation, regulatory genes required for,
    27:385–27:386
  maintenance, regulation by other genes
    homeotic regulatory genes (*Polycomb*,
      extra sex combs), 27:387–388
    homeotic selector genes of ANT-C and
      BX-C, 27:387
    pair-rule *en* gene and, 27:388, 27:396,
    27:397
  negative regulation by pair-rule gene *ftz*,
    27:381–27:383, 27:385–27:386
  positive regulation by other genes
    bcd and, 27:380–27:381
    hb and, 27:381
    pair-rule genes *eve*, *prd*, 27:382–27:384
  head programming function, 27:367
  molecular map
    position in ANT-C, 27:342, 27:367, 27:368
    transcription unit, 27:368–27:369
  mRNA, during embryogenesis, 27:343,
    27:376–27:378

mutant phenotypes, 27:342–27:343,
27:365–27:368
positional function
comparison with other homeotic genes,
27:372–27:374
in hierarchy of anterior-posterior
patterning genes, 27:375–27:376,
27:385–27:386
homeodomain sequences, 27:368–27:372
similarity to *Dfd*-like vertebrate proteins,
27:370–27:372
protein product
during embryogenesis, 27:343–27:344,
27:348, 27:349, 27:378–27:380
Deformed-like genes, vertebrates
evolutionary history, 27:371–27:372
protein homeodomain sequences comparison
with *Dfd* protein, 27:370–27:371
Deinococcus radiodurans, NUV-sensitive, FUV-
resistant, 26:118
Déjerine-Sottas disease
genetic locus of, 36:21
as HMSNIII disease, 36:4
mutations causing, 36:20, 36:25, 36:28
similarity to CMT disease, 36:2, 36:20
Deletion
carbonic anhydrases and, 30:329
mosquitoes and, 30:129, 30:139, 30:146
Mu elements of *Zea mays* and, 30:84, 30:91,
30:96, 30:103, 30:112
somaclonal variation and, 30:49–30:50, 30:59
superoxide dismutases and, 30:269
molecular genetics, 30:273,
30:275–30:276, 30:284
physiology of mutants, 30:288, 30:294,
30:296, 30:301–30:302, 30:305
telomeres and, 30:232
formation, 30:229–30:231
function, 30:203–30:204, 30:208,
30:217–30:218
gene expression, 30:223
structure, 30:191, 30:193, 30:200
Demethylation, *Mu* elements of *Zea mays* and,
30:89
Demyelination
in CMT disease, 36:3, 36:7, 36:8, 36:33
in Déjerine-Sottas disease, 36:4
Dendrites, function of, 36:21
Dense fibrillar component, yeast ribosomes and,
29:86–29:88

Denys-Drash syndrome
mutations implicated in, 36:70
Wilms' tumor with, 36:69
3′-Deoxy-adenosine, RNA synthesis inhibition,
39:74
Deoxyribonucleic acid
exogenous, transformation by,
20:166–20:168
homology studies, between Ti-, Ri- and
other *Agrobacterium* plasmids,
22:242–22:244
kinetoplast
evolution and function of minicircles,
22:65–22:66
general properties, 22:56–22:58
maxicircles, 22:62–22:65
minicircles, 22:58–22:62
modification, transcriptionally active
chromatin and, 22:190–22:192
plasmidlike, 22:71–22:74
87DE region genes, chrommere–gene–loop
relations, 39:157–158
Detoxification, mosquitoes and, 30:147–30:148
Development, *see also* Embryonic development;
specific types
environmental stress effects
in *Drosophila*, heat-induced defects
gene expression and, 28:286–28:291
history, 28:281–28:282
phenocopies, 28:282–28:286
in vertebrates
teratogen- and heat-induced defects
genetic factors and, 28:280–28:281
molecular models, 28:290
in neural tube, 28:277–28:278
n heart, 28:276–28:280
tolerance and, 28:280
Dfd gene, band organization, 39:144
Df(1) genes
band organization, 39:143, 39:147–148
puff development, 39:291–294
Df(2) genes, hormone function-impairing
mutations, 39:168–169
Df(3R) genes, heat-shock puffs, 39:370–371
DHFR, *see* Dihydrofolate reductase
DHFR gene, antisense transcripts of, 36:103
DHR gene, puff development, 39:317
Diabetes Mellitus, *see* Non-insulin-dependent
diabetes mellitus
Diamide, heat-shock puff induction, 39:350

cis-Diamminedichloroplatinum (DDP) effects
on braconid wasp females
oocyte sensitivity to, **25:**169
oogonium sensitivity to, **25:**171
Dianthus chinensis, MGS, experimental,
26:16–**26:**17
Diaphorase, nitrate reductase and, **30:**22
Diaphragm weakness, in CMT2 disease, **36:**6
Dicentrarchus labrax, evolutionary genetics of
fish and, **29:**138
5,6-Dichloro-1-β-D-ribofuranosilbenzimidazole,
RNA synthesis inhibition, **39:**73–74
Dicoumarol, heat-shock puff induction,
39:347
Dictyostelium discoideum
DNA, heat-shock promoter elements,
24:13–**24:**14
mRNAs during early differentiation, **24:**13
transformation system, **23:**154
Dictyostelium, telomeres and, **30:**187, **30:**196
Dicyanidiamide, puff activity effects, **39:**256
Diet
ADH activity in Drosophila and, **25:**56
cysteine and glutathione, female braconid
wasp radioprotection, **25:**157
effect on life-span, braconid wasps, **25:**136
therapy, for phenylketonuria, **32:**202
Diethyldithiocarbamate, inactivation of
CuZnSOD, **26:**69
Diethyl ether, puff activity effects, **39:**253
Differential cloning, diabetes-susceptibility gene
identification, **32:**61–62
Differentiation
mosquitoes and, **30:**126–**30:**137
nuclear envelope role, **24:**264–**24:**267
Digitonin
heat-shock puff induction, **39:**347
puff activity effects, **39:**256
Dihydrofolate reductase
methotrexate-resistant, in transgenic mouse,
24:314
α,β-Dihydroisovalerate dehydratase, protection
by SOD, E. coli, **26:**77
Dihydroxy acid dehydratase, inactivation by
NUV, E. coli, **26:**102, **26:**109, **26:**111
Dihydroxyphenylalanine
Drosophila
conversion from catecholamine X
amd gene-coded enzyme and, **24:**169
pathway of, **24:**170

developmental profile, **24:**151–**24:**153
Dilated cardiomyopathy, **35:**305–310
clinical syndrome, **35:**305–306
definition, **35:**305–306
epidemiology, **35:**306
genetics, **35:**306–309
autosomal dominant form, **35:**308–309
recessive inheritance, **35:**309
X-linked inheritance, **35:**307–308
pathogenesis, **35:**309–310
Dimethylsulfoxide, puff activity effects,
39:256
Diminution, chromatin loss, **37:**78–89
Ascaris megalocephala, **37:**78–81
Cyclops, **37:**81–84
dipteran insects, **37:**84–86
infusoria, **37:**86–88
physiological significance, **37:**89
Dinactin, heat-shock puff induction, **39:**347
Dinitrogen gas, nitrate reductase and,
30:2–**30:**3
2,4-Dinitrophenol, heat-shock puff induction,
39:348
Dioxygen (O_2), superoxide dismutases and,
30:252, **30:**270–**30:**271, **30:**383
physiology, **30:**252–**30:**255
physiology of mutants, **30:**296, **30:**304
dip-1, yeast ribosomes and, **29:**101, **29:**103
Diphosphate kinase, see Nucleoside diphosphate
kinase
Diploidization, Gossypium spp. allotetraploids,
23:347–**23:**349
Diploids
mosquitoes and, **30:**126, **30:**151
nitrate reductase and, **30:**13
somaclonal variation and, **30:**43–**30:**44,
30:48
superoxide dismutases and, **30:**281
telomeres and, **30:**193, **30:**226
Diploidy
classification
mutation rate per haploid genome (u),
24:348–**24:**349
recessive mutations masked at equilibrium,
24:348–**24:**351
life cycle stage in
haplodiploid insects, **24:**352–**24:**353
multicellular haploids (fungi),
24:351–**24:**353
in primitive organisms, **24:**345–**24:**346

Diptera
  chromosome types, 34:130–136
  polyteny occurrence
    adult ovarian nurse cells, 34:46–62
    banding, 34:22
    Drosophila, 34:32, 34:37
    form variance, 34:21–32
    heterochromatin morphology variation,
      34:22–23
    polyploidy, 34:32, 34:37
    pupae
      bristle-forming cells, 34:43–46
      foot pad cells, 34:37–43
Dipteran insects, see also specific species
  band characteristics, 37:234–238
  B chromosomes
    number, 37:295–297
    occurrence, 37:288–294
  centromeric heterochromatin
    amount variation
      mitotic chromosomes, 37:36–39
      polytene chromosomes, 37:121–122
  DNA structure, 37:99
  chromatin diminution, 37:84–86
  chromosomal break characterization,
    37:151–157
  developmental features, 39:161–197
    endocrine system, 39:161–169
    hormone effects, 39:161–169
    puff-related gene mutations
      Df(2R)bw⁵ gene, 39:168–169
      dor gene, 39:167–168
      dre4 gene, 39:169
      ecd1 gene, 39:167
      ecs gene, 39:169
      eyeless^D gene, 39:169
      giant gene, 39:167
      grg gene, 39:168
      l(1)HM40 gene, 39:168
      l(1)su(f)^{ts67g} gene, 39:167
      l(2)ft gene, 39:168
      l(2) gl gene, 39:167
      l(3)3^{DTS} gene, 39:168
      l(3)th gene, 39:169
      sta gene, 39:168
      swi gene, 39:169
    salivary glands
      hormonal regulation, 39:192–197
      physiology, 39:170–192
  ectopic pairing

  nucleolar material, 37:178–179
  polytene chromosomes, 37:171–176,
    37:266–276
  germline limited chromosome occurrence,
    37:87
  intercalary α-heterochromatin, 37:135–138
  morphology, 34:125–127
  polytene chromosomes
    centromeric heterochromatin amount
      variation, 37:121–122
    ectopic pairing, 37:171–176,
      37:266–276
    Q⁺-band occurrence, 37:147–148
    terminal deletion occurrence,
      37:243–244
Diptericin, mosquitoes and, 30:155, 30:171
Diptheria toxin
  bacterial gene encoding, 36:190
  repressor, as possible homolog to Fur,
    36:196–36:197
disconnected (disco) mutant
  Drosophila melanogaster, 31:170–171
Disease, see Pathology
Disease tolerance, Gramineae
  cell line selection from tissue culture,
    24:478–24:480
  pathotoxins as selection agents,
    24:479–24:480
Disjunctions, see Chromosomes, segregation
  fidelity
dissonance (dis) mutant
  Drosophila melanogaster, 31:152–154
Distamycin A, heterochromatin compaction,
    37:11
Distortion factor, autosomes, 37:61–65
Disulfide bonds, nitrate reductase and, 30:4
DMAP-190, 31:102
DMAP60, 31:102
DNA, see also Chromomeres; Interbands;
    Recombinant DNA Advisory Committee
  active chromosome region localization,
    DNA–RNA hybrid antibodies, 39:38,
      39:47–52
  Adh alleles, studies in Drosophila population
    genetics, 25:84–25:86
  allelic recombination, 24:325–24:326
    reduction during evolution,
      24:328–24:329
    sex differences, 24:355
  amplification

DNA (continued)
evolutionary genetics of fish and,
29:129–29:130
mosquitoes and, 30:136, 30:147
Balbiani ring organization, 39:400–407
band content, 34:210–212
binding proteins, trans-acting
in animals and yeast, 28:206
HSF, heat-shock response regulation,
28:245–28:246
in plants, 28:206–28:214
defense response gene regulation,
28:207–28:214
rbcS gene regulation, 28:206–28:207,
28:208
break formation, 38:186–188
CCAAT box, in HSP induction, vertebrates,
24:44–24:45, 24:55–24:56
centromeric heterochromatin structure,
37:98–105
chromomere pattern production, 34:212–213
chromosome structure, 34:216–217
complementary (cDNA), clones
for Cat genes, restriction maps, maize,
28:30–28:31
for cor genes, alfalfa, Arabidopsis,
28:115–28:116
for SOD genes, restriction maps, maize,
28:32–28:33
complimentary
Gaucher disease, 32:21
phenylalanine hydroxylation cloning,
32:204–205
damage
accumulation during asexual phase,
Paramecium tetraurelia,
24:359–24:360
double-strand, 24:330–24:331
in mitotically dividing germ-line cells,
24:354
high cost, meiosis role in repair,
24:354–24:355
mutation and recombination induction,
24:327–24:328
repaired but not replicated,
24:326–24:327
single-strand, 24:329–24:330
-DNA hybridization studies, on genes, 36:139
donor in fungal transformation induction
effects, 23:96–23:97, 23:101–23:103

fate, 23:98–23:101
hybrid plasmid preparation, 23:85–23:86
mechanism, 23:77–23:79
use of preparations
cloned, 23:79
pretreated, 23:86–23:87
total, 23:79
Drosophila transposable elements and, 29:231,
29:281
cis-acting effects of retrotransposons,
29:241, 29:244–29:245
foldback elements, 29:284–29:286, 29:288
P elements, 29:263–29:264, 29:266,
29:269
retrotransposons, 29:231, 29:237–29:238
elimination, infusoria chromosomes,
34:75–76, 34:90–92
evolutionary genetics of fish and, 29:122,
29:201–29:202
detection of variation, 29:123, 29:126,
29:128, 29:130–29:131
development, 29:175
endocrine system, 29:194, 29:196
environmental change, 29:163, 29:169,
29:172–29:173
immune system, 29:181, 29:183,
29:185–29:187
linkage groups, 29:146
nervous system, 29:177
nuclear genomic structures, 29:134,
29:136–29:137, 29:140–29:143
exogenous, direct gene transfer in pollen,
26:46
feminizing element, microinjection into C.
elegans, 27:169–27:170
Feulgen-stained, during braconid wasp
development, 25:124
fingerprinting, evolutionary genetics of fish
and, 29:128–29:1129
5′-flanking sequences
chorion gene regulation
Drosophila, 24:233, 24:239
silk moths, 24:232–24:234, 24:239
role in gene transfer, mouse,
24:301–24:304
foreign, transfer into mouse, see Mouse, gene
transfer
FUV-induced SOS repair, 26:129–26:130
gene distribution, 39:11–12, 39:115–118
gene number calculation, 39:94–113

genomic
  content variation
    in evolution, 28:78–28:79
    intraspecific, plants, 28:78–28:81
    somatoclonal, plant tissue culture,
      28:81–28:83
  5'-flanking sequences, light-inducible
    of *cab* genes, 28:144–28:145
    of *rbcS* genes, 28:141–28:142
  structure
    Cat, maize, 28:31–28:33
    cor, cold-associated changes, *Arabidopsis*,
      28:116
    Sod, maize, 28:32–28:33
  in *Gossypium* spp. chromosomes
    content, 23:339–23:346, 23:351–23:352
    repetitive sequence, 23:341–23:342,
      23:344–23:346
  heterochromatin gene expression
    modification, 37:341
  HSE, *see* Heat-shock elements
  insertion sequences, fungal transformation
    and, 23:122–23:124
  in leaves during development, Gramineae,
    24:448
  -mediated transformation, transgenic strain
    creation, *C. elegans*, 27:73–27:74
  MerR binding to, 36:213–36:214
  mitochondrial (mtDNA), ascomycetes
    content, nuclear gene-controlled, 25:227
    poky mutants, *N. crassa*, 25:239,
      25:240–25:241
    ragged mutants, *Aspergillus amstelodami*,
      25:241
    rho⁻ mutants, *S. cerevisiae*, 25:232–25:238
    ori sequences, 25:236–25:238
    senescence (senDNA)
      Neurospora intermedia, variations,
        25:244
      plasmid-like (plDNA), *Podospora*
        anserina, 25:243–25:244
      stopper mutants, *N. crassa*, 25:240
    synthesis during cell cycle, 25:227–25:228
    polymerase characterization, 25:228
  molecular cloning, *see* Molecular cloning
  mosquitoes and, 30:125, 30:162–30:167
    genetic differentiation, 30:126,
      30:130–30:137
    genome characterization, 30:137,
      30:139–30:146

    physiology, 30:147–30:152, 30:159
  Mu elements of *Zea mays* and, 30:79,
    30:114–30:115
    assays, 30:88, 30:90
    properties of transposition, 30:100,
      30:102–30:106, 30:108
    regulation, 30:97
    structure, 30:93–30:95
  mutations
    reduction during evolution, 24:328
    replicated but not repaired,
      24:326–24:327
  Neurospora crassa and, 29:3–29:5,
    29:47–29:49
    development of, 29:43, 29:46
    genetic material, 29:12–29:13,
      29:15–29:17
    gene transfer, 29:5–29:12
    metabolism, 29:39, 29:41
    mitochondria, 29:26, 29:30,
      29:32–29:35
    transaction, 29:18–29:25
  nitrate reductase and, 30:26
  nuclear, *see* Genomic
  NUV effects, bacteria
    damage and protection, models,
      26:101–26:103
    direct absorption, alterations and,
      26:103–26:105
    distinction from FUV effect,
      26:115–26:117
    DNA-protein cross-links, 26:116, 26:118
    lesions as substrate for exonuclease III,
      26:116, 26:118
    similarity to H_2O_2 effects,
      26:118–26:119
    SOS repair blockage, 26:129–26:131
  oxygen radical-induced damage, 28:6–28:7,
    28:45–28:47
    in mitochondria, *Drosophila*, 28:61
    repair by enzymes, *Drosophila*,
      28:58–28:59
  photolyase, photoprotection against NUV,
    26:110–26:111
  -PK, AT protein homology with, 36:90
  plant genetic transformation
    dicotyledonous species by *Agrobacterium*
      tumefaciens, 24:463–24:464
    Gramineae by delivery into protoplast *in*
      vitro, 24:464–24:465

DNA (continued)
  polymerase
    Drosophila transposable elements and,
      29:231–29:232
    evolutionary genetics of fish and, 29:129
    Neurospora crassa and, 29:19–29:20,
      29:24, 29:34–29:35
    telomeres and, 30:203, 30:213, 30:219,
      30:232
  polymerase F, PCNA activation of, 36:62
  polymorphisms, see specific polymorphism
    in populations, sequence variation,
      23:236–23:246
    multigene families, 23:241–23:242
    single copy genes, 23:236–23:241
      historical information, 23:238–23:239
      molecular marker use, 23:239–23:241
      polymorphic sites, 23:237–23:238
  p53 protein role in repair, 36:59
  protein complexes in phenylketonuria,
    32:251–253
  protein kinase, DNA break repair
    mechanisms
    characteristics, 38:200–201
    components, 38:196–200
    defective mouse models, 38:206–207
    DNA ligase IV, 38:200
    Ku protein, 38:196–198
    repair model, 38:208–210
    XRCC4, 38:200
  puffs, see Puffs
  rDNA gene mutations
    bobbed gene, 38:83–84
    mini gene, 38:83
  recombinational repair
    bacteria
      E. coli, 24:334–24:336, see also
        Escherichia coli
      recA gene function, 24:334–24:336
      various species, 24:336
    double-strand break model,
      24:340–24:341
    promotion by meiosis, 24:341
    Drosophila melanogaster, 24:338–24:339
    fungi
      Ustilago maydis, 24:338
      yeast, 24:337–24:338
    mammalian cells, 24:339
    plants, 24:339–24:340
    premeiotic replication and, 24:356–24:357

  viruses, 24:331–24:333, see also
    Bacteriophages
  repair
    genes
      Drosophila melanogaster
        haywire (hay), 31:114–115
        lodestar, 31:115–116
      induced mutagenesis and, 21:190–21:204
    repair mechanisms, 38:185–211
      DNA-protein kinase
        characteristics, 38:200–201
        components, 38:196–200
        defective mouse models, 38:206–207
        DNA ligase IV, 38:200
        Ku protein, 38:191, 38:196–198
        repair model, 38:208–210
        XRCC4, 38:200
      double-stranded break repair, 38:188–190,
        38:205–206
      homologous recombination, 38:188–190,
        38:205–206
      immune deficiency, 38:207–208
      nonhomologous end-joining
        DNA ligase IV, 38:200
        DNA-protein kinase components,
          38:196–200
        Ku protein, 38:191, 38:196–198
        mammalian cell studies, 38:191–193,
          38:203–206
        mechanisms, 38:190
        model, 38:208–210
        variable–diversity–joining
          recombination, 38:204–205
        XRCC4, 38:194, 38:200
        yeast studies, 38:193–196, 38:201–203,
          38:205
      overview, 38:186, 38:208–211
      radiosensitivity, 38:207–208
      single-stranded break annealing pathway,
        38:190
  repetitive sequences, 37:43–54
    composition, 37:53–54
    location, 37:45–46, 37:51–52
    in situ hybridization, 37:3, 37:51–53,
      37:99–101
    slipping, 37:53
    types, 37:47–49
  replication
    chromomere–replication unit correlation,
      39:436–442

genes
  Drosophila melanogaster
    mutations at *gnu, plu,* and *pgu* loci,
      31:113–114
    for replication enzymes, 31:112–113
    morphological characteristics, 39:425–436
  in *Schizosaccharomyces pombe*
    content, 23:3
    dark repair, 23:26–23:35, 23:38–23:40,
      see also Dark repair
    radiation injuries in sensitive mutants,
      23:24–23:25
    synthesis during growth cycle, 23:6–23:7
    uv-induced injuries in sensitive mutants
      liquid holding recovery, 23:36–23:39
      photorepair, 23:35–23:36
  somaclonal variation and, 30:51–30:60,
    30:64–30:65
  structure, 34:220–224
  superoxide dismutases and, 30:261, 30:267
    molecular genetics, 30:273,
      30:275–30:276, 30:280–30:282,
      30:285
    physiology of mutants, 30:288, 30:298,
      30:300–30:301, 30:303, 30:308
  synthesis
    flagellum regeneration and, *E. coli,* 27:23
    gene expression timing, *Caulobacter,*
      27:17–27:18
  telomeres and, 30:185–30:186,
    30:232–30:233
    formation, 30:226–30:232
    function, 30:201–30:206, 30:208–30:213,
      30:215, 30:217–30:220
    gene expression, 30:222–30:223
    structure, 30:186–30:201
  TF cDNA, human, homology with
    Pyura DNA, 25:6–25:7, 25:8
  TFR cDNA, human, 25:7–25:9
  underrepresentation
    intercalary heterochromatin identification,
      ectopic pairing, 37:189–193
    position effect, 37:414–421
    telomeric heterochromatin, 37:252–255,
      37:280
  Y-chromosomal of *Drosophila hydei,*
    nucleotide sequences, 23:223–23:226
  yeast ribosomes and, 29:64, 29:73, 29:75,
    29:77–29:78
  zeste in *Drosophila melanogaster* and, 29:302

  binding, 29:318–29:326
  chromatin packaging, 29:338–29:340,
    29:343
  function, 29:328–29:330
  protein, 29:330–29:333, 29:336–29:337
  transvection, 29:308–29:309
DNA ligase IV, DNA break repair mechanisms,
  nonhomologous end-joining, 38:200
DNA polymerase
  activity studies
    isolated chromosomes, 34:327–328
DNase I, *Drosophila* transposable elements and,
  29:266, 29:270
DNases
  Neurospora crassa and, 29:23–29:24
  telomeres and, 30:204
Dominance, *Mu* elements of *Zea mays* and, 30:89
Dominant-negative effects, on tumor suppressor
  genes, 36:102
DOPA, *see* Dihydroxyphenylalanine
DOPA decarboxylase, *Drosophila*
  biology and biochemistry, 24:157–24:158
  Ddc gene coding for, 24:158–24:165
  during development
    activity, 24:151–24:153
    control by regulatory genes, 24:99–24:100
    distinction from TDC, 24:166
    in germ-line transformed strains,
      24:163–24:165
  αMD effects
    in vitro, 24:166–24:167
    in vivo, 24:167–24:168
Dopamine
  developmental profile, *Drosophila,*
    24:151–24:153
  oxidative deamination and O-methylation,
    24:136
Dopamine acetyltransferase, *Drosophila*
  DAT locus-coded, 24:197
  during development, 24:196
  localization, 24:196–24:197
DOPA quinone imine conversion factor
  purification from *Manduca sexta,* 24:145
  role in melanization, 24:145–24:146
DOPA quinone imine decarboxylase, *Drosophila,*
  24:147
dor gene
  band organization, 39:142–144
  hormone function-impairing mutations,
    39:167–168, 39:282–283

dor gene (continued)
  puff development, **39**:241, **39**:291, **39**:308
Dorsal-group genes, maternal, *Drosophila*
  dorsal, morphogen-encoding, **27**:289–**27**:291
    interaction with *twist* and *snail*, **27**:293
  zen expression repression, **27**:295–**27**:297
  easter, serine protease-encoding,
    27:291–**27**:292
  late-acting, in early embryo, **27**:287–**27**:288
  snake, serine protease-encoding,
    27:291–**27**:292
  Toll, control of dorsal-ventral morphogen
    gradient in embryo, **27**:288–**27**:291
    ventral activation by *easter* protease, **27**:292
Dorsal involuting marginal zone, *see* Organizer
Dorsalizing genes, zygotic, *twist* and *snail*,
  Drosophila
  functions, **27**:292–**27**:293
  interactions with *dorsal*, **27**:293
Dorsal ventral axis
  genetic control, *Drosophila*, **27**:277–**27**:280,
    see also Ventralizing genes; Zerknüllt *gene*
Dorsoventral patterning
  human malformation genes
    floor plate role, **38**:14–15
    notochord role, **38**:14–15
    sonic hedgehog gene, **38**:15–16
Dosage compensation
  autosomes, **39**:76–79, **39**:83
  C. elegans
    coordinate control with sex determination,
      27:152–**27**:162, *see also* Sex
      determination
    demonstration, approaches,
      27:145–**27**:146
    dumpy (*dpy*) genes, mutations,
      27:124–**27**:125, **27**:147–**27**:150
    dpy-29, comparison with *sdc* locus,
      27:161–**27**:162
    feminizing effect in 2X/3A animals,
      27:166–**27**:169
    mechanism, **27**:151–**27**:152
    timing during embryogenesis, TSP and,
      27:150–**27**:151
  glucose-6-phosphate dehydrogenase, **39**:77,
    39:81
  overview, **39**:76–79
  ribosomal RNA, **39**:423–425
  sex chromosome activity, **39**:79–83
Dosage compensation, *Drosophila*, mechanism,
  27:151, **27**:152

double sex (*dsx*) gene
  alternative splicing
    Drosophila melanogaster, **31**:249–252
Down's syndrome, telomere role, **32**:297–298
DPC
  tumor suppressor gene, characteristics of,
    36:50, **36**:52, **36**:91
  as tumor suppressor gene product, **36**:50,
    36:93
Dp(1) genes, X-chromosome replication,
  39:432–433
dre4 gene, hormone function-impairing
  mutations, **39**:169
Drosophila
  biological rhythm genetics
    arrhythmic phenotypes, **38**:149–157
    brain-behavioral studies, **38**:163–167
    clock-resetting signals, **38**:171–172
    courtship song cycle, **38**:159–160
    egg-to-adult development, **38**:161
    environmental synchronization,
      38:142–145
    fundamentals, **38**:135–142
    long-period phenotypes, **38**:146–148
    non-temporal phenotypes, **38**:161–163
    ovarian diapause, **38**:158–159
    overview, **38**:135–136, **38**:173
    period gene expression, **38**:163–168,
      38:172–173
    short-period phenotypes, **38**:148–149
    visual rhythms, **38**:157–158
  evolutionary genetics of fish and, **29**:179
  gene models, *see specific genes*
  mosquitoes and, **30**:125, **30**:145
    genetic differentiation, **30**:126, **30**:130
    genetic transformation, **30**:162, **30**:165,
      30:167–**30**:170, **30**:172
    physiology, **30**:151, **30**:154
  Neurospora crassa and, **29**:45–**29**:46
  search for nonsense suppressors in,
    21:154–**21**:155
  sex determination in, **20**:19–**20**:220
  somaclonal variation and, **30**:50
  species
    Adh gene
      Australian group, **25**:71–**25**:72
      D. melanogaster group, **25**:52, **25**:69,
        25:73–**25**:74
      D. mulleri group, **25**:52–**25**:53,
        25:70–**25**:71, **25**:74
      D. obscura group, **25**:49, **25**:74

Hawaiian group, **25**:53, **25**:74
structural variation of mitochondrial
genome, **22**:24–**22**:26
superoxide dismutases and, **30**:297–**30**:298,
30:301
telomeres and, **30**:232
formation, **30**:229–**30**:231
function, **30**:201–**30**:204, **30**:214–**30**:216,
30:219
gene expression, **30**:222–**30**:223
nuclear organization, **30**:225
structure, **30**:190, **30**:193–**30**:194, **30**:196,
30:200–**30**:201
transposable elements, **29**:229–**29**:231
foldback elements
chromosomal rearrangements,
29:287–**29**:288
mechanism, **29**:286
structure, **29**:282–**29**:286
hobo
chromosomal rearrangements,
29:277–**29**:278
mechanism, **29**:276–**29**:277
structure, **29**:274–**29**:276
mariner
mechanism, **29**:281–**29**:282
mutations, **29**:279–**29**:281
structure, **29**:278–**29**:279
P elements
gene expression, **29**:269–**29**:274
mechanism, **29**:262–**29**:269
structure, **29**:260–**29**:262
retrotransposons
cis-acting effects, **29**:240–**29**:257
expression, **29**:233–**29**:236
mechanisms, **29**:236–**29**:240
structure, **29**:231–**29**:233
trans-acting effects, **29**:257–**29**:260
yeast ribosomes and, **29**:68–**29**:69, **29**:86
Drosophila aldrichi, hybrid viability in,
36:162–**36**:163
Drosophila americana, hybrid viability in,
36:162–**36**:163
Drosophila americana texana, hybrid viability in,
36:162–**36**:163
Drosophila ananassae transposable elements,
29:235, **29**:239, **29**:248–**29**:249
Drosophila arizonensis, hybrid viability in,
36:162, **36**:163
Drosophila bostrycha, hybrid viability in,
36:163–**36**:164

Drosophila buzzatii, hybrid viability in,
36:162–**36**:163, **36**:164
Drosophila cardini, hybrid viability in, **36**:162
Drosophila crucigera, hybrid viability in,
36:163–**36**:163
Drosophila formella, heterochromatin amount
variation, **37**:35
Drosophila funebris
hybrid viability in, **36**:162
transposable elements, **29**:240
Drosophila hydei
hybrid viablility in, **36**:162
position effect
clonal inactivation, **37**:326–327
eye mosaics, **37**:322
spermatogenesis, Y chromosome during,
23:179–**23**:228
comparison with *D. melanogaster*, **23**:199,
23:201, **23**:227–**23**:228
in hybrid with *D. neohydei*,
23:204–**23**:205, **23**:221–**23**:223
transposable elements, **29**:235
Y chromosome, **37**:68–72
Drosophila imeretensis, intercalary α-
heterochromatin, **37**:137–138
Drosophila immigrans, hybrid viability in, **36**:162
Drosophila koepferae, hybrid viability in,
36:162–**36**:163, **36**:164
Drosophila lummei, hybrid viability in,
36:162–**36**:163, **36**:164
Drosophila mauritiana
genetics of, **36**:166
hybrid viability in, **36**:160, **36**:162, **36**:165,
36:169, **36**:170, **36**:171, **36**:172
Drosophila mauritiana transposable elements,
29:260, **29**:262, **29**:274, **29**:278, **29**:280,
29:282
Drosophila melanica, hybrid viability in, **36**:162
Drosophila melanogaster
ADH, *see* Alcohol dehydrogenase
Adh gene, *see Adh* locus
Adh gene polymorphism, **23**:238
β-alanine metabolism, genetics,
24:197–**24**:198, **24**:200–**24**:202
alcohol tolerance, **25**:65–**25**:70
Adh polymorphism and, **25**:67–**25**:68,
25:79
attraction to ethanol-containing medium
and, **25**:67–**25**:68
comparison with other *Drosophila* species,
25:66–**25**:67

Drosophila melanogaster (*continued*)
  increase in temperate populations, 25:67
  wineries as habitats and, 25:69–25:70
alkaline phosphatase-1, 24:154–24:156
allelic recombination, lower rates in males,
    24:355
alternative RNA splicing
  effects of *cis*-acting mutations
    α-actinin, 31:258–259
    myosin heavy chain, 31:257–258
  in germ line, 31:252
  P element transcript regulation,
    31:254–257
  sex determination gene transcripts,
    31:243–252
  suppressor of sable (*su[s]*) gene, 31:253–254
  suppressor of white apricot mutations,
    31:252–253
  trans-acting factors, 31:259
aneuploid genotypes, viability, 27:213–27:215
ANT-C, *see* Antennapedia complex
anterior–posterior axis segmentation
  gap to pair-rule patterns, 31:11–12
  gradients, 31:10–11
  pair-rule interactions, 31:12–14
anterior-posterior axis
  homeotic gene functional domains,
    27:372–27:374
  maternal-effect gene roles, 27:246–27:248
  positional information genes, hierarchy,
    27:374–27:376
AS-C (*achaete-scute* complex), *see*
    Subdivision 1B of X chromosome
auditory behavior
  cacophony (*cac*) mutant, 31:152–154
  dissonance (*dis*) mutant, 31:152–154
  fruitless (*fru*) mutant, 31:157–158
  period (*per*) gene role, 31:154–155
biogenic amines, metabolism, 24:137–24:145
biological rhythms
  aj42 mutant, 31:171
  Andante (*And*) mutant, 31:169–170
  Clock (*Clk*) mutant, 31:169
  disconnected (*disco*) mutant, 31:170–171
  ebony (*e*) mutant, 31:169–170
  period (*per*) gene
    behavioral effects, 31:161–162
    molecular biology, 31:162–166
    sequence similarities with *arnt, Ahr, and
      sim*, 31:167–169

  threonine–glycine repeats, 31:162–166
    transcript localization, 31:164–166
  PER protein
    circadian cycling, 31:166–167
    expression, 31:164–166
    transcript localization, 31:164–166
body color mutations, 24:194–24:195,
    24:197–24:205
catecholamines during development,
    24:151–24:154
cell cycle genes, 31:80–81
  actin-binding proteins, 31:107
  actin gene family, 31:106–107
  in actin-mediated processes, 31:107–109
    daughterless-abolike, 31:108
    nuclear fall-out, 31:108
    pebble, 31:110
    spaghetti squash (*sqh*), 31:109
    sponge, 31:108
    zipper, 31:110
  in actin-mediated processes, *scrambled*,
    31:108
  cdc2 gene family, 31:81–83
  cyclin A
    genetic studies, 31:85–86
    mitotic behavior during development,
      31:83–88
  cyclin B
    genetic studies, 31:85–86
    maternal transcripts, 31:86–88
    mitotic behavior during development,
      31:83–88
    and pole cell development, 31:86–88
  cyclin C, 31:88–89
  cyclin D, 31:88–89
  cyclin E, 31:88–89
  in cytokinesis, 31:109–110
  kinesin family, 31:103–106
  in meiosis, 31:91–93
  microtubule-associated proteins, 31:99–101
  microtubule organizing centers, 31:101–103
  nuclear envelope, 31:110–111, 31:110–112
    fs(1)Ya, 31:111–112
    lamins, 31:111
  p34^{cdc2} activity
    in cellularized embryo, 31:90–91
    in syncytial embryo, 31:89–90
  polo kinase, 31:94
  protein phosphatase 1, 31:96
  protein phosphatase 2A, 31:96–97

string effects, 31:90–91
tubulin gene family, 31:97–99
twine effects
   in female meiosis, 31:92–93
   in male meiosis, 31:91–92
chorion
   genes, 24:231–24:232
   regulatory intergenic elements, 24:233, 24:235, 24:237, 24:239
   proteins, 24:227–24:229
   structure, 24:224
chromosomal rearrangement
   frequency, 37:199–201
   localization, 37:29–30
chromosome cycle genes
   DNA repair, 31:114–116
   DNA replication, 31:112–114
   pairing and segregation, 31:116–121
compound eye structure, 37:317
courtship behavior
   characterization, 31:151–152
   experience effects on mating, 31:159–160
   female receptivity, 31:158–159
   neurogenic control, 31:160–161
DAT, 24:196–24:197
daughterless gene, multifunctional, 27:165, 27:206–27:207, 27:439–27:440, 27:446
DCC activity, 24:157–24:158, 24:165–24:166
Ddc
   gene, 24:158–24:165
   cluster, 24:173–24:183
developmental defects, heat-induced
   comparison with mammalian systems, 28:286
   history, 28:281–28:283
   phenocopies
      branched hair, 28:283–28:285
      in recessive mutant heterozygotes, 28:285
differential heterochromatin staining, Q-staining, 37:18, 37:20
DNA
   recombinational repair in mutants, 24:338–24:339
   satellite repeating sequences, 37:47–49
dorsal-ventral (DV) axis, genetic control, 27:277–27:280, *see also* Ventralizing genes; *Zerknüllt* gene
Drosophila miranda, telomeres and, 30:194
Drug resistance, mosquitoes and, 30:124

DS1, *Mu* elements of *Zea mays* and, 30:94
embryo differentiation *in vitro*, 24:21
HSP induction by teratogenic drugs, 24:21
gap genes, zygotic
   characteristics, 27:240–27:246
   effects on homeotic genes, 27:266–27:268
   effects on pair-rule genes, 27:261–27:266
   late express of *Kr*, 27:268–27:270
   in anlage of Malpighian tubules, 27:270–27:272
   regulation
      by maternal-effect genes, 27:246–27:254
      in mutant embryos *stau exu* and *vas exu*, 27:257–27:260
      by other gap genes, 27:254–27:257
genes, expression in yeast, 23:136
genetic redundancy in, 36:150
genetics of, 36:166
head development
   abnormalities in *Dfd_* mutants, 27:365–27:368
   from anterior segments, 27:363–27:365
   Dfd role, *see Deformed* gene, homeotic
HSC (heat-shock-cognate) genes, developmental expression, 24:9
HSE
   HSP induction by heat and, 24:42–24:44
   HSTF binding
      in cell extracts, 24:36–24:38
      by chromatin *in vivo*, 24:38–24:39
HSP
   description, 24:3–24:4
   dual regulation by heat shock and ecdysterone, 24:4–24:8
   in *ts* conditional mutant *ecd-1*, 24:5–24:6
   expression during development, 24:5–24:6
   in response to heat shock, 24:9–24:10
HSP-encoding genes
   expression at normal temperature
      early in development, 28:288–28:289
      in mutants, 28:254
HSP70
   amino acid-analog-induced, 28:255
   organization, 28:238
   self-regulation, 28:251
   transcriptional regulation, HSE role, 28:244–28:247
HSP90, organization, 28:239–28:240

Drosophila melanogaster (continued)
HSP genes
  HSP83, developmental regulation, **24**:8,
    24:53–**24**:54
  HSTF and, **24**:53–**24**:54
  HSP70, expression during development,
    24:9
  small, induction by ecdysterone and heat,
    24:4–**24**:8, **24**:47–**24**:50
  control by distinct promoters,
    24:7–**24**:8, **24**:48–**24**:49
hybrid viability of, **36**:160, **36**:162,
  36:164–**36**:166, **36**:167–**36**:168,
  36:169, **36**:172–**36**:173, **36**:176,
  36:177, **36**:179
intercalary heterochromatin features, **37**:228
late replication study, **37**:31–32
learning
  dunce (dnc) mutant
    biochemical analysis, **31**:149–150
    expression patterns, **31**:150–151
    genetic mapping, **31**:148–149
  rutabaga (rut) mutant
    biochemical analysis, **31**:149–150
    expression patterns, **31**:150–151
αMD effects
  dietary, on cuticle, **24**:167–**24**:168
  hypersensitivity to, *amd* locus,
    24:168–**24**:171
  resistance to
    dominant second-chromosome-resistant
      strains, **24**:171–**24**:172
    third-chromosome-resistant mutations,
      24:172–**24**:173
  in vitro on DDC, **24**:166–**24**:167
mei mutants, **26**:150
  asynaptic (as), **26**:159
  genetic analysis using sex-transforming
    mutations, **26**:175
  interaction with *mus* mutations, **26**:180
  male sterility and, **26**:174
  ord gene, **26**:160
  variable (va), **26**:169
mitotic pairing, **37**:26–28
mobile element location, **37**:209–216
mosquitoes and, **30**:125–**30**:126, **30**:130,
  30:140
  genetic transformation, **30**:162–**30**:164,
    30:167, **30**:171–**30**:172
  physiology, **30**:149–**30**:150
multigene families, polymorphism, **23**:242

NBAD metabolism, genetics, **24**:198–**24**:199
neurogenesis
  cell commitment, transplantation studies,
    27:409–**27**:412
  ectodermal cell lineages, **27**:404–**27**:405
  ganglion mother cell identity genes,
    31:17–20
  genetic and molecular aspects
    daughterless gene, **27**:439–**27**:440,
      27:446
    interaction between gene involved,
      27:440–**27**:442
    neurogenic genes, **27**:412–**27**:433
    subdivision 1B of X chromosome,
      27:433–**27**:439
  neuroblast identity genes, **31**:17–20
  neurogenic ectoderm formation,
    27:405–**27**:412
  neuroblasts, segregation and map,
    27:406–**27**:408
  peripheral nervous system development,
    27:408–**27**:409
  proneural genes, **31**:15–17
olfaction
  abnormal chemosensory jump (acj) mutant,
    31:147–148
  anatomy, **31**:144–146
  assays, **31**:143–144
  female receptivity, **31**:158–159
  olfactory (olf) mutant, **31**:146–147
  olfactory-trap-abnormal (ota) mutant,
    31:147–148
oxygen defense mechanisms
  aging and, **28**:61–**28**:62
  ancillary enzymes and proteins,
    28:58–**28**:60
  enzymatic systems, **28**:52–**28**:57
    CAT, **28**:55–**28**:56
    SOD, **28**:52–**28**:55
  genetic approach, **28**:48–**28**:52
  heat-shock response and, **28**:62
  nonenzymatic systems, **28**:57–**28**:58
  radiosensitivity and, **28**:63–**28**:64
P family of transposable elements in,
  36:143–**36**:144
phenol oxidase, properties and genetics,
  24:185–**24**:196
polytene chromosome Q$^+$-band occurrence,
  37:148
position effect
  bw$^+$ locus, **37**:371–376

ci^+ locus, 37:371
clonal inactivation, 37:326–327,
    37:332–333
eye mosaics, 37:322–325
In(2LR)40d locus, 37:376
light locus, 37:362–365
rolled$^+$ gene, 37:362–365
variegation control genes, 37:313–315
prune/Killer of prune
interaction, 35:207–209
    awd gene, 35:209–221
    awd^{Kpn} mutation analysis,
        35:218–221
    early studies, 35:209
    Killer of prune allele, 35:209–210
    neomorphic character, 35:219–221
    nm23 gene comparison, 35:214–216
    nucleoside diphosphate kinase
        activity, 35:216–218
    phenotypes, 35:211–214
    discovery, 35:207–209
    lethal interactions, 35:237–244
    mechanisms, 35:241–244
    sensitivity, 35:238–240
    timing, 35:240–241
    prune gene, 35:222–236
    developmental expression, 35:227
    drosopterin pigment, 35:227–236
    function, 35:222–226
    Killer of prune
interaction rescue, 35:226
    phenotypes, 35:222
    pteridine biosynthesis pathway,
        35:229–234
regulatory genes for enzyme expression,
    24:89–24:100
sex-controlling genes
    linear pathway, 27:141–27:142
    X-chromosome dosage compensation,
        27:151, 27:152
sex determination in soma, see also Sex-
    controlling genes
    from dsx to real sex, 27:216–27:230
    early in development, 27:175–27:176
    genetic hierarchy, 27:190–27:191
    from primary signal to Sxl, 27:206–27:216
    primary signal (X/A ratio),
        27:189–27:192, 27:195–27:196,
        27:200, 27:201, 27:205,
        27:210–27:216
    from Sxl to dsx, 27:192–27:206

somatic sexual fate
    Sxl gene
    spatial regulation, 31:7–10
    X/A signal for, 31:4
    X/A ratio, 31:4–7
spermatogenesis, comparison with D. Hydei,
    23:199, 23:201, 23:227–23:228
TDC and 5HDC activities, 24:165–24:166
telomeres and, 30:190, 30:193–30:194
telomeric heterochromatin, DNA
    underrepresentation, 37:280
transgenic, B. mori chorion gene expression,
    24:235–24:238
transposable elements, 29:236,
    29:239–29:240, 29:263, 29:274,
    29:282
transposons
    activity changes
    dysgenic crosses and, 28:78
    internal effects, 28:77–28:78
    temperature effects, 28:91
    genes, 37:318–319
    population dynamics, 23:247–23:249
    tumor suppressor of, 36:74
tyrosine-O-phosphate metabolism,
    24:154–24:155
    in lethal translucida mutant, 24:156–24:157
visual system genes
    optomotor-blind (omb), 31:141–142
    sevenless (sev), 31:140–141
    small-optic-lobes (sol), 31:142–143
X chromosome, 37:59–60, 37:102–104,
    37:222, see also Chromosome X
X-linked gene dosage compensation,
    24:371–24:377
    cis-acting regulators of, 24:405–24:418
    regulatory mechanisms, 24:418–24:421
    sex determination and, 24:389–24:397
    trans-acting regulators of, 24:399–24:405
    transcription regulation and,
        24:377–24:381
    X chromosome/autosome ratio and,
        24:381–24:389
Y chromosome, 37:65–68, 37:102
zeste in, see zeste in Drosophila melanogaster
Drosophila mesophragmatica, hybrid viability of,
    36:162
Drosophila miranda, neo-Y chromosome
    degeneration, 37:74–76
Drosophila mojavensis, hybrid viability in,
    36:162, 36:163

Drosophila montana, hybrid viability in, 36:162–36:163

Drosophila mulleri, hybrid viability in, 36:162–36:163

Drosophila neohydei hybrids with *D. hydei*, spermatogenesis and Y chromosome, 23:204–23:205, 23:221–23:223

Drosophila neohydei, hybrid viability in, 36:162

Drosophila obscura, hybrid viability in, 36:161, 36:162

Drosophila persimilis, hybrid viability in, 36:161–36:162

Drosophila pseudoobscura heterochromatin amount variation, 37:33–34

hybrid viability in, 36:161–36:162

Drosophila quinaria, hybrid viability in, 36:162

Drosophila repleta, hybrid viability in, 36:162

Drosophila robusta, hybrid viability in, 36:162

Drosophila saltans, hybrid viability in, 36:162

Drosophila sechellia genetics of, 36:166

hybrid viability in, 36:160, 36:165, 36:169, 36:171

Drosophila simulans genetics of, 36:166

hybrid viability in, 36:160, 36:162, 36:164–36:166, 36:167, 36:168, 36:169, 36:170, 36:171, 36:172, 36:174, 36:176, 36:177, 36:179

transposable elements, 29:260, 29:274, 29:278, 29:280, 29:282

Drosophila spp.

chromosome rearrangements in, 36:241

hybrid inviability in, 36:157–36:185

intrachromosomal transpositions in, 36:259

mutant strains of, 36:166

Drosophila teisseiri hybrid viability in, 36:174

transposable elements, 29:278

Drosophila tripunctata, hybrid viability of, 36:162

Drosophila virilis chromosomal rearrangement parental effects, 37:342

Ddc DNA, comparison with *D. melanogaster*, 24:164–24:165

differential heterochromatin staining, Q-staining, 37:17, 37:21

hybrid viability in, 36:162–36:163, 36:164

late replication study, 37:32

phenol oxidase, cuticular, 24:186–24:187

position effect

clonal inactivation, 37:326–327

peach+ locus, 37:366–367

transposable elements, 29:239

zeste in, 29:313–29:315, 29:329–29:330, 29:337

Drosophila willistoni, hybrid viability of, 36:162

Drosophila yakuba transposable elements, 29:278

Drosopterin pigments

accumulation reduction, 35:234–236

GTP role, 35:233–236

prune gene mutations, 35:227–229

pteridine biosynthesis pathway, 35:229–233

Drought

ABA increase induction, 28:119

effect on *cor* gene expression, *Arabidopsis*, 28:120

Drug-metabolizing enzymes

other, multiple forms of, 21:39

phase I and phase II, 21:2–21:3

research directions, 21:40–21:42

Drymona rubra, pollen competition, 26:33

DSF splicing factor, 31:221

dsx gene, X-chromosome replication, 39:433

DTS-3 gene, hormone function-impairing mutations, 39:282, 39:284

Dubunin effect, *ci+* gene dominance, 37:357–362

Duchenne muscular dystrophy, gene therapy, 35:117–142

animal models, 35:123–125

disease characteristics, 35:117–123

apodystrophins, 35:121

clinical features, 35:117–118

DMD gene, 35:118–121

dystrophin, 35:121–123, 35:127–129

dystrophin-associated glycoprotein complex, 35:121–123

future research directions, 35:141–142

gene transfer efficacy, 35:125–127

methodology, 35:129–141

adenoviral vectors, 35:129–134

direct DNA injection, 35:137–139

myoblast transplantation, 35:140–141

retroviral vectors, 35:134–137

Duffy (Fy) blood group, CMT1 disease linkage to, 36:4, 36:5

dunce

gene, band organization, 39:153

mutant
  Drosophila melanogaster
    biochemical analysis, 31:149–150
    expression patterns, 31:150–151
Duplication testing, for CMT disease, 36:34
DV axis, *see* Dorsal-ventral axis
Dystrophin, 33:177–216, 35:121–123,
  35:127–129
  dystrophin-associated proteins, 33:199–203
  future research directions, 33:215–216
  gene characteristics, 33:184–190
    expression regulation, 33:188–190
    identification, 33:184–185
    structure, 33:185–188
  muscular dystrophy
    carrier diagnosis, 33:211–215
    direct diagnosis, 33:212–214
    indirect diagnosis, 33:211–212
    disease characteristics, 33:177–183
      animal models, 33:183
      cardiac muscle, 33:181–182
      mental retardation, 33:180–181
      muscles, 33:177–180
      retina, 33:182–183
    mutational distribution, 33:203–207
    prenatal diagnosis, 33:211–214
  mutational spectra, 33:203–211
    genotype/phenotype correlations
      gross rearrangements, 33:207–209
      point mutations, 33:209–211
    muscular dystrophy distribution,
      33:203–207
  protein characteristics, 33:190–198
    isoforms, 33:194–195
    related forms, 33:195–197
      87K tyrosine kinase substrate, 33:197
      protodystrophin, 33:196–197
      utrophin/DRP, 33:195–196
    structure, 33:190–193
    subcellular localization, 33:197–198

E74 genes
  band organization, 39:153
  cascade regulation, 39:326–327
  hormone function-impairing mutations,
    39:284
  puff development, 39:310–312
E. coli, *see* Escherichia coli
E63 genes, puff development, 39:304

E75 genes, puff development, 39:312–315,
  39:317
E78 genes, puff development, 39:315
E93 genes, puff development, 39:316
E1A oncoprotein, 36:57
  binding to pRb, 36:56, 36:60
  host HSP70 gene induction, 24:19
  in human cells, 24:51–24:52
  inactivation of p27 by, 36:64
EBNA-5 protein, binding of p53 by, 36:57
ebony (e) mutant
  Drosophila melanogaster, 31:169–170
ebony gene, heat-shock puffs, 39:372
E-cadherin, catenin association with,
  36:73–36:74
ecd1 gene, hormone function-impairing
  mutations, 39:167
Ecdysone hypothesis, *minute* genes, 38:78–79
Ecdysterone
  dipteran development role, 39:164–166
  Drosophila melanogaster
    during embryogenesis, 24:4, 24:48
    HSP gene activation, 24:4–24:7,
      24:48–24:50
    promoter sequence responsible for,
      24:7–24:8
  puff association
    ecdysterone receptor characterization,
      39:319–324
    puff induction characterization,
      39:291–319
      5A puff, 39:302–303
      39BC puff, 39:303
      2B3-5 puff, 39:291–299
      25B puff, 39:303
      35B2-5 puff, 39:303
      67B puff, 39:304
      75B puff, 39:312–315
      90B3-8 puff, 39:315–316
      71C3-4-D1-2 puff, 39:308–309
      75CD puff, 39:315
      71CE puff, 39:309
      2C1-3 puff, 39:300
      3C puff, 39:300–302
      68C puff, 39:304–308
      78C puff, 39:315
      Drosophila lummei, 39:317
      Drosophila nasuta X chromosome region
        10 puff, 39:317
      Drosophila virilis 16A puff, 39:317–318
      71EF puff, 39:309–310

Ecdysterone (continued)
  55E puff, 39:319
  74E puff, 39:310–312
  46F puff, 39:304
  63F puff, 39:304
  93F puff, 39:316
  I-18C puff, 39:316–317
  II-9A puff, 39:317
  II-14A puff, 39:317
  IV2B puff, 39:317
  regulation
    activity change cascades, 39:271–281
    analogs, 39:285–287
    mechanisms, 39:267–271
    puff induction, 34:15, 34:238–242, 34:294
    radioimmune analysis, 39:166
    salivary secretion regulation, 39:193–194,
      39:197
ECF family, of sigma factors, 36:226
Ecological factors
  morphology change induction, 34:299–305
EcR gene
  hormone function-impairing mutations,
    39:284
  puff development, 39:303–304
ecs gene
  band organization, 39:142, 39:144
  hormone function-impairing mutations,
    39:169, 39:196, 39:284
  puff development, 39:291
Ectoderm, neurogenic, Drosophila
  cell commitment
    epidermalizing signal, 27:409–27:411
    neurogenic gene functions,
      27:442–27:445
    neuralizing signal, 27:409–27:411
    AS-C gene and da function, 27:446
  formation
    neuroblast segregation and map,
      27:406–27:408
    PNS development, 27:408–27:409
Ectopic pairing
  characteristics, 37:134
  intercalary heterochromatin identification
    chromosomal rearrangement frequency,
      37:204
    DNA underreplication, 37:189–193
    formation mechanisms, 37:183–184
    nucleolar contacts, 37:166, 37:178–179
    nucleoprotein association, 37:184–185

overview, 37:166–168
polytene chromosomes, 37:171–176
properties, 37:168–170, 37:180–182
telomeric heterochromatin, 37:266–279
  characterization, 37:268–275
  properties, 37:267, 37:276–279
E2F transcription factors, pRb regulation of,
  36:55, 36:56, 36:60
Egasyn, β-glucuronidase expression in mouse
  and, 24:80
EGF, see Epidermal growth factor
Eggs
  braconid wasps
    hatchability, effects of
      chemical mutagens
        oocyte sensitivity, 25:168–25:171
        oogonium sensitivity, 25:171–25:172
      irradiation by X rays and g rays,
        25:151–25:153
      radioactive isotope digestion,
        25:161–25:162
      ultraviolet rays, 25:163–25:164
    production pattern
      chemical mutagen effects,
        25:164–25:167
      radiation-induced infecundity,
        25:153–25:155
      in flight simulation experiments,
        25:158–25:168
      hydroxyurea effect on recovery,
        25:157
      orbital flight and, 25:157–25:158
    size, decrease by chemical mutagens,
      25:167–25:168
  determination, nuclear envelope role,
    24:263–24:264
  fertilized, DNA microinjection into
    pronucleus, mouse, 24:286–24:287,
    24:290–24:291
Egp genes, secretory protein expression, 39:183
EGR-1 gene, WT1 effects on, 36:70
EGR-1 transcription factor, WT1 homology
  with, 36:70
Elasmobranch, evolutionary genetics of fish and,
  29:151, 29:167
Elastase, bacterial gene encoding, 36:190
Electrodiagnostic testing, for CMT disease,
  36:2, 36:3–36:4
Electron microscopy
  genetic mapping, 34:202–207

Neurospora crassa and, **29:**22, **29:**45
transcriptionally active chromatin,
  22:170–**22:**171
yeast ribosomes and, **29:**86–**29:**87
Electron transfer
nitrate reductase and, **30:**3–**30:**8,
  30:22–**30:**23, **30:**30
superoxide dismutases and, **30:**252,
  30:266–**30:**268, **30:**295
molecular genetics, **30:**281
physiology, **30:**252–**30:**253, **30:**257,
  30:259, **30:**261
Electrophoresis
carbonic anhydrases and, **30:**336, **30:**347
evolutionary genetics of fish and
  detection of variation, **29:**123, **29:**126,
    29:131
  environmental change, **29:**165
  multigene families, **29:**147, **29:**157
  nomenclature, **29:**134
mosquitoes and, **30:**132, **30:**140, **30:**151
Neurospora crassa and, **29:**4, **29:**10–**29:**11,
  29:13, **29:**15–**29:**16, **29:**48
nitrate reductase and, **30:**20
pollen protein and isozyme analysis,
  26:21–**26:**22
somaclonal variation and, **30:**57–**30:**59
telomeres and, **30:**192, **30:**229
yeast ribosomes and, **29:**73, **29:**88, **29:**101
  ribosomal proteins, **29:**64–**29:**65,
    29:70–**29:**71
zeste in *Drosophila melanogaster* and, **29:**333
Electrophorus electricus, evolutionary genetics of
  fish and, **29:**179
Elicitors
from plant pathogen fungi
  binding to receptors in plants, **28:**202
  characteristics, **28:**203
  interaction with plant elicitors, **28:**202,
    28:204
protoplasting-induced, alfalfa cells, **28:**214
ELISA, nitrate reductase and, **30:**20, **30:**22
Elongation
factors, yeast ribosomes and, **29:**77
telomeres and
  function, **30:**203, **30:**205, **30:**208–**30:**218,
    30:220–**30:**221
  structure, **30:**190, **30:**200–**30:**201
Elongins, VHL homology with, **36:**85
EMBL3, mosquitoes and, **30:**141, **30:**143

Embryogenesis
mosquitoes and, **30:**154
somaclonal variation and, **30:**43–**30:**45
telomeres and, **30:**227
Embryonic development, *see also* Neoplasia
gene inactivation, **37:**355–357
heterochromatin association
  formation, **37:**35–43
  supercompaction, **37:**440–443
Embryos
embryogenic callus production during
  development, Gramineae
  growth hormone levels and, **24:**446
  size and, **24:**445–**24:**446
  tissue specificity and, **24:**447
mosquitoes and, **30:**125, **30:**163–**30:**164,
  30:167–**30:**169
Mu elements of *Zea mays* and, **30:**91
telomeres and, **30:**202, **30:**206, **30:**226,
  30:229
totipotent cells, DNA injection *invitro*,
  mouse, **24:**287, **24:**290
Emetine, yeast ribosomes and, **29:**70
EMS, *see* Ethyl methanesulfonate
EmtB gene, yeast ribosomes and, **29:**65
Emtb gene, yeast ribosomes and, **29:**65
Emx genes, brain patterning role, rostrocaudal
  axis, **38:**3–7
End-joining technique, *see* Nonhomologous
  end-joining
Endocrine system, evolutionary genetics of fish
  and, **29:**190–**29:**200
Endonuclease IV, response to NUV and,
  26:124
Endosperm
Mu elements of *Zea mays* and, **30:**78, **30:**90
somaclonal variation and, **30:**57
telomeres and, **30:**229
Engrailed (en), pair-rule gene, *Drosophila*
  effect on *Dfd* gene expression, **27:**382,
    27:388, **27:**395–**27:**397
  expression pattern
    eve effect, **27:**386
    in *stau exu* and *vas exu* embryos, **27:**258
    male mutant, secondary sex comb formation,
      27:220
Enhancers, mosquitoes and, **30:**154, **30:**163
Enhancer, somaclonal variation and, **30:**53
env, *Drosophila* transposable elements and,
  29:231–**29:**232, **29:**235, **29:**248

Environment
  adversity in, means of coping with
    diversity in organism in responses,
      21:29–21:31
    rapid responses, 21:27–21:28
  contaminated, detoxification of, 36:189
  evolutionary genetics of fish and, 29:158,
    29:191, 29:201–29:202
    antifreeze genes, 29:162–29:163
    cytochrome P-450 genes, 29:167–29:168
    enzyme-synthesizing loci, 29:163–29:167
    heat-shock protein genes,
      29:159–29:162
    metallothionein genes, 29:169–29:170
    oncogenes, 29:170–29:173
Enzymes
  carbonic anhydrases and, 30:233–30:232,
    30:336–30:337
  differential heterochromatin staining,
    chromosome digestion, 37:24
  evolutionary genetics of fish and, 29:126,
    29:140
    development, 29:174–29:175
    environmental change, 29:163–29:167,
      29:169
    linkage groups, 29:144, 29:146
    multigene families, 29:152, 29:154
    nomenclature, 29:132–29:133
  mosquitoes and
    genetic differentiation, 30:131, 30:135
    genetic transformation, 30:169
    genome characterization, 30:142, 30:146
    physiology, 30:151, 30:154–30:161
  Mu elements of Zea mays and, 30:103, 30:112,
    30:114
    assays, 30:81, 30:85–30:86
    regulation, 30:99
    structure, 30:95
  Neurospora crassa and, 29:4, 29:7, 29:49
    DNA transaction, 29:20–29:21,
      29:23–29:24
    metabolism, 29:39–29:41
    mitochondria, 29:34, 29:36
  nitrate reductase and, 30:3, 30:9, 30:31
    biochemistry, 30:4, 30:6–30:8
    genetics, 30:20, 30:23, 30:27
  replacement
    Gaucher disease treatment, 32:29–33
  somaclonal variation and, 30:57, 30:59
  superoxide dismutases and

  molecular genetics, 30:275–30:276,
    30:278, 30:280, 30:282,
    30:285–30:287
  physiology, 30:253, 30:255, 30:259,
    30:261–30:262
  physiology of mutants, 30:289,
    30:293–30:294, 30:296–30:297,
    30:299–30:308
  structure, 30:265–30:268
  telomeres and, 30:209, 30:211,
    30:216–30:217, 30:228, 30:232
  yeast ribosomes and, 29:87, 29:94
Epidermal growth factor
  mammalian, homology to neurogenic gene
    products of Drosophila
    Dl protein and, 27:422
    N protein and, 27:419, 27:422
  p21 induction by, 36:62
Epidermoblasts, cell lineages, Drosophila,
  27:404–27:405
Epigenesis, Mu elements of Zea mays and, 30:91
Epilobium canum, pollen
  competition in natural populations, 26:33
  germination, style effect, 26:29
Epistasis, C. elegans
  cell-type-controlling genes, 27:71–27:72,
    27:105–27:107
  sex-controlling genes, 27:138–27:141
Epithelium
  carbonic anhydrases and, 30:330–30:331
  mosquitoes and, 30:156
Epitopes, nitrate reductase and, 30:22–30:23
  E7 protein, binding to pRb, 36:56, 36:60
Epstein-Barr virus, EBNA-5 protein of, See
  EBNA-36:5 protein
Equinomycin, RNA synthesis inhibition, 39:75
ERCC3 factor, p53 binding of, 36:59
Erythrocytes, carbonic anhydrases and, 30:325,
  30:344, 30:346
Erythrogenesis, carbonic anhydrases and, 30:327
Erythroids
  cells, carbonic anhydrases and, 30:326,
    30:343–30:344, 30:349
  hemin-induced differentiation and HSP, 24:22
  precursors, differentiation, TF role,
    25:22–25:23
Erythropoiesis, abnormal fetal, 20:386–20:387
Escherichia coli, 16S ribosomal RNA mutational
  analysis, 33:1–31
  arsenic detoxification in, 36:218, 36:221

carbonic anhydrases and, 30:323, 30:325
catalase-deficient mutants, NUV resistance
  and, 26:102, 26:112–26:113, 26:119,
  26:121–26:122
conserved nucleotides, 33:19, 33:20
detection methods, 33:2–5
  mutation introduction, 33:4–5
  plasmid expression, 33:2–4
differential heterochromatin staining,
  Q-staining, 37:17
DNA recombinational repair
  during conjugation, 24:335
  cross-links, 24:334
  double-strand breaks, 24:334
  effective against variety of damages,
    24:335
  gaps opposite thymine dimers,
    24:334–24:335
  mismatch repair system, 24:335–24:336
double mutations, 33:19, 33:21–30
evolutionary genetics of fish and, 29:158,
  29:161
flagellar genes, comparison with *Caulobacter*
  cell cycle role in expression, 27:23
  mutations, effects on flagellar assembly,
    27:19–27:22
  organization, regulatory hierarchy,
    27:22–27:23
  promoters, 27:14, 27:25–27:27
flagellum, assembly, 27:19
  hook-associated proteins and,
    27:19–27:20
fungal genes
  detection by complementation,
    23:90–23:93
  expression, 23:126–23:127
  genomic library construction, 23:86
genes
  expression in yeast
    β-galactosidase, 23:129–23:131
    β-lactaminase, 23:127–23:128
    chloramphenicol resistance, 23:128
  for FeSOD and MnSOD
    isolation, 26:80, 26:122–26:123
    lacking in mutants, 26:78, 26:80–26:81
    location on chromosomes, 26:75
    sequencing, 26:80
heat-shock response
  abnormal protein-induced without heat,
    28:253–28:254

groEL HSP
  biochemical function, 28:261
  homology to Rubisco-binding protein,
    28:262
  negative regulation by dnaK protein,
    28:250
  RNA polymerase sigma factor (σ^{32}) role,
    28:244, 28:245
  thermotolerance, impaired in mutants,
    28:256
HSP
  functions, 24:16–24:18
  HSP70, *dnaK*-coded, properties,
    24:17–24:18
  htpR-regulated genes and, 24:16–24:17
  l-phage-activated genes and, 24:17–24:18
hybrid between Mn- and Fe-containing
  SODs, 26:70–26:71, 26:74
iron-containing SOD
  biosynthesis during aerobic and anaerobic
    growth, 26:82, 26:123
  regulation by metals, 26:84–26:85
  isolation, 26:67
  three-dimensional structure, 26:71
iron-regulated gene in, 36:190, 36:191,
  36:193, 36:196, 36:197
iron-sulfur clusters in, 36:199
limitations, 33:30–31
manganese-containing SOD
  amino acid sequences, 26:70
  biosynthesis during aerobic growth,
    O_2`-induced, 26:82–26:83, 26:123
  iron regulatory role, 26:83–26:86
  catalytic mechanisms, 26:78
  isolation, 26:69
mercury resistance protein of, 36:206
molydenum-regulated genes in, 36:200,
  36:201
mosquitoes and, 30:140, 30:152, 30:155
Neurospora crassa and, 29:23
nitrate reductase and, 30:3
NUV effects
  absorption by
    dihydroxy acid dehydratase, 26:102,
      26:109, 26:111
    porphyrins, 26:107
    ribonucleotide reductase, 26:109
    thiolated tRNA, 26:102,
      26:105–26:106
  mutagenic, 26:132–26:134

Escherichia coli (continued)
  physiological
    growth delay, **26:**106, **26:**126
    membrane damage, **26:**128–**26:**129
    protein synthesis induction,
      26:126–**26:**128
  sensitivity in mutants
    gal-latt deletion, **26:**125–**26:**126
    hem (hematins), **26:**125
    katF, katE, KatG (catalase), **26:**112,
      26:119, **26:**121–**26:**122
    nuvA (thiolated tRNA), **26:**106,
      26:126, **26:**127
    polA (5′ to 3′ exonuclease),
      26:124–**26:**125
    RecA (recombinase), **26:**125,
      26:130–**26:**131
    uvr, **26:**125, **26:**129
    xthA (exonuclease III), **26:**123–**26:**124
  oxygen toxicity, protection by SOD
    branched-chain amino acid biosynthesis
      and, **26:**77
    α,β-dihydroisovalerate activity and,
      26:77
    ribonucleotide reductase activity and,
      26:78, **26:**112
  plasmid hybrids with fungal
    characteristics, **23:**148–**23:**151
  expression in bacteria and fungi,
    23:138–**23:**139
  recA gene in, **36:**261
  second-site suppressor mutations, **33:**31
  single mutations, **33:**19, **33:**21–30
  sodA sodB double mutant
    construction and properties, **26:**80–**26:**81
    human CuZnSOD plasmid effect, **26:**78,
      26:114
    hypersensitivity to NUV and H$_2$O$_2$,
      26:114, **26:**123
  somaclonal variation and, **30:**61
  structure–function analysis, **33:**6–19
    central domain mutations, **33:**12–13
    3′ major domain mutations, **33:**13–16
    5′ major domain mutations, **33:**10–12
    3′ minor domain mutations, **33:**16–19
    secondary structure, **33:**6–9
    upstream mutations, **33:**9–10
  superoxide dismutases and
    molecular genetics, **30:**272, **30:**276
    physiology, **30:**257, **30:**261

  physiology of mutants, **30:**288,
    30:293–**30:**294, **30:**298,
    30:307–**30:**308
  structure, **30:**266, **30:**272
  suppression, **30:**304–**30:**305
  transfection by recombinant plasmids,
    23:80–**23:**84
  transposons, population dynamics, **23:**248,
    23:250
  yeast ribosomes and, **29:**63–**29:**64, **29:**74,
    29:93
  ribosomal protein genes, **29:**75, **29:**80,
    29:84
  ribosomal proteins, **29:**65, **29:**68–**29:**69
Esophageal cancer, disruptive mutation in,
  36:66
Esterase
  carbonic anhydrases and, **30:**337
  developmental control by regulatory genes
    Drosophila, **24:**98
    maize, **24:**100
    mosquitoes and, **30:**148–**30:**150,
      30:156–**30:**157
  β-Esterase genes, puff development, **39:**317
Estrogen
  carbonic anhydrases and, **30:**330–**30:**331
  TF synthesis induction
    in liver, chicken, **25:**25, **25:**27
    iron deficiency and, **25:**27
    in oviduct, chicken, **25:**25, **25:**26–**25:**27
    undetected in rat liver, **25:**27
EST1, telomeres and, **30:**204
est1, telomeres and, **30:**206, **30:**209, **30:**216,
  30:219–**30:**220
Ethanol
  developmental defects induction,
    28:278–**28:**279
  heat-shock puff induction, **39:**348
  puff activity effects, **39:**253, **39:**256
  yeast ribosomes and, **29:**84
Ethidium bromide
  differential heterochromatin staining,
    chromosome digestion, **37:**24
  RNA synthesis inhibition, **39:**75
Ethionine, RNA synthesis inhibition, **39:**75
Ethnic groups, CMT disease in, **36:**2
Ethyl carbamate, puff activity effects, **39:**264
Ethyleneimine, effect on braconid wasp egg
  hatchability, **25:**169
Ethyl methanesulfonate

Adh mutant induction, Drosophila, 25:48
effects on braconid wasps
egg production and, 25:166
hatchability and, 25:168
postembryonic lethal mutation induction
in sperm, 25:173–25:174
sperm inactivation, 25:173
Ethyl methane sulfonate, nitrate reductase and,
30:13, 30:15
Euchromatin
definition, 37:2–3
heterochromatization, 37:438–440
zeste in Drosophila melanogaster and, 29:342
Euglena gracilis FeSOD, 26:67
Eukaryotes
carbonic anhydrases and, 30:325
Drosophila transposable elements and, 29:234,
29:243–29:244
evolutionary genetics of fish and, 29:135,
29:140
mosquitoes and, 30:155, 30:165, 30:174
Neurospora crassa and, 29:2, 29:9, 29:38,
29:45, 29:49
DNA transaction, 29:19–29:21,
29:24–29:25
genetic material, 29:15–29:16
nitrate reductase and, 30:3–30:4, 30:6–30:7,
30:9
superoxide dismutases and
physiology, 30:255–30:257,
30:261–30:263
physiology of mutants, 30:289, 30:298,
30:300–30:302
structure, 30:264, 30:266–30:267,
30:271–30:272
telomeres and, 30:186, 30:190, 30:195,
30:200, 30:203
yeast ribosomes and, 29:63–29:65, 29:91,
29:94, 29:103–29:104
nucleolus, 29:86, 29:90
ribosomal protein genes, 29:72–29:73,
29:84
Euplotes, telomeres and, 30:199, 30:227
eve gene
Drosophila melanogaster
in neural fate, 31:17–20
stripe 2 element, 31:11–12
Even-skipped (eve) pair-rule gene, Drosophila
effects on Dfd expression, 27:382–27:384
en activation regulation, 27:386

expression pattern in stau exu and vas exu
embryos, 27:258
Evi2 genes, 36:80
antisense transcripts of, 36:103
Evolution
Adh gene in Drosophila, 25:73–25:76
ADH origin and, 25:75–25:76
in angiosperms, pollen selection role,
26:41–26:43, see also Male
gametophytic selection
carbonic anhydrases and, 30:334–30:335,
30:348
chorion gene regulatory elements,
conservation in insects, 24:233–24:235,
24:237
cis- and trans-acting factor conservation,
24:299–24:300
cultural, 23:261
DNA damage and mutation reduction,
24:328–24:329
factors affecting genetic variability,
23:260–23:261
intron origin, 24:269–24:275
maturases and, 24:270–24:273
pre-mRNA structure and, 24:275
mitochondrial genome, ascomycetes
introns in mosaic genes, 25:226–25:227
ori sequences, scheme, 25:237
mosquitoes and, 30:173
phenotype dynamics
basic models, 23:250–23:253
pleiotropy, 23:253–23:255
polyteny role, 34:20, 34:356
sexual reproduction origin, 24:342–24:355
superoxide dismutases and, 30:270–30:272
superoxide dismutases of three types, 26:68,
26:74–26:75
TF gene
expression in prochordate, 25:5–25:7
intragenic duplication, 25:305
separation from linkage group in higher
primates, 25:11
Evolutionary genetics of fish, see Fish,
evolutionary genetics of
Excision, Mu elements of Zea mays and,
30:100–30:103, 30:106–30:107
Exine pattern, formation during pollen
ontogeny, 26:4–26:6
sporophytic control, 26:7–26:8,
26:10–26:11, 26:47

Exons
definition model, 31:218–220, 31:261–262
Drosophila transposable elements and, 29:245,
29:268, 29:269–29:270
evolutionary genetics of fish and, 29:172,
29:183, 29:186, 29:194–29:197
Exon skipping
during alternative splicing, 31:261
exon definition model, 31:218–220,
31:261–262
Exonuclease III
deficiency in xthA mutants, sensitivity to
NUV and, 26:123–26:124
protection against NUV, 26:112
DNA repair synthesis and, 26:116, 26:118
Exotoxin A, bacterial gene encoding, 36:190
Explant
genotype, somaclonal variation and,
30:46–30:48
source tissue, somaclonal variation and,
30:42–30:43
Expressed sequence tags, mouse libraries,
35:166–168, 191–194
extramacrochaete (emc) gene
Drosophila melanogaster, 31:6
exuperantia (exu) gene, 31:100–101
Eye
color
Drosophila transposable elements and,
29:253, 29:255, 29:278
zeste in Drosophila melanogaster and,
29:328, 29:333
development, human malformation, ocular
anlage patterning
eye formation, 38:21
homeobox genes, 38:21–22
structures
Drosophila transposable elements and,
29:248–29:249
eyeless^D gene, hormone function-impairing
mutations, 39:169
Ezrin, merlin similarity to, 36:83

Factor IX
in hemophilia, 32:100, 32:102–104
Factor VIII
in hemophilia, 32:100, 32:113–116
FAD, nitrate reductase and, 30:5–30:7, 30:23

Familial adenomatous coli
chromosomal linkage of, 36:95
tumor suppressor gene role in, 36:49,
36:72–36:73, 36:75, 36:95
Familial agonadism, 33:313
Familial cancer syndromes, tumor suppressor
gene role in, 36:47, 36:48, 36:49, 36:52,
36:72–36:73, 36:106
Familial cardiomyopathies, 35:285–315
arrhythmogenic right ventricular
cardiomyopathy, 35:310–312
dilated cardiomyopathy, 35:305–310
clinical syndrome, 35:305–306
definition, 35:305–306
epidemiology, 35:306
genetics, 35:306–309
autosomal dominant form, 35:308–309
recessive inheritance, 35:309
X-linked inheritance, 35:307–308
pathogenesis, 35:309–310
future research directions, 35:315
hypertrophic cardiomyopathy, 35:286–305
clinical syndrome, 35:286–287
definition, 35:286–287
epidemiology, 35:288
features, 35:288–289
genetics, 35:289–290
genotype–phenotype correlation, 35:302
mutation characteristics
β-cardiac myosin, 35:290–292, 35:302
cardiac myosin-binding protein C,
35:295–296
etiology, 35:296–297
α-tropomyosin, 35:293–294, 35:302–303
troponin T, 35:294–295, 35:303–305
pathogenesis, 35:297–302
long QT syndrome, 35:313–312
overview, 35:285–286
restrictive cardiomyopathy, 35:312–313
Familial MTC, chromosomal linkage of, 36:95
Familial recurrent polyneuropathy, HNPP
disease
FAP, use in predicting prognosis, 36:106
Far-ultraviolet radiation
damage different from NUV action,
26:115–26:117
mutagenicity, 26:132–26:134
SOS response induction, 26:129–26:130
fa^sbw gene, band organization, 39:148
fa^sub gene, interband organization, 39:89–90

Fat, dietary, role in colon cancer, 36:76
fat gene
  puff development, 39:241
  secretory protein expression, 39:183
Fatty acid-binding protein-2 gene
  non-insulin-dependent diabetes mellitus gene
  candidate, 32:87–88
Fatty acids
  composition in braconid wasps
    adaptability to host and diet, 25:143
  polyunsaturated, oxygen radical production,
    28:45
fep genes, in bacteria, 36:193
Ferricyanide reductase, nitrate reductase and,
  30:8–30:9
Ferrodoxin, bacterial regulation of, 36:198
Fertility factors, position effects, 37:368
Fertilization, telomeres and, 30:202, 30:229
Fertilizers, nitrate reductase and, 30:1, 30:30
α-Fetoprotein, expression in transgenic mouse,
  24:303
FGF, p21 induction by, 36:62
FGF3/int-2 gene
  Xenopus laevis, 31:35, 31:43
Fibrillar center, yeast ribosomes and, 29:86
Fibrillarin, yeast ribosomes and, 29:88–29:92
Fibrillin, mutations on gene for, 36:98
Fibrils, characteristics, 34:249–256
Fibroblasts
  evolutionary genetics of fish and, 29:173
  telomeres and, 30:204–30:208
Filamentous fungi, structural variation and
  organization of mtDNA in, 22:39–22:46
Fish
  evolutionary genetics of, 29:120–29:122,
    29:201–29:202
  detection of variation, 29:123
    DNA amplification, 29:129–29:130
    DNA fingerprinting, 29:128–29:129
    mtDNA, 29:126–29:128
    protein-coding loci, 29:123–29:126
    sequencing, 29:131
  development, 29:173–29:176
  endocrine system, 29:190
    anterior pituitary, 29:190–29:196
    hypothalamus, 29:196–29:200
  environmental change, 29:158
    antifreeze genes, 29:162–29:163
    cytochrome P-450 genes,
      29:167–29:168

enzyme-synthesizing loci,
  29:163–29:167
heat-shock protein genes,
  29:159–29:162
metallothionein genes, 29:169–29:170
oncogenes, 29:170–29:173
immune system
  immunoglobulin gene superfamily,
    29:181–29:185
  immunoglobulins, 29:185–29:188
  MHC antigens, 29:188–29:190
  linkage groups, 29:143–29:147
  multigene families, 29:147
    lactate dehydrogenase, 29:152–29:157
    protamine genes, 29:157–29:158
    vertebrate hemoglobins,
      29:148–29:152
  nervous system, 29:176–29:181
  nomenclature, 29:131–29:134
  nuclear genomic structures,
    29:134–29:135
    isochores, 29:140–29:143
    morphology, 29:137–29:140
    size, 29:135–29:137
  Nomenclature Committee, evolutionary
    genetics of fish and, 29:131,
    29:133–29:134
  tetraploidization in, 36:149–36:150
FISH analysis
  of chromosome, 36:10, 36:17
  radiation hybrid genome mapping, human
    component analysis, 33:79–80
Fixation technique, banding pattern
  identification, 34:190–197
Flagellar genes
  Caulobacter crescentus
    clusters, location, 27:5–27:6
    comparison with
      B. subtilis sporulation genes, 27:25
      E. coli flagellar genes, 27:20
    regulatory interactions
      complexity of control, 27:15–27:17
      methods, 27:7–27:8
      negative, 27:10
      positive three-level hierarchy,
        27:8–27:13
    promoters, 27:13–27:15, 27:16, 27:26
    timing of expression, 27:6–27:7
      DNA synthesis and, 27:17–27:18
      morphogenesis and, 27:18

Flagellar genes (continued)
  Escherichia coli
    hierarchy, 27:22–27:23
    life cycle and, 27:23
    role in flagellar assembly, 27:19–27:22
  S. typhimurium, 27:19, 27:25
Flagellins, see also Flagellar genes
  multiple location in flagellum, C. crescentus,
    27:4–27:6
  single in flagellum, E. coli, 27:19
  synthesis reduction in flagellar gene mutants,
    C. crescentus, 27:8–27:10
Flagellum
  genes required for assembly, see Flagellar genes
  structure
    B. subtilis, 27:4–27:5
    C. crescentus, 27:4–27:6, 27:18–27:19
    E. coli, 27:4–27:5, 27:19
Flavin, nitrate reductase and, 30:4, 30:6, 30:22
Flax
  genome
    intraspecific variation, 28:80–28:81
    size and structure, 28:75, 28:76
  heritable changes
    induction by nutrient regimes,
      28:83–28:86, 28:92
    nuclear DNA in genotrophs and,
      28:86–28:90
    naturally occurring variation and,
      28:89–28:90
fliG gene, oligogene bands, 39:134–135
Floor plate, dorsoventral patterning, human
  malformation genes, 38:14–15
Fluorescence
  Mu elements of Zea mays and, 30:113
  somaclonal variation and, 30:51
Fluorescent imaging, active chromosome region
  localization, DNA–RNA hybrid
  antibodies, 39:38, 39:47–52
Fluorescent in situ hybridization analysis, See
  FISH analysis
Fluorescent sequencing, use in mutation testing,
  36:36
Fluoride, heat-shock puff induction, 39:345,
  39:348
5-Fluorodeoxyuridine (FUdR), effects on
  braconid wasp females
    egg production and, 25:166
    egg size and, 25:167
    oocyte sensitivity to, 25:169

oogonium sensitivity to, 25:171
fmrl gene, mutations in, 36:99
FNR protein, nitrate reductase and, 30:3
Foldback elements, Drosophila transposable
  elements and, 29:282–29:288
Folic acid antagonists, braconid wasp egg
  production and, 25:164
Follistatin gene, Xenopus laevis, 31:41–43
Foot pad cells, polyteny occurrence, 34:37–43
Footprint, somaclonal variation and, 30:55
Formaldehyde, Adh mutant induction,
  Drosophila, 25:48
Forward mutation, Mu elements of Zea mays
  and, 30:80, 30:83–30:84, 30:87–30:88,
  30:99
Founder effect, in phenylketonuria, 32:233–241
Fractionation, somaclonal variation and, 30:57
Fragile X-syndrome, somaclonal variation and,
  30:50, 30:61–30:62
Fragmentation, infusoria chromosomes,
  34:88–96
Framework regions, evolutionary genetics of fish
  and, 29:187
Frataxin gene, see Friedreich ataxia
Freezing tolerance
  cor gene expression and, alfalfa, 28:117
  cycloheximide effect, Brassica napus, 28:100
  plasma membrane role, rye, 28:101–28:103
  woody perennials, 28:99
French bean, genes coding for seed storage
  proteins of, 22:123–22:124
French Canadians, BRCA2 gene mutations in,
  36:86
Friedreich ataxia, 38:49–60
  clinical features, 38:51–52
  disease mechanisms, 38:57–58
  frataxin gene
    GGA triplet repeat expansion, 38:55–57
    point mutations, 38:54–55
  frataxin protein, 38:53–54
  gene characteristics, 38:52–53
  pathology, 38:50–51
  phenotype–genotype correlations, 38:58–60
Fructose, puff activity effects, 39:263
fruitless (fru) mutant
  Drosophila melanogaster, 31:157–158
fs(3)02729 gene, protein synthesis theory,
  38:118–119
fs(1) genes, band organization, 39:135, 39:143
fs(1)Ya gene, 31:111–112

ftz gene
band organization, **39**:144
chromomere–gene–loop relations, **39**:157
dual element region
Drosophila melanogaster, **31**:13
puff development, **39**:315
FUdR, *see* 5-Fluorodeoxyuridine
Function
evolutionary significance, **34**:356
isolated chromosome studies, **34**:320–327
peculiarities, **34**:355–356
physiological development, **34**:356–358
Fundulus heteroclitus, evolutionary genetics of
fish and, **29**:128, **29**:146, **29**:156, **29**:174
environmental change, **29**:159–**29**:161,
29:164–**29**:165
nuclear genomic structures, **29**:139–**29**:140
Fungi, **23**:73–**23**:160, *see also* specific fungi
bacterial gene expression in, **23**:127–**23**:132
chromosome rearrangements in,
36:239–**36**:397
eukaryotic gene expression in, **23**:132–**23**:138
genes, expression in bacteria, **23**:126–**23**:127
Neurospora crassa and, **29**:2, **29**:5, **29**:27,
29:48
development, **29**:42, **29**:45
gene transfer, **29**:5, **29**:10
nitrate reductase and, **30**:2–**30**:3, **30**:11,
30:26–**30**:27, **30**:31
plant pathogen, *see also* specific fungi
avirulence genes, transformation
technology, **28**:171
elicitors from, **28**:202–**28**:204
superoxide dismutases and, **30**:252, **30**:264,
30:269, **30**:275
physiology, **30**:257, **30**:263
physiology of mutants, **30**:296–**30**:297,
30:301–**30**:302, **30**:308
telomeres and, **30**:187, **30**:200
transformation
applications, **23**:103–**23**:125
biochemistry, **23**:139–**23**:140
in different groups of, **23**:140–**23**:155
donor DNA
fate, **23**:98–**23**:101
function, **23**:101–**23**:103
genetic system, **23**:75–**23**:77
mechanism of, **23**:155–**23**:160
methodology, **23**:80–**23**:97
versatile vector for, **23**:138–**23**:139

yeast ribosomes and, **29**:101
Fur
gene, essentiality of, **36**:195–**36**:196
protein, role in bacterial iron regulation,
36:190, **36**:191–**36**:192
titration assay, use for gene identification,
36:194
Fusarium oxysporum resistance
I gene-controlled, tomato, **26**:13
MGS and, alfalfa, **26**:19
Fusarium solani
cutinase gene, cloning and characterization,
23:155
mRNA induction in pea, **28**:180–**28**:181
Fushi tarazu, pair-rule gene
Drosophila
cis-acting regulatory elements,
27:334–**27**:335
expression pattern
Dfd expression and, **27**:377–**27**:378,
27:380–**27**:383, **27**:385–**27**:386
during embryogenesis, **27**:334
gap gene expression and,
27:261–**27**:265
in *stau exu* and *vas exu* embryos, **27**:258
interaction with gap and homeotic genes,
27:267–**27**:268
mutant phenotypes, **27**:332–**27**:333
structure, position in ANT-C, **27**:334,
27:340
effects on pair-rule interactions, **31**:12–13
Fusidic acid, heat-shock puff induction, **39**:348

GADD45, p53 transactivation of, **36**:59
gag, *Drosophila* transposable elements and,
29:231–**29**:235, **29**:238
Galactose, puff activity effects, **39**:256–257,
39:263–264
β-Galactosidase
mouse, developmental control by regulatory
genes, **24**:82–**24**:83
pollen during development, *Brassica*
campestris, **26**:24
superoxide dismutases and, **30**:277, **30**:282,
30:284
yeast ribosomes and, **29**:68–**29**:69
zeste in *Drosophila melanogaster* and, **29**:315,
29:318, **29**:330

α-Galactosidase, mouse, developmental control by regulatory genes, **24**:82–**24**:83

β-Galactosidase genes, artificial bands, **39**:149

GAL, yeast ribosomes and, **29**:81

GAL1, yeast ribosomes and, **29**:74, **29**:83, **29**:89, **29**:98

Gametes, multilocus in plants, **23**:255–**23**:257

Gametic imprinting, mouse models, **35**:180–181

Gametophyte, male, *see* Pollen

Gametophytic-sporophytic genetic overlap, **26**:25–**26**:27

   Hordeum spp., **26**:22

   maize, **26**:26

   Tradescantia, **26**:26

Gamma radiation, puff activity effects, **39**:260

Gamma rays, effects on braconid wasps

   body weight genetic variability, **25**:149

   egg hatchability decline, **25**:152

   in flight simulation experiments, **25**:158–**25**:160

   during orbital flight, **25**:157–**25**:158

   infecundity, **25**:154

   sperm damage, **25**:150

   orbital flight-unaffected, **25**:151–**25**:151

Ganglion mother cell identity genes

   Drosophila melanogaster, **31**:17–20

Gap genes

   transition to pair-rule gene patterns, **31**:11–12

   zygotic, *Drosophila*

      correlation with pair-rule gene expression in maternal-effect mutations, **27**:262–**27**:265

         bcd osk embryos, **27**:264–**27**:265

         bcd osk tsl embryos, **27**:263–**27**:264

         stau exu embryos, **27**:265, **27**:267–**27**:268

         model, **27**:266

         wild type, **27**:261–**27**:262, **27**:263

      effects on homeotic gene expression, **27**:266–**27**:268

      hunchback (hb), expression pattern, **27**:243–**27**:246

         after blastoderm stage, **27**:268

         effect on *Kr* expression, **27**:257

         maternal control by *bcd*, **27**:250–**27**:251, **27**:255, **27**:321–**27**:323, **27**:375

         in mutant embryos *stau exu* and *vas exu*, role of *bcd*, **27**:257–**27**:260

         tll effect, **27**:255–**27**:256

      knirps (kin)

         effects on *Kr* expression, **27**:256–**27**:257

         in anlage of Malpighian tubules, **27**:270–**27**:271

      Krüppel, expression pattern

         in anlage of Malpighian tubules, **27**:266–**27**:272

         control by *caudal* gene, **27**:270, **27**:272

         requirement for *forkhead* and *tailless* genes, **27**:270–**27**:271

         during extended germ band stage, **27**:269–**27**:270

         during gastrulation, **27**:268–**27**:269

         maternal control, negative, **27**:251–**27**:254

         in mutant embryos *stau exu* and *vas exu*, role of *bcd*, **27**:257–**27**:260

         other gap gene effects, **27**:254–**27**:257

      mutant phenotypes, **27**:241–**27**:242

      positional function along AP axis, **27**:375, **27**:376

      as segmentation group of zygotic genes, **27**:240–**27**:241

      sequence analysis, **27**:243

      tailless (tll)

         effects on *hb* expression, **27**:255–**27**:256

         effects on *Kr* expression, **27**:256–**27**:257

         in anlage of Malpighian tubules, **27**:270–**27**:271

         mutant phenotype, **27**:242

Gap junction, connexin role in formation of, **36**:29

GAP proteins, neurofibromin homology with, **36**:80, **36**:81

Gart gene, band organization, **39**:150

Gastropoda, polytene chromosome occurrence, **34**:97–98

Gaucher disease, **32**:17–41

   biology, **32**:20–24

   complementary DNA, **32**:21

   glucocerebrosidase gene characteristics, **32**:20–21

   mutations, **32**:22–24

   pseudogene characteristics, **32**:20–21

   clinical manifestations, **32**:18–19

   controversies, **32**:39–41

   genotype variability, **32**:36–37

heterozygotes, 32:38–39
in Jewish populations, 32:19, 32:25–27
population genetics, 32:24–27
treatment, 32:27–36
dosage regulation, 32:39–41
enzyme replacement, 32:29–33
gene transfer, 32:35–36
marrow transplantation, 32:34–35
skeletal symptoms, 32:28
splenectomy, 32:28–29
symptomatic management, 32:28–29
Gaze palsy, in Gaucher disease, 32:19
GC, evolutionary genetics of fish and,
29:140–29:142
GCN4, Neurospora crassa and, 29:39–29:40,
29:49
Gcr1p, yeast ribosomes and, 29:78–29:79
GCR1, yeast ribosomes and, 29:78
G₁ cyclins, of Saccharomyces cerevisiae,
mutations affecting, 36:139
GDP, yeast ribosomes and, 29:69
Gene expression
carbonic anhydrases and, 30:325, 30:327,
30:331
inactivation
embryonic development, 37:355–357,
37:440–443
historical perspectives, 37:376–378
initiation, 37:429–433
maintenance, 37:433–434
position effect
biochemically identified loci, 37:318
chromosomal rearrangements,
37:310–311, 37:329–330
genes affected, 37:312–319
inactivation levels, 37:327–329
phenotype development control genes,
37:312–316
position effect variegation
characteristics, 37:309–312
spreading, 37:311, 37:330–334
transposon genes, 37:318–319
variegation inactivation, 37:319–327
vital genes, 37:316–318
modification conditions, 37:334–355
chemical modifiers, 37:342–345
genetic modifiers, 37:345–355
chromatin formation control, 37:351,
37:353–355
dose dependence, 37:349–350

identification, 37:346–348
molecular–genetic characteristics,
37:352–353
P-element-mediated mutagenesis,
37:346–347
heterochromatin, 37:335–341
autosomes, 37:339–341
exogenous DNA, 37:341
X chromosome, 37:339–341
Y chromosome, 37:335–339
histone genes, 37:345
parental effects, 37:339, 37:341–342
temperature, 37:325, 37:334–335,
37:342
mosquitoes and, 30:152, 30:161–30:162,
30:168–30:169
Mu elements of Zea mays and, 30:78, 30:91,
30:108–30:112
position effect, 37:306–309
quantitative and temporal regulation,
21:348–21:349
model gene-protein systems,
21:349–21:359
other systems, 21:359–21:361
somaclonal variation and, 30:56–30:57
spatial regulation
tissue specific expression of catalase genes,
21:362–21:363
tissue specificity and the R locus of maize,
21:361–21:362
superoxide dismutases and
molecular genetics, 30:275–30:287
physiology of mutants, 30:299–30:300,
30:303
telomeres and, 30:222–30:226
Gene libraries
human genes, see Human Genome Project
mouse genomics, 35:165–168
yeast artificial chromosome libraries, 35:166,
168
Gene mapping
chromosome region analysis, 39:113–115
individual band organization, 39:118–156
artificial bands, 39:148–150
37C1-2 band, 39:139–145
multiband genes, 39:153–156
oligogene bands, 39:129–139
overlapping gene bands, 39:150–153
polygene bands, 39:126–129
simple bands, 39:145–147

Gene registry
  hemophiliacs, 32:99–100
  therapy patients, 32:3, 32:8, 32:15
Genes, see also DNA; RNA, messenger; specific
  genes; Transcription
  Adh1 (alcohol dehydrogenase), plants
    alleles, expression in sporophyte and
      pollen, 26:11
    gametophytic control of expression,
      26:47
  Adh (alcohol dehydrogenase), polymorphism
    in Drosophila melanogaster, 23:238
  amplification, somaclonal variation and,
    30:60
  of bacteria, metal regulation of,
    36:187–36:238
  bacterial, expression in fungi, 23:127–23:132
  band–loop relations, 39:156–160
    Adh gene, 39:157
    14B region genes, 39:159–160
    15B region genes, 39:159–160
    87DE region genes, 39:157–158
    ftz gene, 39:157
    histone genes, 39:157
    Sgs-4 gene, 39:157
  β-globin family, human polymorphism,
    23:237, 23:239
  CAT-encoding, Drosophila, 28:55–28:56
  CAT (three unlinked loci), maize
    developmental expression, 28:15–28:16
    Cat2 regulation in scutellum,
      28:16–28:17
    localization and properties, 28:13–28:14
    DNA structure, 28:31–28:33
    photoresponses of Cat2 and Cat3,
      28:21–28:23
  cdc (cell division cycle), yeast
    isolation and function, double mutants,
      26:180–26:181
    meiosis initiation control, 26:157
    mutations, 26:163
    sequence homology with human gene,
      26:158
  chimeric, plants
    construction, 28:154–28:155
    photoregulation assay, 28:140–28:141
  chorion, insects, see Chorion, genes
  cis-acting elements, plants, 28:206–28:214
  cloning of, 36:139
  code, in mt tRNA genes, ascomycetes,
    25:211–25:212

conversion
  Neurospora crassa and, 29:4, 29:22
  conversion, telomeres and, 30:213, 30:224
  copper-zinc-containing SOD-encoding
    cloning and sequencing, Ph. leiognathi,
      S. cerevisiae, 26:79
    human, complementing SOD deficiency in
      E. coli, 26:78, 26:114
  copy number, somaclonal variation and,
    30:59–30:60
  cor (cold-regulated), expression
    abscisic acid effects, alfalfa, Arabidopsis,
      28:118–28:119
    in acclimated Arabidopsis, 28:115, 28:116
    comparison with heat-shock response,
      28:121–28:122
    freezing tolerance and, alfalfa cultivars,
      28:117
    water stress and, Arabidopsis, 28:120
  cutinase from Fusarium solani, cloning and
    characterization, 23:155
  de (defective endosperm), pollen mutants,
    maize, 26:13, 26:24, 26:26, 26:40
  defense response, see Defense response genes,
    plants
  disruption in mammals, 36:140–36:143
  distribution, 39:11–12, 39:115–118
  dosage
    applied microbiology and
      gene amplification, 20:65–20:66
      plasmids, 20:67–20:68
      transduction, 20:66–20:67
    somaclonal variation and, 30:46
  Drosophila melanogaster
    amd (α-methyldopa)
      coding for enzyme converting DOPA to
        catecholamine X, 24:169–24:170
      αMD-hypersensitive mutations,
        24:168–24:169
      nucleotide sequence, homology with
        Ddc, 24:169, 24:171
    Aph-1 (alkaline phosphatase-1), alleles,
      24:154–24:156
    autosomal, dosage compensation,
      24:388–24:389
    biogenic amine metabolism-controlling,
      24:130–24:134
    chorion-encoding, see Chorion, genes
    cis-acting regulators of compensation,
      24:405–24:418
    chromosome fragment translocation

from autosome to X chromosome,
24:407
from X chromosome to autosome,
24:406
cloned gene relocation
autosomal sequences to X
chromosome, 24:407–24:410
X chromosome sequences to autosome,
24:409, 24:411–24:413
mechanisms of action, speculations
chromatin conformation changes,
24:415–24:418
transcription enhancement, models,
24:413–24:415
controlling dosage compensation and sex
differentiation
da (daughterless)
interaction with Sxl, 24:392–24:393,
24:396
mutant allele, 24:391–24:392
Dk (Daughterkiller), mutation on
chromosome, 24:3, 24:397
fl (female lethal), mutation on
chromosome, 24:2, 24:397
her (hermaphrodite), mutation on
chromosome, 24:2, 24:397
sis-a (sisterless-a), female-specific lethal
mutation, 24:396–24:397
Sxl (Sex-lethal)
cloned, functions, 24:396
female-specific mutant, 24:392
interaction with da, 24:392–24:393,
24:396
in triploid intersexes, 24:395–24:396
X chromosome transcription and,
24:393–24:395
DAT (dopamine acetyltransferase), 24:197
Ddc cluster, 24:173–24:183
functional relatedness
catecholamine metabolism and,
24:177–24:178
cuticle properties and, 24:178–24:180
female sterility and, 24:180–24:181
melanotic pseudotumors and, 24:180
genetic and molecular organization,
24:174–24:177
malignant brain tumor in l(2)37Cf
mutations, 24:182
sequence homologies within cluster,
24:182–24:183
Ddc (DOPA decarboxylase)

coding for 5–HTDC, 24:165
location, 24:158–24:159
mutant alleles, 24:159–24:161
neurophysiological phenotypes,
24:161–24:162
nucleotide sequences, 24:162–24:163
CNS-specific regulator element, 24:164
comparison with D. virilis DNA,
24:164–24:165
developmental regulation and, 24:164
homology with amd, 24:169, 24:171
Dox-A2 and Dox-3 (diphenol oxidase),
phenol oxidase-coding,
24:187–24:189
HSC (heat-shock cognate), 24:9
melanization-controlling, 24:130–24:134
phenol oxidase-affecting
Phox (Phenol oxidase), 24:193
qs (quicksilver), 24:189–24:190
sp (speck), 24:193–24:194
tyr-1 (tyrosinase), 24:190–24:191
Punch, GTP Ch-coding, 24:137–24:138
regulatory for expression of
alcohol dehydrogenase, 24:89–24:90
aldehyde oxidase, 24:94–24:95
α-amylase, 24:90–24:92
DOPA decarboxylase, 24:99–24:100
esterase, 24:98
glycerol-3-phosphate dehydrogenase,
24:96–24:98
molybdenum hydrolases, 24:92–24:94
xanthine dehydrogenase, 24:95–24:96
ry+ (rosy), XDH-encoding, male/female
activity, 24:407–24:408
transduction to X chromosome and,
24:408–24:410
sclerotization-controlling, 24:130–24:134
TH-coding, 24:139–24:140
trans-acting regulators of compensation,
male-specific, 24:397–24:405
developmental effects, 24:398–24:399
germ-line effects, 24:399
identification by mutant alleles, 24:398
interactions with gene products of
da, 24:402–24:403
sis-a, 24:402–24:403
Sxl, 24:401–24:402
mechanism of action, 24:404–24:405
new loci, 24:403–24:404
X-chromosome activity and,
24:400–24:401

Genes (continued)
from Drosophila melanogaster, expression in
yeast, 23:136
duplication, evolutionary genetics of fish and,
29:147–29:152
lactate dehydrogenase, 29:152–29:157
protamine genes, 29:157–29:158
duplication and polyploidy in, 36:149
effects on plant mating system,
23:258–23:259
eukaryotic
expression in fungi, 23:132–23:138
flow, evolutionary genetics of fish and,
29:126, 29:164–29:165
four routes to, 36:139–36:143
frequency, evolutionary genetics of fish and,
29:164–29:165
for frost hardiness
barley, 28:107
oat, 28:106–28:107
wheat, 28:105–28:107
functions and effects of, 36:138–36:139
fungal
chromosomal location, transformation and,
23:121
expression in bacteria, 23:126–23:127
isolation by transformation,
23:103–23:104
new, discovery by transformation,
23:116–23:118
promoter, nucleotide sequence,
23:109–23:112
resident chromosomal, replacement,
23:121–23:122
unknown, function determination by
transformation, 23:116
Ga (gametophytic factors), alleles expressed
in pollen, maize, 26:13–26:14, 26:40
gal (β-galactosidase), Brassica oleracea
gametophytic control, 26:47
gametophytic-sporophytic genetic overlap,
26:26
phenotypic segregation in pollen mutants,
26:12
of Gossypium spp. mutants
Asiatic diploid, characteristics,
23:276–23:281
New World allotetraploid, characteristics,
23:282–23:289
higher eukaryotic
expression in yeast, 23:134–23:136

lack of expression in Neurospora crassa,
23:134
HSP, see HSP genes
human, expression in yeast, 23:137
immune response
Ir-1 loci of the H-2 complex,
20:323–20:330
loci not linked to H-2, 20:330–20:331
I (resistance to fusarium oxysporium),
distorted segregation, tomato, 26:13
iron-containing SOD-encoding, sodB from
E. coli, sequencing, 26:80
manganese-containing SOD-encoding
from S. cerevisiae, cloning and sequencing,
26:79–26:80
sodA, E. coli
anaerobic expression, 26:85–26:86
NUV resistance induction, 26:123
sequencing, 26:80, 26:85
mei (meiotic)
chain controlling initial steps,
26:184–26:185
consequent activation, 26:177–26:178
hierarchy, 26:181–26:183
independent action, 26:176–26:177
metallothionein-encoding, Drosophila, 28:58
mitochondrial, split organization, yeast,
24:246–24:247
multigene families, polymorphism,
23:241–23:242
in Drosophila melanogaster, 23:242
new combinations
cell fusion, 20:83
heterokaryosis, 20:84–20:85
interspecific recombination, 20:75–20:77
intraspecific recombination, 20:68–20:75
plasmids, 20:79–20:81
transduction, 20:82–20:83
transformation, 20:77–20:79
nif (nitrogen fixation) from Klebsiella
pneumoniae, expression in yeast, 23:130,
23:132
number calculation, 39:94–113
in NUV response, see also Escherichia coli,
NUV effects
katE, katF, katG (catalase), 26:103,
26:112, 26:119–26:122
oxyR (oxydative stress), 26:126–26:127,
26:131–26:132
phenotypes and map positions,
26:119–26:120

xthA (exonuclease III), 26:112, 26:118, 26:119, 26:123–26:124
organelle, transmission, 23:242–23:246
photosynthetic, *see* Photosynthetic genes
possible chance existence of, 36:145
qa (quinic acid) in *Neurospora crassa*
   discovery, 23:116–23:117
   mapping, 23:118
recA, in recombinational repair, bacteria, 24:334–24:336
regulation, chromatin structure and, 22:145–22:154
regulatory, eukaryote, *see* Regulatory genes, eukaryote
Rfe (restorer factor), gametophyte-specific, 26:27
of *Schizosaccharomyces pombe*
   cloning and transformation techniques, 23:52–23:54
   meiotic recombinations, 23:14–23:18
   conversion during, 23:15–23:17
   mutations in meiotic cycle, 23:13–23:14
   switching in homothallic strains, 23:12–23:13
SOD-encoding, *Drosophila*
   for Cu-ZnSOD, 28:53–28:54
   methods, 28:48–28:52
      autosomal screening, 28:51
      localization, 28:49–28:50
      null alleles, identification, 28:50–28:51
      transposon mutants, 28:51–28:52
   for MnSOD, 28:55
Sod (five unlinked loci), maize
   localization and properties, 28:19–28:20
   DNA structure, 28:32–28:33
split, *see* Introns
sp-1 (small pollen), pollen size gametophytic determination, maize, 26:8–26:9
5S rRNA family, variation in flax genotrophs, 28:87–28:89
S (self-incompatibility), expression in pollen and style, maize, 26:13–26:14
tassel seed, interaction with *mei* genes, 26:175–26:176, 26:182–26:183
transfer, *see also* Transformation
   into mouse, 24:285–24:316, *see also* Mouse, gene transfer
   in pollen, 26:45–26:46
tRNA
   localization by *in situ* hybridization, 21:127–21:134

number and diversity of, 21:126–21:127
structure of, 21:134–21:140
Waxy, maize
   expression in pollen and endosperm, 26:2
   gametophytic-sporophytic genetic overlap and, 26:26
   segregating phenotypes in mutants, 26:12
   weak selection role in maintenance of, 36:146–36:147
Zw (Zwischenferment), glucose-6-phosphate dehydrogenase-encoding, *Drosophila*, 28:58
Gene segregation, somaclonal variation and, 30:65
Gene therapy
   adverse experiences
      clinical identification, 32:5–8
      ongoing, 32:8–12
   benefits, 32:12–13
   Duchenne muscular dystrophy, 35:117–142
      animal models, 35:123–125
      disease characteristics, 35:117–123
         apodystrophins, 35:121
         clinical features, 35:117–118
         DMD gene, 35:118–121
         dystrophin, 35:121–123, 35:127–129
         dystrophin-associated glycoprotein complex, 35:121–123
      future research directions, 35:141–142
      gene transfer efficacy, 35:125–127
      methodology, 35:129–141
         adenoviral vectors, 35:129–134
         direct DNA injection, 35:137–139
         myoblast transplantation, 35:140–141
         retroviral vectors, 35:134–137
   Gaucher disease, 32:35–36
   informed consent, 32:9, 32:13–14
   low-density lipoprotein receptor pathway defects, 32:153–156
   ongoing
      adverse experiences, 32:8–12
      clinical benefit, 32:12–13
      patient registry, 32:3, 32:8
   phenylketonuria, 32:224, 32:244–253
      adenoviral vectors, 32:248–251
      DNA/protein complexes, 32:251–253
      retroviral vectors, 32:246–248
   primary immunodeficiency disorders, 35:87–89
   regulation, 32:1–3
   risks, 32:3–5, 32:9, 32:13–14

Genetic defects, see Abnormalities
Genetic disorders, see specific disorders
Genetic diversity, evolutionary genetics of fish
    and, 29:126, 29:164–29:165, 29:183
Genetic drift, evolutionary genetics of fish and,
    29:126, 29:165, 29:189
Genetic engineering
    for cultivated cotton improvement,
        23:352–23:354
    mtDNA and, 22:76–22:79
    nitrate reductase and, 30:28–30:29, 30:31
    of plants with Ti- and Ri-plasmids,
        22:263–22:265
    superoxide dismutases and, 30:288
Genetic hybrids, see Radiation, hybrids
Genetic mapping
    chromomere pattern analysis, 34:187–215
    band mapping
        artificial bands, 34:212–213
        band sizes, 34:207–212
        chromosome morphology relation,
            34:198–202
        cytological repeats, 34:213–215
        interbands, 34:207–213
        methods, 34:202–207
        pattern fixation, 34:190–197
        map building basis, 34:187–190
    historical perspective, 34:7, 34:10–12
    nitrate reductase and, 30:21–30:22
    Ti-plasmids
        conjugation mediated by, 22:232–22:234
        isolation of Ti-plasmid innsertion and
            deletion mutants, 22:234–22:237
        octopine and nopaline utilization,
            22:231–22:232
        physical and genetic maps,
            22:238–22:239
Genetic redundancy, 36:137–36:155
    evidence for, 36:139
    as fail-safe system, 36:151–36:152
    functional type, 36:152–36:153
    mutation effects in, 36:147–36:149
    phenotype changes in, 36:144–36:150
    source of genes in, 36:149–36:150
    true redundancy, 36:143–36:144
Genetic suppression, superoxide dismutases and,
    30:304–30:306
Genetic systems, for A. tumefaciens,
    22:225–22:226
    chromosomal linkage maps, 22:230–22:231

    introduction of plasmids from other bacterial
        species and their expression,
        22:227–22:230
    mutagenesis and isolation of mutants, 22:226
    transformation, transduction, and
        conjugation in, 22:226–22:227
Gene transfer, Neurospora crassa and,
    29:4–29:12
Genome mapping
    apolipoprotein B gene, 32:158–159
    diabetes-susceptibility gene identification,
        32:57–61
    Gaucher disease, 32:20–24
    hemophilia
        factor IX, 32:102–103
        factor VIII, 32:113–116, 32:124–126
    phenylalanine hydroxylase gene, 32:204–207
    radiation hybrids, 33:63–94
        construction methods, 33:71–77
            dosage effects, 33:75–77
            retention frequencies, 33:75–77
            species considerations, 33:75
        future directions, 33:93–94
        Goss and Harris experiments, 33:65–68
            extensions, 33:68–71
                chromosome-specific hybrid panels,
                    33:70–71
                hybrid gene enrichment, 33:69–70
                whole genome experiments, 33:68–69
        human component analysis, 33:77–82
            fluorescence in situ hybridization,
                33:79–80
            interspersed repetitive sequence-
                polymerase chain reaction,
                33:81–82
            single-copy sequence scoring, 33:77–79
        mouse genome maps, 33:92–93
        somatic cell genetics, 33:64
        statistical analysis, 33:82–94
            data collection, 33:83–84
            influential hybrids, 33:91–92
            multipoint analysis, 33:84–91
            two-point analysis, 33:84
Genomes
    characterization, mosquitoes and,
        30:137–30:147
    chloroplast, polymorphism, 23:244–23:245
    Drosophila transposable elements and
        foldback elements, 29:282, 29:285
        hobo, 29:277

mariner, 29:278, 29:280, 29:282
P elements, 29:260, 29:263, 29:267,
    29:270–29:271
retrotransposons, 29:122, 29:231, 29:235,
    29:237, 29:240
eukaryotic of fungi, 23:75–23:77
evolutionary genetics of fish and, 29:122,
    29:201
detection of variation, 29:129–29:131
development, 29:175
endocrine system, 29:195, 29:200
environmental change, 29:162
immune system, 29:186–29:187
multigene families, 29:147
nuclear genomic structures,
    29:134–29:143
of Gossypium spp.
    allotetraploid, origin, 23:327–23:331,
        23:335–23:352
    chromosome size, 23:291, 23:293
    groups of, distribution, 23:291–23:293
    intergenomic hybrids, 23:294–23:295
    phylogeny, 23:296
    stability after chromosome translocations,
        23:306–23:307
haploid, variation, plants, 28:74–28:76
environmental stress possible effects,
    28:90–28:93
nutrient regime-induced, flax,
    28:89–28:90
    comparison with naturally occurred
        variation, 28:89–28:90
    repetitive sequence families and,
        28:86–28:87
    5S rRNA gene families and,
        28:87–28:89
mapping, mosquitoes and, 30:125,
    30:144–30:147, 30:173
mitochondrial, polymorphism
    in animals, 23:243–23:244
    in plants, 23:244
Neurospora crassa and, 29:2–29:3, 29:45,
    29:47
    genetic material, 29:13–29:14, 29:17
    gene transfer, 29:5, 29:11
    mitochondria, 29:26–29:28
    responses to environmental stresses,
        eukaryotes, 28:2–28:3
segmented, of influenza virus, 20:3–20:4
structure in higher plants, 22:110–22:115

yeast ribosomes and, 29:72, 29:77, 29:79,
    29:86, 29:99
zeste in Drosophila melanogaster and, 29:302,
    29:312, 29:330, 29:341
Genomic library, fungal, construction in
    E. Coli, 23:86
Genomic resources
    human genes, see Human Genome Project
    mouse genomics, 35:165–168
    yeast artificial chromosome libraries, 35:166,
        168
Genomic stress, somaclonal variation and,
    30:52
Genotrophs, flax
    DNA, nuclear variation
        repetitive sequences and, 28:86–28:87
        5S ribosomal RNA genes and,
            28:87–28:89
    induction by nutrient regimes, 28:84–28:86
Genotype
    analysis
        for phenylketonuria, 32:225–228
    Drosophila transposable elements and, 29:262,
        29:282
    evolutionary genetics of fish and,
        29:133–29:134, 29:166
    mosquitoes and, 30:128, 30:157
    somaclonal variation and, 30:46–30:48
        genetic consequences, 30:51,
            30:54–30:55, 30:57
        unusual genetic behavior, 30:63
    superoxide dismutases and, 30:273, 30:299,
        30:303
Geranium maculatum, pollen competition,
    quantitative expression, 26:34–26:35
German persons, X-linked inheritance of CMT
    disease in, 36:7
Germ cell
    development
        gametogenesis, 20:263–20:272
        primordial determination, 20:255–20:258
        primordial development, 20:258–20:263
        interaction with somatic cell,
            20:253–20:255
Germinal reversion, Mu elements of Zea mays
    and, 30:107–30:108
Germ plasm, preservation, plant tissue culture
    and, 20:173–20:175
GGA triplet repeat expansion, Friedreich ataxia
    association, 38:55–57

γ_c-Chain gene, severe combined
  immunodeficiency cloning studies, **35:**77
giant gene, hormone function-impairing
  mutations, **31:**167,282
giant (gt) gap gene
  Drosophila melanogaster, **31:**11–12
giant nuclei (gnu) mutant
  Drosophila melanogaster, **31:**113–114
Giardia, telomeres and, **30:**230
Gibberellic acid, puff activity effects, **39:**257
Glaser's dumb-waiter, screening and, **20:**44
Glial cells, function of, **36:**22
Glial tumors, p21 abnormalities in, **36:**63
Globin
  evolutionary genetics of fish and, **29:**148,
    29:150
  genes, telomeres and, **30:**195, **30:**230
  genes encoding, **36:**139, **36:**146
β-Globin
  carbonic anhydrases and, **30:**329
  genes, carbonic anhydrases and, **30:**327
  human, murine
    expression in β-thalassemic transgenic
      mouse, **24:**313–**24:**314
γ-Globin, human fetal expression in transgenic
  mouse, **24:**299, **24:**302–**24:**303
Glucagon-like peptide-1 receptor gene, non-
  insulin-dependent diabetes mellitus gene
  candidate, **32:**81
β-1,3-Glucanase, microspore release from
  tetrads, **26:**5
Glucanase, plants
  pathogen-induced, localization, **28:**178–**28:**179
  structure, homologies, **28:**199
Glucocerebrosidase, *see* Gaucher disease
Glucokinase gene, non-insulin-dependent
  diabetes mellitus gene candidate, **32:**86–87
Glucosamine, puff activity effects, **39:**257
Glucose
  puff activity effects, **39:**263
  superoxide dismutases and
    molecular genetics, **30:**280,
      30:282–**30:**284, **30:**287
    physiology of mutants, **30:**289–**30:**291,
      30:294–**30:**295, **30:**298, **30:**300
  yeast ribosomes and, **29:**84
Glucose-6-phosphate dehydrogenase
  Drosophila, **28:**58
  X-linked
    in autosomal male-specific lethals,
      24:400

  gene for, **24:**373
  in metafemales, **24:**386
  in metamales, **24:**384–**24:**385
  mRNA coding for, **24:**380–**24:**381
  in triploid females, **24:**382
  in triploid intersexes, **24:**382–**24:**383
  X-chromosome segment addition and,
    24:386–**24:**387
  transcription dosage compensation, **39:**77,
    39:81
Glucose-6-phosphate isomerase, mouse
  developmental control by regulatory genes,
    24:88–**24:**89
Glucose transporter gene
  non-insulin-dependent diabetes mellitus gene
    candidate, **32:**76–78
Glucosidase, mosquitoes and, **30:**160, **30:**169
β-Glucuronidase
  expression in transgenic tobacco, **28:**207
  induction by *Pseudomonas syringae,* bean cells,
    28:193
  mouse, developmental control by regulatory
    genes, **24:**75, **24:**80–**24:**82
    egasyn role, **24:**80
  nitrate reductase and, **30:**12
Glutamic amino acid, puff activity effects,
  39:257
Glutamine
  nitrate reductase and, **30:**26
  repeats, *zeste* in *Drosophila melanogaster* and,
    29:336
Glutathione
  in antioxidant metabolism, *Drosophila,* **28:**57,
    28:58
  defense response gene activation in plants
    and, **28:**205, **28:**207
  dietary
    female braconid wasp radioprotection,
      25:157
  S-transferase, properties, *Drosophila,* **28:**57
Glutathione peroxidase, absence in *Drosophila,*
  28:56
Glutathione reductase, stimulation by paraquat,
  maize, **28:**24–**28:**25
Glycerol, puff activity effects, **39:**253, **39:**257
Glycerol-3-phosphate dehydrogenase,
  Drosophila
  developmental control by regulatory genes,
    24:96–**24:**98
Glycerol shock, mosquitoes and, **30:**163
Glycogen synthase gene

non-insulin-dependent diabetes mellitus gene
    candidate, 32:81–83
Glycoprotein, dipteran insect salivary glands
    physiology, 39:170–192
    regulation, 39:192–197
Glycosylation, Neurospora crassa and, 29:11,
    29:46–29:47
Glyoxylate, superoxide dismutases and, 30:296
Glyoxysomes, superoxide dismutases and,
    30:260, 30:269, 30:285, 30:296–30:297
Glyptotendipes barbipes, heterochromatin puff
    induction, 37:106
Gonadal dysgenesis, Drosophila transposable
    elements and, 29:260, 29:262
Gonadoblastoma, Wilms' tumor with, 36:69
Gonadotropin-releasing hormone
    induction in hypogonadal transgenic mouse,
    24:314
Gonads
    sex-determining genes, 33:293–300
    dosage-sensitive sex reversal, 33:299–300
    sex-reversing chromosomal deletions,
        33:300
    SOX9 gene, 33:296–297
    steroidogenic factor 1, 33:297–299
    WT1 gene, 33:294–296
    testis determining factor
    candidates, 33:281–283
    cloning, 33:283–293
    sex-determining Y gene, 33:288–293
    Y chromosome
        deletion mapping, 33:284–287
        structure, 33:283–284
        zinc finger Y gene, 33:287–288
goosecoid gene
    Xenopus laevis, 31:34, 31:36–37
Gorlin syndrome, chromosomal linkage of,
    36:95
Goss and Harris experiments
    radiation hybrid genome mapping
    extensions, 33:68–71
        chromosome-specific hybrid panels,
        33:70–71
        hybrid gene enrichment, 33:69–70
        whole genome experiments, 33:68–69
    later experiments, 33:65–66
    preliminary experiments, 33:66–68
Gossypium hirsutum
    homozygous translocation lines,
        23:300–23:301
    monosomic, 23:307–23:323

breeding behavior, 23:314–23:317
    origin and identification, 23:307–23:314
    uses of, 23:317–23:323
G6PD, see Glucose-6-phosphate
    dehydrogenase
G proteins
    CAP proteins as negative regulators of,
        36:80, 36:81–36:82
    plant transcription regulation, 27, 35:11–13
    yeast cell mating and, 27:35–27:36
G-quartet, telomeres and, 30:187, 30:199,
    30:202, 30:221
Grace medium, puff activity effects, 39:259
Gramineae, see also Maize
    cell phenotype heterogeneity, 24:433–24:434
    protoplast culture, 24:456–24:465
    genetic transformation induction, 24:459,
        24:463–24:465
    resistance to kanamycin and,
        24:464–24:465
    somatic hybridization and, 24:458,
        24:462–24:463
    systems used for production
    callus culture, 24:457, 24:460
    intact plant tissues, 24:457
    nonmorphogenic cell suspension culture,
        24:460–24:462
    regeneration in vitro
    pathways
        direct from explant, 24:435–24:436
        indirect after callus formation,
        24:435–24:444, see also Callus
    selection for somatic variation in vitro
    disease tolerance in presence of
        pathotoxins, 24:478–24:480
    mutants induced by various agents, 24:476
    protein quality improvement, 24:475,
        24:477
    salt tolerance in cell lines accumulating
        proline and glycinebetaine, 24:478
    tissue and cell responses in vitro
    developmental stage effects
        embryo, 24:445–24:447
        leaves, 24:447–24:449
    environmental influences, 24:449–24:452
        nutrients and water, 24:450
        photoperiod, 24:450–24:451
    genotypic influences, 24:453–24:455
        intra- and intervarietal differences, rice,
        24:454
        negative maternal effect, maize, 24:455

Gramineae (continued)
  regenerative competence decrease during
    subculture
    genetic changes and, 24:451
    physiological changes and,
      24:451–24:452
  variability in culture, 24:465–24:474
    genetic variation production, 24:473
    inherited variation selectively perpetuated,
      24:466–24:469, 24:470–24:471
    wide-cross hybrids, 24:469, 24:472–24:473
  in vitro plant production improvement
    perspectives, 24:480–24:482
    problems, 24:431–24:433
  in vivo propagation, 24:434
Granin domains, in BRCA1 and BRCA2
  proteins, 36:88
Granular component, yeast ribosomes and,
  29:86, 29:88
Gregarine parasites
  morphology change induction, 34:285–286
Grf1p, yeast ribosomes and, 29:77
grg gene, hormone function-impairing
  mutations, 39:168
Griseofulvin, heat-shock puff induction, 39:350
Growth-arrest-specific gene (gas-3), peripheral
  myelin protein 22 compared to, 36:28
Growth hormone
  carbonic anhydrases and, 30:331
  evolutionary genetics of fish and,
    29:190–29:196, 29:198, 29:200
  in little mouse
    induction by metallothionein-growth
      hormone construct transfer, 24:313
GTP
  drosopterin biosynthesis, 35:233–236
  yeast ribosomes and, 29:69
GTPase, yeast ribosomes and, 29:69
GTP cyclohydrolase I (GTP CH), Drosophila
  phenylalanine hydroxylase activity and,
    24:138
  Punch-coded, 24:137–24:138
Guanine, telomeres and, 30:187, 30:198,
  30:202, 30:211
GUS, see β-Glucuronidase
Guthrie test, for phenylketonuria, 32:203
Gypsy element Drosophila transposable elements
  and
    cis-acting effects of retrotransposons, 29:241,
      29:243, 29:245, 29:247

retrotransposons, 29:232, 29:234, 29:239,
  29:257, 29:260
Gyrate atrophy, gene mutation causing, 36:98

H. victoriae, tolerance, MGS role, Avena sativa,
  26:19
Habrobracon juglandis (Bracon hebetor), see
  Braconid wasps
Haemophilus ducreyi, iron-regulated gene in,
  36:191
Haemophilus influenzae Rd, molybdenum-
  regulated gene in, 36:191
hair-wing locus, Drosophila transposable elements
  and, 29:241, 29:245–29:247, 29:257,
  29:278
hairy (h) gene
  Drosophila melanogaster
    mutation effects on ftz expression, 31:12–13
    sequence identities with dpn, 31:7–8
Haldane's rule, effect of X chromosome,
  36:173–36:175
Hansteinia blepharorachis, pollen competition,
  26:33
Haploids
  mosquitoes and, 30:137, 30:151
  nitrate reductase and, 30:9, 30:13
  somaclonal variation and, 30:64
  superoxide dismutases and, 30:281
  telomeres and, 30:204
Haploid-specific genes, yeast
  expression in α and a cells, 27:38–27:40
  negative regulation by MATα1 and MATα2
    in a/α cells, 27:40–27:41, 27:51–27:53
Haploidy, evolutionary genetics of fish and,
  29:135, 29:175
Haplopappus, somaclonal variation and, 30:49
Haplotype, mosquitoes and, 30:131
Hardy-Weinberg frequencies, 36:147
Harris, see Goss and Harris experiments
haywire (hay) gene
  Drosophila melanogaster
    in DNA repair, 31:114–115
    and microtubule-associated proteins,
      31:100
HB elements, Drosophila transposable elements
  and, 29:284
Hcf106, Mu elements of Zea mays and, 30:90,
  30:93, 30:109

hcf106, Mu elements of *Zea mays* and, 30:110, 30:113
H-2 complex
Ir-1 loci of, 20:323–20:330
loci not linked to, 20:330–20:331
MHC and, 20:307–20:309
Heart, *see also* Cardiac muscle
defects
congenital, human, 28:281
ethanol-induced, human, mouse, 28:279
heat-induced, chicken embryo, 28:279
TF mRNA, rat, 25:16
Heart disease, *see* Familial cardiomyopathies
Heat, developmental defects induction
comparison between *Drosophila* and mammals, 28:276, 28:286, 28:290–28:291
Drosophila
in embryo, 28:282–28:283
history, 28:281–28:282
molecular models, 28:289–28:290
in pupae
branched hair phenocopy, 28:283
recessive mutant heterozygotes, 28:285
mammals, 28:276–28:277
neural tube and heart defects, 28:277–28:280
prevention by stepwise adaptation, 28:280
Heat shock
elements, HSP regulation
Drosophila, 28:244–28:247, 28:249–28:250
plants, 28:247–28:250
Hsp genes, *see Hsp* genes
mosquitoes and, 30:151, 30:167–30:169
puff induction, 39:336–358
telomeres and, 30:217
treatment
Drosophila
homeotic transformation induction in *hsDfd* embryos, 27:391–27:395
promoter induction near *Dfd* cDNA, ectopic expression of *Dfd* protein and, 27:389–27:393
Heat-shock cognates
developmentally regulated, 28:237
HSC70, expression and function, *Drosophila*, 28:288–28:289
HSE identification, rat, 28:247

Heat-shock elements
regulatory
discovery, 24:32–24:33
function, 24:33, 24:36
in HSP gene developmental regulation, 24:55
in HSP gene induction by heat
long-range effects
Drosophila cells, 24:43–24:44
vertebrate cells, 24:44–24:45
requirements for, 24:42–24:43
structure, 24:33–24:36
Heat-shock factor, binding to HSE
HSP70 gene activation, *Drosophila*, 28:245–28:246
phosphorylation state role, yeast, 28:245
Heat-shock proteins
characteristics, 24:1–24:3
developmental regulation
Drosophila melanogaster, 24:3–24:10
Leischmania, 24:15
rodents, 24:11–24:13
Trypanosoma brucei, 24:15
Xenopus laevis, 24:11
yeast, 24:15–24:16
dnaK, association with RNA polymerase, *E. coli*, 28:250
in *E. coli*, response to NUV and, 26:132
in *Escherichia coli*, 24:16–24:18
g-phage and, 24:17–24:18
evolutionary genetics of fish and, 29:159–29:162
function during normal development, 24:23
high-molecular-weight
groEL, *E. coli*
biochemical function, 28:261
homology to Rubisco-binding protein, 28:262
HSP70
expression early in normal development, 28:288–28:289
role in other protein transport and assembly, 28:260–28:261, 28:288
structure, 28:237–28:239
HSP90
binding to steroid hormone receptor, 28:288
structure, 28:239–28:240

Heat-shock proteins (*continued*)
HSP70
  developmental regulation, 24:9,
    24:11–24:12
  function in heat-shock response,
    24:56–24:60
  accumulation in nucleoli and, 24:58
  ATP binding and, 24:3, 24:58
  immunoglobulin assembly and, 24:59
  preference for abnormal proteins, 24:59,
    24:63
  highly conserved, 24:3, 24:31–24:32,
    24:56–24:57
HSP90, mammalian, comparison with
  Drosophila HSP83, 24:60
induction in cell culture by
  heat shock
  in differentiating teratocarcinomas,
    24:21–24:22
  in myoblasts, quail, 24:20–24:21
hemin in differentiating erythroids, 24:22
teratogenic drugs in differentiating embryo,
  Drosophila, 24:21
large, 24:2, 24:31, 24:80–24:100K
low-molecular-weight (LMW), plants
  15- to 18-kDa
  promoter elements, 28:247–28:249
  structure, 28:240–28:241
  21- to 24-kDa, structure, 28:241–28:242
  26- to 28-kDa, structure, 28:242–28:243
  subcellular localization and function,
    28:262–28:263
in pollen during development, maize, 26:25
reviews, 28:278
role in thermotolerance, *see* Thermotolerance
small, 24:2, 24:15–24:30K, 24:31, 24:60
teratogen-induced, 28:278–28:279, 28:280
thermotolerance and, 28:287–28:288
ubiquitin, 28:253, 28:254, 28:258–28:259
virus-induced in animal cells, 24:18–24:20
Heat-shock response, *see also* Heat-shock
  proteins
  in antioxidant defense, *Drosophila*, 28:62
  comparison with cold acclimation,
    28:121–28:122, 28:124
  conservation during evolution, 28:236,
    28:263–28:264, 28:287
  discovery, 28:235–28:236
  experimental design role, 28:265
  induction without heat
    by abnormal proteins, 28:253–28:254

by other stresses, 28:264
  in plants, 28:10, 28:259–28:260
  genetic transformation study, 28:249,
    28:265–28:266
  transcriptional regulation
    by HSF binding to HSE, eukaryotes,
      28:244–28:250
    by RNA polymerase sigma factor
      ($δ^{32}$), *E. coli*, 28:244, 28:245, 28:250
Heat-shock transcription factor
  activation, model of, 24:39–24:41
  binding to HSE in HSP70 promoter,
    Drosophila
  in cell extracts, 24:36–24:38
  in chromatin *in vivo*, 24:38–24:39
  mechanism of action, 24:45–24:47
  CTF and, 24:46
  in developmental regulation of
    HSP83, *Drosophila*, 24:53–24:54
    HSP70, *Xenopus* oocytes, 24:55–24:56
  stable transcription complex formation,
    24:46–24:47
  purification and characterization,
    24:41–24:42
Helianthus annus, nuclear DNA, intraspecific
  variation, 28:79
Helix-loop-helix-type transcription factors
  achaete-scute (AS-C) complex-related,
    Drosophila melanogaster, 31:5
  during neural plate induction, *Xenopus laevis*,
    31:59–65
Helminthosporium maydis
  pathotoxin, maize resistant cell line selection
    in vitro and, 24:479–24:480
  tolerance in pollen and sporophyte, maize,
    26:15
Hemagogus, mosquitoes and, 30:129
Hemangioblastomas, in von Hippel-Lindau
  disease, 36:84
Hematogenesis, carbonic anhydrases and,
  30:327, 30:329
Heme
  biosynthesis in reticulocytes, TF role, 25:22
  nitrate reductase and, 30:4–30:7,
    30:22–30:23
  superoxide dismutases and, 30:281–30:283,
    30:286
Hemocytes, mosquitoes and, 30:156, 30:158
Hemoglobin
  adult, polymorphism of, 20:366–20:368
  carbonic anhydrases and, 30:336

embryonic, 20:368–20:369
evolutionary genetics of fish and,
  29:147–29:152
Hemoglobinopathies, mutagen induced
  β-chain abnormalities in mice, 20:438
  frequency in human *vs.* mouse,
  20:436–20:438
  Jackson laboratory α-thalassemia,
  20:439–20:440
  Oak Ridge α-thalassemia, 20:438–20:439
Hemolysin, bacterial gene encoding, 36:190
Hemophilia, 32:99–131
  B mutations, 32:100, 32:104–113
    carrier tests, 32:110–113
    detection methods, 32:104–105
    genotype/phenotype correlations,
    32:108–110
    prenatal diagnosis, 32:110–113
    types, 32:105–108
  factor IX, 32:100, 32:102–104
  factor VIII, 32:100, 32:113–116
  forms, 32:99–101
  genetics, 32:101–102
  A mutations, 32:100, 32:116–130
    carrier tests, 32:129–130
    causes
      conventional, 32:118–122
      nonconventional, 32:122–126
    detection methods, 32:116–118
    genotype/phenotype correlations,
    32:126–129
    prenatal diagnosis, 32:129–130
  treatment, 32:100–101, 32:110, 32:130
Hemopoiesis
  in hematologically normal mice
    developmental changes, 20:362–20:364
    embryonic hemoglobins, 20:368–20:369
    erythroid homeostasis, 20:364–20:366
    hemopoiesis in culture, 20:376–20:378
    hemopoietic stem cells and derivatives,
    20:369–20:373
    normal erythroid differentiation,
    20:373–20:376
    normal *vs.* deficient hemopoiesis,
    20:378–20:379
    polymorphism of adult hemoglobins,
    20:366–20:368
Hepatitis B virus
  human, surface antigen expression in yeast,
  23:137–23:138
  X protein of, *See* X protein

Hepatocellar carcinoma, p53 implication in,
  36:57
Hepatogenesis, carbonic anhydrases and, 30:329
Hepatoma x fibroblast, rodents
  gene expression extinction
    serum albumin, 25:28
    TF, 25:28–25:29
Heptochlor, effect on braconid wasp egg
  hatchability, 25:170
2-Heptyl-4-hydroxyquinoline N-oxide,
  heat-shock puff induction, 39:348
Herbicides, bleaching, photosynthetic gene
  expression and, 28:146–28:147
Hereditary ataxias
  autosomal dominant progressive ataxias,
  38:34–49
    classification, 38:35
    clones, 38:40–47
    SCA1 gene, 38:40–43
    SCA2 gene, 38:43–44
    SCA3 gene, 38:44–46
    SCA6 gene, 38:46–47
    epidemiology, 38:49
    Machado–Joseph disease, 38:44–46
    mapped genes, 38:47–49
    SCA4 gene, 38:47–48
    SCA5 gene, 38:48
    SCA7 gene, 38:48–49
    polyglutamine proteins, 38:39–40
    triplet repeat expansions, 38:35–39
  Friedreich ataxia, 38:49–60
    clinical features, 38:51–52
    disease mechanisms, 38:57–58
    frataxin gene
      GGA triplet repeat expansion,
      38:55–57
      point mutations, 38:54–55
    frataxin protein, 38:53–54
    gene characteristics, 38:52–53
    pathology, 38:50–51
    phenotype–genotype correlations,
    38:58–60
  overview, 38:31–34
Hereditary motor and sensory neuropathy, as
  synonym for CMT disease, 36:4
Hereditary neuropathy with liability to pressure
  palsies, *See* HNPP disease
Hereditary nonpolyposis colon cancer
  chromosomal linkage of, 36:95
  genes implicated in, 36:50, 36:76–36:78
  syndromes of, 36:76

Heritability, *see* Inheritance
Hermaphrodites, sex determination,
    33:311–313
Herpes simplex virus
    HSP induction in chicken embryo fibroblasts,
        24:19
HeT-A element, telomeres and
    formation, 30:229–30:231
    function, 30:214–30:217, 30:223
    structure, 30:194, 30:201
Heterochromatin
    apterygotan insect chromosomes, 34:71
    B chromosome association, 37:300–301
    centromeric heterochromatin in polytene
        chromosomes, 37:89–133
        cytogenetics, 37:124–133
        morphology, 37:89–98
        quantity variations, 37:109–124
        structural components, 37:98–109
            DNA, 37:98–105
            proteins, 37:105–106
            structural changes, 37:106–109
    characteristics, 37:434–440
    definition, 37:2, 37:5
    diptera morphology variation, polyteny
        occurrence, 34:22–23
    Drosophila transposable elements and, 29:238
    evolutionary genetics of fish and, 29:138
    gene expression modification, 37:335–341
        autosomes, 37:339–341
        exogenous DNA, 37:341
        X chromosome, 37:339–341
        Y chromosome, 37:335–339
    germline cell chromosomes, 37:304–306
    α-heterochromatin, 37:135–141
        apterygotan insects, 37:138–141
        Bilobella aurantiaca, 37:141
        centromeric heterochromatin in polytene
            chromosomes, 37:124–133
        Chironomus, 37:138
        dipteran insects, 37:135–138
        Drosophila imeretensis, 37:137–138
        infusoria, 37:141
        Neanura monticola, 37:140–141
        Phryne cincta, 37:135–137
    β-heterochromatin cytogenetics, centromeric
        heterochromatin in polytene
        chromosomes, 37:124–133
    historical perspective, 34:18–19
    inactivation

initiation, 37:429–433
intercalary heterochromatin, 37:391–394
maintenance, 37:433–434
pericentromeric heterochromatin,
    37:378–391
    heterochromatin amount effects,
        37:381–382
    inactivation strength, 37:383–385
    rearrangement breaks, 37:385–390
    revertant strain cytological analysis,
        37:379–381, 37:389–390
Prokofyeva–Belgovskaya
    heterochromatization theory,
    37:395–399
telomeric heterochromatin, 37:394–395
infusoria chromosomes, 34:81–82
intercalary heterochromatin
    differential staining identification methods,
        37:141–150
        acridine orange stain, 37:143–145
        acriflavine-nitrate, 37:146–149
        ammoniacal silver stain, 37:150
        C-staining, 37:141
        H-staining, 37:141–143
        methyl green stain, 37:146
        pyronine, 37:146
        Q-staining, 37:141–143
    α-heterochromatin, 37:135–141
        apterygotan insects, 37:138–141
        Bilobella aurantiaca, 37:141
        Chironomus, 37:138
        dipteran insects, 37:135–138
        Drosophila imeretensis, 37:137–138
        infusoria, 37:141
        Neanura monticola, 37:140–141
        Phryne cincta, 37:135–137
    morphological identification methods,
        37:150–225
        chromosomal breaks, 37:150–165
        chromosomal rearrangements,
            37:198–206
        cytological repeats, 37:225
        ectopic pairing, 37:166–193
        gene repeat sequences, 37:208–209
        late replication, 37:193–198
        minute mutations, 37:224–225
        mobile genome elements, 37:209–216
        nuclear membrane contacts, 37:224
        repetitive sequences, 37:207–224
        somatic pairing, 37:206–207

tandem repeats, 37:216–224
tRNA genes, 37:207–208
overview, 37:133–135
property manifestation correlations,
  37:225–232
quantity variations, 37:232–238
mammal tumor cells, 34:105
mitotic genetic content, 37:54–78
autosomes, 37:60–65
crossing over frequency, 37:76–77
neo-Y chromosome degeneration, 37:74–76
overview, 37:54–56
X chromosome, 37:57–60
Y chromosome, 37:65–74
  Drosophila hydei, 37:68–72
  Drosophila melanogaster, 37:65–68
  protein accumulation, 37:73–74
  in situ hybridization, 37:66–72
  Ste gene, 37:66–68
morphology, 37:5–43
chromosomal rearrangement localization,
  37:29–30
compaction degree, 37:5–14
anoxia effects, 37:13
distamycin A effects, 37:11
genetic control, 37:13
Hoechst 33258 effects, 37:9–11
mechanisms, 37:13–14
overview, 37:5–6
permanence, 37:5–6
radiation effects, 37:12–13
temperature effects, 37:11–13
developing animal heterochromatin
  formation, 37:35–43
supercompaction, 37:440–443
differential staining, 37:14–24
C-staining, 37:14–15
enzymatic chromosome digestion, 37:24
heterochromatin heterogeneity, 37:24
H-staining, 37:15–21
N-staining, 37:21–23
Q-staining, 37:15–21
late replication, 37:30–33
pairing, 37:24–28
interphase chromocenter formation,
  37:8, 37:24–25
meiosis, 37:28
mitosis, 37:26–28
quantity variation, 37:33–35
mosquitoes and, 30:126

protein structure, 34:241
research, historical perspectives, 37:2–5
sex-determining factors, 37:306
somaclonal variation and, 30:49–30:50,
  30:61
telomeres and, 30:193, 30:201,
  30:221–30:223, 30:226
telomeric heterochromatin
characteristics, 37:259–282
change manifestations, 37:281
differential staining, 37:279–280
ectopic pairing, 37:266–279
heterochromatin proteins, 37:280
overview, 37:238–248, 37:259–266
repeats, 37:248–259
trophoblast cells, 34:100–103
zeste in Drosophila melanogaster and, 29:309,
  29:317, 29:341–29:343
Heterokaryon, Neurospora crassa and, 29:5,
  29:25, 29:42–29:44, 29:47–29:48
Heterokaryosis, Neurospora crassa and, 29:6,
  29:14, 29:25
Heterologous hosts, nitrate reductase and,
  30:7–30:8
Heterologous plants, Mu elements of Zea mays
  and, 30:116
Heterozygosity
carbonic anhydrases and, 30:345
mosquitoes and, 30:172
Mu elements of Zea mays and, 30:78, 30:90,
  30:107–30:108
nitrate reductase and, 30:17, 30:23
somaclonal variation and, 30:46,
  30:63–30:64
superoxide dismutases and, 30:301
telomeres and, 30:226, 30:231
Heterozygotes
phenylketonuria selection, 32:243–244
selective advantage for Gaucher disease,
  32:38–39
het⁺ gene, Neurospora crassa and, 29:44, 29:48
HFL1, Drosophila transposable elements and,
  29:276–29:277
hfw gene
band organization, 39:142–144
hormone function-impairing mutations,
  39:169, 39:283–284
puff development, 39:241, 39:291
Hibiscus flowers, Drosophila hibisci breeding in,
  25:71–25:72

H19/Igf2 complex
as "controller," 36:102
genetic site of, 36:69, 36:95, 36:104
as possible tumor suppressor gene,
36:91–36:92
High-density lipoproteins, *see* Lipoprotein
metabolism
Higher plants
characterization of transcriptionally active
chromatin in
DNA modification, 22:190–22:192
fractionation and nuclease sensitivity of,
22:171–22:174
nonhistone chromosomal proteins,
22:186–22:190
role of histones in determining active
chromatin structure, 22:174–22:186
visualization by electron microscopy,
22:170–22:171
diversity of mtDNA in
circular molecules, 22:68–22:70
cosmid mapping in maize, 22:70–22:71
plasmidlike DNAs, 22:71–22:74
possible rearrangements in cell and tissue
culture, 22:75–22:76
variation in genome size, 22:66–22:68
variation of ribosomal gene organization,
22:75
general features of chromatin in comparison
to other eukaryotes
histones, 22:157–22:164
nonhistone chromatin proteins,
22:164–22:170
nucleosomes and higher order structure,
22:154–22:157
genes coding for
other proteins of, 22:125
actin, 22:128
lectins, 22:127
leghemoglobin, 22:126
other genes to watch, 22:128–22:129
RuBP carboxylase (small subunit),
22:126–22:127
sucrose synthase, 22:127–22:128
ribosomal RNA, 22:131–22:134
seed storage proteins of, 22:116–22:125
barley, 22:125
French bean, 22:123–22:124
maize, 22:116–22:121
pea, 22:124–22:125
soybean, 22:121–22:123

genome structure in, 22:110–22:115
unidentified genes in regulated sets,
22:129–22:131
Histidine, puff activity effects, 39:253
Histocompatibility loci, non-*H-2*,
20:292–20:296
Histones
in *Drosophila hydei* nuclei during
spermatogenesis, 23:199–23:202
genes
chromomere–gene–loop relations, 39:157
distribution estimation, 39:116
heterochromatin gene expression
modification, 37:345
intercalary heterochromatin identification,
tandem repeats, 37:219
polygene bands, 39:128–129
of higher plants, 22:157–22:164
mosquitoes and, 30:144
RNA synthesis inhibition, 39:75
role in determining active chromatin
structure, 22:174–22:186
structure, 34:225–242
Historical perspectives
Balbiani nuclei, 34:5, 34:15–16
Balbiani rings, 34:14–15
band number estimation, 34:12–14
chromatin compaction, position effect,
37:400–401
chromomere pattern, 34:13–14
chromosome size, 34:9
cloning, 34:20
genetic mapping, 34:7, 34:10–12
heterochromatin, 34:18–19
research, 37:2–5
definitions, 37:2–3
position effect, 37:4–5
inheritance theory, 34:7
isolated chromosome studies, 34:311–314
molecular biology, 34:19
polytene chromosome morphology, 34:16–17
positional gene inactivation, 37:376–378
spireme nuclei, 34:5–9
H loci, MHC, and, 20:309–20:318
Hm1, Mu elements of *Zea mays* and, 30:93
hm1, Mu elements of *Zea mays* and, 30:114
HMGR, *see* Hydroxymethylglutaryl-CoA
reductase
hmr mutation (*Drosophila*), 36:168–36:169,
36:177, 36:178, 36:179
HMR, yeast ribosomes and, 29:77

HMSNI disease, 36:4, *See also* CMT1 disease
HMSNII disease, 36:4, *See also* CMT2 disease
HMSNIII disease, 36:4, *See also* Déjerine-Sottas
 disease
HMSNIV disease, phytanic acid excess in, 36:4
HMSNV disease, spastic paraplegia in, 36:4
HMSNVIa disease (CMT1A disease), linkage
 to chromosome 17, 36:5
HMSNVIb disease (CMT1B disease), linkage to
 chromosome 1, 36:5
HMSNVI disease, optic atrophy in, 36:4
HMSNVII disease, retinitis pigmentosa in, 36:4
HNPCC gene family, 36:76–36:78
 modifier effects on, 36:104
 mutations in, 36:106
 as tumor suppressors, 36:77
HNPP disease
 clinical symptoms of, 36:13
 CMT1A disease comparison to, 36:14–36:16
 crossover region on chromosome for,
  36:14–36:19
 deletion of D17S122 locus in, 36:13–36:14
 genetic locus of, 36:21
 molecular testing for, 36:34–36:36
 underexpression of *peripheral myelin protein 22*
  gene in, 36:28, 36:29
Hobo, *Drosophila* transposable elements and,
 29:243, 29:274–29:278, 29:284, 29:286
Hoechst 33258
 differential heterochromatin staining,
  37:15–21
 heterochromatin compaction effects, 37:9–11
 intercalary heterochromatin identification,
  37:141–143
Holocytochrome, *Neurospora crassa* and, 29:35,
 29:38
Homeobox-containing genes, cell-type
 specification, C. *elegans*, 27:100–27:103,
 27:110
 in QL neuroblast cell lineage, 27:101–27:103
Homeobox genes, *see also specific types*
 human malformation
  brain patterning, rostrocaudal axis, 38:3–7
  limb patterning, 38:18–21
  ocular anlage patterning, 38:21–22
  tooth anlage patterning, 38:23
 in neoplasia
  cancer role, 33:267
  developmental processes, 33:265–266
  expression
   cancers, 33:268–269

leukemia, 33:267–268
 future research directions, 33:269–270
 overview, 33:255–256
 tumorigenesis, *in vivo* model, 33:267
Homeogenetic induction, in *Xenopus*
 neurogenesis, 31:47–48
Homeostasis, *see also* Copper homeostasis
 erythroid, 20:390–20:393
Homeotic regulatory genes, *Drosophila*,
 maintenance of *Dfd* expression pattern
 and, 27:387–27:388
Homeotic selector genes, *Drosophila*, *see also
 specific genes*
 in ANT-C, *see* Antennapedia complex
 functional domains along AP axis in embryo,
  27:372–27:374
 gap gene effects
  during development, 27:266–27:267
  in mutant embryos *stau exu* and *vas exu*,
   27:267–27:268
  in segmentation gene mutants, 27:267
  segmentation process and, 27:268
 interaction with *dsx*, sex comb formation
  and, 27:218, 27:220
 maintenance of *Dfd* expression pattern and,
  27:387
 protein products, homeodomain sequences,
  27:370, 27:371
Homologous chromosomes
 synapsis, 34:157–174
  additional chromosome material effect,
   34:163–165
  asynapsis
   causes, 34:173–174
   occurrence, 34:157–163
  disturbance-controlled tissue differences,
   34:166–169
  factors, 34:170–172
  interspecific hybrid homologs, 34:165–166
  meiotic conjugation relation, 34:172–173
Homologous recombination, DNA break repair
 mechanisms, 38:188–190, 38:203–206
Homology
 carbonic anhydrases and, 30:323, 30:325
 Drosophila transposable elements and
  foldback elements, 29:282, 29:285, 29:287
  P elements, 29:264, 29:271
  retrotransposons, 29:232, 29:234, 29:236,
   29:240, 29:244, 29:257–29:258
 evolutionary genetics of fish and, 29:123,
  29:134, 29:143, 29:179

Homology (continued)
   endocrine system, 29:192, 29:194–29:195
   environmental change, 29:162, 29:167,
      29:172
   immune system, 29:182, 29:186, 29:189
   multigene families, 29:151, 29:154,
      29:156–29:157
   mosquitoes and, 30:125
   genetic differentiation, 30:130, 30:133
   genetic transformation, 30:168–30:169,
      30:171
   genome characterization, 30:142,
      30:144–30:145
   physiology, 30:149–30:150,
      30:153–30:155
   Mu elements of Zea mays and, 30:98,
      30:107–30:108, 30:114
   assays, 30:84–30:85
   structure, 30:91–30:95
   Neurospora crassa and, 29:5, 29:13, 29:23,
      29:33, 29:39, 29:46
   nitrate reductase and, 30:7, 30:12, 30:21,
      30:28–30:29, 30:31
   somaclonal variation and, 30:54–30:57,
      30:64
   superoxide dismutases and
      molecular genetics, 30:273, 30:276,
         30:281–30:282, 30:284, 30:286
      physiology, 30:262
      structure, 30:264–30:266, 30:269–30:270
   telomeres and
      formation, 30:229
      function, 30:211, 30:213–30:216, 30:226
      structure, 30:192–30:193, 30:196
   yeast ribosomes and, 29:102–29:103
      assembly, 29:95, 29:98
      nucleolus, 29:89–29:90
      ribosomal protein genes, 29:72–29:74
      ribosomal proteins, 29:65–29:71
   zeste in Drosophila melanogaster and, 29:303,
      29:313, 29:318, 29:330, 29:340
   transvection, 29:308–29:309
Homozygosity
   carbonic anhydrases and, 30:337, 30:343
   Mu elements of Zea mays and, 30:78, 30:100,
      30:108
   nitrate reductase and, 30:13, 30:23
   somaclonal variation and, 30:58,
      30:63–30:65
   superoxide dismutases and, 30:297–30:298,
      30:307

   telomeres and, 30:230
Hook-associated proteins, in flagellum assembly,
   E. coli, 27:19–27:20
Hordeum spp., gametophytic-sporophytic genetic
   overlap, 26:22
Hordeum vulgare, nitrate reductase and, 30:18
Horizontal supranuclear gaze palsy
   in Gaucher disease, 32:19
Hormone response elements, mosquitoes and,
   30:154
Hormones
   carbonic anhydrases and, 30:325,
      30:330–30:331, 30:349
   evolutionary genetics of fish and, 29:159,
      29:176
   endocrine system, 29:190–29:196,
      29:198–29:199
   mosquitoes and, 30:153
   nitrate reductase and, 30:10
   somaclonal variation and, 30:61
Hox genes
   in anterior–posterior axis formation, Xenopus
      laevis, 31:56–57
   gene expression, 38:8–10
   gene structure, 38:8–10
   limb development, 38:18–21
   mutations, 38:10–13
   polyploidizations in, 36:149
   regulation, 38:13–14
   rhombospinal region patterning, rostrocaudal
      axis, 38:8–14
HPVE6 protein, binding of p53 by, 36:57
HRAS gene, as modifier, 36:104
HRGP, see hydroxyproline-rich glycoproteins
HSC, see Heat-shock cognates
HSE, see Heat-shock elements
α$_2$-HS-glycoprotein, human
   gene linkage to TF on chromosome, 25:3,
      25:11
HSP, see Heat-shock proteins
HSP genes
   activation by heat in eukaryotes
      HSE and, 24:32–24:36, 24:42–24:45
      HSTF and, 24:36–24:42, 24:45–24:47
      ubiquitin and, 24:62–24:63
      band–loop relations, 39:156
   in E. coli
      dnaK, coding for HSP70, 24:17–24:18
      htpR-regulated, 24:16–24:17
   ecdysterone receptors, 39:323
   heat shock puffs, 39:357–369, 39:375–376

homologous features, 39:365–368
hormone function-impairing mutations,
   39:210–211
HSP70
   developmental regulation
     Drosophila, 24:9
     mammalian, 24:11–24:12, 24:50–24:53
     Xenopus oocytes, 24:11
   induction by adenovirus, vertebrates,
     24:19, 24:51–24:52
   promoter elements, vertebrates, 24:19,
     24:54–24:56
HSP71, developmental regulation, rodents,
   24:11–24:13
normal development, 39:375–376
polypeptide-encoding genes, 39:358–369
protein synthesis regulation, 39:380
puff development, 39:299–300, 39:303,
   39:376–379
small, developmental regulation, *Drosophila*
   control elements distinct from HSE,
     24:7–24:8, 24:48–24:49
   ecdysterone and, 24:4–24:7, 24:48–24:50
transcription proteins, 39:56
hsp70, mosquitoes and, 30:167–30:170
hsp82, mosquitoes and, 30:167–30:170
HSTF, *see* Heat-shock transcription factor
H19 tumor suppressor gene, characteristics of,
   36:50, 36:69
Human cancer
   chromosome 2p13 disruptions in, 36:93
   chromosome rearrangements in, 36:241
   9p21 as common deletion region in, 36:65
   p53 disruption role in, 36:56, 36:99
   tumor suppressor gene role in, 36:45–36:136
Human Genome Project
   genomic resources, 35:165–168
   mouse comparisons, 35:155, 35:162–165
Human malformation genes
   body axes establishment, 38:3–16
   dorsoventral patterning
     floor plate role, 38:14–15
     notochord role, 38:14–15
     sonic hedgehog gene, 38:15–16
   rostrocaudal patterning, 38:3–14
     domains, 38:3
     forebrain region, 38:3–7
     Hox gene cluster, 38:8–14
     isthmic region, 38:7–8
     midbrain region, 38:3–7
     rhombospinal region, 38:8–14

limb patterning, 38:16–21
   homeobox genes, 38:18–21
   limb development, 38:16
   secreted molecules, 38:16–18
ocular anlage patterning
   eye formation, 38:21
   homeobox genes, 38:21–22
overview, 38:1–3
tooth anlage patterning
   homeobox genes, 38:23
   tooth development, 38:22–23
Human papilloma virus, E7 protein of, *See* E7
   protein
Humans
   Down's syndrome, SOD excess and, 26:114
   gene for CuZnSOD, effect on *E. coli sodA*
     sodB double mutant, 26:78, 26:114
   mei mutations, male sterility and, 26:159,
     26:163
Humoral immunity, mosquitoes and,
   30:154–30:158
hunchback (hb) gene
   Drosophila melanogaster, 31:11–12
Hutchinson–Gilford syndrome, telomere role,
   32:297–298
Hybrid dysgenesis
   Drosophila transposable elements and,
     29:236–29:237, 29:239, 29:260,
     29:269, 29:276
   mosquitoes and, 30:165, 30:167
Hybrid inviability *(Drosophila)*
   chromosomes and genes affecting,
     36:168–36:175
   gene function in, 36:178–36:179
   genetics of, 36:157–36:185
   maternal effects on, 36:167–36:168
   temperature effects on, 36:166–36:167
Hybridization, *see also in situ* hybridization
   carbonic anhydrases and, 30:348
   Drosophila transposable elements and, 29:248,
     29:271, 29:272
   evolutionary genetics of fish and, 29:147,
     29:171, 29:174, 29:187, 29:200
     detection of variation, 29:124,
      29:128–29:129
     linkage groups, 29:143–29:144
     nuclear genomic structures, 29:139, 29:141
   mosquitoes and, 30:125
     genetic differentiation, 30:133–30:134
     genetic transformation, 30:166, 30:169,
      30:171

Hybridization (continued)
  genome characterization, 30:141–30:146
  physiology, 30:148–30:154, 30:157,
    30:160–30:161
  Mu elements of Zea mays and, 30:80, 30:98,
    30:110
  applications, 30:113–30:114
  structure, 30:94–30:96
  Neurospora crassa and, 29:4, 29:19, 29:48
  genetic material, 29:13, 29:16
  gene transfer, 29:6–29:7
  nitrate reductase and, 30:17, 30:21, 30:28
  somaclonal variation and, 30:57
  somatic, protoplasts and, 20:155–20:163
  telomeres and
    formation, 30:228
    function, 30:206, 30:214–30:215, 30:225
    structure, 30:193, 30:197–30:198
  yeast ribosomes and, 29:72–29:73, 29:75
  zeste in Drosophila melanogaster and, 29:315,
    29:328–29:330
Hybrids
  Drosophila hydei x D. neohydei, Y chromosome
    during spermatogenesis, 23:204–23:205,
    23:221–23:223
  intergenomic in Gossypium spp.,
    23:294–23:295
Hydrocortisone, heat-shock puff induction,
  39:349
Hydrogen, carbonic anhydrases and, 30:321
Hydrogen peroxide
  CAT response, maize, 28:28–28:29
  heat-shock puff induction, 39:349
  induction by NUV, 26:101, 26:111
  irreversible inhibition of
    copper-zinc-containing SOD, 26:69
    iron-containing SOD, 26:72
    manganese-containing SOD unaffected by,
      26:72
  oxygen toxicity and, 26:65–26:66
  production, 28:4–28:5
  superoxide dismutases and
    molecular genetics, 30:287
    physiology, 30:253–30:254,
      30:259–30:260
    physiology of mutants, 30:289,
      30:296–30:297, 30:301–30:302,
      30:307–30:308
  toxicity, 28:5–28:7
  comparison with NUV effect

  catalase role in protection,
    26:111–26:113, 26:122
  DNA damage, 26:118–26:119
  protein synthesis, 26:113
Hydrophobicity
  evolutionary genetics of fish and,
    29:150–29:151
  zeste in Drosophila melanogaster and, 29:334,
    29:336–29:337
20-Hydroxyecdysone, mosquitoes and, 30:154
3-Hydroxykynurenine, in braconid wasp eye
    color mutants, 25:139
Hydroxyl, superoxide dismutases and, 30:253,
    30:255, 30:259–30:261, 30:263, 30:293
Hydroxylamine, heat-shock puff induction,
    39:349
Hydroxyl radical, NUV-induced, toxicity,
    26:114–26:115
Hydroxymethylglutaryl-CoA reductase, elicitor-
    induced, structure, 28:201
Hydroxyproline-rich glycoproteins
    pathogen-induced, 28:178, 28:198
    structures, 28:197–28:198
    wounding-induced, 28:198
5-Hydroxytryptophan decarboxylase, Drosophila
    brain
  Ddc-coded, 24:165
  distinction from TDC, 24:166
Hydroxyurea, puff activity effects, 39:257
hyg, mosquitoes and, 30:170
Hygromycin, mosquitoes and, 30:151–30:152,
    30:170
Hyoscyamus muticus, nitrate reductase and,
    30:13, 30:15, 30:18
Hyper-immunoglobulin M syndrome
  characteristics, 35:84–85
  cloning studies, 35:85–87
  animal studies, 35:86–87
  gene map, 35:85–86
  mutation analysis, 35:86
  future research directions, 35:89–90
  historical perspective, 35:63–65
  overview, 35:57–58
Hypermethylation
  effects on tumor suppressor genes, 36:102
  Mu elements of Zea mays and, 30:86–30:88
Hyperoxia, superoxide dismutases and, 30:283,
    30:289, 30:305
Hyperphenylalaninemia
  clinical aspects, 32:203

frequency in human populations, 32:228–229
genotype/phenotype correlations,
32:225–228
haplotype/phenotype correlations, 32:214
mutations
distribution, 32:217–220
expression analysis, 32:221–225
Hypertrophic cardiomyopathy, 35:286–305
clinical syndrome, 35:286–287
definition, 35:286–287
epidemiology, 35:288
features, 35:288–289
genetics, 35:289–290
genotype–phenotype correlation, 35:302
mutation characteristics
β-cardiac myosin, 35:290–292, 35:302
cardiac myosin-binding protein C,
35:295–296
etiology, 35:296–297
α-tropomyosin, 35:293–294, 35:302–303
troponin T, 35:294–295, 35:303–305
pathogenesis, 35:297–302
Hypomethylation
Mu elements of Zea mays and, 30:84, 30:99,
30:105
somaclonal variation and, 30:58, 30:64
Hypomyelination, in CMT4 disease, 36:6
Hypothalamus, evolutionary genetics of fish
and, 29:190–29:191, 29:196–29:200
Hypoxanthine
braconid wasp feeding
incorporation into urate cells and eggs,
25:143
nitrate reductase and, 30:19

IA1-3B gene, antisense transcripts of, 36:103
Ia loci, MHC and, 20:318–20:320
Iceland, BRCA2 gene mutations in, 36:86
Idiomorphs, Neurospora crassa and, 29:5,
29:43–29:44
Igf2 gene
defective methylation of, 36:91–36:91
genetic site of, 36:104
implication in Wilms' tumor, 36:95
IGF-R protein, repression of, 36:71
Ig-like motif, in peripheral myelin protein zero,
36:22, 36:23
IL-2 gene, as p53 target, 36:59

Immune response, genes of, 20:323–20:331
Immune system
deficiency, DNA repair mechanisms,
radiosensitivity, 38:207–208
evolutionary genetics of fish and,
29:181–29:190
mechanisms, mosquitoes and,
30:154–30:159
Immunodeficiency disorders, see X-linked
immunodeficiency disorders
Immunofluorescence, zeste in Drosophila
melanogaster and, 29:316–29:318, 29:339
Immunofluorescent imaging, active chromosome
region localization, DNA–RNA hybrid
antibodies, 39:38, 39:47–52
Immunoglobulin
carbonic anhydrases and, 30:334
evolutionary genetics of fish and,
29:185–29:188
gene superfamily, evolutionary genetics of fish
and, 29:181–29:185, 29:188
superfamily, ama protein similarity to
members of, 27:326–27:327
in transgenic mouse after introduction of
μ heavy chain gene, 24:310–24:311
heavy chain gene, 24:310
k light chain gene, 24:309–24:311
Immunoglobulin M, see Hyper-immunoglobulin
M syndrome
Immunoglobulin system, comparison with Ah
complex
clinical disease, 21:33–21:34
initaiton of programming in control animal,
21:32–21:33
overlapping specificities, 21:34–21:39
phylogenetic expression, 21:33
reciprocal relationship between P-450 and
immune system, 21:34
Immunoprecipitation zeste in Drosophila
melanogaster and, 29:318–29:319
"Imprinting centers," methylation control by,
36:102
Inactivation, see Gene expression, inactivation
Inbred strains, recombinant, 20:297
Inbreeding
mosquitoes and, 30:156
Mu elements of Zea mays and, 30:87
puff activity effects, 39:257–258
Incompatibility studies, of Agrobacterium
plasmids, 22:239–22:242

Incubation-induced change
  in vitro incubation, 34:297–299
  in vivo incubation, 34:291–297
Infection
  chromosome size variation, 34:279–280
  pathologically-induced morphology change,
    34:280–291
  gregarine parasites, 34:285–286
  microsporidia, 34:281–284
  viruses, 34:286–289
Influenza virus
  assignment of RNA segments to gene
    function, 20:12–20:13
  base sequence studies on individual RNA
    segments
    complementary RNA, 20:5–20:6
    virion RNA, 20:4–20:5
  genetic basis for antigenic variability,
    20:13–20:16
  antigenic drift, 20:18–20:21
  antigenic shift, 20:16–20:18
  model for earliest form of sex,
    24:344–24:345
  multiplicity reactivation, 24:344–24:345
  nomenclature, 20:2–20:3
  practical applications
    amantadine resistance as genetic marker,
      20:25
    host-range mutants, 20:24–20:25
    host-range recombinants, 20:23–20:24
    new pandemic strain (H1N1) from 1977,
      20:21–20:23
    possible application of recombinants and
      mutants for live vaccine production,
      20:26–20:27
  ribonucleic acid, synthesis and regulation,
    20:6–20:7
  RNA, segmented, single-stranded, 24:344
  segmented genome of, 20:3–20:4
  temperature-sensitive mutants
    defects in biological functions, 20:8–20:12
    number of recombination groups,
      20:7–20:8
  virus-specific proteins, structure and number,
    20:3
Infusoria
  chromatin diminution, 37:86–88
  ectopic pairing, polytene chromosomes,
    37:176
  intercalary α-heterochromatin, 37:141

polytene chromosome occurrence
  DNA elimination, 34:75–76, 34:90–92
  fragmentation, 34:88–96
  nuclear apparatus characterization,
    34:73–75
  polytene chromosomes, 34:76–88
  significance, 34:96–97
  vegetative macronucleus organization,
    34:88–96
In(1) genes
  puff development, 39:291–292
  X-chromosome replication, 39:433
Inheritance
  carbonic anhydrases and, 30:336, 30:349
  mosquitoes and, 30:147
  Mu elements of *Zea mays* and, 30:89, 30:99
  somaclonal variation and, 30:60, 30:65
  superoxide dismutases and, 30:301, 30:307
  theory, historical perspective, 34:7
Inhibitors
  carbonic anhydrases and, 30:343
  Drosophila transposable elements and,
    29:265–29:266
  evolutionary genetics of fish and, 29:191,
    29:198
  mosquitoes and, 30:157
  Mu elements of *Zea mays* and, 30:86
  Neurospora crassa and, 29:40–29:41, 29:49
  in situ hybridization, *Drosophila* transposable
    elements and, 29:284–29:285
  superoxide dismutases and, 30:261, 30:263,
    30:308
  telomeres and, 30:187, 30:202, 30:219
  yeast ribosomes and, 29:70, 29:82–29:83,
    29:89
  zeste in *Drosophila melanogaster* and, 29:303,
    29:337
INK4A tumor suppresor gene
  characteristics of, 36:48, 36:52, 36:64–36:68
  complex structure of, 36:67, 36:68
  hypermethylation of, 36:102
  mutations in, 36:65–36:66, 36:68
  as possible *MLM1*, 36:65
  role in cancer, 36:65, 36:95
INK4B tumor suppressor gene
  characterstics of, 36:48, 36:66, 36:68
  complex structure of, 36:67
INK4C tumor suppressor gene
  characteristics of, 36:48
  genetic site of, 36:68

INK4D tumor suppressor gene
  characteristics of, **36**:48
  genetic site of, **36**:68
In(2LR)40d locus, position effects, **37**:376
Insecticide resistance, mosquitoes and,
  30:124–**30**:125, **30**:147–**30**:152, **30**:170
Insects, *see specific order; specific types*
Ins2 gene, defective methylation of,
  36:91–**36**:92
In situ hybridization, *see also* Gene mapping
  67B heat-shock puff detection, **39**:135–136
  37C1-2 band detection, **39**:139–145
  DNA structure analysis
    centromeric heterochromatin, **37**:99–101
    repetitive sequence localization, **37**:3,
      37:51–53
    underrepresentation, **37**:417–418
  interband detection, **39**:88–90
  isolated chromosome studies, **34**:330
  mosquitoes and
    genetic transformation, **30**:166
    genome characterization, **30**:142,
      30:145–**30**:146
    physiology, **30**:149–**30**:151, **30**:153,
      30:160–**30**:161
  telomeres and, **30**:193, **30**:225
  trophoblast cells, **34**:104–105
  Y chromosome, **37**:66–72, **37**:102
Insulin
  in non-insulin-dependent diabetes mellitus
    gene, **32**:63–64
    resistance
      leprechaunism, **32**:68–69
      Rabson–Mendenhall syndrome,
        32:69–70
      type A, **32**:70–74
Insulin-like growth factor II gene, WT1 effects
  on, **36**:70
Insulin receptor gene, **32**:64–75
  function, **32**:65–68
  leprechaunism, **32**:68–69
  mutations, **32**:74–75
  Rabson–Mendenhall syndrome, **32**:69–70
  structure, **32**:65–68
  type A insulin resistance, **32**:70–74
Insulin receptor substrate-1 gene, **32**:75–76
Integradation, evolutionary genetics of fish and,
  29:164–**29**:165
Integrase, *Drosophila* transposable elements and,
  29:232–**29**:233

Interbands, *see also* Bands
  artificial band relation, **34**:212–213
  chromosome structure, **34**:215–217
  function, **39**:12–17
  genetic organization, **39**:87–94
  historical perspective, **34**:12, **34**:16
  molecular organization, **39**:87–94
  overview, **39**:84–87
  size characteristics, **34**:207–212
Intercalary heterochromatin
  differential staining identification methods,
    37:141–150
    acridine orange stain, **37**:143–145
    acriflavine-nitrate, **37**:146–149
    ammoniacal silver stain, **37**:150
    C-staining, **37**:141
    H-staining, **37**:141–143
    methyl green stain, **37**:146
    pyronine, **37**:146
    Q-staining, **37**:141–143
  α-heterochromatin, **37**:135–141
    apterygotan insects, **37**:138–141
    Bilobella aurantiaca, **37**:141
    Chironomus, **37**:138
    dipteran insects, **37**:135–138
    Drosophila imeretensis, **37**:137–138
    infusoria, **37**:141
    Neanura monticola, **37**:140–141
    Phryne cincta, **37**:135–137
  heterochromatin inactivation, **37**:391–394
  morphological identification methods,
    37:150–225
    chromosomal breaks, **37**:150–165
      constrictions, **37**:150, 158
      fissures, **37**:158–159
      frequency, **37**:161–165
      shift, **37**:159–160
    chromosomal rearrangements, **37**:198–206
    cytological repeats, **37**:225
    ectopic pairing, **37**:166–193
    gene repeat sequences, **37**:208–209
    late replication, **37**:193–198
    minute mutations, **37**:224–225
    mobile genome elements, **37**:209–216
    nuclear membrane contacts, **37**:224
    repetitive sequences, **37**:207–224
    somatic pairing, **37**:206–207
    tandem repeats, **37**:216–224
    tRNA genes, **37**:207–208
  overview, **37**:133–135

Intercalary heterochromatin (continued)
property manifestation correlations,
37:225–232
quantity variations, 37:232–238
Intercrossing, Mu elements of Zea mays and,
30:86–30:87, 30:89
Intergenic spacer, mosquitoes and,
30:127–30:129, 30:135–30:136
Interleukin 2 (IL-2), in activated T cells
aging and, 25:23
TF synthesis and, 25:20–25:21
Interleukins, genetic redundancy in,
36:142–36:143
Intermediate filaments
neural plate
Xenopus laevis, 31:67
Internal transcribed spacer, mosquitoes and,
30:128–30:129, 30:135–30:137
Internet resources, mouse genomics,
35:165–168
Interphase, chromocenter formation,
heterochromatin pairing, 37:8, 37:24–25
Interspersed repetitive sequence-polymerase
chain reaction
radiation hybrid genome mapping
human component analysis, 33:81–82
Intestine
hermaphrodite, yolk protein gene expression,
C. elegans, 27:174, 27:178–27:179
TF mRNA during development, rat,
25:16–25:18
int-2 gene
Xenopus laevis, 31:35, 31:43
Intrachromosomal transpositions, in N. crassa,
36:245, 36:246
Introns
classes of, 24:245
Drosophila transposable elements and
P elements, 29:265–29:270,
29:273–29:274
retrotransposons, 29:245, 29:247,
29:250–29:251, 29:253,
29:255–29:257
evolutionary genetics of fish and, 29:186,
29:194–29:197, 29:200
mitochondrial gene splicing, yeast,
24:246–24:247
Neurospora crassa and, 29:4, 29:43
genetic material, 29:15, 29:18
mitochondria, 29:27, 29:30–29:31, 29:35

nuclear RNA splicing, 24:250–24:253
consensus sequences, 24:251–24:252
coptosome role, 24:253
lariat formation, 24:251, 24:274
ontogeny
aging and cancer, 24:267–24:268
cell differentiation and, 24:264–24:267
egg determination and, 24:263–24:264
open reading frames (ORF)
detection, 24:246, 24:248–24:249
proteins encoded by, see Maturases
phylogeny
localization in genes and, 24:273
maturases, functions and descent,
24:270–24:273
mRNA translocation and, 24:274
origin, hypotheses, 24:269
pre-mRNA structure and, 24:275
yeast ribosomes and, 29:73, 29:82
zeste in Drosophila melanogaster and, 29:313
Invertase, superoxide dismutases and, 30:299
In vitro studies
isolated chromosomes
antibody localization, 34:329
chromosome stretching, 34:330–332
DNA polymerase activity, 34:327–328
genome function, 34:320–327
historical perspective, 34:311–314
microcloning, 34:329
restrictase effects, 34:328
RNA polymerase activity, 34:328
in situ hybridization, 34:330
solution effects
hydrogen ions, 34:318–320
tonicity, 34:314–318
terminal transferase, 34:327–328
morphology change induction, cell
incubation, 34:297–299
Iodoacetamide, heat-shock puff induction,
39:345
Iodoacetate, heat-shock puff induction, 39:349
Iris pseudacorus, SOD response to anoxia, 28:30
Iron
during aging in rat brain, TF and,
25:23–25:24
defects in utilization, 20:411–20:412
microcytic anemia, 20:420–20:424
sex-linked anemia, 20:417–20:420
transitory siderocytic anemia of flexed
mice, 20:412–20:417

deficiency, TF synthesis in rat liver and, 25:25–25:26
estrogen synergism, 25:27
evolutionary genetics of fish and, 29:148
ferrous, MnSOD biosynthesis regulation, *E. coli*, 26:83–26:85
nitrate reductase and, 30:6
photosynthetic gene expression and, 28:151–28:152
in proteins, 36:188
role in bacterial gene regulation, 36:190–36:199
-sulfur clusters, as bacterial iron sensors, 36:199
superoxide dismutases and, 30:280, 30:294
physiology, 30:254, 30:256–30:258, 30:261–30:262
structure, 30:268, 30:270–30:272
Irradiation, sublethal, effect on pollen genes in intraspecific crosses, 26:45–26:46
Islet amyloid polypeptide gene, non-insulin-dependent diabetes mellitus gene candidate, 32:80–81
Isochores, evolutionary genetics of fish and, 29:122, 29:140–29:143
Isolated chromosomes
in vitro studies
antibody localization, 34:329
chromosome stretching, 34:330–332
DNA polymerase activity, 34:327–328
genome function, 34:320–327
historical perspective, 34:311–314
microcloning, 34:329
restrictase effects, 34:328
RNA polymerase activity, 34:328
in situ hybridization, 34:330
solution effects
hydrogen ions, 34:318–320
tonicity, 34:314–318
terminal transferase, 34:327–328
Isotocin, evolutionary genetics of fish and, 29:196–29:197
Isozymes
evolutionary genetics of fish and
detection of variation, 29:123–29:128
environmental change, 29:164–29:167
multigene families, 29:152–29:157
nomenclature, 29:133
in pollen, postmeiotic gene expression, 26:20–26:22

Istanbul hypothesis
coiling patterns, 34:14
Isthmic region patterning, rostrocaudal axis, 38:7–8
ix gene, X-chromosome replication, 39:433

JC virus, human
early region, in transgenic mouse, 24:306–24:307, 24:315
in immunocompromised patients, symptoms, 24:306–24:307
Jockey, *Drosophila* transposable elements and, 29:243
Joseph–Machado disease, autosomal dominant progressive ataxia role, 38:44–46
Juglone, effects on SOD and CAT, maize, 28:24
Juvenile chronic myeloid leukemia (JCML), in neurofibromatosis type 1, 36:82
Juvenile hormone
analogs, effects on braconid wasp females
egg production and, 25:167
oocyte sensitivity to, 25:170
puff regulation, 39:287–291

Kanamycin, protoplast colony growth inhibition, Gramineae, 24:464–24:465
resistance in transformed lines to, 24:464–24:465
Karyotype
evolutionary genetics of fish and, 29:122, 29:137–29:139, 29:146–29:147
Neurospora crassa and, 29:13–29:14
Kerr, John, apoptosis concept development, 35:35–53
acceptance, 35:49–53
applications, 35:50–52
definition, 35:40–41
morphology, 35:41–46
overview, 35:35–36
shrinkage necrosis, 35:36–40
studies, 35:46–49
Kidney
cancer, tumor suppressor gene mutations in, 36:96
evolutionary genetics of fish and, 29:169, 29:190–29:191

Kidney (continued)
    telomeres and, 30:206
    TF synthesis during development, 25:16,
        25:18
    Wilms' tumor of, See Wilms' tumor
Killer of prune gene, see prune/Killer of prune
    Interaction
Kimura equation, 36:144–36:145
kinase heavy chain (khc) gene, 31:104
Kinases, role in pRb regulation, 36:55
Kinesin family motor proteins
    genes for
        Drosophila melanogaster, 31:103–106
Kinetoplast, DNA
    evolution and function of minicircles,
        22:65–22:66
    general properties, 22:56–22:58
    maxicircles, 22:62–22:65
    minicircles, 22:58–22:62
KIP1 tumor suppressor gene, See also CIP/KIP
    gene family
    characteristics of, 36:47, 36:102
    implication in Wilms' tumor, 36:95
    search for mutations on, 36:63
KIP2 tumor suppressor gene, see also CIP/KIP
    gene family
    characteristics of, 36:47, 36:64, 36:69
    genetic site of, 36:104
Klebsiella pneumoniae
    nif gene, expression in yeast, 23:130, 23:132
Kn, Mu elements of Zea mays and, 30:109,
    30:115
Kn1, Mu elements of Zea mays and, 30:93
Knockout mice
    peripheral neuropathy studies on, 36:34
    tumor suppressor gene studies on, 36:47,
        36:52, 36:57
"Knockouts," as gene-targeted disruptions,
    36:140
Knudson two-hit model, for tumorigenesis,
    36:52, 36:53, 36:54, 36:69, 36:81, 36:87
KP elements, Drosophila transposable elements
    and, 29:269
Kruppel (Kr) gap gene
    Drosophila melanogaster, 31:11–12
Ku protein, DNA break repair mechanisms,
    nonhomologous end-joining, 38:191,
    38:196–198
Kynurenine, in braconid wasp eye color
    mutants, 25:138–25:139

L71 genes, puff development, 39:309–310
L16, yeast ribosomes and, 29:68
l(1)10Ae gene, oligogene bands, 39:134–135
Labial (lab) gene, homeotic, Drosophila
    deficiency, effect on development,
        27:347–27:348
    molecular map, 27:346–27:347
    mRNA accumulation pattern, 27:347, 27:348
    protein product accumulation,
        27:347–27:349
Lactate dehydrogenase, evolutionary genetics of
    fish and, 29:125–29:157, 29:147, 29:166,
    29:174–29:175
Lactose, puff activity effects, 39:263
lacZ
    gene
        interband organization, 39:94
        puff development, 39:209, 39:211
        secretory protein expression, 39:183
    superoxide dismutases and, 30:272, 30:282
    yeast ribosomes and, 29:85
    zeste in Drosophila melanogaster and, 29:315,
        29:324
l(1)9Fe gene, oligogene bands, 39:135
l(1)HM40 gene, hormone function-impairing
    mutations, 39:168
Lamins
    nuclear envelope, genes encoding Drosophila
        melanogaster, 31:111
    telomeres and, 30:223
Lampbrush loops
    in Drosophila hydei Y chromosome during
        spermatogenesis, 23:181, 23:184,
        23:188–23:209
    functions, 23:207–23:209
    proteins, 23:199–23:204, 23:206–23:207
    ultrastructure, 23:192–23:199, 23:205
l(1)nprl gene
    DNA–RNA hybrid antibodies, 39:51–52
    puff development, 39:295–297
l(1)pplt10 gene, puff development, 39:297
La protein, yeast ribosomes and, 29:95–29:96
Larvae
    Drosophila transposable elements and, 29:241,
        29:249–29:250, 29:254
    evolutionary genetics of fish and, 29:123,
        29:127, 29:150
    zeste in Drosophila melanogaster and,
        29:315–29:316
Late replication

dividing cell heterochromatin morphology,
  37:30–33
intercalary heterochromatin identification,
  37:193–198
l(1)su(f)^{ts67g} gene
  heat-shock puffs, 39:384
  hormone function-impairing mutations,
    39:167, 39:193
  puff development, 39:308
l(2)ft gene, hormone function-impairing
  mutations, 39:168
l(2)gl gene
  hormone function-impairing mutations,
    39:167, 39:192, 39:195, 39:281, 39:284
  puff development, 39:241, 39:267, 39:308
l(3)3^{DTS} gene, hormone function-impairing
  mutations, 39:168
l(3)tl gene
  DNA–RNA hybrid antibodies, 39:52
  hormone function-impairing mutations,
    39:169, 39:281–282, 39:284
  polytene chromosome organization,
    39:35–38, 39:40
  puff development, 39:308
  X-chromosome replication, 39:436
Lead
  bacterial gene induction by, 36:221
  biological toxicity of, 36:188
Lead nitrate, puff activity effects, 39:260
Learning behavior
  Drosophila melanogaster
    dunce (dnc) mutant
      biochemical analysis, 31:149–150
      expression patterns, 31:150–151
      genetic mapping, 31:148–149
    rutabaga (rut) mutant
      biochemical analysis, 31:149–150
      expression patterns, 31:150–151
Leaves, Gramineae
  embryogenic callus production during
    development
    cell cycle stage and, 24:449
    DNA changes and, 24:448
    growth hormone levels and, 24:448–24:449
    morphogenic competence and,
      24:447–24:448
Lectins, genes coding for, 22:127
Leghemoglobin, genes coding for, 22:126
Legionella pneumophila, iron-regulated gene in,
  36:191

Leischmania, HSP during development, 24:15
Lemna gibba, photosynthetic gene expression,
  benzyladenine effect, 28:152–28:153
Lepidopteran order, polyteny occurrence,
  34:62–63
Lepomis, evolutionary genetics of fish and,
  29:127, 29:145
Leprechaunism
  insulin resistance, 32:68–69
lethal of scute (T3) gene
  Drosophila melanogaster
    role in neurogenesis, 31:16
    role in sex determination, 31:8
Leucaena leucocephala, pollen, competition-
  intensifying mechanisms, 26:42, 26:48
Leukemias, see also Acute myeloid leukemia
  DCC gene implication in, 36:78
  homeobox gene expression, 33:267–268
  pRb aberrations in, 36:54
  search for chromosome 12p13 mutations in,
    36:63
  tumor suppressor gene mutations in, 36:96
Lgp genes, puff development, 39:306, 39:317
L2/HNK-1 epitope
  implication in adhesion, 36:23, 36:27
  in peripheral myelin protein, 36:22, 36:27
  in peripheral myelin protein zero, 36:23
Lhr mutation (Drosophila), 36:168–36:169,
  36:177
  genetic models of, 36:175–36:177
Libraries
  human genes, see Human Genome Project
  mouse genomics, 35:165–168
  yeast artificial chromosome libraries, 35:166,
    168
Li-Fraumeni syndrome
  chromosomal linkage of, 36:95
  TP53 gene mutation in, 36:47, 36:57,
    36:95
Ligands, superoxide dismutases and, 30:264,
  30:267–30:268
Light
  effects on Cat2 and Cat3 genes, maize,
    28:21–28:23
  nitrate reductase and, 30:10–30:11, 30:26,
    30:28
  photosynthetic gene regulation, 28:12,
    28:134–28:146
    in nucleus, 28:11, 28:138–28:146
    in plastids, 28:135–28:138

light locus, position effect, 37:362–365
Lignification, pathogen-induced, in plants,
    28:177–28:178
Lilium henryi, pollen ontogeny, 26:4–26:5
Limb patterning, human malformation genes,
    38:16–21
  homeobox genes, 38:18–21
  limb development, 38:16
  secreted molecules, 38:16–18
LINES (Long-interspersed elements), telomeres
    and, 30:194, 30:216
Linkage
  evolutionary genetics of fish and, 29:122,
    29:143–29:147
  mosquitoes and, 30:144–30:145, 30:147
  Mu elements of Zea mays and, 30:105
  telomeres and, 30:195, 30:197
Linkage analysis
  chromosome proterminal regions,
    32:275–276
  diabetes-susceptibility gene identification,
    32:59–61
Lipids
  during plant cold hardening, 28:99–28:100
  in plasma membranes, 28:103–28:104
  superoxide dismutases and, 30:260, 30:263,
    30:288, 30:300, 30:307
Lipoprotein metabolism, 32:141–191
  apolipoprotein B, 32:156–164
  apolipoprotein E, 32:164–175
  atherogenesis, 32:185–186
  high-density lipoprotein metabolism,
    32:175–183
    cholesterol ester transfer protein,
      32:180–183
    transgenic mouse genetics, 32:178–180
  historical perspective, 32:142–147
  lipoprotein (a) metabolism, 32:183–185
  low-density lipoprotein receptor pathway,
    32:147–164
    apolipoprotein B, 32:156–164
    defect therapy, 32:153–156
    transgenic mouse genetics, 32:152–153,
      32:185
  macrophage scavenger receptors, 32:186–190
  remnant metabolism, 32:164–175
Listeria monocytogenes, CadC protein from,
    36:220, 36:221, 36:222–36:223
Liver
  antigens of, 20:305–20:306

cancer, tumor suppressor gene mutations in,
    36:96
  carbonic anhydrases and, 30:331
  cells, shrinkage necrosis, 35:37–38
  evolutionary genetics of fish and,
    29:167–29:170, 29:172–29:174
  TF mRNA, rodents
    during aging, 25:23, 25:24
    cAMP and, 25:27
    estrogen administration and, 25:27
    iron deficiency and, 25:25
  TF synthesis
    human, 25:13–25:14
    mouse, during aging, 25:23–25:24
    rat, 25:16
LOH, regions involved in human cancers,
    36:78, 36:83, 36:84, 36:94
Long–Evans Cinnamin rat
  Wilson disease model, 33:246–247
Long QT syndrome, 35:313–312
Long-term clinical care, 32:1–15
  adverse experiences
    clinical identification, 32:5–8
    ongoing, 32:8–12
  benefit, 32:12–13
  gene therapy risks, 32:3–5, 32:9, 32:13–14
  informed consent, 32:9, 32:13–14
Long terminal repeats
  Drosophila transposable elements and
    cis-acting effects, 29:244, 29:246–29:247,
      29:253–29:257
    retrotransposons, 29:231–29:234,
      29:238–29:240
  mosquitoes and, 30:166
  telomeres and, 30:192
Looping model, zeste in Drosophila melanogaster
    and, 29:322–29:323
Loops, band–gene relations, 39:156–160
  Adh gene, 39:157
  14B region genes, 39:159–160
  15B region genes, 39:159–160
  87DE region genes, 39:157–158
  ftz gene, 39:157
  histone genes, 39:157
  Sgs-4 gene, 39:157
Lotus carniculatus, MGS, excess pollination and,
    26:16
Low-density lipoproteins, see Lipoprotein
    metabolism
Low-temperature tolerance, MGS, tomato, 26:18

LTF (lactoferrin) gene, linkage with *TR* on
  chromosome 3
  human, **25:**9–**25:**10
  mouse, **25:**11
Luciferase
  bacterial gene encoding, **36:**189
  Mu elements of *Zea mays* and, **30:**112
Lung
  cancer
    p21 suppression of, **36:**62
    tumor suppressor gene mutations in, **36:**96
  TF mRNA, rat, **25:**16
Lycopersicon esculentum
  mei mutants in *pc* gene, **26:**160
  MGS, mixed pollination
    cross with *Lycopersicon hirsutum*, low-
      temperature tolerance and, **26:**18
    cross with *Solanum pennelii*, salinity
      tolerance and, **26:**19
  pollen
    competition, **26:**36
    distorted phenotype segregation in
      mutants, **26:**13
    enzyme systems, gene expression and,
      26:22
Lycospersicon esculentum, nitrate reductase and,
  30:18
Lymphocytes, miscellaneous antigens of,
  20:304–**20:**305, **20:**341–**20:**342
Lymphomas
  p53 implication in, **36:**57
  PMS2 implication in, **36:**77
  pRb aberrations in, **36:**54
Lynch syndromes, in hereditary nonpolyposis
  colon cancer, **36:**76, **36:**104
Lysine
  plus threonine, as selection agents
    high-quality protein mutant isolation from
      Gramineae cell lines, **24:**475, **24:**477
    puff activity effects, **39:**260
Lysosomes
  enzymes, salivary secretion regulation, **39:**197
  mosquitoes and, **30:**154

Machado–Joseph disease, autosomal dominant
  progressive ataxia role, **38:**44–46
Macrophage scavenger receptors
  low-density lipoprotein uptake, **32:**186–190

MAD protein
  DPC4 gene homology with, **36:**91
  as MYC regulator, **36:**93
Magnaporthe grisea, chromosome rearrangements
  in, **36:**264, **36:**281–**36:**282
Magnesium
  ions, puff activity effects, **39:**260
  role in cellular integrity, **36:**188
Magnesium chloride, heat-shock puff induction,
  39:349
Magnetic fields, puff activity effects, **39:**261
Maize
  CAT gene-enzyme system
    biochemistry, **28:**13
    developmental expression, **28:**15–**28:**17
    environmental stress effects, **28:**23–**28:**29
    genetics, **28:**13–**28:**14
    molecular biology, **28:**30–**28:**34
    photoresponse, **28:**21–**28:**23
    subcellular localization, **28:**15
  chromosome rearrangements in, **36:**242,
    36:256
  chromosomes B, recombinational repair
    enhancement, **24:**339
  embryogenic callus production *in vitro*
    negative maternal effect, **24:**455
    type I and type II, morphology,
      24:439–**24:**440
  genes coding for seed storage proteins of,
    22:116–**22:**121
  genome
    size and structure, **28:**75, **28:**76
    transposons, **28:**77
      internal effects, **28:**78
      in tissue culture, **28:**82–**28:**83, **28:**91
  meiosis
    in *mei mutants, see* Meiotic mutants, maize
    in normal plants, **26:**152, **26:**166,
      26:172–**26:**173
  mtDNA, cosmid mapping of, **22:**70–**22:**71
  Mu elements of, *see Mu* elements of *Zea mays*
  mutant cell line selection *in vitro*
    disease tolerance and, **24:**479–**24:**480
    high-quality protein and, **24:**477
    nitrate reductase and, **30:**10, **30:**12
    oxygen, intracellular in leaf tissues, **28:**9–**28:**10
  photosynthetic gene expression
    developmental regulation, **28:**153
    photoregulation, **28:**136
    phytochrome role, **28:**140

Maize (continued)
  pollen
    alcohol dehydrogenase during
      development, 26:21, 26:24–26:25
    competition, 26:36
    in mixture from tow lines, style effect,
      26:30
    de mutants, pre- and postpollination
      effects, 26:13, 26:24, 26:26, 26:40
    distorted phenotypic segregation in
      mutants, 26:12, 26:13
    enzyme systems, gene expression and,
      26:22
    gametophytic mutants, 26:12–26:14,
      26:24
    germinating in vitro, tolerance to
      pathotoxin, 26:15
    growth rate
      correlation with kernel and seedling
        weight, 26:15
      effect on sporophyte qualities, 26:3
      variability, inbreeding and, 26:14
    heat-shock protein synthesis, 26:25
    irradiation, effects on crosses between
      lines, 26:45
    MGS, experimental, 26:17
    sporophyte role, 26:39–26:40
    size control
      gametophytic, sp-1 gene study,
        26:8–26:9
      pollen tube growth and, 26:10
      sporophytic, 26:9–26:10
    threonine content, inverse correlation with
      content in styles, 26:29
    Waxy gene expression, 26:2, 26:12, 26:26
  protoplast culture, DNA delivery into,
    24:464–24:465
  regulatory genes for expression of
    alcohol dehydrogenase, 24:103–24:105
    catalase, 24:100–24:103
    esterase, 24:100
    UDPglucose : flavonol 3-O-
      glycosyltransferase, 24:105–24:108
    zein, 24:108–24:110
  R locus, tissue specificity and, 21:361–21:362
  SOD gene-enzyme system
    biochemistry, 28:17–28:18
    environmental stress effects, 28:23–28:30
    genetics, 28:19–28:20
    intracellular localization, 28:19

  molecular biology, 28:32–28:34
  somaclonal variation and
    genetic consequences, 30:50,
      30:52–30:55, 30:57–30:59, 30:61
    genotype, 30:43–30:44, 30:47
    superoxide dismutases and, 30:268, 30:306
    telomeres and, 30:229
Major histocompatibility complex
  adjacent loci and, 20:306–20:307
  H-2 complex, 20:307–20:309
  H loci, 20:309–20:319, 20:342–20:343
  Ia loci, 20:318–20:320, 20:343–20:344
  T complex, 20:320–20:322
  in cell-cell interactions, 20:334–20:341
  evolutionary genetics of fish and,
    29:188–29:189
Malaria, mosquitoes and, 30:124, 30:132,
  30:156–30:157
Malate dehydrogenase, evolutionary genetics of
  fish and, 29:132, 29:166
Malathion, mosquitoes and, 30:150
Malathion carboxylesterase, mosquitoes and,
  30:150
Male fertility factors, position effects, 37:368
Male gametophytic selection
  in breeding programs
    advantages, 26:43–26:44
    efficiency evaluation, 26:44
  evolutionary significance
    angiosperm evolutionary rise and,
      26:41–26:43
    effectiveness
      comparison with sporophytic selection,
        26:39
      models, 26:38–26:39
    genetic load and, 26:40–26:41
    gene transmission opportunity and ability,
      26:37
    haploid state and, 26:36, 26:38, 26:41
    large population size and, 26:37–26:38,
      26:41
    pollen selective values, 26:39
  experimental
    distance-relating for competing pollen,
      26:15–26:17
    excess pollination treatment, 26:15, 26:16
    mixing pollen from various sources,
      26:16–26:18
    sporophyte role, maize, 26:39–26:40
    storage effect, 26:20

tolerance to environmental stresses,
26:18–26:20
Male-specific transcripts, paragonial, control by
dsx, Drosophila, 27:223–27:224
Malformation genes, see Human malformation
genes; specific types
mal gene, Neurospora crassa and, 29:27
mall, mosquitoes and, 30:159–30:161
Malic enzyme
evolutionary genetics of fish and, 29:132
mitochondrial, mouse, developmental control
by regulatory genes, 24:87–24:88
Malonaldehyde, detoxification, Drosophila,
28:59–28:60
Malonate, heat-shock puff induction, 39:345
Malpighian tubules, Krüppel gene expression,
Drosophila
absence in Kr-deficient mutants, 27:270
control by other zygotic genes
caudal, 27:270, 27:272
forkhead and tailless, 27:270–27:271
MAL, telomeres and, 30:192, 30:224
Maltose, puff activity effects, 39:263
Mammalian cells, HSP and thermotolerance
antibody to HSP70 effect, 28:257–28:258,
28:287
Chinese hamster ovary, 28:257, 28:259
mouse mammary ts85, 28:253, 28:258
Mammals
polytene chromosome occurrence
trophoblast cells, 34:98–105
tumor cells, 34:105
sex determination in, 20:220
structural variation of mitochondrial genome,
22:15–22:24
Mammary gland, F synthesis, rodents, 25:15
Man
BK virus in immunocompromised patients,
24:307
β-globin gene family, polymorphism, 23:237,
23:239
HSP70 gene
family of, distinct regulation pattern,
24:52–24:53
inducibility
by adenovirus protein E1A,
24:51–24:52
by heat and during development,
24:50–24:53
by serum, 24:51

interferon gene, expression in yeast, 23:137
JC virus in immunocompromised patients,
24:306–24:307
viral disease, transgenic mouse as model of,
24:314–24:315
Manduca sexta, melanization, 24:145–24:147
DOPA QICF and, 24:145–24:146
Manganese
in bacterial superoxide dismutase, 36:194
competition with iron in MnSOD
biosynthesis, 26:84–26:85
superoxide dismutases and, see Superoxide
dismutases
Mannose
dependent receptors
Gaucher disease treatment, 32:30–32
puff activity effects, 39:263
MAO, see Monoaminoxidase
Mapping, see also Genetic mapping; Genome
mapping
evolutionary genetics of fish and,
29:129–29:131, 29:143–29:144,
29:146
genome, mosquitoes and, 30:124,
30:144–30:147, 30:173
superoxide dismutases and, 30:272–30:275,
30:280–30:287, 30:301
telomeres and, 30:195, 30:197–30:198
Marfan syndrome, gene mutation causing, 36:98
Mariner
Drosophila transposable elements and,
29:278–29:282
insect transposon-like element
on chromosome for CMT1A disease,
36:18
hypothesized function for, 36:18–36:19
Markers
apoptosis detection, 35:48–49
expressed sequence tags, mouse libraries,
35:166–168, 35:191–194
Maternal-effect genes, Drosophila
anterior organizers, 27:246–27:249
gap gene regulation, 27:250–27:255
in mutant embryos stau exu and vas exu,
27:257–27:260
mutant phenotypes, 27:246–27:250
posterior organizers, 27:248, 27:249
terminal organizers, 27:248
effects on Kr expression, 27:251–27:253,
27:256

Maternally inherited diabetes and deafness,
32:78–80
Mating
between α and a cells, yeast, 27:34–27:37,
27:41
systems
in plant populations, 23:255–23:259
genetic modification, 23:257–23:258
mixed model modification,
23:257–23:258
multilocus data, 23:255–23:257
pollination, 23:257–23:259
Mating-type locus, yeast, see Proteins, MATα1
and MATα2
Mating types, Neurospora crassa and,
29:42–29:44
Matrix attachment regions(MARs), zeste in
Drosophila melanogaster and, 29:338
Maturases
intron ORF-encoded, 24:249
RNA-maturase activity, 24:249–24:250
mitochondrial RNA splicing, 24:249,
24:250
S. cerevisiae
intron mutations in cob gene and,
25:220–25:222
Maturity-onset diabetes of the young, 32:83–86
MCC gene, implication in colon cancer, 36:73
αMD, see α-Methyldopa
mdm-2 gene
overexpression in human cancers, 36:57
p53 transactivation of, 36:59
mdm-2 protein, p53 interaction with, 36:102
MDR-1 gene, p53 protein mutant effects on,
36:61
MECI gene, AT protein homology with, 36:90
Medicago media, somaclonal variation and,
30:47
Medicago sativa, tolerance to Fusarium, MGS
and, 26:19
mei-41 gene, AT protein homology with, 36:90
mei gene, Neurospora crassa and, 29:45
Meiosis, see also specific phases
in apomixis, replacement by mitotic division,
24:350
in a/α cells, yeast, 27:34, 27:42
in Drosophila hydei spermatocytes,
23:210–23:211
elementary steps, control by mei genes,
26:177–26:178
in endomixis, diploid egg production, 24:350
evolutionary genetics of fish and, 29:147
genetic control pathways, 26:177–26:178,
26:183–26:185
in germ line, 24:353–24:355
DNA damage in mitotically dividing cells
and, 24:354
timing, stage of costly unrepaired DNA
damages, 24:354–24:355
heterochromatin pairing, 37:28
in mei mutants
abnormalities
cytokinesis impairments, 26:169
nonspecific multiple, 26:169–26:173
second division control, 26:168–26:169
blockage
after pachytene, 26:160–26:163
at prophase I, 26:164
first division substitution for mitosis,
26:158–26:160
initiation control
maize, 26:153, 26:156
yeast, 26:157–26:158
mosquitoes and, 30:142, 30:149, 30:172
Mu elements of Zea mays and, 30:91
mutation rate during, 21:216–21:217
Neurospora crassa and, 29:2, 29:14, 29:19,
29:48
development, 29:42–29:43, 29:45
gene transfer, 29:5–29:8
in normal plants, maize, 26:152, 26:166,
26:172–26:173
physical recombination without allelic
recombination, 24:325, 24:357–24:358
premeiotic replication, function of,
24:356–24:357
recombinational repair promotion, 24:341
somaclonal variation and, 30:49
telomeres and, 30:195–30:196, 30:202,
30:224, 30:226, 30:229
in triticales, 21:291–21:307
Meiotic mutants, maize
afd, first meiotic division substitution for
meiosis
crosses with am, 26:178–26:179
crosses with dsy, 26:179–26:180
cytology, 26:158–26:159
allelic relationships, 26:156
ameiotic (am), meiosis blockage
biochemistry, 26:156

crosses with *afd*, 26:178–26:179
cytology, 26:153
in double *mei* mutants, 26:181–26:183
asynaptic (as) crossing over increase,
  26:164–26:165
crosses with *ms43*, 26:176–26:177
characteristics, 26:154–26:155
desynaptic (dsy), abnormal chromosomal
  disjunction and segregation, 26:160,
  26:165–26:167
cross with *afd*, 26:179–26:180
divergent (dv), spindle shape and function
  defect, 26:166, 26:167
double
  am gene epistasis over ms43, 26:181–26:183
  segregation ratio, 26:174–26:175
  with *tassel seed* mutants, 26:175–26:176,
    26:182–26:183
elongate (el), second division control,
  26:168–26:169
tetraploid mutant production, 26:185
inheritance, 26:155
male sterility and, 26:174
Mei025, meiosis blockage after pachytene
  crosses with inbred W64A line,
    26:160–26:161
cytological analysis, 26:161–26:163
sticky mutations and, 26:164
ms43, disturbance in two spindle orientation,
  26:167–26:168
crosses with *as*, 26:176–26:177
in double *mei* mutants, 26:181–26:183
ms28, spindle fibril depolymerization delay,
  26:166, 26:167–26:168
pam1, *pam2*, multiple abnormalities, 26:169,
  26:171, 26:173
polymitotic (po), precocious postmeiotic
  mitosis, 26:172–26:173
variable (va) cytokinesis impairment, 26:169
Meiotic prophase I, telomere function,
  32:276–278
Meiotic reciprocal recombination, chromosome
  segregation fidelity, 35:253–278
chiasma formation, 35:273–276
chromosome segregation studies, 35:276–277
disjunction enhancement, 35:265–271
  bivalents, 35:268–269
  chiasma binder, 35:271–273
  pairing, 35:265–268
  partner recognition, 35:265–268

spindle attachment, 35:269–271
exchange contributions, 35:255–265
  crossover cytology, 35:259–261
  recombination mutant use, 35:256–257
  spontaneous nondisjunctions, 35:257–259
  yeast chromosome model, 35:261–265
  overview, 35:253–255
recombination intermediates, 35:273–276
Meiotic recombination
in *Schizosaccharomyces pombe*, 23:14–23:18
  gene conversion, 23:15–23:17
  induced, 23:15
  mitotic recombination and, 23:18
  reciprocal, 23:17–23:18
  spontaneous, 23:14
sister chromatids, 33:41–59
  cytological analysis, 33:52–55
  genetic analysis, 33:43–50
    chromosome repeats, 33:50
    circular chromosomes, 33:48
    duplicated gene exchange, 33:44–47
    nonsister chromatid competition, 33:49
    ribosomal DNA crossovers, 33:43–44
  genetic control, 33:50–52
  nonsister chromatid comparison, 33:55–59
  recombination intermediates, 33:48–49
mei-S332 mutant
Drosophila melanogaster, 31:120
Melanin-concentrating hormone, evolutionary
  genetics of fish and, 29:200
Melanization, insects
Drosophila melanogaster
  Ddc gene cluster role, 24:178–24:180
  genes coding for, 24:130–24:134
Manduca sexta, pathway
  catecholamine oxidation, 24:145–24:147
  DOPA QICF and, 24:145–24:146
  tyrosine oxidation, 24:147
Melanocyte-stimulating hormones, evolutionary
  genetics of fish and, 29:200
Melanoma
  chromosomal linkage of, 36:95
  NF1 implication in, 36:80, 36:81
  9p21 as linkage in, 36:65
  stimulating hormones, evolutionary genetics
    of fish and, 29:144, 29:171, 29:173
  susceptibility gene (*MLM1*), 9p21 as possible
    locus for, 36:65
  tumor suppressor gene role in, 36:47, 36:48,
    36:95

Melanoplus diferentialis, late replication study, 37:30
Melanotic capsules, mosquitoes and, 30:156–30:159
Melanotic pseudotumors, morphology change induction, 34:306–307, 34:311
Menadione, heat-shock puff induction, 39:349
Menkes disease, 33:233–248
  clinical findings, 33:235–237
  copper homeostasis, 33:233–235
  future research directions, 33:247–248
  molecular genetics, 33:238–242
  mottled mouse model, 33:245–246
Mental retardation
  with CMT1 disease, 36:8
  muscular dystrophy, 33:180–181
Menthol, puff activity effects, 39:261
Mentor pollen
  incompatibility overcoming technique, 26:46
  style indirect effect, 26:30–26:31
Mercury
  bacterial detoxification of, 36:205–36:216
  bacterial gene induction by, 36:221
  biological toxicity of, 36:188
  mer gene, role in bacterial mercury resistance, 36:205–36:206
Meristem, somaclonal variation and, 30:43
Merlin, *NF2* gene encoding of, 36:83
MeR protein
  role in bacterial mercury resistance, 36:206–36:207
  structure of, 36:209–36:212
merry-go-round mutant, 31:102–103
Messenger RNA, *see* RNA, messenger
Metabolic pathways, parallel, genetics of, 36:152–36:153
Metabolism
  Neurospora crassa and, 29:38–29:42
  nitrate reductase and, 30:3
Metallothionein
  Drosophila, 28:58
  genes
    evolutionary genetics of fish and, 29:169–29:170
    mouse
      transcription, regulation by Cd and Zn, 25:25, 25:26
Metals, role in bacterial gene expression, 36:187–36:238
Methionine, puff activity effects, 39:253

Methotrexate
  mosquitoes and, 30:151
  tolerance, somaclonal variation and, 30:60
Methoxyethyl mercuric acetate, puff activity effects, 39:261
Methylated chemotaxis proteins (MC), flagellar genes and, *Caulobacter*, 27:12
Methylation
  Mu elements of *Zea mays* and, 30:78, 30:100, 30:115
  assays for monitoring, 30:85–30:86
  characteristics, 30:87, 30:89
  regulation, 30:99–30:100
  somaclonal variation and, 30:54–30:59, 30:62, 30:64–30:66
  superoxide dismutases and, 30:282
  telomeres and, 30:187
  yeast ribosomes and, 29:71, 29:87
5-Methylcytosine, somaclonal variation and, 30:62
α-Methyldopa (αMD)
  dietary, *Drosophila*
    abnormal cuticle induction, 24:167–24:168
    DDC activity and, 24:168
    hypersensitivity to, 24:168–24:171
    resistance to, 24:171–24:173
    in vitro interaction with DDC, 24:166–24:167
Methylene blue, heat-shock puff induction, 39:349
Methyl green stain
  intercalary heterochromatin identification, 37:146
  RNA staining, 39:41
Methyl methanesulfonate, effect on braconid wasp egg hatchability, 25:169
Methyl methane sulfonate (MMS), *Neurospora crassa* and, 29:21–29:22
5-Methyltryptophan, as selection agent
  high-quality protein mutant isolation from Gramineae cell lines, 24:477
M(1) genes, protein synthesis theory
  M(1)1B gene, 38:91
  M(1)7C gene, 38:102–106, 38:120–121
  M(1)15D gene, 38:101–102
M(2) genes, protein synthesis theory
  M(2)23B gene, 38:108–109
  M(2)30D/E gene, 38:93–95
  M(2)32A gene, 38:106–108

M(2)32D gene, 38:109–110

M(2)60E gene, 38:114–115

M(3) genes, protein synthesis theory

M(3)95A gene, 38:95–97

M(3)95A^{prvll} gene, 38:97–101

M(3)66D gene, 38:110–114

M(3)99D gene, 38:90

M(3)80 gene, 38:117–118

M(3)Q-III gene, 38:117–118

mhr mutation (Drosophila), chromosome linkage of, 36:170

Mice, use in CMT1 disease studies, 36:9–36:10

Microbodies, superoxide dismutases and, 30:296–30:297

Microfilariae, mosquitoes and, 30:158–30:159

Microorganisms

    screening methods

        agar plate method, 20:40–20:41

        chemostat, 20:43

        colony morphology, 20:41–20:42

        glaser's dumb-waiter, 20:44

        pigment changes and colony color, 20:42–20:43

    transfer, protoplasts and, 20:163–20:166

Micropterus salmoides, evolutionary genetics of fish and, 29:129

Microseris douglasii, DNA, nuclear content changes, 28:80

Microsomes, evolutionary genetics of fish and, 29:167–29:169

Microsporidia, morphology change induction, 34:281–284

Microsporidian infection, puff activity effects, 39:261

Microtubule-associated proteins

    genes for Drosophila melanogaster, 31:99–101

    microtubule interacting protein A (mipA) gene, 31:101–102

Microtubule organizing centers

    genes for Drosophila melanogaster, 31:101–103

Midgut, postembryonal development, braconid wasps, 25:122, 25:123

Mimulus guttatus, copper tolerance

    in germinating in vitro pollen and growing roots, 26:15

    MGS and, 26:19–26:20

Minichromosomes

    fungal, during transformation, 23:101–23:102, 23:113–23:114

    Neurospora crassa and, 29:13–29:14

Mini gene, rDNA gene mutations, 38:83

Minirepeat polymorphisms

    diabetes-susceptibility gene identification, 32:58

Minisatellite repeat sequences, 32:282–283

Minisatellites

    evolutionary genetics of fish and, 29:128–29:129

    telomeres and, 30:197–30:198, 30:218, 30:223

Minute genes

    development studies, 38:84–88

    mitotic recombination

        cell competition, 38:85–86

        maternal effects, 38:86

        parameters, 38:85

        suppressor function, 38:86–88

    future research directions, 38:122–124

    historical perspectives, 38:76–84

        ecdysone hypothesis, 38:78–79

        minute phenotype, 38:76–77

        minute reaction, 38:76–78

        minute–tRNA hypothesis, 38:81–82

        oxidative phosphorylation hypothesis, 38:79–81

        rDNA gene mutations

            bobbed gene, 38:83–84

            mini gene, 38:83

    overview, 38:70–76, 38:122–124

    protein synthesis theory, 38:88–122

        molecular research, 38:89–92

        antisense mRNA, 38:91

        M(1)1B gene, 38:91

        M(3)99D gene, 38:90

        Rp49 gene, 38:89–91

        RpL32 gene, 38:90–91

        RpL36 gene, 38:91

        non-minute phenotype ribosomal protein mutations, 38:118–119

        nonribosomal protein genes, 38:121–122

        recessive minutes, 38:116–118

        M(3)80 gene, 38:117–118

        M(3)Q-III gene, 38:117–118

        short-bristle gene, 38:117

        ribosomal protein genes, 38:119–121

        transposon clone method, 38:92–116

        M(1)7C gene, 38:102–106

        M(1)15D gene, 38:101–102

        M(2)23B gene, 38:108–109

        M(2)30D/E gene, 38:93–95

Minute genes (continued)
  M(2)32A gene, 38:106–108
  M(2)32D gene, 38:109–110
  M(2)60E gene, 38:114–115
  M(3)66D gene, 38:110–114
  M(3)95A gene, 38:95–97
  M(3)95A^{prvll} gene, 38:97–101
  oho23B gene, 38:108–109
  RpL9 gene, 38:109–110
  RpL14 gene, 38:110–114
  RpL19 gene, 38:114–115
  RpS2 gene, 38:93–95
  RpS3 gene, 38:95–97
  RpS3^{prvll} gene, 38:97–98
  RpS3^{prv99} gene, 38:98–101
  RpS5gene, 38:101–102
  RpS6 gene, 38:102–106
  RpS13 gene, 38:106–108
  string of pearls gene, 38:93–95
  stubarista gene, 38:115–116
Minute mutations, see also B chromosomes
  intercalary heterochromatin identification,
    37:224–225
Mitochondria
  carbonic anhydrases and, 30:321–30:322,
    30:325
  evolutionary genetics of fish and, 29:134
  genome polymorphism
    in animals, 23:243–23:244
    in plants, 23:244
  mosquitoes and, 30:130–30:132,
    30:135–30:137, 30:144
  mutagenesis of, 21:217–21:220
  Neurospora crassa and, 29:2, 29:4–29:5,
    29:25–29:26, 29:46
    DNA transaction, 29:23–29:24
    genetic material, 29:12–29:13
    gene transfer, 29:11
    genome, 29:26–29:28
    metabolism, 29:40–29:41
    mutants, 29:30–29:33
    nuclear interactions, 29:35–29:38
    plasmids, 29:33–29:35
    transcription, 29:29–29:30
    tRNA, 29:28–29:29
  in Schizosaccharomyces pombe during growth
    cycle, 23:7–23:8
  SOD-3 localization, maize, 28:19
  somaclonal variation and, 30:42
  superoxide dismutases and
    antioxidant enzymes, 30:306–30:307

  metabolism, 30:294–30:296
  molecular genetics, 30:280–30:282,
    30:284, 30:287
  physiology, 30:252–30:257, 30:259–30:260
  structure, 30:267–30:269
  telomeres and, 30:192, 30:214
  yeast ribosomes and, 29:73, 29:77
Mitochondrial DNA
  diversity in higher plants
    circular molecules in, 22:68–22:70
    cosmid mapping in maize, 22:70–22:71
    plasmidlike DNAs, 22:71–22:74
    possible rearrangements in cell and tissue
     culture, 22:75–22:76
    variation in genome size, 22:66–22:68
    variation of ribosomal gene organization,
     22:75
  evolutionary genetics of fish and,
    29:126–29:131, 29:139–29:140, 29:165
  fungal, amplified circular molecules in
    Aspergillus and Neurospora, 22:54–22:56
  heterogeneity in senescent cultures of
    Podospora, 22:52–22:53
  petites, 22:47–22:52
  genetic engineering and, 22:76–22:79
  Neurospora crassa and, 29:11–29:13,
    29:26–29:30, 29:32–29:35, 29:46
  organization in Achlya, 22:46
  structural diversity in yeast
    Saccharomyces cerevisiae, 22:32–22:38
    Schizosaccharomyces pombe, 22:38–22:39
    variation in size and organization,
     22:29–22:32
  structural variation and organization in
    filamentous fungi, 22:39–22:46
Mitochondrial genes, ascomycetes, see also
  Saccharomyces cerevisiae
  protein-coding
    continuous
     atp6, 8, and 9 (ATPase subunits),
      25:213–25:214
     cox2 and cox3 (cytochrome c oxidase
      subunits), 25:212–25:213
    mosaic, intron locations
     atp6, Neurospora crassa, 25:216
     cob (cytochrome b), 25:218–25:223
     cox1, variability, 25:216–25:218
  ribosomal RNA
    rnl (large rRNA-coding), introns,
     25:205–25:208
    intronic orf expression, 25:207–25:208

polarity in drug-resistant mutants and,
25:206–25:207
rns (small rRNA-coding), structure,
25:208–25:209
transfer RNA (tRNA)
clustering, 25:199
genetic code, deviation from universal,
25:211–25:212
mapping and sequencing, 25:209–25:210
tsl (tRNA synthesis locus), location and
function, 25:210–25:211
vari, ribosomal protein-coding
allele genotypes, 25:215
location, 25:214–25:215
product variability, 25:214
sequencing, 25:215–25:216
Mitochondrial genome
ascomycetes, see also Saccharomyces cerevisiae
chromosomes, organization and replication,
25:227–25:228
introns
-encoded protein, function,
25:225–25:226
evolution and, 25:226–25:227
self-catalyzing splicing, 25:224–25:225
structure of group I and group II,
25:223–25:224
rearrangements
poky and related mutations, N. crassa,
25:238–25:241
rho_ petite mutation, S. cerevisiae,
25:232–25:238
during senescence
Neurospora intermedia, 25:244
Podospora anserina, 25:241–25:244
structural diversity
duplication number, 25:192–25:193
gene order, 25:199–25:200
gene presence, 25:193, 25:194–25:195
insertion/deletion, 25:193, 25:196
intergenic "spacers," 25:188–25:189
linearity and circularity, 25:188
mapping using mutants, 25:201–25:204
size, 25:190–25:191, 25:192
transcription
initiation, 25:229–25:230
processing, 25:230–25:231
RNA polymerase, DNA-dependent,
25:228–25:229
mammalian, 25:187
protozoa, 22:26–22:28

structural variation
in animals, Drosophila species,
22:24–22:26
in animals, mammals, 22:15–22:24
and functional conservation of,
22:2–22:15
Mitochondria suspension, heat-shock puff
induction, 39:351
Mitomycin C, effect on braconid wasp sperm
postembryonic lethal mutation induction,
25:173
Mitosis
mosquitoes and, 30:132, 30:142
Mu elements of Zea mays and, 30:90
Neurospora crassa and, 29:14
somaclonal variation and, 30:49, 30:58,
30:61
telomeres and, 30:193, 30:202, 30:218,
30:225–30:226
in triticales, 21:287–21:291
yeast ribosomes and, 29:88
zeste in Drosophila melanogaster and, 29:318
Mitotic heterochromatin
genetic content, 37:54–78
autosomes, 37:60–65
crossing over frequency, 37:76–77
neo-Y chromosome degeneration,
37:74–76
overview, 37:54–56
X chromosome, 37:57–60
Y chromosome, 37:65–74
heterochromatinized region properties,
37:436
pairing, 37:26–28
Mitotic recombination
minute genes
cell competition, 38:85–86
maternal effects, 38:86
parameters, 38:85
in Schizosaccharomyces pombe, meiotic
recombination and, 23:18
mle gene, dosage compensation, 39:79–80
MLH1 protein
DNA repair function of, 36:77
as tumor suppressor gene product, 36:50
MLH1 tumor suppressor gene
characteristics of, 36:50
implication in colon cancer, 36:76, 36:77,
36:95
MLM1 tumor suppressor gene, characteristics of,
36:48

MMTV, *see* Mouse mammary tumor virus
MNNG, nitrate reductase and, 30:13
Models, *see specific model*
ModE protein, as bacterial molybdate repressor,
    36:202–36:203
Moesin, merlin similarity to, 36:83
Molecular biology, historical perspective, 34:19
Molecular cloning
    for fungal transformation, 23:80–23:88
    DNA preparations, 23:85–23:86
    fungal gene expression in *E. coli*,
        23:90–23:93
    genomic library, 23:86
    vectors, 23:81–23:85, *see also* Vectors
    for *Schizosaccharomyces pombe* repair assay
        gene isolation, 23:54
    spheroplastic procedures, 23:52
    transformation systems, 23:53–23:54, *see
        also* Transformation
Molecular markers, in DNA polymorphism
    assay, 23:239–23:241
mol gene, of bacteria, 36:204
Mollusks, polytene chromosome occurrence,
    34:97–98
Molybdenoenzymes, antioxidant role,
    Drosophila, 28:59–28:60
Molybdenum
    cellular function of, 36:199–36:200
    cofactor, as bacterial corepressor, 36:203
    cofactor, nitrate reductase and
        apoenzyme mutants, 30:21–30:23
        biochemistry, 30:4–30:8
        genetics, 30:17, 30:19–30:20, 30:27
    hydrolases, *Drosophila*
        developmental control by regulatory genes,
            24:92–24:94
    nitrate reductase and, 30:6–30:7,
        30:18–30:19
    in proteins, 36:188
    role in bacterial gene regulation, 36:190,
        36:200–36:205
Molybdopterin, nitrate reductase and, 30:6,
    30:19
Mom-1 gene, isolation of, 36:75–36:76
Monoaminoxidase, *Drosophila*
    catecholamine oxidative deamination, 24:141
Monoclonal antibodies
    nitrate reductase and, 30:6, 30:20,
        30:22–30:23
    yeast ribosomes and, 29:68, 29:88

Monoisodisomes
    Gossypium spp., 23:325–23:326
Monooxygenase activity, nature of, 21:4–21:7
Monophenolamines, synthesis and metabolism,
    24:128–24:129, 24:135
Monosomes
    Gossypium hirsutum, 23:307–23:323
    breeding, 23:314–23:317
    origin and identification, 23:307–23:317
    uses for
        chromosome substitution line synthesis,
            23:322–23:323
        dominant gene identification,
            23:317–23:319
        duplicate linkage group separation,
            23:322
        recessive mutant gene identification,
            23:317–23:319
Monotelodisomes
    Gossypium spp., 23:323–23:325
Morone americana, evolutionary genetics of fish
    and, 29:123
Morone saxatilis, evolutionary genetics of fish
    and, 29:123
Morphogenesis, *Drosophila* transposable
    elements and, 29:248–29:249
Morphology
    chromatid synapsis-induced variation,
        34:125–130, 34:150–157
    chromomere pattern, mapping procedures,
        34:198–202
    diptera chromosomes, 34:22–23, 34:130–136
    evolutionary genetics of fish and, 29:144,
        29:173–29:174
    detection of variation, 29:123–29:124,
        29:128
    nuclear genomic structures,
        29:137–29:140
    historical perspective, 34:16–17
    pathologically-induced change
        ecological factor effects, 34:299–305
        infections, 34:280–291
        gregarine parasites, 34:285–286
        microsporidia, 34:281–284
        viruses, 34:286–289
    long-term cell incubation
        in vitro incubation, 34:297–299
        in vivo incubation, 34:291–297
    melanotic pseudotumors, 34:306–307,
        34:311

mutation effects, 34:305–311
polytene chromosome types, 34:127–130
polyteny, 34:125–127
pompon-like chromosomes, 34:137–150
yeast ribosomes and, 29:86, 29:91
Mortality, evolutionary genetics of fish and,
29:166
Mos1, *Drosophila* transposable elements and,
29:280–29:282
Mosaicism
clonal inactivation, 37:323–328
Drosophila transposable elements and,
29:280–29:282
hereditary change association, 37:4
specificity, 37:320–322
Mosquitoes, 30:123–30:125, 30:173–30:174
genetic differentiation
classification, 30:126–30:127
cryptic species, 30:132–30:137
patterns, 30:127–30:132
genetic transformation, 30:162–30:163
DNA delivery, 30:163–30:164
DNA integration, 30:164–30:167
promoters, 30:167–30:169
reporter genes, 30:169–30:170
target genes, 30:170–30:172
genome characterization
mapping, 30:144–30:147
organization, 30:137–30:144
physiology
immune mechanisms, 30:154–30:159
oogenesis, 30:152–30:154
resistance, 30:147–30:152
salivation, 30:159–30:162
Motor conduction velocities, in CMT4 disease,
36:6
Motor nerves, demyelination of, in CMT
disease, 36:3
Mouse, *see also* Transgenic mouse, models
gene transfer
chromosomal translocations and,
24:293–24:295
future research, 24:315–24:316
gene expression in transgenics
developmental stage-specific
αA-crystallin-CAT fusion gene,
24:303–24:304
fetal g-globin gene, human, 24:299,
24:302–24:303
α-fetoprotein gene, murine, 24:303

5′-flanking sequences and,
24:302–24:304
tissue-specific, 24:298–24:302
cis- and trans-acting factors, evolution
and, 24:299–24:300
5′-flanking sequences, 24:301–24:302
strain differences, 24:300
genetic deficiency complementation
β-globin human and murine genes in
β-thallasemia line, 24:313–24:314
GnRH gene in hypogonadal line, 24:314
metallothionein-growth hormone
construct in *little* line, 24:313
methotrexate-resistant DHFR gene,
24:314
MHC class II E_a gene in
immunodeficient line, 24:313
immunocompetence induction
Ig genes, 24:309–24:312
μ heavy chain, 24:310–24:311
heavy chain, 24:310
κ light chain, from myeloma,
24:309–24:311
MHC antigen genes
class I, 24:312–24:313
class II, 24:312
insertional mutation generation,
24:295–24:298
integration into genome
list of genes, 24:288–24:289
pattern variety, 24:292–24:293
model of human viral disease,
24:314–24:315
techniques
introduction into embryo via totipotent
stem cells, 24:287, 24:290
microinjection into fertilized egg
pronucleus, 24:286–24:287,
24:290–24:291
virus introduction, 24:287, 24:290
tumor induction by
bovine papilloma virus, 24:307
human papovaviruses BK and JC, early
region, 24:306–24:307
myc-MMTV construct, 24:307–24:308
SV40
early region, T antigen-coding,
24:305–24:306
T antigen-rat insulin gene construct,
24:306

Mouse (continued)
  heat-induced mRNAs for HSP70 and
    ubiquitin, 24:12
  HSP70 and HSP68 during embryogenesis,
    24:11–24:12
  inbred line, meiosis blockage under genetic
    control, 26:164
  models, 35:155–197
    future research directions, 35:183–184,
      35:195–197
    genomic resources, 35:165–168
    historical perspective, 35:156–157
    human disorder modeling, 35:184–195
      model differences, 35:194–195
      mouse germ line manipulation,
        35:185–194
      DNA sequence targeting, 35:191–194
      gene targeting, 35:188–191
      transgenic animals, 35:185–188
    human genetic disease advances,
      35:168–184
      chromosomal syndromes, 35:175–177
      future research directions, 35:183–184
      gametic imprinting, 35:180–181
      polygenic disease, 35:177–180
      position effects, 35:181–183
      single gene disorders, 35:168–175
        assays, 35:171–173
        candidate gene cloning, 35:169–170
        causal gene determination,
          35:173–175
        functional disease loci cloning,
          35:169
        positional cloning, 35:170–171
        triplet repeat mutation, 35:181–183
    model attributes, 35:157–162
      genetic studies, 35:159–160
      mutations, 35:160–162
      mouse–human comparative map,
        35:162–165
    overview, 35:155–156
  regulatory genes for expression of
    alcohol dehydrogenase, 24:86–24:87
    aminolevulinate dehydrogenase, 24:86
    arylsulfatase B, 24:84
    catalase, 24:86
    α-galactosidase, 24:82
    β-galactosidase, 24:82–24:83
    glucose-6-phosphate isomerase,
      24:88–24:89
    β-glucuronidase, 24:75, 24:80–24:82

  H-2 antigen, 24:84–24:85
  malic enzyme (mitochondrial),
    24:87–24:88
Mouse mammary tumor virus
  constructs with myc oncogene, in transgenic
    mouse, 24:307–24:308
Mouth hooks, Drosophila
  development from maxillary segment, 27:365
  in hsDfd larvae, 27:391, 27:393, 27:394
  missing in Dfd_ mutants, 27:366–27:367
MRS-A, Mu elements of Zea mays and, 30:96
MSH2 protein
  DNA repair function of, 36:77
  as tumor suppressor gene product, 36:50
MSH2 tumor repressor gene
  antisense transcripts of, 36:103
  characteristics of, 36:50, 36:95
  implication in colon cancer (HNPCC),,
    36:76, 36:77
msl genes, dosage compensation, 39:79–80
MS strain, Drosophila transposable elements and,
  29:239
M strain, Drosophila transposable elements and,
  29:262–29:264, 29:268
MTS1 tumor suppressor gene, characteristics of,
  36:48
MTS2 tumor suppressor gene, characteristics of,
  36:48, 36:95
Mucor racemosus
  transformation system, 23:154–23:155
Mu elements of Zea mays, 30:77–30:78
  applications
    mutagenesis, 30:112–30:113
    transposon tagging, 30:113–30:115
  characteristics, 30:86–30:91
  discovery, 30:78–30:80
  future directions, 30:115–30:116
  gene expression, 30:108–30:112
  monitoring, 30:80
    genetic assays, 30:80–30:84
    molecular assays, 30:84–30:86
Mu1
  applications, 30:114–30:115
  assays, 30:84–30:86
  characteristics, 30:87–30:88, 30:90–30:91
  future directions, 30:115
  gene expression, 30:109–30:112
  properties of transposition, 30:100, 30:103,
    30:105–30:106, 30:108
  regulation, 30:97, 30:99
  structure, 30:92–30:93, 30:95–30:96

Mu2, 30:93, 30:96
Mu3, 30:93, 30:109–30:110
Mu4, 30:93, 30:95–30:96
Mu5, 30:93–30:96
Mu6, 30:93–30:94
Mu7, 30:93–30:94, 30:103, 30:115
Mu8, 30:94, 30:103, 30:115
Mu9, 30:94, 30:98–30:99, 30:115
MuA, 30:94, 30:98
MuA2, 30:99, 30:115
MuR, 30:94, 30:96, 30:98, 30:107
MuR1, 30:97, 30:99, 30:115
properties of transposition, 30:100–30:108
regulation, 30:97–30:100
structure
  classes, 30:91–30:94
  distribution, 30:94–30:96
Muir-Torre syndrome
  chromosomal linkage of, 36:95
  MSH2 gene role in, 36:77, 36:95
Multigene families, evolutionary genetics of fish
  and
  environmental change, 29:162–29:163,
    29:167–29:168
  gene duplication, 29:147–29:158
Multiple endocrine neoplasis, chromosomal
  linkage of, 36:95
Multiple-tissue tumor suppressor gene (*MTS1*),
  possible locus for, 36:65
Multistrandedness, 34:174–187
  degrees, 34:179–186
  evidence, 34:174–179
  incomplete polytenization, 34:187
Muscina stabulans, *zeste* in *Drosophila
  melanogaster* and, 29:329
Muscle
  carbonic anhydrases and, 30:331, 30:333
  TF mRNA during development, rat, 25:16,
    25:18
  weakness and atrophy, in CMT disease, 36:3,
    36:8
Muscular dystrophy, *see also* Becker muscular
  dystrophy; Duchenne muscular dystrophy
  carrier diagnosis, 33:211–215
  direct diagnosis, 33:212–214
  indirect diagnosis, 33:211–212
  disease characteristics, 33:177–183
  animal models, 33:183
  cardiac muscle, 33:181–182
  mental retardation, 33:180–181
  muscles, 33:177–180

retina, 33:182–183
mutational distribution, 33:203–207
prenatal diagnosis, 33:211–214
Mustard, nitrate reductase and, 30:10
Mutagen
  anemias induced by, 20:436–20:440
  specificity, nonrandomness and,
    21:204–21:211
Mutagenesis
  applied microbiology and, 20:44–20:46
  carbonic anhydrases and, 30:349
  Drosophila transposable elements and, 29:229,
    29:231
  P elements, 29:264–29:265
  retrotransposons, 29:233, 29:235,
    29:240–29:257
  fungal, transformation and, 23:102–23:103,
    23:117, 23:119–23:122
  Mu elements of *Zea mays* and, 30:78,
    30:112–30:113
  Neurospora crassa and, 29:4, 29:20–29:22,
    29:24–29:25, 29:40
  nitrate reductase and, 30:7, 30:12–30:14
  in *Saccharomyces cerevisiae*
    comparison with other organisms,
      21:228–21:240
    experimental methods, 21:174–21:186
    induced, 21:186–21:211
    mechanisms of induction,
      21:220–21:228
    mitochondrial, 21:217–21:220
    spontaneous, 21:211–21:217
  Schizosaccharomyces pombe, 23:41–23:52
    enrichment technique, 23:41–23:43
    genetic recombination, 23:44–23:46
    mutators, 23:43–23:44
    repair and, 23:46–23:52
      caffeine effects, 23:50–23:51
      cell stage and mutation frequency,
        23:48–23:49
      mosaicism and lethal sectoring,
        23:46–23:47
      radiosensitive mutants, 23:49–23:50
  somaclonal variation and, 30:65
  superoxide dismutases and, 30:268, 30:298,
    30:304
  telomeres and, 30:232
  in Y chromosome of *Drosophila hydei*
    spermatozoa, 23:217–23:221
  zeste in *Drosophila melanogaster* and, 29:312,
    29:324

Mutants
  with ability to generate molecules with
    altered biological activities,
    20:59–20:63
  auxotrophic and suppressor, 20:51–20:52
  constitutive, 20:52–20:53
  enzyme-specificity, 20:55–20:57
  Gossypium spp.
    Asiatic diploid, 23:274, 23:276–23:281
    New World allotetraploid, 23:274–23:275,
      23:281–23:290, *see also*
      Allotetraploids
  host-range, of influenza virus, 20:24–20:25
  with increased resistance to own metabolites,
    20:59
  inhibitor-resistant, 20:46–20:51
  permeability, 20:57–20:58
  Schizosaccharomyces pombe
    double, response to uv, 23:26
    of meiotic cycle, 23:13–23:14
    radiosensitive, 23:22–23:26
  temperature-sensitive, of influenza virus,
    20:7–20:12
  up-promotor, 20:53–20:55
  viruses and, 20:63–20:64
Mutational analysis
  agammaglobulinemia cloning studies,
    35:71–72
  dystrophin, 33:203–211
    genotype/phenotype correlations
    gross rearrangements, 33:207–209
    point mutations, 33:209–211
    muscular dystrophy distribution,
      33:203–207
  hyper-immunoglobulin M syndrome, 35:186
  mouse models, 35:160–162
  prune/Killer of prune interaction, *awd* gene,
    35:218–221
  severe combined immunodeficiency disorder,
    35:77
  16S ribosomal RNA, 33:1–31
    conserved nucleotides, 33:19, 33:20
    detection methods, 33:2–5
      mutation introduction, 33:4–5
      plasmid expression, 33:2–4
    double mutations, 33:19, 33:21–30
    limitations, 33:30–31
    second-site suppressor mutations, 33:31
    single mutations, 33:19, 33:21–30
    structure–function analysis, 33:6–19

    central domain mutations, 33:12–13
    3′ major domain mutations, 33:13–16
    5′ major domain mutations, 33:10–12
    3′ minor domain mutations, 33:16–19
    secondary structure, 33:6–9
    upstream mutations, 33:9–10
  Wiskott–Aldrich syndrome, 35:82–83
Mutations, *see also specific disease*
  affecting dosage compensation and sex
    differentiation, *Drosophila*
    Daughterkiller, 24:397
    daughterless, 24:391–24:393, 24:396
    female lethal, 24:397
    hermaphrodite, 24:397
    Sex-lethal, female-specific, 24:392–24:396
    sisterless-a, female-specific, lethal,
      24:396–24:397
  body color, *Drosophila*
    black
      β-alanine metabolism, 24:197–24:198
      synthesis, 24:200–24:202
      phenol oxidase, 24:194–24:195
    ebony
      β-alanine metabolism, 24:197–24:198
      BAH activity, 24:199
      BAS activity, 24:198–24:199
      neurological effect, 24:200
      phenol oxidase, 24:194–24:195
    silver
      gene mapping, 24:203–24:204
      light avoidance, 24:203
      NADA accumulation, 24:203
    tan
      BAS and BAH activities, 24:199
      neurological effect, 24:200
    yellow
      mating behavior, 24:204
      phenol oxidase, 24:194
      pigmentation pattern, 24:204
      yellow protein functions, 24:205
  carbonic anhydrases and, 30:326,
    30:336–30:346
  Drosophila embryos, occurrence, 34:32,
    34:36–57
  Drosophila transposable elements and,
    29:229–29:231
    cis-acting effects of retrotransposons,
      29:240–29:241, 29:243–29:252
    foldback elements, 29:287–29:288
    hobo, 29:277–29:278

mariner, 29:279–29:281
P elements, 29:260, 29:266,
    29:268–29:274
retrotransposons, 29:234, 29:236, 29:239,
    29:253–29:258
evolutionary genetics of fish and, 29:122
development of, 29:175–29:176
environmental change, 29:172–29:173
immune system, 29:183, 29:185, 29:189
nuclear genomic structures, 29:135,
    29:142
forward, Mu elements of Zea mays and, 30:80,
    30:83–30:84, 30:87–30:88, 30:99
insertional, gene transfer-induced, mouse
    frequency, 24:297–24:298
non-lethal, 24:297
prenatal homozygous-lethal,
    24:295–24:296
recessiveness, 24:297
lethal translucida, tyrosine-O-phosphate
    accumulation, Drosophila,
    24:156–24:157
male-specific lethal, autosomal, Drosophila
    mle (maleless), 24:398–24:401
msl-1, msl-2 (male-specific lethal),
    24:398–24:401
morphology change induction, 34:305–311
mosquitoes and, 30:147, 30:163, 30:167,
    30:170
Mu elements of Zea mays and, see Mu
    elements of Zea mays
Neurospora crassa and, 29:5, 29:48
development, 29:43, 29:46
DNA transaction, 29:18–29:25
gene transfer, 29:7–29:10, 29:12
metabolism, 29:40–29:41
mitochondria, 29:29–29:33, 29:35–29:36,
    29:38
nitrate reductase and, 30:2, 30:28, 30:31
apoenzyme mutants, 30:21–30:28
genetics, 30:12–30:20
pleiotropic effects on phenotype from, 36:138
recessive, masking outcrossing maintenance,
    24:347–24:353
reduction during evolution, 24:328
redundant genes, 36:146
saturation, 34:13
somaclonal variation and, 30:65
genetics consequences, 30:50, 30:56,
    30:58, 30:60, 30:62

genotype, 30:44–30:47
unusual genetic behavior, 30:63–30:65
superoxide dismutases and, 30:259, 30:263,
    30:269
antioxidant enzymes, 30:306–30:308
genetics consequences, 30:297–30:300
metabolism, 30:289, 30:292–30:297
molecular genetics, 30:273, 30:277,
    30:282, 30:285–30:288
physiology, 30:288–30:291
senescence, 30:300–30:303
suppression, 30:303–30:306
telomeres and
formation, 30:227, 30:230–30:232
function, 30:204, 30:207–30:209, 30:213,
    30:216, 30:219–30:221
of tumor suppressor genes, 36:51,
    36:95–36:99
yeast ribosomes and, 29:103–29:104
assembly, 29:95–29:96, 29:98
genetic analysis, 29:98–29:103
nucleolus, 29:69–29:71, 29:89–29:91
ribosomal protein genes, 29:74,
    29:77–29:78, 29:81–29:82
zeste in Drosophila melanogaster and
chromatin packaging, 29:339–29:342
discovery, 29:303–29:305
DNA binding, 29:318, 29:320,
    29:324–29:325
molecular biology, 29:313, 29:315
polytene chromosomes, 29:317
protein, 29:333–29:334, 29:336–29:337
transvection, 29:306, 29:308–29:312
Mutator, see also Mu elements of Zea mays
somaclonal variation and, 30:55, 30:64
MutL tumor suppressor gene, implication in
colon cancer, 36:76
Mxil gene, as possible tumor suppressor, 36:93
Mycobacterium smegmatis, dtxR homolg of,
    36:197
Mycobacterium tuberculosis, dtxR homolog of,
    36:197
MYC oncogene, negative regulation of, 36:93
Mycorrhizae, nitrate reductase and, 30:2
Myelin
composition of, 36:22
peripheral myelin protein 22 role in,
    36:26–36:28
peripheral myelin protein zero in compaction
of, 36:23

Myelin-associated glycoprotein (MAG)
  abnormal expression of, 36:24
  as major myelin protein, 36:22
Myelin basic protein (MBP)
  lack of, in *shiverer* mouse, 36:22
  as major myelin protein, 36:22
Myelin proteins, function of, 36:21–36:34
Myelodysplasia, *NF1* implication in, 36:80
Myelodysplastic syndrome, search for
  chromosome 12p13 mutations in, 36:63
Myf-5 protein
  expression of, 36:153
  mouse gene encoding, 36:141,
    36:150–36:151
Myoblasts
  Duchenne muscular dystrophy gene therapy,
    35:140–141
  HSP response to heat shock, 24:20–24:21
myoD gene
  mutation effects on, 36:153
  redundancy in, 36:141
MyoD protein, expression of, 36:151,
  36:152–36:153
MyoD transcription factor, pRb regulation of,
  36:55
Myogenic regulatory factors (MRFs), mouse
  gene encoding, 36:141
Myogenin, mouse gene encoding, 36:141,
  36:150
Myoglobin, evolutionary genetics of fish and,
  29:148–29:151
Myosin, hypertrophic cardiomyopathy role,
  35:290–292, 35:302
Myosin heavy chain
  cis-acting mutations
    effects on alternative splicing, 31:257–258

N. rustica, pollen sublethal irradiation, effects
  on crosses between lines, 26:45
N. tabacum, ozone tolerance in pollen and
  sporophyte, 26:15
NAD, evolutionary genetics of fish and, 29:132,
  29:152
NADA, *see* N-Acetyldopamine
NADH
  nitrate reductase and
    biochemistry, 30:4–30:5, 30:7–30:9
    genetics, 30:19, 30:21–30:22

  superoxide dismutases and, 30:257, 30:259
NADP, evolutionary genetics of fish and,
  29:132, 29:152, 29:166
NADPH
  nitrate reductase and, 30:4–30:5,
    30:21–30:22
  superoxide dismutases and, 30:259
nar mutants, nitrate reductase and,
  30:20–30:21
NarX/NarL, as bacterial gene repressor, 36:202,
  36:204
Nasopharyngeal carcinomas, p53 implication in,
  36:57
NAT, *see* N-Acetyltransferase
Natural selection, 36:138
  evolutionary genetics of fish and,
    29:125–29:127, 29:147, 29:164–29:166
NBAD, *see* N-β-Alanyldopamine
NCAD gene
  Xenopus laevis, 31:62, 31:66–67
NCAM gene
  Xenopus laevis, 31:62, 31:66
Neanura monticola, intercalary α-
  heterochromatin, 37:140–141
Near-ultraviolet radiation
  absorption by
    dehydroxy acid dehydratase, 26:102,
      26:109, 26:111
    DNA, 26:103–26:105
    heme-containing porphyrins and catalase,
      26:107
    N-acetlcysteinamide-containing peptide,
      phase, T7, 26:108–26:109
    riboflavin, 26:107
    ribonucleotide reductase, 26:109
    thiolated tRNA, effect on DNA, 26:102,
      26:105–26:107
  DNA damage, 26:115–26:119
    distinction from FUV lesions,
      26:115–26:117
    induction and repair, models,
      26:101–26:103
    similarity to H$_2$O$_2$ effect, 26:118–26:119
  mutagenicity, 26:132–26:135
  oxidative photoproducts
    detoxification by catalase and SOD,
      26:111–26:112
    hydrogen peroxide, 26:112–26:113
    singlet oxygen, 26:115
    superoxide anion radical, 26:114–26:115

photoprotection by DNA photolyase,
26:110–26:111
physiological effects, E. coli
growth delay, 26:106, 26:126
membrane damage, 26:128–26:129
protein synthesis induction,
26:126–26:128
regulons involved in response to, se also
Regulons, 26:129–26:131
sensitivity in mutants, 26:119–26:126, see
also Escherichia coli, NUV effects
sources, natural and artificial, 26:100–26:101
Neisseria gonorrheae, iron-regulated gene in,
36:190, 36:191, 36:195, 36:196
Neisseria meningitidis, iron regulated gene in,
36:191, 36:195
Neisseria sicca, carbonic anhydrases and, 30:323
Neogenome, evolutionary genetics of fish and,
29:142–29:143
neo, mosquitoes and, 30:170
Neomycin, mosquitoes and, 30:168, 30:170
Neomycin sulfate, puff activity effects, 39:261
Neonatal screening, for phenylketonuria, 32:203
Neoplasia, 33:255–270
future research directions, 33:269–270
homeobox genes
cancer role, 33:267
developmental processes, 33:265–266
expression
cancers, 33:268–269
leukemia, 33:267–268
tumorigenesis, in vivo model, 33:267
paired-box genes
embryonic development role, 33:256–259
expression
brain cancers, 33:260–263
primary human tumors, 33:260
rhabdomyosarcoma, 33:264–265
Wilms' tumor, 33:263–264
oncogene classification, 33:259
tumorigenesis, in vivo model, 33:259–260
telomeres and, 30:206, 30:208
Neoplasmins, evolutionary genetics of fish and,
29:171–29:172
Neo-Y chromosome, mitotic heterochromatin
degeneration, 37:74–76
Nerve cells, structure of, 36:21–36:22
Nerve conduction velocities
in CMT disease diagnosis, 36:3, 36:4, 36:7,
36:8

in hereditary neuropathy with liability to
pressure palsies, 36:13
Nerve growth factor, receptor for, 36:79
Nerve pathology, in CMT disease, 36:3–36:4
Nervous system, evolutionary genetics of fish
and, 29:176–29:181
Neural cell adhesion molecule (N-CAM)
abnormal expression of, 36:24
homology with DCC gene structure, 36:79
Ig-like motif in, 36:22
Neural plate
Xenopus laevis
cadherins, 31:66–67
cell adhesion molecules, 31:66
channels, 31:67–68
intermediate filaments, 31:67
transcription factors
helix-loop-helix, 31:59–65
paired domain, 31:65
POU domain, 31:65
zinc-finger, 31:65
Xwnt genes, 31:65–66
Neural tube, environmental stress-induced
defects, mammals, 28:277–28:278,
28:281
Neural tumors
gene dysregulation in, 36:79
tumor suppressor gene mutations in, 36:96
Neuroblasts
cell lineages, Drosophila, 27:404–27:405
distinction between three classes, Drosophila,
27:407–27:408
identity genes, Drosophila melanogaster,
31:17–20
QL cell lineage, homeobox gene actions,
C. elegans, 27:101–27:103
segregation from ectodermal cells, Drosophila,
27:406–27:407
Neurofibromatosis type 1
cancers with, 36:82
chromosomal linkage of, 36:95
symptoms of, 36:79, 36:104
tumor suppressor gene role in, 36:49, 36:80,
36:95
Neurofibromatosis type 2
chromosomal linkage of, 36:95
symptoms of, 36:79
tumor suppressor gene role in, 36:49
Neurofibromin, as tumor suppressor gene
product, 36:49, 36:81

Neurogenesis
  in *Drosophila*
    neural lineage estabilishment, 31:17–20
    neuroblast identity genes, 31:17–20
    proneural genes, 31:15–17
    schematic diagram, 31:15
  in *Xenopus*
    anterior–posterior axis formation
      Hox gene role, 31:56–57
      pattern
        induction, 31:54–55
        lability, 31:53–54
        posterior dominance, 31:55–56
        prepattern, 31:53–54
        retinoic acid role, 31:56–57
    competence
      protein kinase C function, 31:51
      temporal, 31:48–49
      Xotch function, 31:51–53
    neural plate response
      structural and physiological proteins,
        31:66–68
      transcription factors, 31:59–65
      Xwnt genes, 31:65–66
    organizer
      characterization, 31:33–36
      secreted proteins, 31:41–43
      transcription factors, 31:36–40
    signaling
      combined, 31:45–47
      homeogenetic induction, 31:47–48
      planar, 31:45
      vertical, 31:44–45
Neurogenic genes
  class, 31:16
  Drosophila
    big brain (bib), functional difference from
      other neurogenic genes,
      27:412–27:414, 27:433, 27:445
    Delta (Dl)
      molecular organization, 27:421–27:422
      mutant phenotypes, 27:412,
        27:420–27:421, 27:430
      discovery, 27:412
    Enhancer of split [E(spl)] locus
      cluster of several genes, 27:424
      epidermalizing signal reception by
        protein products, 27:428,
        27:444–27:445
      molecular organization, 27:425–27:428

        mutant phenotypes, 27:423–27:425,
          27:428, 27:430
        functional interactions, 27:430–27:433
          in heterozygotes, 27:431–27:432
          in homozygotes, duplication effects,
            27:432–27:433
        mutant phenotypes
          neural hyperplasia, 27:423–27:424
          neuralized (neu), mutant phenotypes,
            27:430
      Notch (N)
        molecular organization,
          27:418–27:420
        mutant phenotypes, 27:412,
          27:416–27:418
        protein products, epidermalizing
          function, 27:442–27:445, see also
          under Proteins
        transcripts, see RNA, *Drosophila*
        interactions with AS-C and *da* genes,
          double mutant studies,
          27:440–27:442
      master mind (mam), mutant phenotype and
        structure, 27:429
      mutant phenotypes
        mosaic analysis
          cellular autonomy of expression and,
            27:415–27:416
          imaginal disc morphogenesis and,
            27:414–27:415
Neurohypophysis, evolutionary genetics of fish
  and, 29:197
Neuron, anatomy of, 36:21–36:22
Neurophysin, evolutionary genetics of fish and,
  29:197
Neurospora
  amplified mtDNAs in, 22:54–22:56
  superoxide dismutases and, 30:265, 30:268,
    30:288, 30:301–30:302
Neurospora artificial chromosomes, 29:12,
  29:14, 29:16–29:17
Neurospora crassa
  and, 29:2–29:5, 29:47–29:49
  biotechnology, 29:47
  development, 29:42–29:46
  DNA transaction, 29:18
  enzymology, 29:23–29:24
  mutagenesis, 29:24–29:25
  recombination, 29:22–29:23
  repair, 29:20–29:22

replication, 29:19–29:20
    transcription, 29:20
genetic material, 29:12–29:13
    centromeres, 29:15–29:16
    chromosomes, 29:13–29:15
    organization, 29:17–29:18
    replicators, 29:15, 29:17
    telomeres, 29:15–29:17
gene transfer
    artificial chromosome, 29:12
    DNA transformation, 29:5–29:6
    meiotic instability, 29:6–29:8
    self-replicating vector, 29:11–29:12
    transformation, 29:9–29:11
membrane, 29:38
metabolism, 29:38
    amino acid, 29:40–29:41
    nitrogen, 29:39
    phosphate, 29:39–29:40
    quinic acid, 29:41–29:42
    sulfur, 29:39
mitochondria, 29:25–29:26
    genome, 29:26–29:28
    mutants, 29:30–29:33
    nuclear-mitochondrial interactions,
        29:35–29:38
    plasmids, 29:33–29:35
    transcription, 29:29–29:30
    translation, 29:29–29:30
    tRNA, 29:28–29:29
    transposons, 29:46–29:47
centromeres, 23:113
chromosome rearrangements, 36:239–36:397
    ascospore abnormalities from,
        36:271–36:271, 36:274–36:275
    balancers in, 36:269–36:270
    breakpoint distribution in, 36:247–36:249
    complex rearrangements, 36:265–36:267
    complex translocations, 36:245, 36:292
    crossing-over suppression, 36:267–36:269
    cryptic rearrangements, 36:267–36:269
    database for, 36:245–36:247
    duplication from, 36:294–36:295
    duplication instability in, 36:262–36:263
    electrophoretic separation, 36:263–36:264
    identification of progeny with duplications,
        36:275
    insertional translocations, 36:245–36:246,
        36:248, 36:261, 36:276–36:277,
        36:291

intrachromosomal transpositions, 36:245,
        36:246, 36:258–36:259
    junction sequences in, 36:260–36:261
    length factors in, 36:249–36:254
    lethal deficienceis from, 36:265
    list of, 36:287–36:383
    markers, maps, and normal sequence
        strains for, 36:286–36:287
    mutant phenotypes from, 36:295–36:296
    mutual insertions, 36:290
    nonterminal inversions, 36:290
    in NOR region, 36:244, 36:249,
        36:256–36:258, 36:262, 36:292
    pericentric inversions, 36:245, 36:246
    phenotype effects of, 36:251–36:253
    problems in identification of,
        36:271–36:277
    quasiterminal translocations,
        36:245–36:246, 36:247,
        36:291–36:292
    reciprocal translocations, 36:245,
        36:272–36:274, 36:288–36:290
    repeat induced point mutations,
        36:258–36:259
    symbols and conventions used for, 36:285
    transcriptional-repression release by,
        36:260
    transvection in, 36:270–36:271
    uses of, 36:243–36:244
genome complexity, 23:76
mei mutants, 26:150
meiosis arrest after pachytene, 26:163
mitochondrial genome
    genes
        atp6, mosaic, 25:216
        atp9 and 8,, continuous, 25:213,
            25:214
        cob, mosaic, 25:222
        cox1, 2, and 3, continuous,
            25:212–25:213
        duplicate, 25:193
        nontranscribed, 25:193
        rnl, mosaic, 25:208
        tRNA
            clustering, 25:199
            structure and genetic code, 25:210,
                25:211
        urf1, mosaic, 25:223
        vari, 25:214
    mapping using mutants, 25:203

Neurospora crassa (continued)
  mutants
    classification, 25:238–25:239
    poky
      cytochromes aa_3 and b,
        25:238–25:239
      DNA of two types, 25:240–25:241
      protein synthesis impairment, 25:239
    stopper, description, 25:240
      cytochrome aa_3 deficiency, 25:240
    palindromic sequences, 25:189
    transcription, initiation and processing,
      25:230
    unassigned intergenic orfs, 25:197–25:198
  nitrate reductase and, 30:26
  nonfunctional genes
    higher eukaryotic, 23:134
    from yeast, 23:132–23:134
  outcrossing maintenance, 24:352
  plasmid combined with those from *E. coli*
    characteristics, 23:151
    replication in fungi and bacteria, 23:139
  qa (quinic acid) genes
    discovery, 23:116–23:117
    mapping, 23:118
  recessive mutations affecting diploid stage,
    24:352
  sulfur regulation
    alternative sulfur sources, 31:196
    aromatic sulfate utilization, 31:192–194
    aryl sulfatase role, 31:192–194
    assimilation pathway, 31:189
    choline-O-sulfate utilization, 31:195–196
    circuit design, 31:190
    cys-3 gene
      characterization, 31:198–199
      control of, 31:201
    CYS3 protein
      autogenous regulation, 31:201
      DNA binding, 31:199–200
      as DNA-binding nuclear protein,
        31:201–202
      molecular characterization, 31:202–203
      mutation studies, 31:200–201
    genetic controls, 31:190–192
    metabolic repressors of sulfur catabolic
      expression, 31:196–197
    negative control genes, 31:197–198
    physiological basis, 31:190
    positive control genes, 31:197–198
    structural genes affecting, 31:191–192

  sulfate permease II role, 31:194–195
  sulfate permease I role, 31:194–195
  superoxide dismutases and
    molecular genetics, 30:288
    physiology, 30:261–30:262
    physiology of mutants, 30:301, 30:306
    structure, 30:263, 30:266
  transformation
    ars significance, 23:109
    with cloned DNA, 23:145–23:147
    DNA
      donor, fate after, 23:100–23:102
      treatment during, 23:86–23:88
    evidence for, 23:74, 23:78
    frequency, 23:95–23:97
    methods, 23:79
    mutation during, 23:102–23:103
    plasmids and, 23:85
    promoter isolation, 23:109–23:111
    with total DNA preparations,
      23:140–23:143
    transformant genetics, 23:143–23:144
Neurospora intermedia, mitochondrial genome
  rearrangement in senescent cultures, 25:244
Neurospora tetrasperma, 29:42–29:43
  chromosome rearrangements, 36:265, 36:269
Neurotransmitters, evolutionary genetics of fish
  and, 29:178
Neutralist view, evolutionary genetics of fish
  and, 29:164–29:165
Newcastle disease virus, chicken embryo
  HSP-related protein induction, 24:20
NF1 protein, tumor-suppressor gene effect on,
  36:46
NF1 tumor suppressor gene
  antisense transcripts of, 36:103
  characteristics of, 36:49, 36:52,
    36:79–36:84, 36:95
  complex structure of, 36:67
  modifier effects on, 36:104
  mutations on, 36:79–36:80, 36:82, 36:96
  translocations affecting, 36:93
NF2 tumor suppressor gene, characteristics of,
  36:49, 36:79–36:84, 36:95
ng-1 gene
  band organization, 39:153
  puff development, 39:300
Nia genes, nitrate reductase and
  gene expression, 30:9–30:11
  genetic engineering, 30:28–30:29
  genetics, 30:13, 30:20–30:24, 30:26–30:28

nia mutants, nitrate reductase and, 30:15,
  30:21, 30:23, 30:25–30:28, 30:30–30:31
Nickel
  bacterial resistance to, 36:221,
    36:223–36:226
  DtxR activation by, 36:196, 36:197
  in proteins, 36:188
Nickel-63, braconid wasp feeding effects,
  25:161
Nick translation, *Neurospora crassa* and, 29:7,
  29:13
Nicotiana langsdorfii, resistance to apple scab
  fungus, MGS and, 26:18
Nicotiana, nitrate reductase and, 30:17, 30:21,
  30:27
Nicotiana plumbaginifolia
  cabE gene, photoregulation, 28:145–28:146
  glucanase, structure and homologies, 28:199
  nitrate reductase and, 30:2, 30:4,
    30:27–30:28, 30:30–30:31
  apoenzyme mutants, 30:21–30:23, 30:26
  gene expression, 30:10, 30:12
  genetics, 30:13–30:15, 30:17–30:20
  superoxide dismutases and, 30:271, 30:306
Nicotiana tabacum, nitrate reductase and, 30:4,
  30:14, 30:17–30:18, 30:21
Niemann–Pick disease
  in Jewish populations, 32:27
NirA, nitrate reductase and, 30:27
Nit1 genes, nitrate reductase and, 30:9
Nitrate
  superoxide dismutases and, 30:252–30:253
  utilization auxotrophy, nitrate reductase and,
    30:15
Nitrate reductase in higher plants, 30:1–30:2,
  30:30–30:32
  biochemistry
    apoenzyme, 30:4
    cDNA analysis, 30:6–30:7
    cofactors, 30:4–30:6
    intracellular localization, 30:8–30:9
    structure, 30:7–30:8
  function, 30:3
  gene expression, 30:9–30:12
  genetic engineering, 30:28–30:29
  genetics, 30:12
    apoenzyme mutants, 30:21–30:26
    cDNA, 30:27–30:28
    cofactor mutants, 30:17–30:20
    complementation groups, 30:15–30:17
    mutagenesis, 30:12–30:14

nitrate assimilation, 30:26–30:27
  selection for mutants, 30:14–30:15
  transcription, 30:26
Nitrite, nitrate reductase and, 30:3–30:4, 30:26
Nitrite reductase in higher plants, 30:2, 30:9,
  30:11–30:12, 30:27
Nitrogen
  braconid wasp protections from X rays,
    25:156
  fixation, by plant tissue cultures,
    20:168–20:173
  metabolism, bacterial, genetic control,
    27:13–27:14, 27:26–27:27
  mustard, effects on braconid wasps
    oocyte sensitivity to, 25:168
    sperm inactivation, 25:173
  Neurospora crassa and, 29:38
  nitrate reductase and, 30:1–30:2
    function, 30:3, 30:5
    gene expression, 30:10–30:11, 30:15,
      30:18, 30:21, 30:26
    genetic engineering, 30:28
  photosynthetic gene expression and, 28:151
  superoxide dismutases and
    physiology, 30:255, 30:260
    physiology of mutants, 30:289, 30:293,
      30:298, 30:300, 30:304
  yeast ribosomes and, 29:84–29:85
Nitrogenase, nitrate reductase and, 30:6
nm23 Gene, *prune/Killer of prune* interaction,
  awd gene comparison, 35:214–216
nm23 protein, as possible tumor suppressor,
  36:92–36:93
nmr gene, *Neurospora crassa* and, 29:39
Nocodazole, heat-shock puff induction,
  39:350
Nodes of Ranvier
  connexin32 expression at, 36:29
  role in neural activity, 36:22
no distributive disjunction (nod) mutation,
  31:105–106
NOF sequence, *Drosophila* transposable elements
  and, 29:284–29:286
Noggin gene
  Xenopus laevis, 31:35, 31:41
nonclaret disjunctional (ncd) mutation,
  31:104–105
Nonhistone chromatin proteins
  of higher plants, 22:164–22:170
  transcriptionally active crhomatin and,
    22:186–22:190

Nonhomologous end-joining, DNA repair
  mechanisms
  DNA ligase IV, 38:200
  DNA-protein kinase components,
    38:196–200
  Ku protein, 38:191, 38:196–198
  mammalian cell studies, 38:191–193,
    38:203–206
  mechanisms, 38:190
  repair model, 38:208–210
  variable–diversity–joining recombination,
    38:204–205
  XRCC4, 38:194, 38:200
  yeast studies, 38:193–196, 38:201–203,
    38:205
Non-insulin-dependent diabetes mellitus,
  32:51–89
  candidate genes, 32:63–88
    fatty acid-binding protein-2, 32:87–88
    glucagon-like peptide-1 receptor, 32:81
    glucokinase regulatory protein, 32:87
    glucose transporter genes, 32:76–78
    glycogen synthase, 32:81–83
    insulin gene, 32:63–64
    insulin receptor, 32:64–75
      function, 32:65–68
      leprechaunism, 32:68–69
      mutations, 32:74–75
      Rabson–Mendenhall syndrome,
        32:69–70
      structure, 32:65–68
      type A insulin resistance, 32:70–74
    insulin receptor substrate-1, 32:75–76
    islet amyloid polypeptide, 32:80–81
    maternally inherited diabetes and deafness,
      32:78–80
    maturity-onset diabetes of the young,
      32:83–86
    susceptibility, 32:55–57
  etiology, 32:54–55
  gene susceptibility identification strategies,
    32:55–62
    animal models, 32:62
    candidate gene approach, 32:55–57
    differential cloning, 32:61–62
    genome mapping, 32:57–61
    positional cloning, 32:57, 32:60
    subtraction cloning, 32:61–62
  history of development, 32:52–54
  polymorphism, 32:88

thrifty gene hypotheses, 32:88
Nonpolytene chromosomes
  chromatid structure, 34:243–247
  spatial organization, 34:332–335
Nonsense mutations, of tumor suppressor genes,
  36:98
Nontranscribed spacers, organization, 39:423
Nopaline, utilization, Ti-plasmid and,
  22:231–22:232
Nop1p, yeast ribosomes and, 29:89, 29:91
NOP1, yeast ribosomes and, 29:89
Norepinephrine, oxidative deamination and
  O-methylation, 24:136
Norrbottnian disease, 32:19, 32:29
Notch gene
  artificial bands, 39:149
  band organization, 39:147
  distribution estimation, 39:118
  interband organization, 39:89–90
Notochord, dorsoventral patterning, human
  malformation genes, 38:14–15
NPAT gene, antisense transcripts of, 36:103
npr1 gene
  DNA–RNA hybrid antibodies, 39:51–52
  puff development, 39:295–297, 39:308
N-staining
  centromeric heterochromatin nonhistone
    protein analysis, 37:105–106
  differential heterochromatin staining,
    37:21–23
Nuclear DNA, evolutionary genetics of fish and,
  29:134–29:135, 29:138
Nuclear envelope
  Drosophila melanogaster
    fs(1)Ya mutant, 31:111–112
    lamin genes, 31:111
    in mitotic cycle, 31:110–111
  genome expression heredity and,
    24:257–24:258, 24:262–24:263
    aging and cancer, 24:267–24:268
    cell differentiation, 24:264–24:267
    pathogenic deviations, 24:266–24:267
    egg determination, 24:263–24:264
    model, 24:258
    nuclear RNA processing, 24:259–24:260
    m-protein-dependent splicing, 24:258,
      24:260–24:263
    translation in pores, 24:253–24:256,
      24:261–24:262
    organization, 24:258–24:261

double-membrane structure, 24:259
telomeres and, 30:185, 30:225–30:226
Nuclear factor IV, telomeres and, 30:200
nuclear fall-out mutation, 31:108
Nuclear localization signals (NLSs), yeast
   ribosomes and, 29:98
Nuclear matrix, *zeste* in *Drosophila melanogaster*
   and, 29:337–29:339
Nuclear membrane, intercalary heterochromatin
   identification, contact points, 37:224
Nuclear organizing regions *Neurospora crassa*
   and, 29:2, 29:7, 29:28
Nucleases, sensitivity of transcriptionally active
   chromatin and, 22:171–22:174
Nuclei
   during *Drosophila hydei* spermatogenesis,
      ultrastructure in
   advanced spermatids, 23:214–23:215
   primary spermatids, 23:188–23:198,
      23:205–23:206
   secondary spermatocytes, 23:210–23:211
   young spermatids, 23:211–23:214
Nucleolar organizer
   heterochromatin cytogenetics, 37:124–133
   intercalary heterochromatin identification,
      ectopic pairing, 37:166, 37:178–179
   position effects, 37:368–370
   regions
      evolutionary genetics of fish and, 29:138
      in *N. crassa*
         breakpoints in, 36:244, 36:249,
            36:256–36:258, 36:262
         rearrangements in, 36:246
      somaclonal variation and, 30:49
      yeast ribosomes and, 29:85–29:86
Nucleolar RNA, yeast ribosomes and, 29:64
Nucleoli
   [³H]uridine labeling method, 39:41–47
   molecular organization, 39:418–425
   morphology, 39:407–418
   organization, 34:16
   ribosomal RNA gene expression,
      39:418–425
Nucleolus
   yeast ribosomes and, 29:82, 29:85–29:87,
      29:103–29:104
   assembly, 29:98
   proteins, 29:87–29:90
   small nucleolar RNAs, 29:90–29:91
Nucleoplasmin, yeast ribosomes and, 29:88

Nucleoside diphosphate kinase
   awd gene, 35:216
   awd^{Kpn} mutation analysis, 35:218–221
   characteristics, 35:216–218
Nucleosomes, of higher plants, 22:154–22:157
Nucleotides
   carbonic anhydrases and, 30:330, 30:334,
      30:336, 30:343, 30:346–30:347
   Drosophila transposable elements and, 29:235,
      29:262, 29:265, 29:278,
      29:281–29:282
   evolutionary genetics of fish and, 29:142,
      29:185
   detection of variation, 29:127, 29:130
   endocrine system, 29:199–29:200
   nervous system, 29:177–29:178
   mosquitoes and, 30:131, 30:142, 30:144
   Mu elements of *Zea mays* and, 30:11, 30:93,
      30:109
   Neurospora crassa and, 29:2, 29:5, 29:7,
      29:23, 29:43
   genetic material, 29:13, 29:15,
      29:17–29:18
   mitochondria, 29:26–29:27, 29:29–29:30,
      29:34–29:35
   somaclonal variation and, 30:50, 30:58, 30:61
   tandem repeats, intercalary heterochromatin
      identification
   dinucleotide repeats, 37:222–223
   mononucleotide repeats, 37:222–223
   nucleotide sequences, 37:246
   poly(A) nucleotide complexes,
      37:220–222
   telomeres and
      function, 30:204–30:205, 30:207,
         30:215–30:217
      structure, 30:191, 30:200
   yeast ribosomes and, 29:65, 29:72–29:73,
      29:75, 29:94
   zeste in *Drosophila melanogaster* and, 29:313,
      29:319, 29:321, 29:324,
      29:329–29:330
Nucleotide sequences
   Adh locus, *Drosophila melanogaster*
      flanking regions, 25:48–25:49
      variant differences, 25:47–25:48
      comparison with other *Drosophila*
         species, 25:74–25:75
      experimentally induced mutations, 25:48
      haplotype diversity, 25:84–25:86

Nucleotide sequences (*continued*)
ascomycete mt DNA, *see* Mitochondrial
genes, ascomycetes
Pyura DNA, homology with human TF
cDNA, 25:5–25:7
TF promoter, human, homology with chicken
TF promoter, 25:11–25:12
metallothionein promoter, human,
25:25–25:26
TFR promoter, human, 25:11–25:12,
25:13
Nucleus
characteristics
protozoan nuclear apparatus, 34:73–75
vegetative macronucleus, 34:88–96
experimental studies
chromosome stretching, 34:330–332
genome function, 34:320–327
historical perspective, 34:311–314
isolated polytene chromosomes
antibody localization, 34:329
DNA polymerase activity, 34:327–328
microcloning, 34:329
restrictase effects, 34:328
RNA polymerase activity, 34:328
in situ hybridization, 34:330
terminal transferase, 34:327–328
solution effects
hydrogen ions, 34:318–320
tonicity, 34:314–318
historical perspective
Balbiani nuclei, 34:5, 34:15–16
spireme nuclei, 34:5–9
size, 34:260–280
spatial organization
interphase nonpolytene nuclei,
34:332–335
polytene nuclei
chromosome fields, 34:340–344
chromosome polarity, 34:335–340
ectopic contacts, 34:351
longitudinal coiling, 34:344
nuclear architectonics, 34:353–355
nuclear arrangement, 34:344–350
three-dimensional structure
maintenance, 34:351–353
nuc mutants, *Neurospora crassa* and,
29:9–29:10, 29:23, 29:40
Nuphar luteum, iron-containing SOD, 26:67
Nurse cells
chromatid synapsis variation, 34:153–154

homologous chromosomes, 34:169
mutations, 34:56–57
ovarian tumors, 34:58–59
polyploidy, 34:51–52
polyteny occurrence, 34:46–62
Nutrient regimes
heritable change induction, flax,
28:84–28:86, 28:92
nuclear DNA variation and, 28:86–28:90
photosynthetic gene expression and,
28:151–28:152
NUV, *see* Near-ultraviolet radiation
Nyssorhynchus, mosquitoes and, 30:129

Oats
frost hardiness, gene control, 28:106–28:107
root-tip tissue culture, chromosome changes,
28:82
somaclonal variation and, 30:47, 30:49,
30:61
Occurrence
apterygotan insects, 34:64–72
ascarid worms, 34:97
dipteran order
adult ovarian nurse cells, 34:46–62
banding, 34:22
Drosophila embryo mutations, 34:32,
34:37, 34:56–57
form variance, 34:21–32
heterochromatin morphology variation,
34:22–23
polyploidy, 34:32–37
pupae
bristle-forming cells, 34:43–46
foot pad cells, 34:37–43
homologous chromosomes, asynapsis,
34:157–163
infusoria
DNA elimination, first stage, 34:75–76
fragmentation, 34:88–96
nuclear apparatus characterization,
34:73–75
polytene chromosomes, 34:76–88
significance, 34:96–97
vegetative macronucleus organization,
34:88–96
lepidopteran order, 34:62–63
mammals
trophoblast cells, 34:98–105

tumor cells, 34:105
mollusks, 34:97–98
orthopteran order, 34:62–63
plants
  chromosome organization, 34:110–125
  polyploidy, 34:107–110
Octopine, utilization, Ti-plasmid and,
  22:231–22:232
Ocular anlage patterning, human malformation
  genes
  eye formation, 38:21
  homeobox genes, 38:21–22
Oenocytes, ploidy appearance, 34:62–63
Oenothera, somaclonal variation and, 30:50
Oleic acid, superoxide dismutases and, 30:285,
  30:297
Olfaction
  Drosophila melanogaster
    abnormal chemosensory jump (acj) mutant,
      31:147–148
    anatomy of, 31:144–146
    assays for, 31:143–144
    and female receptivity, 31:158–159
    olfactory (olf) mutant, 31:146–147
    olfactory-trap-abnormal (ota) mutant,
      31:147–148
olfactory mutant
  Drosophila melanogaster, 31:146–47
olfactory-trap-abnormal (ota) mutant
  Drosophila melanogaster, 31:147–148
Oligodendrocytes, function of, 36:22
Oligogalacturonides, plants
  elicitor activities, 28:202
  interaction with fungal elicitors, 28:202,
    28:204
Oligomycin, heat-shock puff induction,
  39:349–350, 39:352
Oligonucleotides
  evolutionary genetics of fish and, 29:129
  mosquitoes and, 30:133, 30:150, 30:155,
    30:157, 30:166, 30:171
  Neurospora crassa and, 29:17, 29:32
  superoxide dismutases and, 30:272
  telomeres and, 30:190, 30:209, 30:214
  yeast ribosomes and, 29:90, 29:99
  zeste in Drosophila melanogaster and,
    29:318–29:319
Om, Drosophila transposable elements and,
  29:248–29:249
OMgp gene, 36:80
  antisense transcripts of, 36:103

Ommochrome, synthesis in braconid wasp eye
  color mutants, 25:138–25:140
Oncodazole, heat-shock puff induction, 39:350
Oncogenes
  discovery of, 36:46
  evolutionary genetics of fish and, 29:144,
    29:170–29:173
  isolation and characteristics of, 36:46–36:50
  myc, construct with MMTV, in transgenic
    mouse, 24:307–24:308
  tumor suppressor protein interaction with,
    36:105
Oncoproteins, binding by tumor suppressor
  proteins, 36:56
Onion bulb formation (neural)
  in animal models, 36:27, 36:32
  in CMT1A disease, 36:26, 36:27
  in CMT2A disease, 36:3
  in CMT4 disease, 36:6
Oocysts, mosquitoes and, 30:156–30:157
Oocytes
  braconid wasps
    cytology during oogenesis, 25:111–25:112
    metaphase and prophase sensitivity to
      chemical mutagens, 25:168–25:169
    radiation, 25:151–25:153
  telomeres and, 30:201
Oogenesis, mosquitoes and, 30:152–30:154
Oogonia, chemical mutagen effects, braconid
  wasps, 25:170–25:171
Oomycetes, evolution of, 36:245
Open reading frames
  carbonic anhydrases and, 30:343
  Drosophila transposable elements and, 29:275,
    29:278, 29:285
  P elements, 29:260, 29:264–29:269,
    29:273
  retrotransposons, 29:231–29:232, 29:235,
    29:237–29:238
  length of, 36:145, 36:150
  mitochondrial genome
    intron expression, S. cerevisiae,
      25:207–25:208
    location, S. cerevisiae, 25:196–25:197
  unassigned (urf)
    Aspergillus nidulans, 25:196–25:197
    Neurospora crassa, 25:197–25:198,
      25:199
    Schizosaccharomyces pombe, 25:198
  mosquitoes and, 30:154, 30:160
  Mu elements of Zea mays and, 30:98

Open reading frames (*continued*)
Neurospora crassa and, **29**:34–**29**:35, **29**:43, **29**:46
Optic atrophy, in HMSNVI disease, **36**:4
in redundant genes, **36**:145–**36**:146
telomeres and, **30**:191–**30**:192, **30**:194, **30**:216
Optic gliomas, with neurofibromatosis type 1, **36**:104
Optic lobe, differentiation, *Drosophila*
absence in *zen_* mutants, **27**:281, **27**:285, **27**:317
zen target genes and, **27**:303
optomotor-blind (omb) mutant
Drosophila melanogaster, **31**:141–142
Orbital flight, effects on irradiated braconid wasps
hatchability and, **25**:157–**25**:158
simulation experiments
embryonic death induction, **25**:159–**25**:160
treatment selection, **25**:158–**25**:159
sperm damage and, **25**:150–**25**:151
xanthine dehydrogenase and, **25**:141–**25**:142
Orcein, RNA synthesis inhibition, **39**:75
ORF, *see* Introns, open reading frames
Orfs, *see* Open reading frames
Organelles
gene transmission, **23**:242–**23**:246
transfer, protoplasts and, **20**:163–**20**:166
Organizer
induction, **31**:31–33
Xenopus laevis
genes, table, **31**:34–35
secreted proteins, **31**:41–43
transcription factors, **31**:36–40
Organogenesis, somaclonal variation and, **30**:43–**30**:44
Organophosphate, mosquitoes and, **30**:147–**30**:150
orientation disruptor (ord) mutant
Drosophila melanogaster, **31**:120–121
Ornithine-δ-aminotransferase, mutation on gene for, **36**:98
Orthologous gene loci, evolutionary genetics of fish and, **29**:133
Orthopteran order
polyteny occurrence, **34**:62–63
Osmoregulation evolutionary genetics of fish and, **29**:190–**29**:196, **29**:198
Osteosarcoma, pRb aberrations in, **36**:54

otu gene, polytene chromosome organization, **39**:33
Otx genes, brain patterning role, rostrocaudal axis, **38**:3–7
Outcrossing, *Mu* elements of *Zea mays* and, **30**:85–**30**:89, **30**:99, **30**:114–**30**:115
Ovarian cancer
BRC2 gene mutations in, **36**:90
chromosomal linkages of, **36**:95
modified-gene role in, **36**:104
tumor suppressor gene role in, **36**:49, **36**:86, **36**:87, **36**:95, **36**:96
Ovarian diapause, *Drosophila* biological rhythm genetics, **38**:158–159
Ovaries
interaction with germinating pollen, *Petunia* hybrids, **26**:31
nurse cells
chromatid synapsis variation, **34**:153–154
homologous chromosomes, **34**:169
mutations, **34**:56–57
ovarian tumors, **34**:58–59
polyploidy, **34**:51–52
polyteny occurrence, **34**:46–62
tumors, *Drosophila*, **34**:58–59
Ovarioles, postembryonic development, braconid wasps, **25**:125–**25**:126
Overview, **34**:1–20
historical perspective, **34**:2–11
Balbiani nuclei, **34**:5
cell cycle, **34**:9
chromosomes
inheritance theory, **34**:7
origin, **34**:9
size, **34**:9
genetic maps, **34**:7, **34**:10
spireme nuclei, **34**:5–9
research problems, **34**:11–20
Balbiani ring role, **34**:15–16
band number estimation, **34**:12–14
chromosome morphology, **34**:16–17
cloning methods, **34**:20
cytogenetic maps, **34**:11–12
gene mapping, **34**:11–12
heterochromatin role, **34**:18–19
interband activity, **34**:12, **34**:16
molecular biology studies, **34**:19
puff activity, **34**:15–16
Oxatocin, evolutionary genetics of fish and, **29**:197

Oxidation, *Neurospora crassa* and, 29:25–29:28
Oxidative phosphorylation hypothesis, *minute*
  genes, 38:79–81
Oxidative stress
  induction, 28:8–28:9
  protection by SOD and CAT, 28:9
  in plants, 28:20–28:30, 28:34–28:35
Oxidization, nitrate reductase and, 30:2–30:3
Oxygen, *see also* Superoxide dismutases
  active species
    biological sources, 28:4–28:6,
      28:44–28:45
    cytotoxicity
      biological consequences, 28:5–28:6,
        28:46–28:47
      radical basis, 28:4–28:7, 28:44–28:46
    environmental stress induction, *see*
      Oxidative stress
  braconid wasp protection from X rays,
    25:155
  consumption during development, *Drosophila*,
    28:52
  defense systems
    in *Drosophila*, 28:48–28:64
    in maize, 28:12–28:33
    overview, 28:6–28:8, 28:47–28:48
  deprivation, telomeres and, 30:226
  in Earth atmosphere, 28:3
  evolutionary genetics of fish and,
    29:196–29:197, 29:200
  high concentration, SOD induction in
    bacteria and yeast, 26:81
  intracellular concentration, maize leaves,
    28:9–28:10
  nitrate reductase and, 30:3
  SOD isozyme responses to, maize,
    28:26–28:27
  toxicity
    bacteriostatic effects, 26:77–26:78
    superoxide radical production and,
      26:65–26:66, 26:77, *see also*
      Superoxide anion radical
Oxytetracycline, puff activity effects, 39:261
Oxytricha, telomeres and, 30:187,
  30:198–30:199, 30:202, 30:213, 30:227
Ozone
  depletion in stratosphere, NUV excess and,
    26:100, 26:134
  effects on SOD and CAT, plants, 28:20
  tolerance, in pollen and sporophyte, 26:15

P. deltoides, pollen as mentor for *P. alba*, 26:30,
  26:31, 26:46
P. ovalis, iron-containing SOC, 26:70, 26:71
PAB1, yeast ribosomes and, 29:102
Pactamycine, puff activity effects, 39:261
Paired-box genes
  in neoplasia
    embryonic development role,
      33:256–259
    expression
      brain cancers, 33:260–263
      primary human tumors, 33:260
      rhabdomyosarcoma, 33:264–265
      Wilms' tumor, 33:263–264
    future research directions, 33:269–270
    oncogene classification, 33:259
    overview, 33:255–256
    tumorigenesis, *in vivo* model, 33:259–260
Paired domain transcription factors
  during neural plate induction *Xenopus laevis*,
    31:65
Pairing
  B chromosome homology, 37:299–300
  dividing cell heterochromatin morphology,
    37:24–28
    interphase chromocenter formation, 37:8,
      37:24–25
    meiosis, 37:28
    mitosis, 37:26–28
  ectopic strands
    characteristics, 37:134
    intercalary heterochromatin identification,
      37:166–193
    DNA underreplication, 37:189–193
    formation mechanisms, 37:183–184
    nucleolar contacts, 37:166,
      37:178–179
    nucleoprotein association, 37:184–185
    polytene chromosomes, 37:171–176
    properties, 37:168–170, 37:180–182
    telomeric heterochromatin, 37:266–279
    characterization, 37:268–275
    properties, 37:267, 37:276–279
  intercalary heterochromatin identification
    ectopic pairing, 37:166–193
    somatic pairing, 37:206–207
Pair-rule genes
  Drosophila, *see also Fushi tarazu; other specific*
    genes
    effects on *Dfd* expression, 27:381–27:384

Pair-rule genes (*continued*)
    gap gene effects on expression
        in maternal-effect mutations,
            27:262–27:265
        bcd osk embryos, 27:264–27:265
        bcd osk tsl embryos, 27:263–27:264
        stau exu embryos, 27:265,
            27:267–27:268
        model, 27:266
        in wild type, 27:261–27:262, 27:263
    positional function along AP axis, 27:375,
        27:376
    patterns
        gene interactions, 31:12–14
        transition from gap genes, 31:11–12
PAL, see Phenylalanine ammonia-lyase
Paleogenome, evolutionary genetics of fish and,
    29:142–29:143
Palindromes, *Neurospora crassa* and, 29:27
Pancreas, evolutionary genetics of fish and,
    29:188–29:189
Pancreatic cancer
    DCC gene implication in, 36:78
    DPC4 gene implication in, 36:91
    tumor suppressor gene mutations in, 36:96
pan gu (pgu) mutant
    Drosophila melanogaster, 31:113–114
Papovaviruses, HSP induction in animal cells,
    24:18–24:19
Paraamino benzoic acid, puff activity effects,
    39:261
Paracetamol, heat-shock puff induction, 39:350
Paracoccus dinitrificans, copper-zinc-containing
    SOD, 26:67
parallel sister chromatids (pasc) gene
    Drosophila melanogaster, 31:121
Paramecium, telomeres and, 30:227–30:228
Paramecium tetraurelia
    asexual phase, DNA damage during,
        24:359–24:360
    sexual phase, DNA repair during,
        24:359–24:360
Paraquat
    copper-zinc-containing SOD biosynthesis
        induction, *S. cerevisiae*, 26:82
    endonuclease IV induction, 26:124
    enzyme stimulation, maize
        CAT activity, 28:23–28:25
        SOD activity, 28:23–28:26
    manganese-containing SOD biosynthesis
        induction

    in *E. coli*, 26:85
    in *S. cerevisiae*, 26:82
    oxidative stress induction, 28:9, 28:23
    superoxide dismutases and, 30:259, 30:273,
        30:276, 30:289, 30:291, 30:294
Parascaris univalens, chromatin diminution,
    37:78–81
Parasites
    morphology change induction
        gregarines, 34:285–286
        microsporidia, 34:281–284
        mosquitoes and, 30:155, 30:172
Parental effects
    chromatin compaction, 37:408–409
    gene expression modification, 37:339,
        37:341–342
Paromomycin, HSP induction, yeast, 28:254
Parsley, defense response genes
    4CL, 28:195
    PAL, 28:194
Parthenogenesis
    apomixis, 24:350
    cost of shifting from outcrossing to,
        24:350–24:351
    endomitosis, 24:350
    survivorship, 24:348
PAS reaction, salivary secretion detection,
    39:175–177, 39:181
Pathogenesis-related proteins
    characterization, 28:10, 28:179–28:180
    PR-1
        induction by TMV and cytokinins, 28:190,
            28:192
        structure, homologies, 28:200
        in transgenic tobacco, 28:215
Pathogens, mosquitoes and, 30:123–30:125,
    30:159, 30:171–30:172
Pathology
    morphology change
        ecological factor effects, 34:299–305
        infections, 34:280–291
            gregarine parasites, 34:285–286
            microsporidia, 34:281–284
            viruses, 34:286–289
        long-term cell incubation
            in vitro incubation, 34:297–299
            in vivo incubation, 34:291–297
        melanotic pseudotumors, 34:306–307,
            34:311
        mutation effects, 34:305–311
Pathotoxin tolerance, MGS and, 26:18–26:19

Pax-6 gene
Xenopus laevis, 31:62, 31:65
Pax genes
eye anlage patterning, 38:21–22
isthmic region development, 38:7–8
PDGA, p21 induction by, 36:62
Pea
Fusarium-infected, mRNA induction, 28:180–28:181
genes coding for seed storage proteins of, 22:124–22:125
HSP, in chloroplasts, 28:243
nitrate reductase and, 30:13
photosynthetic genes, expression
iron deficiency and, 28:151–28:152
rbcL, photoregulation, 28:137
rbcS, photoregulation, 28:140–28:142
peach+ locus, position effect, 37:366–367
Pearl millet, somaclonal variation and, 30:44, 30:47
pebble gene
Drosophila melanogaster, 31:110
Pedigree analysis
diabetes-susceptibility gene identification, 32:59
hemophilia, 32:111–112
P-element-mediated transformation
banding pattern variation induction, 39:28–32, 39:90–94
Sgs gene puff induction, 39:306
P elements
Drosophila melanogaster
transcript splicing, 31:254–257
mapping of cis-regulatory regions, 31:255
trans-acting factors, 31:256–257
Drosophila transposable elements and
chromosomes, 29:276–29:277
foldback elements, 29:284, 29:286
gene expression, 29:269–29:274
mariner, 29:279
mechanism, 29:262–29:269
retrotransposons, 29:238–29:239, 29:252
structure, 29:260–29:262
gene expression modification, mutagenesis, 37:346–347
mosquitoes and, 30:162, 30:164–30:165, 30:172
position effect, 37:308–309, 37:311
telomeres and, 30:203, 30:232
zeste in Drosophila melanogaster and, 29:328

Pennisetum glaucum, somaclonal variation and, 30:47
pep3 gene, band organization, 39:144
Peptides
Drosophila transposable elements and, 29:285
evolutionary genetics of fish and, 29:178, 29:196–29:200
zeste in Drosophila melanogaster and, 29:336
per genes, Neurospora crassa and, 29:46
Period gene
chronogenetics regulation
arrhythmic phenotypes, 38:149–157
brain-behavioral studies, 38:163–167
clock-resetting signals, 38:171–172
courtship song cycle, 38:159–160
egg-to-adult development, 38:161
environmental synchronization, 38:142–145
expression, 38:163–168, 38:172–173
fundamentals, 38:135–142
long-period phenotypes, 38:146–148
non-temporal phenotypes, 38:161–163
ovarian diapause, 38:158–159
overview, 38:135–136, 38:173
short-period phenotypes, 38:148–149
visual rhythms, 38:157–158
Drosophila melanogaster
behavioral effects, 31:161–162
molecular biology, 31:162–166
role in song patterning, 31:154–155
sequence similarities with arnt, Ahr, and sim, 31:167–169
threonine–glycine repeats, 31:162–166
transcript localization, 31:164–166
Peripheral myelin protein 22
distribution and structure of, 36:26–36:29, 36:30
gene
as causal gene for CMT1A disease, 36:9–36:11, 36:21
deletion in HNPP disease, 36:13–36:14
duplication of, 36:10, 36:12
genotypical alterations in, 36:28–36:29
mutation screening for, 36:35
null mutation in, 36:26–36:27
point mutation of, 36:10–36:11
12/HNK-1 epitope in, 36:23
implication in CMT1A, 36:10–36:11, 36:21, 36:22
as major myelin protein, 36:22, 36:23, 36:26
mutation effects on, 36:28

Peripheral myelin protein 22 *(continued)*
possible role in cell growth, **36:**28
role in peripheral neuropathies, **36:**33–**36:**34
Peripheral myelin protein zero
distribution in myelin sheath, **36:**31
functional domains of, **36:**23, **36:**24
gene
as causal gene for CMT1B disease, **36:**19,
36:21, **36:**22
mouse model with disruption in,
36:23–**36:**24, **36:**33–**36:**34
mutation screening on, **36:**35
mutations in, **36:**19, **36:**21, **36:**26
overexpression of, **36:**27
genotypic/phenotypic correlation in mice and
humans, **36:**25–**36:**26
12/HNK-1 epitope of, **36:**23, **36:**27
mutation effects on, **36:**25, **36:**26
role in myelin formation, **36:**25, **36:**28
role in peripheral neuropathies, **36:**33–**36:**34
role in *shiverer* mouse, **36:**23
structural features of, **36:**22–**36:**26
Peripheral nervous system
Cx32 gene mutation expression in,
36:32–**36:**33
Drosophila
defects in AS-C mutants, **27:**434–**27:**436
development, **27:**408–**27:**409
daughterless gene role, **27:**440, **27:**446
proteins expressed in, **36:**23
Peripheral neuropathies, *See also* CMT diseases;
HNPP disease
genetic loci of, **36:**21
molecular genetics of, **36:**1–**36:**44
Peroneal muscular atrophy, *See also* CMT disease
as hereditary disease, **36:**2
Peroxisomes, superoxide dismutases and,
30:260, **30:**269
molecular genetics, **30:**280, **30:**285, **30:**287
physiology of mutants, **30:**288,
30:296–**30:**297
PER protein
Drosophila melanogaster
circadian cycling, **31:**166–167
expression, **31:**164–166
transcript localization, **31:**164–166
Pes cavus foot deformity, in CMT disease, **36:**3,
36:7
Petites, amplified circular molecules of mtDNA
in, **22:**47–**22:**52

Petunia
defense response genes, structure
CHI, **28:**196–**28:**197
CHS, **28:**195–**28:**196
HSP70 genes, organization, **28:**238
somaclonal variation and, **30:**57
Petunia hybrida and hybrids
ozone tolerance in pollen and sporophyte,
26:15
pollen
-ovary interaction, **26:**31
selection, effect on sporophytic growth,
26:3
P family of transposable elements, disruption
effects on, **36:**143–**36:**144
PFGE, duplication testing by, **36:**34
6PGD, *see* 6-Phosphogluconate dehydrogenase
PGK1, mutations of genes encoding, **36:**96
pH
isolated chromosome studies, **34:**318–320
Phagocytes, mosquitoes and, **30:**154, **30:**158
Phenocopies, heat-induced, *Drosophila*
branched hair, **28:**283–**28:**284
prevention by preshock, **28:**284–**28:**285
in recessive mutant heterozygotes, **28:**285
Phenol oxidase
cuticular, from *D. virilis*, **24:**186–**24:**187
Drosophila
in body color mutations, **24:**194–**24:**195
in crystal cell-affecting mutations,
24:191–**24:**193
Bc (*Black cells*), **24:**192
lz (*lozenge*), **24:**192–**24:**193
during development, **24:**186
loci with effects on, **24:**189–**24:**191,
24:193–**24:**194
PPF effects, **24:**195–**24:**196
properties, **24:**185–**24:**186
structural loci coding for, **24:**187–**24:**189
types in insects, **24:**183–**24:**185
Phenotype
development, position effect, **37:**312–316
Drosophila transposable elements and,
29:230–**29:**231
cis-acting effects of retrotransposons,
29:241, **29:**243–**29:**249,
29:251–**29:**257
foldback elements, **29:**287–**29:**288
hobo, **29:**278
mariner, **29:**279–**29:**280

P elements, 29:262–29:263,
  29:268–29:274
retrotransposons, 29:235–29:236
trans-acting effects of retrotransposons,
  29:257–29:258, 29:260
mosquitoes and, 30:139, 30:156, 30:169
Mu elements of Zea mays and, 30:78, 30:80,
  30:84, 30:90
applications, 30:113–30:114
gene expression, 30:108–30:109
mutation effects on, 36:138
Neurospora crassa and, 29:9, 29:19,
  29:31–29:32, 29:45
nitrate reductase and, 30:15–30:17,
  30:19–30:20, 30:27
somaclonal variation and, 30:42–30:44,
  30:46
genetic consequences, 30:50, 30:53,
  30:55, 30:57, 30:59–30:62
unusual genetic behavior, 30:63–30:64
superoxide dismutases and, 30:257, 30:263,
  30:269
molecular genetics, 30:273, 30:281,
  30:288
physiology of mutants, 30:288–30:289,
  30:294, 30:296, 30:301–30:305,
  30:308
telomeres and, 30:207–30:208, 30:219
yeast ribosomes and
assembly, 29:98
genetic analysis, 29:98, 29:100–29:101
nucleolus, 29:89–29:90
ribosomal protein genes, 29:72, 29:74
ribosomal proteins, 29:70–29:71
zeste in Drosophila melanogaster and
chromatin packaging, 29:339–29:341
discovery, 29:303–29:305
function, 29:327–29:329
molecular biology, 29:316
protein, 29:333, 29:337
Phenylalanine ammonia-lyase
cinnamic acid production and, 28:189
induction by infection/elicitor,
  28:188–28:189
timing, 28:190–28:191
isozymes, 28:177
in phytoalexin biosynthesis, 28:176
Phenylalanine hydroxylase, Drosophila
during development, 24:137
Punch-coded GTP CH and, 24:137–24:138

Phenylketonuria, 32:199–254
clinical aspects, 32:203–204
dietary therapy, 32:202, 32:244–245
discovery, 32:199–200
gene therapy, 32:244–253
adenoviral vectors, 32:248–251
DNA/protein complexes, 32:251–253
retroviral vectors, 32:246–248
molecular genetics, 32:208–228
expression analysis, 32:221–225
extended haplotypes, 32:209–210
genotype/phenotype correlations,
  32:225–228
haplotype analysis, 32:210–211
haplotype/phenotype correlations, 32:214
phenylalanine hydroxylation gene
  mutations, 32:214–220
deletion, 32:214
distribution, 32:217–220
genotype heterogeneity, 32:214–215
molecular lesions, 32:215–217
restriction fragment length polymorphism
  haplotypes, 32:208–209
restriction fragment length polymorphism
  haplotypes
mutant chromosomes, 32:211–214
normal chromosomes, 32:211–214
phenylalanine hydroxylation locus,
  32:208–209
newborn screening, 32:203
phenylalanine hydroxylation, 32:200–202,
  32:204–208
cDNA cloning, 32:204–205
chromosomal location, 32:206
encoding gene, 32:205–206
gene structure, 32:206–207
pterin-dependent hydroxylase homologs,
  32:207–208
population genetics, 32:228–244
Asian populations, 32:240–243
European populations, 32:233–240
frequency, 32:228–229
heterozygote selection, 32:243–244
Middle Eastern populations, 32:233–240
mutation/haplotype association,
  32:229–233
Pheochromocytomas, in von Hippel-Lindau
  disease, 36:84
Pheromone response element, in cell-specific
  genes, yeast, 27:53–27:54

Pheromones
and receptor transcription factor, yeast
binding to P box of UAS, 27:54–27:56
in a-specific genes, 27:46–27:49
repression by MATα2, 27:47–27:48
in α-specific genes, facilitation by
MATα1, 27:42–27:46
MCM1 gene-encoded, 27:49–27:50
yeast
cell-specific gene transcription induction,
27:53–27:54
role in mating between a and α cells,
27:34–27:47
Phosphate, Neurospora crassa and, 29:39–29:41
6-Phosphate dehydrogenase, transcription
dosage compensation, 39:77, 39:81
Phosphoglucomutase, evolutionary genetics of
fish and, 29:174
Phosphoglucomutase, rainbow trout
developmental control by regulatory genes,
24:111
6-Phosphogluconate dehydrogenase, X-linked,
Drosophila
in autosomal male-specific lethal mutations,
24:400
fast and slow variants in heterozygous female,
24:376–24:377
in metafemales, 24:386
in metamales, 24:385
in triploid females, 24:382
in triploid intersexes, 24:382–24:383
X-chromosome segment addition and,
24:386–24:387
X-linked, gene dosage effect, 24:373
Phospholipase (A2s), Mom-1 gene control of,
36:76
Phosphorus, Neurospora crassa and, 29:38
Phosphorylation
Neurospora crassa and, 29:25–29:28
yeast ribosomes and, 29:69, 29:71,
29:87–29:89
Phosphorylation hypothesis, minute genes,
38:79–81
Phosvitin, RNA synthesis inhibition, 39:75
Photobacterium leiognathi
copper-zinc-containing SOD isolation, 26:67
gene for CuZnSOD, cloning and sequencing,
26:79
iron-containing SOD, amino acid sequences,
26:70

Photosynthesis, nitrate reductase and,
30:30–30:31
Photosynthetic genes, expression
circadian rhythm, 28:147–28:150
cytotoxins and, 28:152–28:153
developmental regulation, 28:153–28:154
nutrition and, 28:149, 28:151–28:152
photoregulation, 28:134–28:146
in nucleus, 28:138–28:146
in plastids, 28:135–28:138
plastid factors and, 28:146–28:147
regulatory mechanisms, 28:154–28:157
Photosystem II, 32-kDa protein (psbA)
developmental regulation, fruits, 28:153
photoregulation, seedlings, 28:135–28:137
Phototransduction pathways
future research directions, 35:25–28
genetic analysis, 35:15–17
Phryne cincta, intercalary α-heterochromatin,
37:135–137
Physarum, telomeres and, 30:196, 30:199,
30:214
Physiology, developmental role, 34:356–358
Phytanic acid excess, in HMSNIV disease, 36:4
Phytoalexins
biosynthesis, pathway, 28:175–28:177
pathogen-induced accumulation,
28:167–28:168
Phytochrome
in photosynthetic gene regulation, 28:134,
28:135
cab mRNA and, 28:144–28:145
rbcS mRNA and, 28:139–28:140
plant transcription regulation, 35:6–9
Phytophthera, chromosome rearrangements in,
36:245
Phytophtora megasperma, in soybean
elicitor, binding to plant receptor, 28:202,
28:203
induction of CHS and PAL, 28:188, 28:189
Phytotoxin tolerance, in in vitro germinating
pollen and sporophyte tissues, 26:15
Pig1 gene
band organization, 39:153
puff development, 39:300–301
Pigment changes, screening and, 20:42–20:43
Pigment-producing factor (PPF), Drosophila
isolation and properties, 24:195
melanin formation induction in vivo, 24:195
phenol oxidase and, 24:196

tyrosinase activity and, **24:**195
Pilocarpine, puff activity effects, **39:**261
Pintallavis gene
  Xenopus laevis, **31:**34, **31:**38–39
Pioneer pollen effect, style role, apple, **26:**31
Pistil, effects on pollen behavior, **26:**47–**26:**48,
  see also Stigma; Style
Pisum sativum
  nitrate reductase and, **30:**13–**30:**14, **30:**18
  telomeres and, **30:**225
Pituitary gland
  anterior, evolutionary genetics of fish and,
    29:190–**29:**196
  evolutionary genetics of fish and,
    29:190–**29:**192, **29:**195–**29:**196,
    29:198, **29:**200
Placental lactogen, evolutionary genetics of fish
  and, **29:**192, **29:**194–**29:**195
Plant-pathogen interactions, *see also* Resistance,
  pathogen-induced
  genes involved, *see also* Defense response genes
    classes, **28:**169–**28:**170
    methods of definition
      avirulent genes in pathogen,
        28:170–**28:**173
      resistance genes in host, **28:**171,
        28:174–**28:**175
  hypersensitive response, phytoalexins and,
    28:167–**28:**168
  resistance, race-specific, **28:**168–**28:**169
  reviews, **28:**166
Plants
  cells
    polytene chromosome occurrence
      organization, **34:**110–125
      polyploidy, **34:**107–110
  mating systems, **23:**255–**23:**259
    genetic modifications, **23:**258–**23:**259
    mixed model modification, **23:**257–**23:**258
    multilocus data, **23:**255–**23:**257
  tissue
    culture and haploidy, **20:**138–**20:**139
    nutritional requirements for
      androgenesis, **20:**145–**20:**146
    origin of androgenetic haploids,
      20:139–**20:**145
    physiology of androgenesis,
      20:146–**20:**148
    uses of androgenetic plants,
      20:148–**20:**151

cultures
  germ plasm preservation and,
    20:173–**20:**175
  nitrogen fixation and, **20:**168–**20:**173
  direct transformation by exogenous DNA,
    20:166–**20:**168
  protoplasts in genetics and breeding,
    20:151–**20:**152
  fusion of protoplasts and somatic
    hybridization, **20:**155–**20:**163
  isolation and culture of protoplasts,
    20:152–**20:**155
  protoplasts as tools for the transfer of
    cell organelles or microorganisms,
    20:163–**20:**166
  rapid clonal propagation, **20:**128–**20:**138
transcription regulation, circadian clock
  pathways, **35:**1–28
  CAB gene characteristics, **35:**2–6
  cis- and *trans*-acting element requirements,
    35:20–25
  cyanobacteria model, **35:**17–20
  future research directions, **35:**25–28
  overview, **35:**1–2
  photoreceptors, **35:**6–11
    blue-light receptors, **35:**9–11
    phytochrome, **35:**6–9
  phototransduction pathway analysis,
    35:15–17
  signal transduction intermediate
    identification, **35:**11–14
Plasma membrane
  cold acclimation effects, **28:**101–**28:**104
  lipid composition and, **28:**103–**28:**104
  Neurospora crassa and, **29:**38, **29:**40
Plasmids, **33:**2–4, **33:**16S ribosomal RNA
  detection
  Drosophila transposable elements and, **29:**263
  hybrid
    for fungal transformation, preparation,
      23:85–**23:**86
    between fungi and *E. coli*
      characteristics, **23:**148–**23:**151
      expression in bacteria and fungi,
        23:138–**23:**139
  molecular cloning, **23:**81–**23:**84
    in fungi, **23:**84–**23:**85
  mosquitoes and, **30:**151–**30:**152, **30:**164,
    30:166
  Neurospora crassa and, **29:**4, **29:**46–**29:**47

Plasmids (continued)
  genetic material, 29:12–29:13
  genetic transfer, 29:9, 29:11–29:12
  mitochondria, 29:33–29:35
  superoxide dismutases and, 30:272, 30:301,
    30:308
  telomeres and
    formation, 30:226
    function, 30:207, 30:213, 30:219–30:220
    structure, 30:191, 30:200
  tRNA gene structure and, 21:134–21:140
  tumor-inducing and root-in inducing
    detection and isolation in *Agrobacterium*
      species, 22:218–22:219
    functions determined by Ti- and
      Ri-plasmids, 22:221–22:225
    role of plasmids, 22:219–22:221
  yeast ribosomes and, 29:80, 29:86, 29:99
  zeste in *Drosophila melanogaster* and, 29:323
Plasmodium
  mosquitoes and, 30:123, 30:156–30:157
  telomeres and, 30:190, 30:196, 30:217,
    30:230
Plastidic factor, nitrate reductase and, 30:30
Plastids
  development, photosynthetic gene expression
    and, 28:146–28:147
  mRNA, light effect during development,
    28:135–28:137
  transformed, *Chlamydomonas*, 28:138
Platypoecilus maculatus, evolutionary genetics of
    fish and, 29:171
Pleiotropy, evolutionary background of,
    36:138–36:139
Pleuronectes vetulus, evolutionary genetics of fish
    and, 29:170
Plexiform neurofibromas, with
    neurofibromatosis type 1, 36:104
Ploidy, somaclonal variation and, 30:49
Plutonium-239, braconid wasp feeding effects,
    25:162
plutonium (*plu*) mutant
  Drosophila melanogaster, 31:113–114
pma-1, *Neurospora crassa* and, 29:38
PML protein
  aberrant subcellular localization of,
    36:104–36:105
  regulation of, 36:99
PML tumor suppressor gene, translocations
  affecting, 36:93

PMS1 and PMS2 proteins
  DNA repair function of, 36:77
  as tumor suppressor gene products, 36:50
PMS1 and *PMS2* tumor suppressor genes
  characteristics of, 36:50
  implication in colon cancer, 36:76, 36:77,
    36:95
  implication in lymphomas and sarcomas,
    36:77
PNS, *see* Peripheral nervous system
Pocket, of pRb protein, as site of oncoprotein
    binding, 36:56
Podophyllotoxin, heat-shock puff induction,
    39:350
Podospora, senescent cultures, heterogeneity of
    mtDNA in, 22:52–22:53
Podospora anserina
  chromosome translocations in, 36:265,
    36:282–36:283
  mei mutants
    chromosome stickiness, 26:164
    meiosis arrest after pachytene, 26:163
  mitochondrial genome
    introns, 25:198
    mapping using mutants, 25:203–25:204
    rearrangement during senescence,
      25:241–25:244
    cytochrome *aa₃* decrease and, 25:242
    longevity and, 25:242
    senDNA
      circular, origin, 25:242
      plasmid-like, sequencing,
        25:243–25:244
    rnl gene with two introns, 25:208
  plasmid combined with those from *E. coli*
    characteristics, 23:151
    replication in fungi and bacteria, 23:139
    transformation
      with recombinant plasmids, 23:153–23:154
Poeciliopsis, evolutionary genetics of fish and,
    29:144, 29:161, 29:166
pogo, *Neurospora crassa* and, 29:46
poky, *Neurospora crassa* and, 29:29–29:31
pol, *Drosophila* transposable elements and,
    29:231–29:234, 29:248
Polarity
  polytene chromosomes, 34:335–340
Pollen, *see also specific plants*
  competition in natural populations
    crop plants, 26:35–26:36

intensifying mechanisms, **26:**42
wild species, **26:**32–**26:**35, **26:**48
gametophytic gene expression
distorted phenotype segregation in
mutants, **26:**12–**26:**13
gametophytic factors and, **26:**13–**26:**14
overlap with sporophytic genes, **26:**22,
26:25–**26:**27, *see also* Gametophytic-
sporophytic genetic overlap
postmeiotic, **26:**14
timing during development, **26:**23–**26:**25
gene transfer, practical application,
26:45–**26:**46
genome, comparison with that of sporophyte,
26:2
interaction with pistil, **26:**27–**26:**32
isozyme analysis, **26:**20–**26:**22
mentor, *see* Mentor pollen
mRNA analysis, **26:**22–**26:**23
ontogeny
developmental stages, **26:**4–**26:**6
exine pattern, sporophyte control,
26:7–**26:**8, **26:**10–**26:**11, **26:**47
meiocyte interconnections, *Orchidaceae*,
26:6–**26:**7
microspore isolation in callose, **26:**7
pioneer, *see* Pioneer pollen
properties during germination, correlation
with those of sporophyte, **26:**15
selection, *see also* Male gametophytic selection
application in breeding, **26:**43–**26:**44
effects on sporophyte, **26:**3
evolutionary significance, **26:**36–**26:**43
angiosperm evolutionary rise and,
26:41–**26:**43
effectiveness, **26:**38–**26:**39
genetic load and, **26:**40–**26:**41
large population size and, **26:**37–**26:**38,
26:41
experimental, **26:**16–**26:**20
Pollen tube
chemotropism *in vitro* and *in vivo*, **26:**32
growth rate
correlation with kernel and seedling
weight, maize, **26:**15
difference between X and Y chromosome-
bearers, *Silene alba*, **26:**3
effect on sporophytic qualities, maize, **26:**3
in natural populations, **26:**34–**26:**35
variability, inbreeding effect, maize, **26:**14

in vitro, correlation with pollen size, maize,
26:10
polo kinase
role in cell cycle
Drosophila melanogaster, **31:**93–94, **31:**94
Polyacrylamide gel electrophoresis
secretory protein detection, **39:**180
use in duplication and deletion testing, **36:**35
Polyadenylation
Mu elements of *Zea mays* and, **30:**111–**30:**112
role in alternative splicing, **31:**238–241
Polyamines, mosquitoes and, **30:**153
Polycomb group genes, *zeste* in *Drosophila
melanogaster* and, **29:**340–**29:**342
Polyethylene glycol (PEG), *Neurospora crassa*
and, **29:**10, **29:**48
Polygenic disease, mouse models, **35:**177–180
Polyglutamine proteins, autosomal dominant
progressive ataxias association, **38:**39–40
Polylysines, RNA synthesis inhibition, **39:**75
Polymerase chain reaction, *see also* Interspersed
repetitive sequence-polymerase chain
reaction
carbonic anhydrases and, **30:**348
Drosophila transposable elements and, **29:**280
evolutionary genetics of fish and,
29:128–**29:**131
hemophilia detection, **32:**104–105,
32:117–118, **32:**122–123
mosquitoes and, **30:**125, **30:**154, **30:**166
genetic differentiation, **30:**132, **30:**136
genome characterization, **30:**145, **30:**147
Mu elements of *Zea mays* and, **30:**100, **30:**102
Neurospora crassa and, **29:**33
nitrate reductase and, **30:**23
phenylalanine hydroxylase gene haplotype
detection, **32:**209–210
somaclonal variation and, **30:**58
superoxide dismutases and, **30:**273
telomere subterminal sequence isolation,
32:286
Polymorphism, *see also* Restriction fragment
length polymorphism
carbonic anhydrases and, **30:**334, **30:**336,
30:343, **30:**346–**30:**348
DNA, *see specific polymorphism*
evolutionary genetics of fish and, **29:**144,
29:189
detection of variation, **29:**128, **29:**130
environmental change, **29:**163–**29:**165

Polymorphism (continued)
hypotheses, 32:88
mosquitoes and
genetic differentiation, 30:129,
30:131–30:132
genetic transformation, 30:166
genome characterization, 30:147
physiology, 30:153, 30:156
telomeres and, 30:191, 30:195–30:198,
30:218
zeste in Drosophila melanogaster and, 29:313
Polypeptides
Drosophila transposable elements and, 29:237,
29:265, 29:269
evolutionary genetics of fish and
endocrine system, 29:191, 29:194–29:196
immune system, 29:181, 29:183–29:184
multigene families, 29:148, 29:151
mosquitoes and, 30:158–30:159
Neurospora crassa and, 29:17, 29:43
nitrate reductase and, 30:6, 30:8
superoxide dismutases and, 30:268–30:269,
30:273, 30:276
telomeres and, 30:191, 30:216
yeast ribosomes and, 29:88
zeste in Drosophila melanogaster and, 29:316,
29:328, 29:330, 29:336
Polyploidization, of genes, 36:149
Polyploidy
Drosophila, 34:32, 34:37
evolutionary genetics of fish and,
29:136–29:137, 29:146–29:147
homologous chromosomes, 34:164–165
insect oenocytes, 34:62–63
nurse cells, 34:51–52
plant cells, 34:107–110
polyteny morphology, 34:125–127
somaclonal variation and, 30:43, 30:48,
30:60–30:61
trophoblast cells, 34:99–101
Polypyrimidines, intercalary heterochromatin
repetitive sequences, 37:219
Polypyrimidine tract binding protein, 31:222
associated splicing factor, 31:223
Polytene chromosomes
Balbiani rings
molecular organization, 39:397–407
morphology, 39:387–397
bands, see Chromomeres
centromeric heterochromatin, 37:89–133
cytogenetics, 37:124–133

morphology, 37:89–98
quantity variations, 37:109–124
structural components, 37:98–109
DNA, 37:98–105
proteins, 37:105–106
structural changes, 37:106–109
DNA puffs, see Puffs
Drosophila, 36:140
heterochromatinized region properties,
37:436
historical perspectives, 39:9–20
interbands
function, 39:12–17
genetic organization, 39:87–94
molecular organization, 39:87–94
overview, 39:84–87
intercalary heterochromatin identification,
ectopic contacts, 37:171–176
nucleoli
molecular organization, 39:418–425
morphology, 39:407–418
ribosomal RNA gene expression,
39:418–425
organization
banding pattern constancy and variability,
39:20–40
chromomere definition, 39:3–9
chromomeric concept development,
39:9–20
overview, 39:1–3
Q^+-band occurrence, 37:147–148
telomeric heterochromatin
DNA sequence locations, 37:252–255
ectopic pairing characterization,
37:266–276
terminal deletion occurrence, 37:243–244
transcription, see Transcription
zeste in Drosophila melanogaster and,
29:316–29:318, 29:326
Polyteny evolutionary genetics of fish and,
29:136–29:137
Polyteny occurrence, see Occurrence
Pompon-like chromosomes
morphology, 34:137–150
temperature effects, 34:154–157
Population genetics, 23:235–23:261
braconid wasps, natural selection,
25:143–25:146
gene frequency fluctuation,
25:144–25:145
intraspecific competition, 25:145–25:146

long- and short-winged substrain
production, **25**:144
DNA sequence variation, **23**:236–**23**:246
Drosophila melanogaster, *Adh* alleles
biochemical model, ADH allozymes,
25:80–**25**:81
DNA studies
evidence of large-scale migration, **25**:85
restriction mapping, **25**:84–**25**:85
sequencing, **25**:85–**25**:86
environmental factors
climatic conditions and alcohol, **25**:79
short- and long-term selection
experiments, **25**:80
geographical pattern, latitude and,
25:77–**25**:78
natural selection
fitness estimates, **25**:82–**25**:84
heterozygote advantage, **25**:81–**25**:83
evolutionary genetics of fish and,
29:124–**29**:130, **29**:165, **29**:189
Gaucher disease, **32**:24–27
mosquitoes and, **30**:125, **30**:173
phenylketonuria, **32**:228–244
Asian populations, **32**:240–243
European populations, **32**:233–240
frequency, **32**:228–229
heterozygote selection, **32**:243–244
Middle Eastern populations, **32**:233–240
mutation/haplotype association,
32:229–233
quantitation, models, **23**:250–**23**:255
transposon dynamics, **23**:246–**23**:250
variability, distribution, **23**:259–**23**:261
evolutionary factor effects, **23**:260–**23**:261
substructure, **23**:259–**23**:260
variability, spatial analysis, **23**:259–**23**:261
Populations
genetics, *see* Population genetics
plant mating system, **23**:255–**23**:259
Populus, pollen, enzyme-encoding gene
expression, **26**:22
Porphyrins
deficiency in *hem mutants, resistance to NUV
and,* **26**:107, **26**:125
NUV absorption, *E. coli,* **26**:107
Positional cloning
diabetes-susceptibility gene identification,
32:57, **32**:60
Position effect
chromatid pompon formation, **37**:421–422

chromatin
compaction, **37**:400–413, **37**:428–429
characteristics, **37**:402–404
discontinuous compaction, **37**:406–407,
37:410
formation, **37**:404–406, **37**:410
historical perspectives, **37**:400–401
late-replication, **37**:410
occurrence frequencies, **37**:411–413
parental effects, **37**:408–409
temperature effects, **37**:407–408
state changes, **37**:422–428
DNA underrepresentation, **37**:414–421
dominant position effects, **37**:370–376
bw⁺ locus, **37**:371–376
ci⁺ locus, **37**:371
In(2LR)40d locus, **37**:376
Dubunin effect, **37**:357–362
gene expression changes, **37**:306–309
gene expression modification conditions,
37:334–355
chemical modifiers, **37**:342–345
chromatin formation control, **37**:351,
37:353–355
dose dependence, **37**:349–350
genetic modifiers, **37**:345–355
heterochromatin, **37**:335–341
autosomes, **37**:339–341
exogenous DNA, **37**:341
X chromosome, **37**:339–341
Y chromosome, **37**:335–339
histone genes, **37**:345
identification, **37**:346–348
molecular–genetic characteristics,
37:352–353
parental effects, **37**:339, **37**:341–342
P-element-mediated mutagenesis,
37:346–347
temperature, **37**:325, **37**:334–335, **37**:342
gene inactivation
chromosomal rearrangements, **37**:310–311,
37:316–318, **37**:329–330
embryonic development, **37**:355–357
37:440–443
genes affected, **37**:312–319
biochemically identified loci, **37**:318
phenotype development control genes,
37:312–316
transposon genes, **37**:318–319
vital genes, **37**:316–318
historical perspectives, **37**:376–378

Position effect (*continued*)
  inactivation levels, **37**:327–329
  initiation, **37**:429–433
  intercalary heterochromatin, **37**:391–394
  maintenance, **37**:433–434
  model, **37**:427
  pericentromeric heterochromatin,
    37:378–391
    heterochromatin amount effects,
      37:381–382
    inactivation strength, **37**:383–385
    rearrangement breaks, **37**:385–390
    revertant strain cytological analysis,
      37:379–381, **37**:389–390
  position effect variegation characteristics,
    37:309–312
  spreading, **37**:311, **37**:330–334
  telomeric heterochromatin, **37**:394–395
  variegation inactivation, **37**:319–327
  historical perspectives, **37**:4–5, **37**:376–378,
    37:400–401
  light locus, **37**:362–365
  male fertility factors, **37**:368
  nucleolar organizer, **37**:368–370
  peach+ locus, **37**:366–367
  Prokofyeva–Belgovskaya
    heterochromatization theory,
    37:395–399
  rolled+ gene, **37**:365–366
Position effect varigation, in tumor suppressor
  genes, **36**:100
Postdiauxic shift, superoxide dismutases and,
  30:279
Potassium
  evolutionary genetics of fish and, **29**:179
  role in cellular integrity, **36**:188
Potassium channels
  neural plate
    Xenopus laevis, **31**:68
Potassium cyanide, heat-shock puff induction,
  39:350
Potassium ions, puff activity effects, **39**:260
Potato
  mei mutants, *parallel spindle (ps)*, **26**:168
  somaclonal variation and, **30**:43, **30**:52,
    30:61
POU domain transcription factors
  during neural plate induction
    Xenopus laevis, **31**:65
PPF, *see* Pigment-producing factor

PP2 gene, band organization, **39**:147
PP1 (phosphatase), role in pRb
  dephosphorylation, **36**:55, **36**:56
p16 protein
  ankyrin repeats in, **36**:64
  as tumor suppressor gene product, **36**:47,
    36:93
p21 protein
  functions of, **36**:62
  induction of, **36**:60, **36**:62
  inhibition of CDK activity by, **36**:61
  isolation of, **36**:61–**36**:62
  as tumor suppressor gene product, **36**:47
p53 protein
  aberrant subcellular locallization of, **36**:58,
    36:104
  apoptosis mediated by, **36**:55, **36**:60
  disruption of, in human cancer, **36**:56,
    36:98–**36**:99
  future research on, **36**:105
  gene therapy using, **36**:107
  mdm-2 interaction with, **36**:57, **36**:102
  mutations of, **36**:60–**36**:61
  overexpression of, **36**:60
  p21 effect on, **36**:61–**36**:62
  role in transcription, **36**:58, **36**:59–**36**:60
  self-association of, **36**:57–**36**:68
  structure of, **36**:58
  as TP53 gene product, **36**:47, **36**:56
p57 protein
  structure of, **36**:64
  as tumor suppresor protein, **36**:64, **36**:92
p15 protein, as tumor suppressor gene product,
  36:47
p18 protein, as tumor suppressor gene product,
  36:47
p19 protein, as tumor suppressor gene product,
  36:47
p27 protein, as tumor suppressor gene product,
  36:47, **36**:63
p107 protein, role in cell cycle, **36**:55
p130 protein, role in cell cycle, **36**:55
p54 protein, tranlocation of, **36**:84
PP1 transcription factor, pRb regulation of,
  36:55
pRb protein
  binding to tumor-virus proteins, **36**:56
  functions of, **36**:54–**36**:55, **36**:64, **36**:93
  growth-suppression function of, **36**:56, **36**:60
  mutations affecting, **36**:54

pocket of, 36:55, 36:56
as *RB* gene product, 36:47
Precursor RNA processing mutant
for RNA splicing studies, 31:226–228
Prenatal diagnosis, hemophilia, 32:110–113,
32:129–130
Prepropeptides, evolutionary genetics of fish
and, 29:200
Prevalence, *see* Occurrence
Proboscipedia (pb) gene, homeotic, *Drosophila*
molecular map, position in ANT-C, 27:344,
27:345
mRNA during embryogenesis, 27:344,
27:349
protein product, accumulation pattern,
27:344, 27:346
Proflavin, puff activity effects, 39:262
Programmed cell death
apoptosis, *see* Apoptosis
shrinkage necrosis, 35:39–40
Progressive ataxias, *see* Autosomal dominant
progressive ataxias
Prokaryotes
nitrate reductase and, 30:2, 30:6, 30:12
superoxide dismutases and, 30:253,
30:256–30:257, 30:263,
30:270–30:271
telomeres and, 30:228
yeast ribosomes and, 29:65, 29:70
Prokofyeva–Belgovskaya, heterochromatization
theory, 37:395–399
Prolactin, evolutionary genetics of fish and,
29:190–29:197
Proliferating cell nuclear antigen (PCNA)
p21 interaction with, 36:62, 36:63
as possible p53 target, 36:59
Proline, cold acclimation and, 28:104
Prolyl hydroxylase, in HRGP biosynthesis,
28:178
Promoter mutations, in tumor suppressor genes,
36:99
Promoters
Antp locus, P1 and P2 with distinct functions,
27:335, 27:337
activation by gap genes, 27:267, 27:268
carbonic anhydrases and, 30:325–30:326,
30:333–30:334, 30:343, 30:349
elicitor-inducible
CHS gene l15, bean, 28:207,
28:210–28:213

PAL gene, bean, 28:210–28:213
eukaryotic fungal, 23:109–23:112
flagellar genes, bacterial, 27:13–27:16,
27:25–27:27
heat-shock-inducible of *Dfd, Drosophila,*
27:389–27:393
light-inducible, *rbcS 3a* gene, pea,
28:206–28:207
MATα1, haploid-specific gene negative
regulation, yeast, 27:52
mosquitoes and, 30:167–30:169
Mu elements of *Zea mays* and,
30:109–30:110, 30:112
nitrate reductase and, 30:12, 30:28, 30:31
nitrogen metabolism genes, *Rhizobium,*
enterics, 27:13–27:14, 27:26–27:27
superoxide dismutases and, 30:276–30:277,
30:279, 30:283, 30:285
zeste in *Drosophila melanogaster* and,
29:321–29:322
Promyelocytic leukemia (PML), chromosomal
translocation in, 36:93
Proneural genes, role in cell fate, *Drosophila
melanogaster,* 31:15–17
Prophase, heterochromatic staining, 37:6
Prophase I
telomere function, 32:276–278
n-Propionate, heterochromatin gene expression
modification, 37:343
Propionibacterium shermanii, metal substitution
in Fe-MnSODs, 26:71
Prostate cancer
DCC gene implication in, 36:78
pRb aberrations in, 36:54
p21 suppression of, 36:62, 36:63
tumor suppressor gene mutations in, 36:96
Prosthetic groups, nitrate reductase and,
30:5–30:7
Protamine genes, evolutionary genetics of fish
and, 29:157–29:158
Protease
Drosophila transposable elements and,
29:231–29:233
Neurospora crassa and, 29:24, 29:38–29:39
yeast ribosomes and, 29:82
Proteinase inhibitors, wound-induced in plants,
28:180, 28:196, 28:206, 28:209, 28:213
Protein C
in thrombophilia
activation, 33:142–143

Protein C (continued)
  anticoagulant properties, 33:138–140
  deficiency effects, 33:147–148
  overview, 33:136–138
  resistance
    discovery, 33:150–157
    elucidation, 33:163–168
    overview, 33:138
    prevalence, 33:168–169
  thromboembolic disease, 33:157–162
Protein-encoding genes, Neurospora crassa and,
  29:17–29:18
Protein kinase A, superoxide dismutases and,
  30:279, 30:286
Protein kinase C
  during neural induction
    Xenopus laevis, 31:51
Protein kinases, see also DNA, protein kinase
  defense response gene activation and, 28:204,
    28:205
Protein phosphatase 1
  effects on Drosophila mitosis, 31:96
Protein phosphatase 2A
  effects on Drosophila mitosis, 31:96–97
Protein S
  in thrombophilia
    C4b-binding protein interactions,
      33:144–147
    deficiency effects, 33:148–150
    protein C activation, 33:142–143
Proteins, see also specific proteins; specific types
  active chromosome transcription region
    localization
      ribonucleoprotein products, 39:56–67
      transcription proteins, 39:52–56
  ama, Drosophila embryo
    association with cell membrane, 27:325
    localization during embryogenesis,
      27:330–27:332
    organization in five domains, 27:326
    sequences similar to members of
      immunoglobulin superfamily,
      27:326–27:327
  analysis, 34:17
  antifreeze, fish, 28:121
  Antp, Drosophila embryo
    accumulation during development, 27:338
    homeodomain sequences, 27:370, 27:371
    in stau exu and vas exu mutants, 27:258,
      27:267–27:268, 27:338

AS-C genes, neuralizing function, Drosophila,
  27:446
  in ascomycetes
    mt intron-encoded, functions,
      25:225–25:226
    ribosomal, mitochondrial vari gene
      product, 25:214–25:216
    synthesis impairment in poky mutants,
      N. crassa, 25:239
  bcd, Drosophila embryo
    organization in four domains, 27:322
    spatial distribution, 27:249, 27:321,
      27:323
  in braconid wasps, electrophoretic pattern,
    25:140–25:141
  cab, see Chlorophyll a/b-binding proteins
  carbonic anhydrase genes and, 30:321
    chromosomal localization, 30:335
    genes, 30:322, 30:325, 30:331–30:332
    genetic variation, 30:336–30:337, 30:343,
      30:345
  centromeric heterochromatin structure,
    37:105–106
  cold acclimation effects on content,
    28:109–28:110
  da, homology to myc, AS-C, and E(spl)
    proteins, Drosophila, 27:207, 27:440
  dehydrins, boiling-stable, barley, 28:121
  Dfd, Drosophila embryo
    accumulation during development,
      27:343–27:344, 27:348, 27:349,
      27:378–27:380
  dipteran insect salivary glands
    physiology, 39:170–192
    regulation, 39:192–197
  Dl, Drosophila embryo
    function, 27:422
    structure homology to
      EGF, mammalian, 27:419, 27:422
      N protein, Drosophila, 27:421–27:422
  dorsal, DV gradient in embryo, Drosophila,
    27:289–27:292
    repression of zen expression,
      27:295–27:297
    Toll regulatory role, 27:289–27:292
  during Drosophila hydei spermatogenesis in
    Y-chromosomal lampbrush loops
      autosomal origin, 23:202–23:207
      coding by chromosomal sites,
        23:215–23:217

comparison with *D. melanogaster*,
23:199–23:201
histone identification, 23:199–23:202
interaction with transcripts,
23:206–23:207
Drosophila transposable elements and, 29:230
cis-acting effects of retrotransposons,
29:241, 29:244–29:247, 29:249,
29:252, 29:254–29:257
foldback elements, 29:285
hobo, 29:277–29:278
mariner, 29:278
P elements, 29:265–29:269,
29:273–29:275
retrotransposons, 29:235, 29:238, 29:260
dsx, **M** and **F** products, sex-controlling
functions, *Drosophila*, 27:216–27:220
elav, neural specificity, *Drosophila*, 27:439
E(spl), encoded by several mRNAs, structure,
27:427–27:428
similarity to AS-C and *da* gene products,
27:427
evolutionary genetics of fish and, 29:122,
29:178, 29:194, 29:201
detection of variation, 29:123–29:126
environmental change, 29:162–29:164,
29:167–29:170
immune system, 29:181, 29:186, 29:188
linkage groups, 29:144
multigene families, 29:156–29:158
nomenclature, 29:131, 29:133–29:134
nuclear genomic structures, 29:142
in flagellum, *see also* Flagellins
distribution, *C. crescentum*, *E. coli*,
S. typhimurium, 27:4–27:6
hook-associated (HAP), *E. coli*,
27:19–27:20
ftz, *Drosophila embryo*
accumulation during development, 27:334
in *stau exu* and *vas exu* mutants, 27:258
in Gramineae cell lines, improvement by
lysine analog AEC, 24:475
lysine plus threonine, 24:475, 24:477
5-methyltyrptophan, 24:477
GTP-binding, *see* G protein
heat-shock, *see* Heat-shock proteins
heat-shock puff organization, hsp proteins,
39:375–376
HHox c13, human, structural homology to
Dfd protein, 27:370, 27:371

homeodomain sequences, 27:368–27:372
similarity to *Dfd*-like vertebrate proteins,
27:370–27:372
influenza virus-specific, structure and number,
20:3
intercalary heterochromatin identification,
ectopic pairing association, 37:184–185
lab, during embryogenesis, *Drosophila*,
27:347–27:349
MATα1, yeast
haploid-specific gene repression in a/α
cells, 27:51–27:53
PRTF binding to UAS and, 27:42–27:46
α-specific gene activation, 27:37–27:38
MATα2, yeast
haploid-specific gene repression in a/α
cells, 27:51–27:53
a-specific gene repression
in a/α cells, 27:40, 27:48
in α cells, 27:37–27:38, 27:47–27:48
MCM1, yeast, 27:49–27:50
homology to mammalian SRF,
27:50–27:51
messenger (m-proteins), in nuclear envelope
aging and cancer, 24:267–24:268
cell differentiation and, 24:264–24:267
egg determination and, 24:263–24:264
pre-mRNA splicing and, 24:258,
24:260–24:263
translation in pores, 24:261–24:262
MHox-1.4, mouse, structural homology to
Dfd protein, 27:370, 27:371
mitochondrial, intron-encoded
RNA-maturase activity, 24:249–24:250
mosquitoes and
genetic transformation, 30:167–30:169
physiology, 30:151–30:161
N, *Drosophila embryo*
function, 27:422
structure homology to
EGF, mammalian, 27:419, 27:422
lin-12 protein of *C. elegans*,
27:419–27:420
Neurospora crassa and, 29:4, 29:10, 29:43,
29:47, 29:49
DNA transaction, 29:19, 29:24
genetic material, 29:17–29:18
membrane, 29:38
metabolism, 29:39–29:42
mitochondria, 29:28, 29:30, 29:34–29:38

Proteins (continued)
nitrate reductase and
biochemistry, 30:4, 30:7
function, 30:3
gene expression, 30:10–30:11
genetics, 30:20, 30:22, 30:26–30:28
pb, during embryogenesis, Drosophila
polypeptide composition, see Cold-regulated
polypeptides, plants
PR, see Pathogenesis-related proteins
psbA, see Photosystem II, 32-kDa protein
RME1 (meiosis inhibition), yeast
absence in a/α cells, 27:42
in α and a cells, 27:41
Scr, Drosophila embryo
accumulation during development,
27:341–27:342, 27:349
homeodomain sequences, 27:370, 27:371
Sgs-4-encoded, Drosophila
dosage compensation effect,
24:374–24:375
X-chromosome fragment relocation to
autosome and, 24:412
somaclonal variation and, 30:58, 30:64
STE group, in yeast mating, 27:35–27:36,
27:41
STE12, pheromone response and,
27:53–27:54
structure, 34:225–242
subcellular compartmentation of,
21:363–21:364
superoxide dismutases and, 30:288, 30:307
molecular genetics, 30:273,
30:275–30:277, 30:280–30:286,
30:288
physiology, 30:256–30:257,
30:261–30:263
physiology of mutants, 30:297, 30:300,
30:303, 30:306–30:308
structure, 30:263, 30:265–30:268,
30:270–30:272
telomeres and, 30:186, 30:191,
30:194–30:195, 30:198–30:201,
30:232
function, 30:203–30:204, 30:207, 30:216,
30:220–30:221
gene expression, 30:222–30:224
telomeric heterochromatin protein
characteristics, 37:280
Toll, structure and function, Drosophila,
27:289–27:290

Ubx, homeodomain sequences, Drosophila,
27:370, 27:371
Xhox 1A, Xenopus, structural homology to
Dfd protein, 27:370, 27:371
Y chromosome mitotic heterochromatin,
protein accumulation, 37:73–74
yeast ribosomes and, 29:63–29:64
assembly, 29:93–29:96, 29:98
genetic analysis, 29:100–29:103
nucleous, 29:87–29:90
ribosomal protein genes, 29:71–29:84
ribosomal proteins, 29:64–29:71
synthesis changes, 29:84–29:85
zen, during embryogenesis, Drosophila,
27:285–27:287, 27:319
zeste in Drosophila melanogaster and, 29:302,
29:313, 29:316
chromatin packaging, 29:337–29:338,
29:340
DNA binding, 29:318–29:320,
29:323–29:324, 29:326
function, 29:328
polytene chromosomes, 29:316, 29:318
structure, 29:330–29:337
Protein synthesis
cold-regulated, 28:109–28:113
heat-shock-induced, 28:10–28:27
NUV-induced, bacteria
comparison with H_2O_2 effect,
26:126–26:128
oxyR mutations and, 26:126–26:127,
26:131–26:132
pathogenesis-related, 28:10
in Schizosaccharomyces pombe during growth
cycle, 23:6–23:7
theory, minute genes, 38:88–122
molecular research, 38:89–92
antisense mRNA, 38:91
Rp49 gene, 38:89–91
RpL36 gene, 38:91
non-minute phenotype ribosomal protein
mutations, 38:118–119
nonribosomal protein genes, 38:121–122
recessive minutes, 38:116–118
M(3)80 gene, 38:117–118
short-bristle gene, 38:117
ribosomal protein genes, 38:119–121
RpS4 gene, 38:119–120
RpS14 gene, 38:120–121
transposon clone method, 38:92–116
M(1)7C gene, 38:102–106

M(1)15D gene, **38:**101–102
M(2)23B gene, **38:**108–109
M(2)30D/E gene, **38:**93–95
M(2)32A gene, **38:**106–108
M(2)32D gene, **38:**109–110
M(2)60E gene, **38:**114–115
M(3)66D gene, **38:**110–114
M(3)95A gene, **38:**95–97
M(3)95A^{prv11} gene, **38:**97–101
oho23B gene, **38:**108–109
RpL9 gene, **38:**109–110
RpL14 gene, **38:**110–114
RpL19 gene, **38:**114–115
RpS2 gene, **38:**93–95
RpS3 gene, **38:**95–97
RpS3^{prv11} gene, **38:**97–98
RpS3^{prv99} gene, **38:**98–101
RpS5 gene, **38:**101–102
RpS6 gene, **38:**102–106
RpS13 gene, **38:**106–108
string of pearls gene, **38:**93–95
stubarista gene, **38:**115–116
transcriptional control, **28:**12
translational control, **28:**11–**28:**12
Proteolysis
  Drosophila transposable elements and, **29:**235
  Neurospora crassa and, **29:**24
  nitrate reductase and, **30:**6–**30:**7, **30:**20
  yeast ribosomes and, **29:**88
Proterminal chromosome regions, **32:**273–306
  chromosome ends from other primates,
    32:295–296
  function, **32:**275–278
  genetic disease role, **32:**296–305
    cancer, **32:**298–300
    chromosome healing *in vivo*, **32:**301–303
    contiguous gene syndromes, **32:**303–305
    cryptic translocations, **32:**303–305
    telomere repeat loss, **32:**296–301
  structure, **32:**281–294
    associated sequences, **32:**282–283
    chromosome end sequence organization,
      32:289–294
    minisatellites, **32:**284–285
    properties, **32:**281–282
    subterminal repeat sequences, **32:**287–289
    subterminal sequence isolation,
      32:285–287
Protodystrophin, characteristics, **33:**196–197
Protooncogenes, evolutionary genetics of fish
  and, **29:**170, **29:**172–**29:**173

Protoplasts
  fusion and somatic hybridization,
    20:155–**20:**163
  isolation and culture, **20:**152–**20:**155
  Mu elements *Zea mays* and, **30:**112
  nitrate reductase and, **30:**13
  somaclonal variation and, **30:**43,
    30:46–**30:**47, **30:**53
  as tools for transfer of cell organelles or
    microorganisms, **20:**163–**20:**166
Protozoa
  ciliated, linear mitochondrial genomes of,
    22:26–**22:**28
  infusoria, polytene chromosome occurrence
    DNA elimination, **34:**75–76
    fragmentation, **34:**88–96
    nuclear apparatus characterization,
      34:73–75
    polytene chromosomes, **34:**76–88
    significance, **34:**96–97
    vegetative macronucleus organization,
      34:88–96
  morphology change induction
    gregarine parasites, **34:**285–286
    microsporidia, **34:**281–284
PRP mutant, *see* Precursor RNA processing
  mutant
PRP8 splicing factor, **31:**224
PRTF, *see* Pheromone, and receptor
  transcription factor
prune/Killer of prune Interaction, **35:**207–209
  awd gene, **35:**209–221
    awd^{Kpn} mutation analysis, **35:**218–221
    early studies, **35:**209
    Killer of prune allele, **35:**209–210
    neomorphic character, **35:**219–221
    nm23 gene comparison, **35:**214–216
    nucleoside diphosphate kinase activity,
      35:216–218
    phenotypes, **35:**211–214
  discovery, **35:**207–209
  lethal interactions, **35:**237–244
    mechanisms, **35:**241–244
    sensitivity, **35:**238–240
    timing, **35:**240–241
  prune gene, **35:**222–236
    developmental expression, **35:**227
    drosopterin pigment
      accumulation reduction, **35:**234–236
      content, **35:**227–229
      GTP role, **35:**233–236

prune/Killer of prune Interaction *(continued)*
  pteridine biosynthesis pathway,
    35:229–234
  function, 35:222–226
  phenotypes, 35:222
  prune/Killer of prune interaction rescue,
    35:226
Pseudoautosomal region, telomeres and,
  30:194–30:197
Pseudogenes
  Drosophila transposable elements and, 29:233
  evolutionary genetics of fish and, 29:134,
    29:178, 29:187
  formation of, 36:149, 36:150
Pseudomonas, copper-zinc-containing SOD,
  26:67
Pseudomonas aeruginosa
  iron-regulated gene in, 36:191, 36:192,
    36:193, 36:194, 36:195, 36:196, 36:197
  metal detoxification in, 36:205, 36:226
Pseudomonas fluorescens, iron-regulated gene in,
  36:195
Pseudomonas putida, iron-regulated gene in,
  36:191, 36:195
Pseudomonas syringae
  avirulence genes, cloning, 28:170–28:173
  GUS induction, bean cells, 28:193
Pseudo-nurse chromosomes, heterochromatin
  DNA underrepresentation, 37:128–130
Pseudopleuronectes americanus, evolutionary
  genetics of fish and, 29:170
P strain, *Drosophila* transposable elements and,
  29:267–29:269, 29:286
PTC gene, implication in Gorlin syndrome,
  36:95
Pteridine, biosynthesis pathway, 35:229–234
Puffs
  activity, historical perspective, 34:15–16
  developmental activity, 39:213–267
    genetic control, 39:235–251
    heterozygous puff classification,
      39:250–251
    influencing factors, 39:251–267
    puff stage, 39:215, 39:222
    salivary gland chromosomes, 39:213–224
    tissue specificity, 39:224–235
  dipteran insect developmental features,
    39:161–197
    endocrine system, 39:161–169
    gene mutations
      Df(2R)bw^5 gene, 39:168–169

dor gene, 39:167–168
dre4 gene, 39:169
ecd1 gene, 39:167
ecs gene, 39:169
eyeless^D gene, 39:169
giant gene, 39:167
grg gene, 39:168
l(1)HM40 gene, 39:168
l(1)su(f)^{ts67g} gene, 39:167
l(2)ft gene, 39:168
l(2) gl gene, 39:167
l (3)3^{DTS} gene, 39:168
l(3)tl gene, 39:169
sta gene, 39:168
swi gene, 39:169
  hormone effects, 39:161–169
  salivary glands
    hormonal regulation, 39:192–197
    physiology, 39:170–192
  DNA puffs, 39:328–336
  gene activation–puff formation relationship,
    39:380–386
  heat-shock puffs
    characteristics, 39:336–358
    molecular organization, 39:358–380
    hsp gene induction, 39:376–379
    hsp proteins, 39:375–376
    polypeptide encoding genes,
      39:358–369
    unusual heat-shock puffs, 39:369–374
  hormonal control, 39:267–291
    ecdysterone analogs, 39:285–287
    ecdysterone role
      activity change cascades, 39:271–281
      mechanisms, 39:267–271
    juvenile hormone, 39:287–291
    mutation effects, 39:281–285
      dor gene, 39:282–283
      DTS-3 gene, 39:282
      EcR gene, 39:284
      E74 gene, 39:284
      giant gene, 39:282
      l(2)gl gene, 39:281
      l(3)tl gene, 39:281–282
      swi gene, 39:283
    vertebrate steroid hormones, 39:285–287
  hormonal induction characterization,
    39:291–327
    accessibility model, 39:324–326
    cascade gene regulation, 39:326–327
    ecdysterone puff organization, 39:291–319

5A puff, **39:**302–303
2B3-5 puff, **39:**291–299
25B puff, **39:**303
35B2-5 puff, **39:**303
67B puff, **39:**304
75B puff, **39:**312–315
90B3-8 puff, **39:**315–316
39BC puff, **39:**303
2C1-3 puff, **39:**300
3C puff, **39:**300–302
68C puff, **39:**304–308
78C puff, **39:**315
71C3-4-D1-2 puff, **39:**308–309
75CD puff, **39:**315
71CE puff, **39:**309
Drosophila lummei, **39:**317
Drosophila nasuta X chromosome region
    10 puff, **39:**317
Drosophila virilis 16A puff, **39:**317–318
55E puff, **39:**319
74E puff, **39:**310–312
71EF puff, **39:**309–310
46F puff, **39:**304
63F puff, **39:**304
93F puff, **39:**316
I-18C puff, **39:**316–317
II-9A puff, **39:**317
II-14A puff, **39:**317
IV2B puff, **39:**317
ecdysterone receptors, **39:**319–324
[3H]uridine labeling method, **39:**41–47
infusoria chromosomes, **34:**84–87
isolated nuclei, **34:**324–326
long-term incubation, **34:**292–294,
    34:298–299
morphological aspects, **39:**197–212
    chromosomal involvement, **39:**200–210
    historical perspectives, **39:**197–200
    puff size estimation methods, **39:**210–212
morphology, **34:**137–150
mutation effects, **34:**309–310
overview, **39:**1–3, **39:**160–161
plant chromosomes, **34:**119, **34:**123
protein structure, **34:**238–240, **34:**242
springtail chromosomes, **34:**71
Pulsed-field gel electrophoresis, *Neurospora
    crassa* and, **29:**4, **29:**10–**29:**11, **29:**13,
    29:48
Puromycin
    heat-shock puff induction, **39:**350
    puff activity effects, **39:**262

Pyronine
    intercalary heterochromatin identification,
        37:146
    RNA staining, **39:**40–41
Pyruvate kinase gene
    in Gaucher disease, **32:**24
Pyura
    DNA homology with human TF cDNA,
        25:5–**25:**7
    TF mRNA transcript localization, **25:**7, **25:**8

qa gene cluster, *Neurospora crassa* and,
    29:41–**29:**42
Q-staining
    differential heterochromatin staining,
        37:15–21
    Drosophila melanogaster, **37:**18, **37:**20
    Drosophila virilis, **37:**17, **37:**21
    Escherichia coli, **37:**17
    Samoaia leonensis, **37:**16
    intercalary heterochromatin identification,
        37:141–143, **37:**147–148
Quasiterminal translocations, in *N. crassa,*
    36:245–**36:**246, **36:**247
Quinic acid
    in *E. coli,* pathway, **23:**146
    in *Neurospora crassa,* **29:**41–**29:**42
    pathway, **23:**145–**23:**146

Rabson–Mendenhall syndrome
    insulin resistance, **32:**69–70
Radiation, *see also* Ultraviolet
    eye mosaics, **37:**322
    heterochromatin compaction, **37:**12–13
    hybrids
        genome mapping, **33:**63–94
            construction methods, **33:**71–77
            dosage effects, **33:**75–77
            retention frequencies, **33:**75–77
            species considerations, **33:**75
            future directions, **33:**93–94
            Goss and Harris experiments,
                33:65–68
            extensions, **33:**68–71
            chromosome-specific hybrid panels,
                33:70–71
            hybrid gene enrichment, **33:**69–70

Radiation (continued)
  whole genome experiments, 33:68–69
    human component analysis, 33:77–82
    fluorescence in situ hybridization,
      33:79–80
    interspersed repetitive sequence-
      polymerase chain reaction,
      33:81–82
    single-copy sequence scoring,
      33:77–79
  mouse genome maps, 33:92–93
  somatic cell genetics, 33:64
  statistical analysis, 33:82–94
    data collection, 33:83–84
    influential hybrids, 33:91–92
    multipoint analysis, 33:84–91
    two-point analysis, 33:84
  Neurospora crassa and, 29:25
  Schizosaccharomyces pombe
    caffeine effects on injuries, 23:27–23:33,
      23:35, 23:38–23:40, 23:50–23:51
    resistance during cell cycle, 23:19–23:22
    sensitivity
      comparison with other organisms, 23:19,
        23:20
      mutant, 23:22–23:26
  superoxide dismutases and, 30:252, 30:254,
    30:297, 30:299
  telomeres and, 30:201
Radiography
  [³H]uridine labeling method, 39:41–47
  interband detection, 39:87
Radiosensitivity
  Drosophila
    Cu-ZnSOD role, 28:64
    radical-generating reactions, 28:63
  immune deficiency role, DNA repair
    mechanisms, 38:207–208
Radixin, merlin similarity to, 36:83
RAD9, telomeres and, 30:202
RAD52, telomeres and, 30:213
rad52, telomeres and, 30:218
Rainbow trout, phosphoglucomutase, regulatory
  genes and, 24:111
Random repetitive probes, mosquitoes and,
  30:133–30:135
RAP1
  telomeres and, 30:220
  yeast ribosomes and, 29:77
RAP1, telomeres and, 30:199–30:200, 30:207,
  30:220

rap1, telomeres and, 30:220
RAPD-PCR, mosquitoes and, 30:132
Rapid amplification of cDNA ends (RACE), use
  in APC gene studies, 36:74
Rap1p, yeast ribosomes and, 29:78–29:79,
  29:84, 29:103
ras genes, evolutionary genetics of fish and,
  29:172–29:173
Raspberry, pollen germination
  in vitro, density effect, 26:27
  in vivo
    stigmatic nutrient effects, 26:27–26:28
    stylar and pollen genotype role, 26:30
Rat
  heat-treated embryos, developmental
    abnormalities, 24:12–24:13
  HSP71 during postnatal development, 24:12
  ubiquitin mRNA during late embryogenesis,
    24:12
Raus sarcoma virus, puff activity effects, 39:262
Razisea spicata, pollen competition, 26:33
rbc, see Ribulose bisphosphate carboxylase
rbp genes
  band organization, 39:142
  hormone expression regulation, 39:196–197
  puff development, 39:297, 39:299, 39:304,
    39:316
RB protein, See pRb
RB tumor suppressor gene
  characteristics of, 36:46, 36:71
  implication in human cancers, 36:53–36:56,
    36:95
  inactivation of, 36:56, 36:102
  isolation of, 36:46, 36:69
  p53 as negative regulator of, 36:60
rDNA
  mosquitoes and, 30:126–30:129,
    30:135–30:137, 30:166
  telomeres and, 30:193, 30:214
  yeast ribosomes and, 29:64, 29:79, 29:96,
    29:99, 29:103
    nucleolus, 29:86, 29:89
Reb1p, yeast ribosomes and, 29:79
Recessive inheritance
  dilated cardiomyopathy, 35:309
Reciprocal recombination, telomeres and, 30:213
Recombinant DNA Advisory Committee
  ongoing patient therapy, 32:10–11
  patient registry, 32:3, 32:8, 32:15
Recombinants, host-range, of influenza virus,
  20:23–20:24

Recombination, *see also* Meiotic reciprocal
recombination; Meiotic recombination
carbonic anhydrases and, **30**:335
Drosophila transposable elements and
foldback elements, **29**:285–**29**:288
hobo, **29**:275
P elements, **29**:260, **29**:264, **29**:271
evolutionary genetics of fish and, **29**:135,
29:143, **29**:184–**29**:185, **29**:187
fungal, transformation and, **23**:124–**23**:125
homologous recombination, DNA break
repair mechanisms, **38**:188–190,
38:203–206
meiotic, *see* Meiotic recombination
mitotic, *see* Mitotic recombination
mitotic recombination, *minute* genes
cell competition, **38**:85–86
maternal effects, **38**:86
parameters, **38**:85
mosquitoes and, **30**:125
genetic transformation, **30**:162, **30**:164,
30:167
physiology, **30**:149, **30**:152, **30**:160
Mu elements of *Zea mays* and, **30**:90, **30**:97,
30:106
Neurospora crassa and, **29**:4, **29**:15, **29**:18,
29:20–**29**:24, **29**:32
nitrate reductase and, **30**:29
somaclonal variation and, **30**:52, **30**:58
superoxide dismutases and, **30**:261, **30**:273,
30:281
telomeres and, **30**:232
formation, **30**:228–**30**:229, **30**:231
function, **30**:205–**30**:206, **30**:208–**30**:209,
30:211, **30**:213–**30**:214, **30**:218
gene expression, **30**:224
nuclear organization, **30**:226
structure, **30**:191–**30**:193, **30**:196, **30**:198
variable–diversity–joining recombination,
DNA break repair mechanisms
break formation, **38**:186–188
nonhomologous end-joining, **38**:204–205
zeste in *Drosophila melanogaster* and, **29**:337
Recombination groups, of influenza virus,
20:7–**20**:8
Recombination nodules
function, **32**:276–277
Redox proteins, nitrate reductase and, **30**:7
Redundancy
in sex determination
Drosophila melanogaster, **31**:7–10

Refractoriness, mosquitoes and, **30**:156–**30**:157,
30:159
Regenerated plants, somaclonal variation and,
30:65–**30**:66
genetic consequences, **30**:52–**30**:59
unusual genetic behavior, **30**:63–**30**:64
Regeneration, in plant tissue culture, *see* Callus,
Gramineae
Registry, *see* Gene registry
Regulation, *Mu* elements of *Zea mays* and,
30:97–**30**:100
Regulatory elements
carbonic anhydrases and, **30**:349
superoxide dismutases and, **30**:272
Regulatory genes, eukaryote
classification based on mechanism of action
effector response, **24**:74–**24**:75, **24**:115
processing, **24**:74, **24**:114
systemic, **24**:74, **24**:114–**24**:115
temporal, **24**:75, **24**:115–**24**:116
in *Drosophila*, **24**:89–**24**:100, *see also*
Drosophila melanogaster
identification, methods, **24**:111–**24**:113
in maize, **24**:100–**24**:110
in mouse, **24**:75, **24**:80–**24**:89
properties, **24**:76–**24**:79
in rainbow trout, **24**:111
Regulons, in bacterial response to NUV
heat-shock control and, **26**:132
oxidative stress control (*oxyR*) and, **26**:113,
26:126–**26**:127, **26**:131–**26**:132
SOS control and, **26**:129–**26**:131, **26**:134
stringent response control and, **26**:132
Remethylation, somaclonal variation and,
30:54
Renal cell carcinoma, in von Hippel-Lindau
disease, **36**:84
Reovirus
multiplicity reactivation, **24**:344
RNA, segmented, double-stranded, **24**:344
Repeat expansions, *see* Triplet repeat expansions
Repeat induced point mechanism, *Neurospora
crassa* and, **29**:5–**29**:7, **29**:9,
29:47–**29**:48
Repeat induced point mutations, in *N. crassa*,
36:259–**36**:260
Repeats
chromomere patterns, **34**:213–215
sources, **34**:95–96
Repetitive DNA, mosquitoes and,
30:139–**30**:145, **30**:148

Repetitive sequences
  heterochromatin induction, 37:426–428
  intercalary heterochromatin identification,
    37:207–224
  cytological repeats, 37:225
  gene repeats, 37:208–209
  mobile genome elements, 37:209–216
  tandem repeats
    Chironomus thummi Cla-elements,
      37:105, 37:219–220
    dinucleotide repeats, 37:222–223
    Drosophila melanogaster X chromosome
      repeats, 37:222
    histone encoding genes, 37:219
    mononucleotide repeats, 37:222–223
    pDv family repeats, 37:223
    poly(A) nucleotide complexes,
      37:220–222
    polypyrimidines, 37:219
    rRNA genes, 37:218–219
    scrambled repeats, 37:223–224
    tRNA genes, 37:207–208
  satellite DNA, 37:43–54
    composition, 37:53–54
    location, 37:45–46, 37:51–52
    in situ hybridization, 37:51–53
    slipping, 37:53
    types, 37:47–49
  telomeres and, 30:186, 30:190, 30:204,
    30:206, 30:228
  telomeric heterochromatin, 37:248–259
Replication
  Drosophila transposable elements and, 29:260
  evolutionary genetics of fish and, 29:142,
    29:147
  mosquitoes and, 30:130, 30:145, 30:149,
    30:171–30:172
  Mu elements of Zea mays and,
    30:105–30:108, 30:116
  Neurospora crassa and, 29:9, 29:11–29:12,
    29:19–29:20, 29:24
  somaclonal variation and, 30:49, 30:51,
    30:61
  telomeres and, 30:186, 30:222,
    30:227–30:229, 30:233
    function, 30:203–30:206, 30:208, 30:215,
      30:218–30:219, 30:221–30:222
    structure, 30:190, 30:192, 30:200
  zeste in Drosophila melanogaster and, 29:336,
    29:338

Replicators, Neurospora crassa and, 29:15–29:17
Research problems, 34:11–20
  Balbiani ring role, 34:15–16
  band number estimation, 34:12–14
  chromosome morphology, 34:16–17
  cloning methods, 34:20
  cytogenetic maps, 34:11–12
  gene mapping, 34:11–12
  heterochromatin role, 34:18–19
  interband activity, 34:12, 34:16
  molecular biology studies, 34:19
  puff activity, 34:15–16
Resistance
  hybrid or hemopoietic, 20:331–20:334
  pathogen-induced
    cell wall modification
      HRGP accumulation, 28:178
      phenolic material deposition,
        28:177–28:178
    phytoalexin biosynthesis, 28:175–28:177
    protein synthesis
      chitinase and, 28:178–28:179
      glucanase and, 28:178–28:179
      proteinase inhibitors and, 28:180
      PR proteins and, 28:179–28:180
Respiratory enzymes
  iron-regulated genes encoding, 36:197
  molybdenum-regulated genes encoding,
    36:204–36:205
Restrictase, isolated chromosome studies,
  34:328
Restriction endonuclease maps
  Cat cDNAs, maize, 28:31
  SOD cDNAs, maize, 28:33
Restriction enzymes, differential
  heterochromatin staining, chromosome
  digestion, 37:24
Restriction fragment, Mu elements of Zea mays
  and, 30:85–30:87, 30:95, 30:97–30:98,
  30:114
Restriction fragment length polymorphisms
  apolipoprotein B gene, 32:161–162
  carbonic anhydrases and, 30:336,
    30:347–30:348
  diabetes-susceptibility gene identification,
    32:58, 32:74
  duplication testing by, 36:34
  evolutionary genetics of fish and,
    29:126–29:131, 29:144
  formation in cell culture, soybean, 28:83

low-density lipoprotein receptor gene
identification, 32:149
mapping, C. elegans, 27:73
mosquitoes and, 30:130–30:131, 30:135,
30:146, 30:157, 30:159
Neurospora crassa and, 29:10, 29:13, 29:17
nitrate reductase and, 30:21
phenylalanine hydroxylase gene haplotypes,
32:208–214
somaclonal variation and, 30:59
Restriction mapping
evolutionary genetics of fish and, 29:129,
29:146
mosquitoes and, 30:142, 30:153
Mu elements of Zea mays and, 30:94, 30:98
telomeres and, 30:198
Restrictive cardiomyopathy, 35:312–313
Retardation, relationship to muscular dystrophy,
33:180–181
RET gene, implication in neoplasias, 36:95
Reticulocytes, heme biosynthesis, TF role,
25:22
Retina
evolutionary genetics of fish and, 29:177
pathology in muscular dystrophy,
33:182–183
Retinitis pigmentosa
in HMSNVII disease, 36:4
mutation role in, 36:25
Retinoblastoma
chromosomal linkage of, 36:95
RB tumor suppressor gene role in, 36:47,
36:53–36:56, 36:95
telomeres and, 30:208
Wilms' tumor similarity to, 36:69
Retinoic acid
in anterior–posterior axis formation
Xenopus laevis, 31:56–57
Hox gene regulation, 38:14
Retinoic acid receptors
chromosomal translocation effects on, 36:93
genetic redundancy in, 36:143, 36:151
Retrotransposable elements, telomeres and,
30:192, 30:195
Retrotransposons, Drosophila transposable
elements and
cis-acting effects, 29:240–29:257
expression, 29:233–29:236
mechanisms, 29:236–29:240
structure, 29:231–29:233

trans-acting effects, 29:257–29:260
Retrovirus, see also Viral vectors
Drosophila transposable elements and,
29:231–29:233, 29:235, 29:248
Duchenne muscular dystrophy gene therapy,
35:134–137
mosquitoes and, 30:166–30:167
Reverse transcriptase
Drosophila transposable elements and, 29:232,
29:237
mosquitoes and, 30:166
Neurospora crassa and, 29:34–29:35
telomeres and, 30:185
function, 30:204, 30:209, 30:216–30:217
structure, 30:186–30:187, 30:192
Reversion, superoxide dismutases and, 30:298
Rhabdomyosarcoma
paired-box gene expression, 33:264–265
Rh4 gene, band organization, 39:151
Rhizobium, δ54 promoter, in nitrogen
metabolism regulation, 27:13,
27:26–27:27
Rhizobium japonicum, nitrate reductase and,
30:3
Rhizobium meliloti, NolR protein from, 36:220
Rhizopus stolonifer, casbene synthase induction,
castor bean, 28:201
Rhodobacter capsulatus, molybdenum-regulated
gene in, 36:201–36:202
Rhodopsin, mutations affecting, 36:25
Rhombospinal region patterning, rostrocaudal
axis, Hox genes role, 38:8–14
gene expression, 38:8–10
gene structure, 38:8–10
mutations, 38:10–13
regulation, 38:13–14
Rhosopseudomonas capsulata, nitrate reductase
and, 30:3
Riboflavin, NUV sensitivity and, 26:107
Ribonuclease, puff activity effects, 39:262
Ribonuclease protection analysis, of WT1 gene,
36:72
Ribonucleic acid
influenza virus
assignment of segments to gene function,
20:12–20:13
base sequence studies, 20:4–20:6
synthesis and regulation, 20:6–20:7
ribosomal, genes coding for in higher plants,
22:131–22:134

Ribonucleoprotein
active chromosome region localization,
39:56–67
transcription involvement, 39:55–56
Ribonucleoprotein particles
heterogeneous, role in RNA splicing,
31:225–226
small nuclear
role in exon definition, 31:218–220
role in RNA splicing, 31:214–218
Ribonucleotide reductase, E. coli
activation by SOD, 26:78, 26:112
inactivation by NUV, 26:109
Ribosomal DNA, see rDNA
Ribosomal genes
measurements of transcription and translation
of, 21:77–21:78
expression of r-protein genes,
21:80–21:82
expression of rRNA genes, 21:78–21:80
gene dosage experiments, 21:82–21:85
regulation of transcription, 21:102–21:107
Ribosomal protein genes
expression of, 21:80–21:82
protein synthesis theory
Rp49 gene, 38:89–91
RpL genes
RpL9 gene, 38:109–110
RpL14 gene, 38:110–114
RpL15 gene, 38:118–119
RpL19 gene, 38:114–115
RpL32 gene, 38:90–91
RpL36 gene, 38:91
RpS genes
RpS2 gene, 38:93–95
RpS3 gene, 38:95–97
RpS3^prvII gene, 38:97–98
RpS3^prv99 gene, 38:98–101
RpS4 gene, 38:119–120
RpS5 gene, 38:101–102
RpS6 gene, 38:102–106
RpS13 gene, 38:106–108
RpS14 gene, 38:120–121
Ribosomal proteins, yeast ribosomes and,
29:64–29:71, 29:103
ribosomal proteins genes, 29:71–29:84
Ribosomal protein synthesis, autogenous
regulation
identification of proteins, 21:85–21:92
mechanisms for, 21:92–21:98
significance of, 21:98–21:102

Ribosomal RNA, 33:mutational analysis,
33:1–31, 33:16S
conserved nucleotides, 33:19, 33:20
detection methods, 33:2–5
mutation introduction, 33:4–5
plasmid expression, 33:2–4
double mutations, 33:19, 33:21–30
evolutionary genetics of fish and, 29:130
limitations, 33:30–31
Neurospora crassa and, 29:7, 29:18, 29:27,
29:29–29:30
second-site suppressor mutations, 33:31
single mutations, 33:19, 33:21–30
structure–function analysis, 33:6–19
central domain mutations, 33:12–13
3' major domain mutations, 33:13–16
5' major domain mutations, 33:10–12
3' minor domain mutations, 33:16–19
secondary structure, 33:6–9
upstream mutations, 33:9–10
yeast ribosomes and, 29:64,
29:103–29:104
assembly, 29:93–29:95, 29:98
genetic analysis, 29:98–29:103
nucleolus, 29:85–29:91
processing, 29:91–29:93
ribosomal protein genes, 29:73–29:74,
29:80–29:83
ribosomal proteins, 29:68–29:71
synthesis changes, 29:84–29:85
Ribosomal RNA genes, expression of,
21:78–21:80
Ribosomes, see also Yeast, ribosomes
of E. coli
fine structure analysis of rRNA and
4-protein operons, 21:62–21:65
implications of genetic organization of
r-protein, 21:65–21:77
isolation of mutants, 21:61–21:62
mosquitoes and, 30:126, 30:153
Neurospora crassa and, 29:28, 29:30,
29:35–29:36
phenomenological description of
accumulation, 21:54–21:55
growth rate-dependent regulation,
21:55–21:59
stringent response, 21:59–21:60
somaclonal variation and, 30:57, 30:60
synthesis, regulation, current status of
understanding of, 21:107–21:110
telomeres and, 30:199

Ribulose, 1,5-biphosphate carboxylase (small
    subunit), genes coding for, 22:126–22:127
Ribulose bisphosphate carboxylase
    homology to groEL of *E. coli*, 28:262
    isozyme profiles, cold acclimation effect
      cabbage, 28:109
      rye, 28:108–28:109
    large unit (rbcL)
      developmental regulation, 28:153–28:154
      photoregulation, 28:135–28:138
      oxygen concentration in maize leaf cells and,
        28:9–28:10
    small unit (rcbS)
      circadian rhythm, 28:148
      cytokinins and, 28:152
      developmental regulation, 28:153–28:154
      photoregulation, 28:12, 28:139–28:143
      plastid factors and, 28:146–28:147
Rice
    genome changes in suspension culture, 28:81
    nitrate reductase and, 30:5, 30:9
    somaclonal variation and, 30:46, 30:57,
      30:59–30:61, 30:63
Rifampicin, RNA synthesis inhibition, 39:75
RING finger, in BRCA1 protein, 36:88
RLP, yeast ribosomes and, 29:102–29:103
    assembly, 29:96
    ribosomal protein genes, 29:71,
      29:74–29:75, 29:79, 29:81–29:83
    synthesis changes, 29:84–29:85
RNA, *see also* Ribosomal RNA
    active chromosome region localization,
      DNA–RNA hybrid antibodies, 39:38,
      39:47–52
    ADH mRNA, *Drosophila*
      transcription pattern, 25:46–25:47
      during development, 25:50–25:51
    antisense mRNA, protein synthesis theory,
      38:91
    Balbiani ring organization, 39:397–400
    carbonic anhydrases and, 30:326, 30:345
    cob gene transcripts, processing in *S.*
      cerevisiae, 25:220–25:222
    dependent DNA polymerase, *Drosophila*
      transposable elements and,
      29:231–29:233
    dosage compensation, 39:423–425
    Drosophila
      mRNA
        ama, accumulation during embryogenesis,
          27:327–27:329

Antp, accumulation during
    embryogenesis, 27:338
    AS-C multiple transcripts, spatial
      distribution, 27:437–27:439
      in neurogenic mutants, 27:438,
        27:441–27:442
    bcd, localization
      in embryo during development,
        27:322–27:325
      in oocyte, 27:278
    Dfd, during embryogenesis, 27:343,
      27:376–27:378
    Dl, structure and distribution, 27:421
    dorsal, selective translation in ventral
      region of embryo, 27:291, 27:292
    E(spl), multiple units, spatial
      distribution, 27:427
    ftz, during embryogenesis, 27:334
    lab, during embryogenesis, 27:347,
      27:458
    mam, two major units, expression,
      27:429
    N, structure and processing, 27:419
    pb, during embryogenesis, 27:344,
      27:349
    Scr, during embryogenesis, 27:341,
      27:349
    zen, during embryogenesis, 27:285
      spaciotemporal distribution,
        27:317–27:319
      in wild-type and mutant,
        27:293–27:295
    pre-mRNA, sex-specific splicing
      dsx, 27:200–27:201
      regulation, 27:202, 27:204
      Sxl, 27:199–27:200, 27:205
      tra, 27:200
      regulation, 27:202, 27:203
      tra-2, 27:201–27:202
      regulation, 27:202–27:203
Drosophila transposable elements and
    cis-acting effects of retrotransposons,
      29:241, 29:244–29:247
    foldback elements, 29:286
    P elements, 29:265–29:266, 29:271,
      29:273–29:274
    retrotransposons, 29:231, 29:233–29:237,
      29:258
editing
    tumor suppressor genes, 36:100
    WT1 gene studies using, 36:72

RNA (continued)
evolutionary genetics of fish and, 29:126,
29:142, 29:170, 29:183
heat-shock puff responses, 39:353–356
helicases
in RNA splicing, 31:226–228
histochemical staining, 39:40–41
messenger
ADH, equal level in males and females,
Drosophila, 24:380–24:381
carbonic anhydrases and, 30:343, 30:347
Cat, light effects, maize, 28:21–28:23
cold acclimation-associated changes
Northern blot analysis, 28:115–28:116
in vitro translation, 28:114
Ddc, Drosophila
during development, 24:162–24:163
tissue-specific, 24:163
Drosophila transposable elements and
P elements, 29:265–29:267, 29:271
retrotransposons, 29:235, 29:252,
29:254–29:256
E1A, similar to heat-shock-induced,
Dictyostelium, 24:13
evolutionary genetics of fish and, 29:168,
29:170
G6PD, equal level in males and females,
Drosophila, 24:380–24:381
heat-shock-induced
developmental defects and,
28:289–28:290
self-regulation, soybean,
28:251–28:252
synthesis inhibition and resumption,
Drosophila, 28:283–28:284
heat-shock-induced in Dictyostelium,
24:13
HSP70, hyperthermia effects, rodents,
24:12
HSP and HSC during development,
Drosophila, 24:4–24:6, 24:8–24:9
infection/elicitor-induced
CAD, 28:189–28:190
casbein synthase, Rhizopus stoloniferus-
induced, 28:201
CHI, 28:189
CHS, 28:188–28:190
4CL, 28:189
HMGR, elicitor-induced, 28:201
PAL, 28:188–28:190

organ specificity, 28:194, 28:195
spatial accumulation, 28:192
population changes, 28:180–28:181
PR-1, 28:190, 28:192
timing of induction, 28:190–28:191
mosquitoes and, 30:148, 30:151–30:152,
30:154
Mu elements of Zea mays and,
30:109–30:112
Neurospora crassa and, 29:18, 29:20,
29:28
nitrate reductase and, 30:10–30:12,
30:26
photosynthesis-connected
cab, nuclear
circadian rhythm, 28:148–28:150
cytokinins and, 28:152–28:153
photoregulation, 28:139,
28:144–28:146
plastid development role,
28:146–28:147
psbA, plastid
developmental regulation, fruits,
28:153
photoregulation, seedlings,
28:135–28:137
rbcL, plastid
developmental regulation,
28:153–28:154
photoregulation, 28:135–28:138
rbcS, nuclear
circadian rhythm, 28:148
cytokinins and, 28:152
developmental regulation,
28:153–28:154
photoregulation, 28:139–28:143
plastid factors and, 28:146–28:147
in pollen
long-lived, production during
maturation, 26:23
postmeiotic transcription, 26:22
post-transcriptional editing
apolipoprotein B, 32:159–161
Sgs-4, equal level in males and females,
Drosophila, 24:381
SOD, maize
oxygen treatment and, 28:26–28:27
paraquat effects, 28:24, 28:26
superoxide dismutases and, 30:273,
30:276–30:277, 30:299–30:300

ubiquitin, hyperthermia effects, rodents,
24:12
yeast ribosomes and, 29:99, 29:104
nucleolus, 29:89
ribosomal protein genes, 29:72, 29:75,
29:79–29:80, 29:82–29:83
synthesis changes, 29:84–29:85
zeste in Drosophila melanogaster and,
29:316, 29:328, 29:339
mitochondrial, yeast
introns, 24:247–24:248
splicing by maturases, 24:249–24:250
mosquitoes and, 30:125, 30:127, 30:144
genetic transformation, 30:166, 30:171
physiology, 30:159–30:161
Mu elements of Zea mays and,
30:109–30:110
Neurospora crassa and, 29:2, 29:4, 29:7,
29:18, 29:23
mitochondria, 29:27–29:30
nuclear
pre-mRNA, splicing in envelope, 24:258,
24:260–24:263
aging and cancer, 24:267–24:268
cell differentiation and, 24:264–24:267
egg determination and, 24:263–24:264
evolution and, 24:274–24:275
splicing
consensus sequences in introns and,
24:251–24:252
coptosomes (complex of small RNA)
and, 24:253
mechanism of, 24:250–24:251
p53 binding of, 36:59
post-transcriptional editing
apolipoprotein B, 32:159–161
ribosomal, mt gene-encoded, ascomycetes,
25:205–25:209
ribosomal RNA gene expression, 39:418–425
rRNA genes
molecular organization, 39:418–425
nucleolus function, 39:408, 39:415–418
polygene bands, 39:126–128
size variation, 39:118
splicing
alternative
constitutive intron removal, 31:208–210
exon recognition, 31:218–220
hnRNP protein role, 31:225–226
snRNP role, 31:214–218

in spliceosomes, 31:211–213
splice site usage, 31:213
splicing factor interactions,
31:218–220
Drosophila melanogaster
effects of cis-acting mutations
α-actinin, 31:258–259
myosin heavy chain, 31:257–258
in germ line, 31:252
P element transcript regulation,
31:254–257
sex determination gene transcripts,
31:243–252
suppressor of sable (su[s]) gene,
31:253–254
suppressor of white apricot mutations,
31:252–253
trans-acting factors, 31:259
mechanism
alternative 5′ splice sites, 31:229–231
exon inclusion and exclusion,
31:231–233
mutually exclusive exons, 31:234–238
polyadenylation role, 31:238–241
secondary structure role, 31:241–243
polyadenylation role, 31:238–241
splice site mutation effects
cryptic splice site activation,
31:260–261
exon definition model, 31:218–220,
31:261–262
exon skipping, 31:261
intron retention, 31:260
structure, 34:224–225
superoxide dismutases and, 30:277, 30:280
synthesis
infusoria chromosomes, 34:87–88
in Schizosaccharomyces pombe during
growth cycle, 23:6–23:7
by X chromosome, Drosophila
in males and females, 24:378–24:380
reduction in autosomal male-specific
lethals, 24:400–24:401
X-chromosome segment addition and,
24:387–24:388
telomeres and
formation, 30:227, 30:230
function, 30:203, 30:205, 30:207, 30:209,
30:216–30:217, 30:219–30:221
structure, 30:187, 30:191–30:192, 30:194

RNA (continued)
TF mRNA
  distribution in tissues, 25:14–25:17, see
    also TF gene, expression sites
  extinction in intertypic cell hybrids, 25:28
    in liver, rodents
  during aging, 25:23, 25:24
  cAMP and, 25:27
  estrogen administration and, 25:27
  iron deficiency and, 25:25
  transcript localization, Pyura, 25:7, 25:8
  thiolated tRNA, bacterial
    deficiency in nuvA mutants, sensitivity to
      NUV and, 26:106, 26:126–26:127
    NUV absorption, 26:102, 26:105–26:107
    growth delay and, 26:106, 26:126
  transcription, see Transcription
  transfer
    equal level in males and females,
      Drosophila, 24:380
    mt gene-encoded, ascomycetes,
      25:209–25:212
    translation in nuclear pores, hypothesis,
      24:253–24:256, 24:261–24:263
    tRNA, minute gene hypothesis, 38:81–82
  tRNA genes
    localization, 39:125
    polygene bands, 39:126
  yeast ribosomes and, 29:103–29:104
    assembly, 29:93–29:96
    genetic analysis, 29:99, 29:101–29:102
    nucleolus, 29:88–29:91
    ribosomal protein genes, 29:74–29:75,
      29:83
  zeste in Drosophila melanogaster and,
    29:308–29:310, 29:315–29:316,
    29:319, 29:338
RNA polymerase
  activity studies
    infusoria chromosomes, 34:95
    isolated chromosomes, 34:328
  Drosophila transposable elements and, 29:233,
    29:236
  Neurospora crassa and, 29:20, 29:29–29:30,
    29:34
  sigma (l^{32}) factor, E. coli
    association with dnaK protein, 28:250
    HSP gene control, 28:244, 28:245
  from yeast mitochondria, 25:228–25:229
  yeast ribosomes and, 29:81–29:82,
    29:85–29:89, 29:103

zeste in Drosophila melanogaster and, 29:302,
    29:308, 29:310
RNA polymerase II, transcription involvement,
    39:53–55
RNA recognition motif (RRM), yeast ribosomes
    and, 29:89
RNase
  H, Drosophila transposable elements and,
    29:232–29:233
  Mu elements of Zea mays and, 30:112
  Neurospora crassa and, 29:23
  RNA synthesis inhibition, 39:75
RND family, role in bacterial metal resistance,
    36:223
RNPs, yeast ribosomes and, 29:95–29:96
Robb's medium, puff activity effects, 39:259
rolled$^+$ gene, position effect, 37:365–366
Rostrocaudal patterning, human malformation
    genes, 38:3–14
  domains, 38:3
  forebrain region, 38:3–7
  Hox gene cluster, 38:8–14
  isthmic region, 38:7–8
  midbrain region, 38:3–7
  rhombospinal region, 38:8–14
rosy gene
  artificial bands, 39:149–150
  dosage compensation, 39:78
  oligogene bands, 39:136
  puff development, 39:209–210
  recombination size estimation, 39:96
Rotenone, heat-shock puff induction, 39:351
roughest gene, band organization, 39:147
Roussy-Lévy syndrome
  as clinical variant of HMSN1 disease, 36:4
  as CMT disease, 36:2
RPA protein, p53 binding of, 36:59
RPS, yeast ribosomes and, 29:71, 29:75, 29:79,
    29:84–29:85
RRP1, yeast ribosomes and, 29:100
Rubisco, see Ribulose bisphosphate carboxylase
rudimentary gene, distribution estimation,
    39:118
runt gene
  Drosophila melanogaster
    interactions with eve and h, 31:12–13
    mutation effects on ftz, 31:12–13
    as numerator element, 31:5
    role in neural fate, 31:17–20
    role in sex determination, 31:5–6
rutabaga (rut) mutant

Drosophila melanogaster
  biochemical analysis, **31**:149–150
  expression patterns, **31**:150–151
Rye, cold acclimation
  plasma membrane behavior, **28**:101–**28**:103
  Rubisco isozymes and, **28**:108–**28**:109

S. dioica
  zinc tolerance
    MGS and, **26**:19–**26**:20
    in *in vitro* germinating pollen and growing
      roots, **26**:15
S3034, *Mu* elements of *Zea mays* and, **30**:111
S14, yeast ribosomes and, **29**:65
Saccharomyces
  chromosome rearrangements in, **36**:245
  superoxide dismutases and, **30**:288
  telomeres and, **30**:187, **30**:191, **30**:199,
    30:213, **30**:228
Saccharomyces cerevisiae
  cdc genes
    epistatic group, cell cycle step control,
      26:180–**26**:181
    meiosis initiation control, **26**:157, **26**:158
    mutant *cdc5*, meiosis arrest after pachytene,
      26:163
  copper-zinc-containing SOD
    amino acid sequences, **26**:68–**26**:70
    inhibitors, **26**:69
  double *mus* mutants, **26**:180
  experimental methods for mutagenesis
    estimation of mutation frequencies,
      21:178–**21**:186
    mutant strains, **21**:174–**21**:178
  g_1 cyclins of, **36**:139
  gene for CuZnSOD, cloning and sequencing,
    26:79
  genome sequencing project of, **36**:140
  induced mutagenesis
    misrepair and misreplication,
      21:186–**21**:190
    nonrandomness and mutagen specificity,
      21:204–**21**:211
    relationship to DNA repair,
      21:190–**21**:204
  manganese-containing SOD
    amino acid sequences, **26**:70
    biosynthesis, induction by oxygen,
      26:81–**26**:82

  localization in mitochondrial matrix, **26**:79
  mechanisms of induced mutagenesis
    dose-response kinetics, **21**:227–**21**:228
    formation of pure mutant clones,
      21:223–**21**:224
    inducibility of mutagenic process, **21**:227
    time of mutation induction,
      21:220–**21**:223
    untargeted mutagenesis, **21**:224–**21**:227
mei mutants, *asynaptic (as)*, **26**:159
meiosis model, chromosome segregation
  fidelity, **35**:261–265
mitochondrial genome
  chromosomes
    DNA synthesis
      continuous during cell cycle, **25**:227
      polymerase, nuclear gene-encoded,
        25:228
    organization, **25**:227
  continuous genes
    atp, **25**:213–**25**:214
    cox, **25**:212, **25**:213
  introns
    -encoded protein functions,
      25:225–**25**:226
    group I and group II, **25**:223
    nucleotide sequences, **25**:223–**25**:224
    self-catalyzing splicing, **25**:224–**25**:225
  mosaic genes
    cob, **25**:218–**25**:222
      exon mutations, apocytochrome *b*
        forms and, **25**:219–**25**:220
      intron mutations, maturase synthesis
        and, **25**:220–**25**:222
      mRNA processing, **25**:220–**25**:222
    cox1, intron locations, **25**:216–**25**:217
  organization
    genetic map, **25**:197
    mapping using mutants, **25**:201–**25**:202
    model, **25**:188–**25**:189
    strain differences
      intron number, **25**:198
      physical maps, **25**:193
      size, **25**:189, **25**:192
  *rho_* mutants, petite
    behavior in crosses with *rho*+ strain
      hypersensitive *(HS)*, **25**:236–**25**:238
      neutral, **25**:234
      suppressive, **25**:234, **25**:236
    ori sequences, in *HS* mutant crosses with
      wild type

Saccharomyces cerevisiae (continued)
  deletions affecting suppressivity,
    25:237–25:238
  evolutionary origin, scheme, 25:237
  replication origin outside
    mitochondria, 25:238
  structure, 25:236
  palindromic, model of origin, 25:234,
    25:235
  sequence analysis, 25:232–25:234
  spontaneous and induced, 25:232
  rRNA genes
    rnl, mosaic in omega⁺ strains,
      25:205–25:208
    antibiotic-resistant mutants and,
      25:205–25:206
    intronic orf expression,
      25:207–25:208
    polarity in crosses with omega⁻ strains,
      25:206–25:207
    rns, continuous, 25:205,
      25:208–25:209
  transcript pattern, sporulation and, 25:231
  tRNA genes
    clustering, 25:199
    genetic code, 25:211–25:212
    mapping and sequencing,
      25:209–25:210
    tsl, location and function, 25:210–25:211
    vari genes, ribosomal protein-encoding,
      25:214–25:216
  mitochondrial mutagenesis in,
    21:217–21:220
  mosquitoes and, 30:162
  Neurospora crassa and, 29:22–29:23
  nitrate reductase and, 30:8, 30:20, 30:23
  spontaneous mutagenesis
    genetic analysis, 21:211–21:216
    mutation rate during meiosis,
      21:216–21:217
  superoxide dismutases and
    molecular genetics, 30:272–30:277,
      30:280–30:287
    physiology, 30:257, 30:259,
      30:261–30:262
    physiology of mutants, 30:288–30:291,
      30:293, 30:296–30:300, 30:307
    senescence, 30:302–30:303
    structure, 30:263–30:269
    suppression, 30:304, 30:306

telomeres and
  formation, 30:229
  function, 30:204, 30:213, 30:218–30:220
  gene expression, 30:223–30:224
  structure, 30:190–30:192, 30:201
  variation of mtDNA in, 22:32–22:38
Sacharose, puff activity effects, 39:263
sal gene, puff development, 39:251
Salinity tolerance, MGS role in interspecific
  crosses, plants, 26:19
Salivary glands
  chromosomal puffs
    developmental activity, 39:213–224
    dipteran insect development
      hormonal regulation, 39:192–197
      physiology, 39:170–192
    mosquitoes and, 30:159–30:162, 30:169,
      30:171
  telomeres and, 30:225
Salmonella thyphymurium
  flagellar genes, regulation, 27:19, 27:25
  iron-regulated gene in, 36:190, 36:191,
    36:193–36:194
  molybdenum-regulated genes in, 36:200
  nitrate reductase and, 30:3
  nitrogen metabolism genes, regulation, 27:26
  NUV effects
    absorption by thiolated tRNA, 26:106
    protein synthesis induction, 26:126
Salmonids
  evolutionary genetics of fish and,
    29:146–29:147, 29:161, 29:195
  endocrine system, 29:191, 29:194–29:195
  nuclear genomic structures,
    29:137–29:139
Salt tolerance, Gramineae
  cell line selection from tissue culture, 24:478
  proline or glycinebetaine high levels and,
    24:478
sam gene, band organization, 39:153
Samoaia leonensis, differential heterochromatin
  staining, Q-staining, 37:16
Sarcomas
  PMS2 implication in, 36:77
  pRb aberrations in, 36:54
  tumor suppressor gene role in, 36:57
Satellite chromosomes, somaclonal variation
  and, 30:49
Satellite-like repeats, telomeres and,
  30:196–30:197

Sau3A, mosquitoes and, 30:141, 30:143
Scaffold-associated regions, 39:156–160
Scaffold attachment regions, zeste in Drosophila
   melanogaster and, 29:338
SCA genes, autosomal dominant progressive
   ataxias
   clones
      SCA1 gene, 38:40–43
      SCA2 gene, 38:43–44
      SCA3 gene, 38:44–46
      SCA6 gene, 38:46–47
   mapped genes
      SCA4 gene, 38:47–48
      SCA5 gene, 38:48
      SCA7 gene, 38:48–49
   triplet repeat expansions, 38:35–39
Scanning electron microscopy, Neurospora crassa
   and, 29:45
Schizosaccharomyces pombe, 23:1–23:55
   cell cycle, 23:3–23:19
   chromosome rearrangements in, 36:245,
      36:255
   cloning and transformation, 23:52–23:54
   meiosis initiation, cdc gene control,
      26:157–26:158
   mitochondrial genome
      continuous genes, atp, 25:213, 25:214
      DNA synthesis
         inhibition by ethidium bromide, 25:228
         periodic during cell cycle, 25:227
      introns, 25:198
      mosaic genes, intron locations
         cob, 25:217, 25:223
         cox1, 25:218
      mutants and maps, 25:204
      rRNA genes, continuous
         rnl, 25:208
         rns, 25:209
      size, 25:192
      transcription, processing, 25:230–25:231
      tRNA genes
         clusters, 25:199
         structure and genetic code, 25:210,
            25:211, 25:212
      unassigned orf, 25:198
   mutagenesis, 23:41–23:52
   Neurospora crassa and, 29:12
   postradiation recovery, 23:19–23:40
   superoxide dismutases and, 30:261
   telomeres and, 30:229

transformation system, 23:154
variation of mtDNA in, 22:38–22:39
yeast ribosomes and, 29:69
Schmidt-Lanterman incisures, connexin32
   expression at, 36:29
Schwann cells
   abnormalities in CMT1A disease, 36:10
   abnormalities in mouse models, 36:24,
      36:28
   axon association with, 36:24
   function of, 36:22
   myelin protein role in biology of,
      36:26–36:28, 36:30, 36:33–36:34
   peripheral myelin protein 22 in, 36:26
   tumors derived from, 36:79, 36:82
Sclerotization, insects
   β-, pathway of, 24:148–24:150
   cuticle hardening and, 24:147–24:148
   Ddc gene cluster role, Drosophila,
      24:178–24:180
   genes coding for, Drosophila, 24:130–24:134
   quinone, pathway of, 24:148–24:149
scon-1 gene
   (Neurospora crassa)
      control of cys-3 expression, 31:201
      negative sulfur control by, 31:197–198
      in sulfur circuit, 31:190–192
scon-2 gene
   Neurospora crassa
      control of cys expression, 31:201
      negative sulfur control by, 31:197–198
      in sulfur circuit, 31:190–192, 31:191–192
scrambled gene
   Drosophila melanogaster, 31:108
Scr gene, band organization, 39:144
SC35 splicing factor, 31:223
SD11 tumor suppressor gene, characteristics of,
   36:47
Secale cereale, mei mutants
   asynaptic (as), 26:159
   elongate (el), 26:169
   sticky, 26:164
Sectoring, somaclonal variation and, 30:63,
   30:65
Seed storage proteins, gene coding for
   barley, 22:125
   French bean, 22:123–22:124
   maize, 22:116–22:121
   pea, 22:124–22:125
   soybena, 22:121–22:123

Segmentation
    anterior–posterior axis in Drosophila
        melanogaster
        gap to pair-rule gene patterns, 31:11–12
        pair-rule interactions, 31:12–14
        periodicity gradients, 31:10–11
    Segment polarity genes (gooseberry), positional
        function along AP axis, Drosophila, 27:375,
        27:376
Segregation distorter
    Drosophila transposable elements and, 29:260
    Neurospora crassa and, 29:45
Segregation distortion
    autosomes, 37:61–65
    Mu elements of Zea mays and, 30:79
Selection
    ADH activity change, Drosophila,
        25:57–25:58
    ADh population genetics, D. melanogaster
    natural selection, two-allele polymorphism,
        25:81–25:84
    short- and long-term experiments, 25:80
    carbonic anhydrases and, 30:333
    mosquitoes and
        genetic transformation, 30:162–30:164,
            30:168–30:170, 30:172
        genome characterization, 30:141
        physiology, 30:155
    Mu elements of Zea mays and, 30:99
    nitrate reductase and, 30:14–30:15, 30:28,
        30:31
    somaclonal variation and, 30:45–30:46,
        30:60, 30:65–30:66
    superoxide dismutases and, 30:297,
        30:304–30:305, 30:308
    telomeres and, 30:217
Selectionist view, evolutionary genetics of fish
    and, 29:164–29:165
Selective advantage
    Gaucher disease, 32:38–39
    non-insulin-dependent diabetes mellitus,
        32:88
Selenium
    heat-shock puff induction, 39:351
    in proteins, 36:188
Selfing
    Mu elements of Zea mays and, 30:83
    somaclonal variation and, 30:57, 30:64
Self-pollination, Mu elements of Zea mays and,
    30:78

applications, 30:113–30:114
    assays, 30:80–30:81, 30:85–30:86
    characteristics, 30:86–30:87, 30:89
    regulation, 30:99
Sensory nerves, demyelination of, in CMT
    disease, 36:3
Sequences
    carbonic anhydrases and, 30:323
    genes, 30:326–30:327, 30:329–30:330,
        30:333–30:334
    genetic variation, 30:337, 30:346–30:347
    Drosophila transposable elements and
        cis-acting effects, 29:253–29:254,
            29:256–29:257
        foldback elements, 29:282,
            29:284–29:288
        hobo, 29:274–29:277
        mariner, 29:279, 29:281–29:282
        P elements, 29:262–29:266,
            29:268–29:271, 29:273–29:274
        retrotransposons, 29:231–29:236
        transcription rate, 29:241,
            29:243–29:245, 29:247–29:248,
            29:250–29:251
    evolutionary genetics of fish and, 29:122,
        29:201–29:202
        detection of variation, 29:123, 29:126,
            29:128–29:131
        endocrine system, 29:195–29:200
        environmental change, 29:162–29:163,
            29:167–29:169, 29:171–29:172
        immune system, 29:181, 29:183–29:187,
            29:189
        multigene families, 29:148,
            29:150–29:151, 29:154,
            29:157–29:158
        nervous system, 29:177–29:179
        nuclear genomic structures, 29:140, 29:143
    mosquitoes and, 30:125, 30:162–30:167,
        30:169, 30:171
        genetic differentiation, 30:127–30:134
        genome characterization, 30:137,
            30:139–30:147
        physiology, 30:148–30:154, 30:157,
            30:159–30:160
    Mu elements of Zea mays and, 30:79–30:80
        assays, 30:85–30:86
        gene expression, 30:108–30:110, 30:112
        properties of transposition,
            30:100–30:106, 30:108

regulation, 30:97–30:98
structure, 30:91–30:96
Neurospora crassa and, 29:2–29:5, 29:23,
29:46–29:49
genetic material, 29:14, 29:17–29:18
genetic transfer, 29:6–29:7, 29:11
mitrochondria, 29:27–29:30, 29:32,
29:34–29:35
nitrate reductase and, 30:7, 30:9, 30:12,
30:23
somaclonal variation and, 30:54–30:58,
30:60
superoxide dismutases and, 30:262, 30:301,
30:307
molecular genetics, 30:272–30:273,
30:276, 30:280–30:281, 30:284,
30:286–30:288
structure, 30:263–30:269, 30:272
telomeres and, 30:185–30:186,
30:222–30:224, 30:226–30:230,
30:232–30:233
function, 30:203–30:204, 30:206–30:209,
30:211, 30:213–30:216
length, 30:218–30:219, 30:221
replication, 30:221–30:222
structure, 30:186, 30:190–30:201
yeast ribosomes and, 29:65, 29:103
assembly, 29:94–29:95, 29:98
genetic analysis, 29:98–29:101
nucleous, 29:90
ribosomal protein genes, 29:72–29:73,
29:75–29:79
ribosomal RNA processing, 29:93
synthesis changes, 29:84–29:85
zeste in *Drosophila melanogaster* and, 29:302,
29:308, 29:340
DNA binding, 29:318–29:319, 29:321,
29:326
function, 29:238–29:329
molecular biology, 29:313, 29:315
protein, 29:330–29:332
Serine proteases, encoded by *snake* and *easter*, in
embryo, *Drosophila*, 27:291–27:292
Serotonin, synthesis and metabolism, 24:135
Sertoli cells, testis, human
TF synthesis *in vitro* and *in vivo*, 25:14–15
Serum response factor, mammalian, homology
to yeast MCM1, 27:50–27:51
sevenless (sev) mutant
Drosophila melanogaster, 31:140–141

Severe combined immunodeficiency disorder
cloning studies, 35:74–78
animal models, 35:77–78
cytokine receptor signaling, 35:76–77
gene map, 35:74–76
γ_c-chain gene organization, 35:77
mutation analysis, 35:77
future research directions, 35:89–90
historical perspective, 35:59–61
overview, 35:57–58
phenotype, 35:73–74
sev gene
distribution estimation, 39:118
oligogene bands, 39:131–135
Sex chromosome
chromatid synapsis variation, 34:154–156
diptera morphology, 34:132–133
long-term incubation, 34:297
mutation effects, 34:307–308
pompon-like chromosomes, 34:140–150
Sex comb, control by *dsx* and homeotic genes,
Drosophila, 27:217–27:218, 27:220
Sex combs reduced (Scr) gene, homeotic,
Drosophila
molecular map, position in ANT-C,
27:339–27:441
mRNA accumulation in embryo, 27:341,
27:349
mutations, recovery and characterization,
27:339
protein product
accumulation, 27:341–27:342, 27:349
homeodomain sequences, 27:370,
27:371
Sex-controlling genes
C. elegans
egg-laying *(egl-41)*, 27:137
epistasis, 27:138–27:141
feminization *(fem)*, 27:132–27:137
fem-1, 27:133–27:134
fem-2, 27:134–27:135
fem-3, 27:135–27:137
regulation, 27:181
germ line-specific role, 27:142–27:143,
27:178
germ line-specific role
fog-1, 27:142–27:143
fog-2, 27:143
hermaphroditization *(her-1)*
function in adult male, 27:178

Sex-controlling genes (continued)
    interaction with sdc genes,
        27:157–27:158
    mutant phenotypes, 27:131–27:132,
        27:137–27:138
    transformer (tra)
    tra-1
        autonomous activity, 27:170–27:171
        mechanism of action, approaches,
            27:144–27:145
        mutant phenotypes, 27:126–27:128
    tra-2
        germ line-specific role, 27:143
        mutant phenotypes, 27:128–27:130
    tra-3, mutant phenotypes,
        27:130–27:131
Drosophila
    dsx (double-sex)
        homeotic genes and, 27:218, 27:220
        locus structure and function, scheme,
            27:219
        male-determining (M) and females-
            determining (F) products,
            27:216–27:217
        repression of sex-specific differentiation
            genes by, 27:217–27:219
        positional information and, 27:220
        regulation of sex-specific products,
            27:220–27:224
        male-specific transcripts and,
            27:223–27:224
        yolk protein in fat body and, 27:221,
            27:223
    linear pathway, 27:141–27:142
    from primary signal to Sxl
    liz (snf), with maternal and zygotic
        components, 27:207–27:208,
        27:213–27:215
    maternal genes
        Daughterkiller (Dk), 27:207
        daughterless (da), 27:206–27:207
    sisterless (sis-a, sis-b), zygotic,
        27:209–27:210, 27:212–27:215
    X/A ratio role, 27:210–27:216
    from Sxl to dsx (ix, tra, vir)
        cell autonomous differentiation and,
            27:195–27:196
        hierarchical arrangement,
            27:190–27:191, 27:198–27:199
        on alternative splicing level,
            27:202–27:204

    mutant phenotypes, 27:192–27:194
    X/A ratio and, 27:194–27:195
    permanent requirement during
        development, 27:196–27:198
    sex-specific transcripts, regulation,
        27:199–27:202
    alternative splicing and,
        27:202–27:204
    Sxl pivotal role, 27:204–27:206
Sex determination, 33:275–314
    abnormalities, 33:300–313
        familial agonadism, 33:313
        hermaphrodites, 33:311–313
        XX males, 33:308–313
        XY females, 33:301–308
    C. elegans
        comparison with Drosophila
            molecular characterization,
                27:180–27:181
            phylogenetic criteria, 27:181
            X/A ratio role, 27:175–27:177,
                27:179–27:180
            yolk protein regulation, 27:181
        in germ line, 27:142–27:143, 27:178
        in intestine, 27:178–27:179
        X/A ratio role, 27:122–27:125,
            27:166–27:169
    and dosage compensation, coordinate control,
        C. elegans
    number of genes involved, 27:163–27:165
    pathway, 27:154 (scheme)
    sdc genes
        comparison with dpy-29, 27:161–27:162
        sdc-1, 27:153–27:157
        sdc-2, 27:153–27:155
        sex determination pathway and,
            27:157–27:158
    xol-1 gene
        molecular cloning, 27:161
        X/A ratio and, 27:166
        XO (male) phenotypes, 27:158–27:160
        XX (hermaphrodite) phenotypes,
            27:160–27:161
    evolutionary genetics of fish and, 29:175
    factors, germline cell chromosomes,
        37:304–306
    genetic
        in birds, 20:221–20:223
        in Drosophila, 20:219–20:220
        early studies, 20:218–20:219
        in mammals, 20:220

models of, 20:223–20:230
molecular genetics, 33:278–300
  chromosomal basis, 33:278–281
  gonad-determining genes, 33:293–300
    dosage-sensitive sex reversal, 33:299–300
    sex-reversing chromosomal deletions,
      33:300
    SOX9 gene, 33:296–297
    steroidogenic factor 1, 33:297–299
    WT1 gene, 33:294–296
  testis determining factor
    candidates, 33:281–283
    cloning, 33:283–293
    sex-determining Y gene, 33:288–293
    Y chromosome analysis, 33:283–287
    zinc finger Y gene, 33:287–288
  overview, 33:275–278
Sex differentiation
  Drosophila
    effects on X-linked genes
      dosage compensation, 24:390–24:391
      expression, 24:389–24:391
      genes contributing to, 24:391–24:397, *see
        also* Genes, *Drosophila melanogaster*
    gonadal, 20:230–20:231
    descriptive embryology, 20:231–20:234
    dominant sex *versus* neutral sex,
      20:234–20:238
    models of, 20:238–20:253
    somatic cell-germ cell interction,
      20:253–20:255
Sex lethal (Sxl) gene
  Drosophila melanogaster
    alternative splicing, 31:244–247
    spatial regulation, 31:7–10
    and X/A ratio in sexual fate determination,
      31:4–10
Sex-specifically regulated genes, *Drosophila*
  model of regulation by *dsx*, TTAF role,
    27:227–27:229
  msts (male-specific transcripts), indirect
    control by *dsx*, 27:223–27:224
  s15-1 (chorion protein)
    germ line effect on expression, 27:224
    structure, 27:225–27:227
  yp1-yp2 (yolk protein)
    germ line effect on expression, 27:224
    regulation by *dsx*, 27:221, 27:223
    structure, 27:225–27:227
Sexual differentiation
  Caenorhabditis elegans

autonomous *tra-1* activity, 27:171–27:172
  irreversibility *versus* plasticity,
    27:177–27:179
  in germ line, 27:178
  in intestine, 27:178–27:179
  maternal environment role,
    27:173–27:174
  nonindependence of cells, 27:172–27:173
  positional information and, 27:174
  Drosophila melanogaster, cell autonomy and,
    27:171
  mammalian, autonomous and
    nonautonomous steps, 27:170–27:171
Sexual inducer, in heat-shock response, *Volvox*,
  24:14–24:15
Sexual reproduction
  allelic recombinations, lower rates in males,
    24:355
  benefits
    group selection, 24:324
    neutral modifier approach, 24:324–24:325
    short-term costs to individuals, 24:324
  DNA damage and mutation, *see* DNA
  germ lines
    meiosis, 24:353–24:355
    potential immortality, 24:359, 24:361
  hypotheses
    parasitic DNA, 24:358–24:359
    repair, 24:323, 24:329, 24:356–24:358,
      24:360
    variation, 24:323–24:324,
      24:355–24:358, 24:360
  origin and early evolution
    DNA viruses, recombinatorial repair,
      24:345
    primitive haploid organism coping with
      lethal mutations, 24:345–24:346
    diploidy, transient to dominant stage,
      24:345–24:346
    protocell, genome damage, 24:343
    reactivation by fusion to transient
      diploidy, 24:344
    RNA replicator, 24:342
    encapsulated hypercycles, 24:343
    RNA viruses, multiplicity reactivation,
      24:344–24:345
  outcrossing
    favored among other reproductive systems,
      24:349–24:350
    in haplodiploid insects, 24:352–24:353
    in multicellular haploids, 24:351–24:353

Sexual reproduction (continued)
  recessive mutations masked at equilibrium,
    24:347–24:348
  short-term costs, 24:346–24:347
  switching to parthenogenesis or vegetative
    reproduction, costs of,
    24:350–24:351
X-linked genes, dosage compensation, see
  X-linked genes, Drosophila
SF1 splicing factor, 31:222
SF3 splicing factor, 31:222
Sgs genes
  band organization, 39:153
  cascade regulation, 39:326–327
  chromomere–gene–loop relations, 39:157
  dosage compensation, 39:77–78
  puff development, 39:209, 39:211,
    39:299–309, 39:315
  secretory protein expression, 39:180–182,
    39:193
  sequence homology, 39:323
  transcription proteins, 39:55
Sh1, Mu elements of Zea mays and,
  30:93–30:94, 30:110
sh1, Mu elements of Zea mays and, 30:110
sh9026, Mu elements of Zea mays and, 30:110
Sh1-A83, Mu elements of Zea mays and, 30:97
Shifting mode, evolutionary genetics of fish and,
  29:142
Shigella flexneri, mercury resistance gene of,
  36:205
Shiverer mouse, myelin basic protein lack in,
  36:22
Short-bristle gene, protein synthesis theory,
  38:117
Short interspersed nuclear elements (SINES),
  Drosophila transposable elements and,
  29:233
Shrinkage necrosis, apoptosis concept
  development, 35:36–40
  hormone regulation, 35:39
  identification, 35:36–39
    cancer cells, 35:38–39
    ischaemic liver cells, 35:37–38
    normal tissues, 35:38–39
    programmed cell death, 35:39–40
Signaling
  during neural induction
    Xenopus laevis
      combined, 31:45–47

homeogenetic induction, 31:47–48
    planar, 31:45
    vertical, 31:44–45
Silencing, transcriptional domain repression
  maintenance, 37:424–426
Silene alba, pollen
  bearing X and Y chromosomes, growth rate
    difference, 26:3
  germinating in vitro, zinc tolerance, 26:15
Silk moths, see also Bombyx mori
  chorion, structure, 24:224
  chorion genes, 24:226, 24:228–24:231
    expression in transgenic Drosophila,
      24:235–24:238
    regulatory intergenic elements,
      24:232–24:235, 24:237–24:239
  chorion proteins, 24:225–24:228
Silver stain, intercalary heterochromatin
  identification, 37:150
Simian virus 40
  large T and small t antigen production by
    alternative splice sites, 31:229–231
  T anigen of, See T antigen
  in transgenic mouse
    early region, 24:305–24:306
    T antigen expression, 24:305
    T antigen-rat insulin gene construct,
      24:306
Simulium morsitans, B chromosome studies,
  37:283, 37:286, 37:293–299
sina gene, band organization, 39:151
SINE, telomeres and, 30:217
Sine wales, puff activity effects, 39:263
singed wings gene, hormone function-impairing
  mutations, 39:169
Single gene disorders, mouse models,
  35:168–175
  assays, 35:171–173
  candidate gene cloning, 35:169–170
  causal gene determination, 35:173–175
  functional disease loci cloning, 35:169
  positional cloning, 35:170–171
Single-stranded conformational polymorphism
  analysis
    diabetes-susceptibility gene identification,
      32:55–56
    use in mutation screening, 36:35, 36:36
Singlet oxygen, NUV-induced, toxicity, 26:115
Sister chromatid exchange, somaclonal
  variation and, 30:51

Sister chromatids
exchange
meiotic recombination, 33:41–59
cytological analysis, 33:52–55
genetic analysis, 33:43–50
chromosome repeats, 33:50
circular chromosomes, 33:48
duplicated gene exchange, 33:44–47
nonsister chromatid competition, 33:49
ribosomal DNA crossovers, 33:43–44
genetic control, 33:50–52
nonsister chromatid comparison, 33:55–59
physical assay, recombination intermediates, 33:48–49
Mu elements of Zea mays and, 30:107
sisterless-a (sis-a) gene
Drosophila melanogaster, 31:5
sisterless-b (sis-b) gene
Drosophila melanogaster, 31:5
Sisterless (sis-a, sis-b) genes, zygotic, Drosophila
as numerator elements of X/A ratio, 27:166, 27:212–27:215
sex-controlling function, 27:166, 27:209–27:210
Size
chromomere pattern analysis, 34:207–212
historical perspective, 34:9
nuclei, 34:260–280
Skeletal muscles, disorders, see Duchenne muscular dystrophy
sk gene, Neurospora crassa and, 29:45
Skin, antigens of, 20:305–20:306
Skin cancer, tumor suppressor gene mutations in, 36:96
Slipping, satellite DNA, 37:53
Small nucleolar RNA, yeast ribosomes and, 29:74, 29:88–29:91
small-optic-lobes (sol) mutant
Drosophila melanogaster, 31:142–143
Smooth muscle, pathology in muscular dystrophy, 33:182
SmtB protein, as bacterial metal responsive protein, 36:220–36:222, 36:226
snRNP, yeast ribosomes and, 29:89, 29:91–29:93
SOD, see Superoxide dismutases
sodA gene, Fur negative regulation of, 36:194

Sodium
evolutionary genetics of fish and, 29:191
role in cellular integrity, 36:188
Sodium arsenate, puff activity effects, 39:263
Sodium azide, heat-shock puff induction, 39:351
Sodium butyrate, heterochromatin gene expression modification, 37:343
Sodium cacodylate, heat-shock puff induction, 39:351
Sodium chennel genes, evolutionary genetics of fish and, 29:178–29:181
Sodium perchlorate, puff activity effects, 39:263
Sodium rodanid, puff activity effects, 39:263
Sodium salicylate, heat-shock puff induction, 39:351
Sodium tetraborate, puff activity effects, 39:263
Somaclonal variation in plants, 30:41–30:42, 30:65–30:66
genetic consequences
cell cycle disturbance, 30:61–30:62
chromosomal aberrations, 30:48–30:52
DNA-level aberrations, 30:58–30:60
methylation changes, 30:56–30:58
phenotype, 30:60–30:61
transposable elements, 30:52–30:56
genotype, 30:46–30:48
culture age, 30:45–30:46
culture type, 30:43–30:45
explant source tissue, 30:42–30:43
unusual genetic behavior, 30:62
altered transmission, 30:64–30:65
homozygosity, 30:62–30:63
sectoring, 30:62
unstable mutations, 30:64
Somatic excision products, Mu elements of Zea mays and, 30:100–30:103, 30:107–30:108
Somatic pairing, intercalary heterochromatin identification, 37:206–207
Somatic reversion, Mu elements of Zea mays and, 30:97, 30:107
assays for monitoring, 30:80–30:84
characteristics, 30:87–30:89
Somatic synapsis, see Synapsis
Somatolactin, evolutionary genetics of fish and, 29:195–29:196
Somatostatin, evolutionary genetics of fish and, 29:198–29:200
Song cycles, Drosophila rhythm genetics, 38:159–160

Sonic hedgehog gene, human malformation role
  dorsoventral patterning, **38**:15–16
  limb patterning, **38**:17–18
Sordaria brevicollis, chromosome rearrangements
  in, **36**:283
Sordaria fimicola, chromosome rearrangements
  in, **36**:283–**36**:284
Sordaria macrospora, chromosome rearrangements
  in, **36**:244, **36**:284–**36**:285
Sorghum, somaclonal variation and, **30**:61
Southern blot, DNA underrepresentation
  analysis, **37**:418–419
SOX9 gene, gonad determination, **33**:296–297
Soybean
  genes coding for seed storage proteins of,
    22:121–**22**:123
  genome, changes in tissue culture, **28**:81,
    28:83
  HS mRNA synthesis, self-regulation,
    28:251–**28**:253
  HSP-encoding genes, **28**:239–**28**:243
  nitrate reductase and, **30**:5, **30**:14
  receptor for fungal elicitor, **28**:202
  somaclonal variation and, **30**:57, **30**:60
spaghetti squash gene, **31**:109
Spastic paraplegia, in HMSNV disease, **36**:4
spb mutants, yeast ribosomes and,
  29:102–**29**:103
SPB2, yeast ribosomes and, **29**:102
SPB4, yeast ribosomes and, **29**:102
Species specificity, telomeres and, **30**:186
Spemann's organizer, *see* Organizer
Sperm
  braconid wasps
    inactivation by alkylating agents,
      25:172–**25**:173
    lethal mutation induction by EMS,
      25:173–**25**:174
    radiation damage, **25**:150
    orbital flight-unaffected, **25**:150–**25**:151
  telomeres and, **30**:201, **30**:206
Spermatocytes
  Drosophila hydei
    primary
      nuclear ultrastructure, **23**:188–**23**:198,
        23:205–**23**:206
      transcription, **23**:192, **23**:194–**23**:199
      Y-chromosomal lampbrush loops,
        23:181, **23**:184, **23**:188–**23**:209
    secondary, meiosis, **23**:210–**23**:211

Spermatogenesis
  in *Drosophila hydei*, **23**:178–**23**:228
    comparison with *D. melanogaster*, **23**:199,
      23:201, **23**:227–**23**:228
    meiotic, **23**:210–**23**:211
    morphogenesis, **23**:181–**23**:189
    nuclear ultrastructure during,
      23:188–**23**:198, **23**:205–**23**:206
    postmeiotic, **23**:211–**23**:215
      advanced spermatids, **23**:214–**23**:215
      young spermatids, **23**:211–**23**:214
    premeiotic, **23**:188–**23**:210
    transcriptional pattern during, **23**:192,
      23:194–**23**:199
  Y chromosome, *see* Chromosome Y
Spermine, superoxide dismutases and,
  30:293–**30**:294
Spheroplasts
  effect on fungal transformation frequency,
    23:96–**23**:97
  Neurospora crassa and, **29**:10, **29**:48
  yeast ribosomes and, **29**:95
Spinach
  cold acclimation
    COR polypeptides
      boiling-stable property, **28**:121
      composition, **28**:110, **28**:111, **28**:113
      distribution in tissues, **28**:122
      mRNA populations and, **28**:114
    nitrate reductase and, **30**:12, **30**:30
    photosynthetic genes, photoregulation,
      28:136–**28**:138
Spinal development, *see* Body plan genes
Spireme nuclei
  historical perspective, **34**:5–9
  infusoria chromosomes, **34**:77
Spleen, TF mRNA, rat, **25**:16
Spleen colony formation, macrocytic anemia
  and, **20**:395–**20**:401
Splenectomy, Gaucher disease treatment,
  32:28–29
Spliceosomes, RNA splicing, **31**:211–213
Splice-site mutations, in tumor suppressor genes,
  36:99
Splicing factors
  constitutive
    in alternative splicing, **31**:220–225
    interactions, **31**:218–220
Spm, *Mu* elements of *Zea mays* and, **30**:81,
  30:91, **30**:113, **30**:115

sponge gene, effects on actin structures,
Drosophila melanogaster, 31:108
Spore killer, *Neurospora crassa* and, 29:45
Sporophyte
effect on
exine pattern, 26:7–26:8, 26:10–26:11,
26:47
MGS, maize, 26:39–26:40
pollen size, 26:9–26:10
growth, pollen selection effect, 26:3
selection, comparison with MGS, 26:39
Sporopollenin, deposition on exine, 26:5
Sporulation
in a/α cells, yeast, 27:34, 27:42
specific genes, B. *subtilis*
regulatory cascade, 27:24–27:25
septum formation and, 27:18
SPP-2 splicing factor, 31:221
Springtail, chromosome characteristics, 34:69,
34:71
Squash, nitrate reductase and, 30:4, 30:7,
30:10–30:11
src oncogene, discovery of, 36:46
SRF, *see* Serum response factor
SRP gene, APC as neighbor of, 36:74
5S rRNA, yeast ribosomes and, 29:95–29:96
Ssb1p, yeast ribosomes and, 29:89, 29:91
SSB1, yeast ribosomes and, 29:88
SSP-1 splicing factor, 31:221
SstI, Mu elements of Zea mays and, 30:99
sta gene, hormone function-impairing
mutations, 39:168
Staining methods
differential heterochromatin staining
acridine orange stain, 37:143–145
acriflavine-nitrate, 37:146–149
ammoniacal silver stain, 37:150
C-staining, 37:14–15, 37:141
enzymatic chromosome digestion, 37:24
heterochromatin heterogeneity, 37:24
H-staining, 37:15–21, 37:141–143
methyl green stain, 37:146
N-staining, 37:21–23
pyronine, 37:146
Q-staining, 37:15–21
Drosophila melanogaster, 37:18, 37:20
Drosophila virilis, 37:17, 37:21
Escherichia coli, 37:17
intercalary heterochromatin,
37:141–143

Samoaia leonensis, 37:16
telomeric heterochromatin identification,
37:279–280
histochemical RNA staining, 39:40–41
Staphylococcus aureus
arsenic detoxification in, 36:216
CadC protein from, 36:220, 36:221,
36:222–36:223
Staphylococcus epidermis, iron-regulated gene in,
36:191
Staphylococcus marcescens, iron-regulated gene
in, 36:193
Staphylococcus xylosus, arsenic detoxification in,
36:216, 36:218
Statistical analysis
radiation hybrid genome maps, 33:82–94
data collection, 33:83–84
influential hybrids, 33:91–92
multipoint analysis, 33:84–91
two-point analysis, 33:84
Ste gene, Y chromosome, 37:66–68
Stem cells, hemopoietic, 20:369–20:373
Sterility, female, Drosophila, Ddc gene cluster
role, 24:180–24:181
Steroidogenic factor 1, gonad determination,
33:297–299
Steroids, evolutionary genetics of fish and, 29:197
Sterol regulatory element-1, low-density
lipoprotein receptor protein transcription,
32:150–152
Stigma
nutrients, effects on pollen germination
raspberry, 26:27–26:28
Turnera ulmifolia, 26:28
pollen loads, hummingbird-pollinated forest
species, 26:32–26:33
Stomach cancer, DCC gene implication in,
36:78
stopper mutant, Neurospora crassa and, 29:31,
29:33
Strain stability
storage and, 20:85
tandem duplications and unstable phenotype,
20:87–20:89
viruses and, 20:85–20:87
Streptococcus mutans, metal substitution in
Fe-MnSODs, 26:71–26:72
Streptomyces lividans
dtxR homolog of, 36:197
mercury resistance gene of, 36:205, 36:206

Streptomyces pilosus, dtxR homolog of, **36**:197
Stress, somaclonal variation and, **30**:41, **30**:60
Stretching, chromosomes, isolated chromosome
    studies, **34**:330–332
Striation, *see* Bands
string gene, in G2-M regulation, *Drosophila
    melanogaster,* **31**:90–91
String of pearls gene, protein synthesis theory,
    38:93–95
Strontium-85, *see* Gamma rays
Strontium-89, braconid wasp feeding effects,
    25:161
Structure, *see also* Bands
    chromatids
        nonpolytene chromosomes, **34**:243–247
        polytene chromosomes, **34**:247–260
    DNA, **34**:220–224
    general characterization, **34**:215–219
    minor components, **34**:242–243
    protein, **34**:225–242
    RNA, **34**:224–225
    spatial organization
        interphase nonpolytene nuclei,
            34:332–335
        polytene nuclei
            chromosome fields, **34**:340–344
            chromosome polarity, **34**:335–340
            ectopic contacts, **34**:351
            longitudinal coiling, **34**:344
            nuclear architectonics, **34**:353–355
            nuclear arrangement, **34**:344–350
            three-dimensional structure
                maintenance, **34**:351–353
Stubarista gene, protein synthesis theory,
    38:115–116
Style
    effects on pollen germination, **26**:3,
        26:29–**26**:30
    mediation of pollen-pollen interaction
        chemotropism for pollen tubes and,
            26:32
        mentor effect and, **26**:30–**26**:31
        pioneer pollen effect and, **26**:31
        pollen mixture from two lines and, **26**:30
Stylonchia, telomeres and, **30**:199
Subdivision 1B of X chromosome
    Drosophila
        achaete-scute complex
            interaction with *da* and neurogenic
                genes, **27**:440–**27**:441

    multiple transcripts, spatial distribution,
        27:437–**27**:439
    in neurogenic mutants, **27**:438,
        27:441–**27**:442
    protein products, neuralizing function,
        27:446
    structure, **27**:436–**27**:439
    embryonic lethal and visual system defective,
        molecular organization, **27**:439
    genes required for neural development,
        27:433–**27**:435
    genetic map, **27**:434
Subtelomeric regions
    formation, **30**:231
    function, **30**:224
    structure, **30**:195
Subtelomeric repeats
    formation, **30**:230, **30**:232
    function, **30**:218
    interspersed, **30**:196
    structure, **30**:197–**30**:198
Subterminal sequences
    isolation, **32**:285–287
    repeat sequences, **32**:287–289
Subtraction cloning, diabetes-susceptibility gene
    identification, **32**:61–62
SUC, telomeres and, **30**:192, **30**:195,
    30:223–**30**:224
Succinoxidase system, in braconid wasps,
    25:141
Sucrose synthetase, genes coding for,
    22:127–**22**:128
Sugar beet, *mei* mutants, *parallel spindle (ps),*
    26:168
Sugarcane, somaclonal variation and,
    30:44–**30**:45
Suicide vectors, risk of use, **32**:4
Sulfate oxidase, as antioxidant, *Drosophila,*
    28:60
Sulfate permease I, regulation in, *Neurospora
    crassa,* **31**:194–195
Sulfate permease II
    regulation in
        Neurospora crassa, **31**:194–195
Sulfates
    aromatic, as sulfur source for *Neurospora
        crassa,* **31**:192–194
    superoxide dismutases and, **30**:252–**30**:253
Sulfite oxidase, nitrate reductase and, **30**:7
Sulfur

Neurospora crassa and, 29:38–29:39
regulation
  in *Neurospora crassa*
    alternative sulfur sources, 31:196
    aromatic sulfate utilization, 31:192–194
    aryl sulfatase role, 31:192–194
    assimilation pathway, 31:189
    choline-O-sulfate utilization,
      31:195–196
    circuit design, 31:190
    cys-3 gene
      characterization, 31:198–199
      control of, 31:201
    CYS3 protein
      autogenous regulation, 31:201
      DNA binding, 31:199–200
      as DNA-binding nuclear protein,
        31:201–202
      molecular characterization,
        31:202–203
      mutation studies, 31:200–201
    environmental sulfur sources,
      31:192–194
    genetic controls, 31:190–192
    metabolic repressors of sulfur catabolic
      expression, 31:196–197
    negative control genes, 31:197–198
    physiological basis, 31:190
    positive control genes, 31:197–198
    structural genes affecting, 31:191–192
    sulfate permease II role, 31:194–195
    sulfate permease I role, 31:194–195
  in *Saccharomyces cerevisiae*, 31:203–204
superoxide dismutases and, 30:261, 30:280,
  30:293
Supernumerary chromosomes, *see* B
  chromosomes
Superoxide anion radical
  elimination by SOD, 26:66, 26:74,
    26:77–26:79, 26:111–26:112,
    26:122–26:123
  catalytic mechanisms, 26:75–26:76
  mutagenicity, 26:133
  NUV-induced, toxicity, 26:111,
    26:113–26:114, 26:116, 26:122–26:123
  SOD effects, 26:111, 26:114, 26:123
  SOD induction during aerobic growth, E.
    coli, 26:83–26:84, 26:86
Superoxide dismutases, 30:251–30:252
  anoxic stress effect, *Iris pseudacorus*, 28:30

antioxidant action, 28:6–28:8
biosynthesis in microorganisms
  oxygen-induced, 26:81–26:82
  superoxide-induced, E. *coli*, 26:82–26:86
  metal cofactor availability and,
    26:84–26:85
  negatively controlled operon and,
    26:83–26:86
catalysis, 30:267–30:268
copper-zinc-containing, eukaryotic
  amino acid sequences, 26:68–26:70,
    26:79
  distribution in bacteria, 26:67
  induction by copper and $O_2^{\cdot}$, 26:82
  specific inhibitors, 26:69
  in yeast, *see Saccharomyces cerevisiae*
Cu-ZnSOD, *Drosophila*
  biological role, 28:54
  properties, 28:53–28:54
  radioprotection and, 28:64
evolution, 26:68, 26:74–26:75,
  30:270–30:272
function, 30:268–30:270
function of, 36:194
genes coding for, 26:79–26:80,
  26:85–26:86, 26:122–26:123
isozymes, maize
  biochemistry, properties, 28:17–28:18
  genetics, 28:19–28:20
  intracellular compartmentalization, 28:19
  responses to
    oxygen, 28:26–28:27
    paraquat, 28:23–28:26
manganese-iron-containing(Mn-FeSODs),
    procaryotic, *see also Escherichia coli*
  amino acid sequences, 26:68–26:70
  Cambialistic forms, 26:72, 26:75
  distribution
    in bacteria, 26:72–26:74
    iron-containing SOD in plants, 26:67
  inhibitors, 26:72
  metal substitution, 26:71–26:72
molecular genetics, 30:287–30:288
  catalases, 30:287
  Cu,ZnSOD, 30:272–30:280
  MnSOD, 30:280–30:287
  peroxidases, 30:287
  mutants defective for, E. *coli*, 26:78,
    26:80–26:81, 26:114, 26:123
  oxidative stress and, 28:9, 28:20

Superoxide dismutases (*continued*)
  physiology
    antioxidant defense, 30:262–30:263
    dioxygen, 30:252–30:255
    oxygen defense mechanisms,
      30:255–30:257
    superoxide, 30:257–30:262
  physiology of mutants, 30:288–30:289
    antioxidant enzymes, 30:306–30:308
    genetic consequences, 30:297–30:300
    metabolism, 30:289, 30:292–30:297
    oxidant sensitivity, 30:289–30:291
    senescence, 30:300–30:303
    suppression, 30:303–30:306
  ribonucleotide reductase activation, *E. coli*,
    26:112
  SOD1
    antioxidant enzymes, 30:306
    molecular genetics, 30:272–30:273,
      30:272–30:281, 30:285–30:286,
      30:288
    physiology, 30:259, 30:262–30:263
    physiology of mutants, 30:288–30:291,
      30:289, 30:293–30:295,
      30:294–30:295, 30:297–30:299,
      30:298–30:300, 30:307
    structure, 30:263–30:266,
      30:268–30:269, 30:272
    suppression, 30:303–30:304
  SOD1
    molecular genetics, 30:279–30:280
    physiology, 30:262–30:263
    physiology, 30:297, 30:307
    structure, 30:268–30:269, 30:269,
      30:271
  Sod1, 30:268
  SOD2
    molecular genetics, 30:285
    physiology, 30:306
    structure, 30:268–30:270
  SOD2
    physiology, 30:262, 30:297, 30:299,
      30:306
    structure, 30:276, 30:280–30:288
  SOD3, 30:306
  sod2, 30:288–30:291, 30:293,
    30:295–30:296, 30:298, 30:304,
    30:306
  sodA, 30:298, 30:305, 30:308
  sodB, 30:272, 30:298, 30:305, 30:308

    structure, 30:263–30:267
    superoxide radical elimination, 26:66, 26:74,
      26:77–26:79, 26:111–26:112,
      26:122–26:123
    catalytic mechanisms, 26:75–26:76
    protection against NUV, 26:111, 26:114,
      26:123
Superoxide (O$_2$)
  molecular genetics, 30:284
  physiology, 30:257–30:263
    of mutants, 30:293–30:302,
      30:304–30:305, 30:308
  structure, 30:268, 30:270
Superoxide radical (O^2_)
  cytotoxicity, 28:4–28:7
  production, 28:4–28:5
    in plants, 28:5–28:6
    induction by paraquat, 28:9, 28:23,
      28:24, 28:26
"Super-repressors," of bacterial genes, 36:203
Suppressor genes, position effect modification,
  37:350–355
Suppressor-mutator, somaclonal variation and,
  30:52–30:53, 30:56
suppressor of sable (su[s]) gene
  alternative splicing
    Drosophila melanogaster, 31:253–254
suppressor of white apricot su[w^a]$^+$) gene
  alternative splicing
    Drosophila melanogaster, 31:252–253
SUP44, yeast ribosomes and, 29:69,
  29:72–29:73, 29:75
SUP46, yeast ribosomes and, 29:69,
  29:72–29:73, 29:75
Susceptibility, mosquitoes and, 30:155,
  30:159
SV40, *see* Simian virus 40
Swedish population, *BRCA1* gene mutations in,
  36:86
swi gene
  band organization, 39:142–144
  hormone function-impairing mutations,
    39:169, 39:283–284
  puff development, 39:241, 39:291
sx gene, X-chromosome replication, 39:433
sxl gene, dosage compensation, 39:80
Synapsis
  chromatids
    chromosome variation, 34:150–157
    polyteny morphology, 34:125–130

homologous chromosomes
additional chromosome material effect,
34:163–165
asynapsis
causes, 34:173–174
occurrence, 34:157–163
disturbance-controlled tissue differences,
34:166–169
factors, 34:170–172
interspecific hybrid homologs,
34:165–166
meiotic conjugation relation,
34:172–173
Synaptic adjustment, in *N. crassa* rearrangement
heterozygotes, 36:264–36:265
Synechococcus
carbonic anhydrases and, 30:323, 30:325
iron-regulated gene in, 36:191
SmtB protein from, 36:220–36:222,
36:226

T. paludosa, pollen, mRNA classes, 26:22,
26:24
tad, *Neurospora crassa* and, 29:46
Talinum mengesii, pollen, competition-
intensifying mechanisms, 26:42–26:48
Tandem repeats, intercalary heterochromatin
identification, 37:216–224
Chironomus thummi Cla-elements, 37:105,
37:219–220
dinucleotide repeats, 37:222–223
Drosophila melanogaster X chromosome
repeats, 37:222
histone encoding genes, 37:219
mononucleotide repeats, 37:222–223
nucleotide sequences, 37:246
pDv family repeats, 37:223
poly(A) nucleotide complexes, 37:220–222
polypyrimidines, 37:219
rRNA genes, 37:218–219
scrambled repeats, 37:223–224
T antigen, inactivation of p53 by, 36:57
Target genes, mosquitoes and, 30:170–30:172
Target site preference, *Mu* elements of *Zea mays*
and, 30:103, 30:116
Taxonomy, evolutionary genetics of fish and,
29:135, 29:138, 29:155–29:156, 29:160,
29:188

Tay–Sachs disease, in Jewish populations,
32:27
T cell receptor, evolutionary genetics of fish
and, 29:181, 29:188–29:189
T cells
evolutionary genetics of fish and, 29:181,
29:188–29:189
human
cytotoxicity induction, TF and TFR
functions, 25:22
helper-inducer (T4⁺), activated
IL-2 autocrine cycle, 25:20–25:21
TF mRNA, 25:15, 25:20
TF synthesis
proliferation and, 25:21
truncated 62-kDA protein, 25:22
Ly antigens of, 20:300–20:303,
20:341–20:342
TCM1, yeast ribosomes and, 29:70, 29:75
tcm1, yeast ribosomes and, 29:70,
29:72–29:73
T complex, MHC and, 20:320–20:322
TDC, *see* Tyrosine decarboxylase
TE elements, *Drosophila* transposable elements
and, 29:284, 29:286
TEF1, yeast ribosomes and, 29:77–29:78
TEF2, yeast ribosomes and, 29:77–29:78
TEL1, telomeres and, 30:218
TEL2, telomeres and, 30:218
Teleosts, evolutionary genetics of fish and,
29:197
environmental change, 29:159, 29:163,
29:167–29:168
immune system, 29:187–29:189
multigene families, 29:151–29:157
nuclear genomic structures, 29:137, 29:139
Tellurium, bacterial detoxification of, 36:216
Telomerase, 30:232
formation, 30:227–30:228, 30:230
function, 30:204–30:205, 30:207,
30:209, 30:211, 30:215–30:218,
30:220–30:221
structure, 30:187, 30:190
Telomere-associated DNA, structure, 30:186,
30:193
Telomeres, 30:185–30:186, 30:232–30:233,
32:273–306
binding proteins, 32:280–281
in cancer, 32:298–300
carbonic anhydrases and, 30:334

Telomeres (continued)
  chromosome ends from other primates,
    32:295–296
  chromosome healing in vivo, 32:301–303
    telomerase activity, 32:301–302
    telomerase inactivity in somatic tissues,
      32:302–303
    telomere capture, 32:303
  contiguous gene syndromes, 32:303–305
  cryptic translocation, 32:303–305
  evolutionary genetics of fish and, 29:141
  formation, 30:226–30:227
    artificial induction, 30:228–30:232
    developmental regulation, 30:227–30:228
  function, 30:201, 32:273–275
    cellular senescence, 30:206–30:208
    chromosome capping, 30:201–30:203
    control length, 30:217–30:221
    elongation, 30:208–30:217
    gene expression, 30:222–30:224
    nuclear organization, 30:224–30:226
    replication, 30:203–30:206,
      30:221–30:222
  heterochromatin
    characteristics, 37:259–282
      change manifestations, 37:281
      differential staining, 37:279–280
      ectopic pairing, 37:266–279
      heterochromatin proteins, 37:280
      DNA underrepresentation, 37:252–255,
        37:280
      inactivation, position effect, 37:394–395
      overview, 37:238–248, 37:259–266
      polytene chromosome DNA sequence
        locations, 37:252–255
      repeats, 37:248–259
  isolation, 32:279–281
  mosquitoes and, 30:150
  Neurospora crassa and, 29:12, 29:14–29:17,
    29:34, 29:46
  reintroduction into mammalian cells,
    32:300–301
  repeat loss, 32:296–301
  somaclonal variation and, 30:49
  structure, 30:186, 30:200–30:201,
    32:279–281
    DNA components, 30:186–30:198
    protein, 30:198–30:200
  4p telomere, 32:290–291
  16p telomere, 32:291–293
  7q telomere, 32:291
  21q telomere, 32:293–294
  Xp/Yp pseudoautosomal region,
    32:289–290
  yeast ribosomes and, 29:77–29:78
Telomeric repeats, 30:233
  formation, 30:227–30:231
  function, 30:211, 30:213–30:214, 30:216,
    30:218, 30:220–30:221
  structure, 30:186, 30:190
  TEL1 protein, AT protein homology with,
    36:90
tel1, telomeres and, 30:219
Temperature
  banding pattern variation induction,
    39:33–34
  chronic elevation, CAT response, maize
    seeds, 28:28–28:29
  embryonic development, 37:355–357
  enzyme structure and, 28:108
  evolutionary genetics of fish and,
    29:158–29:163, 29:165–29:166
  gene expression modification, 37:325,
    37:334–335, 37:342
  heat shock
    Hsp genes, 39:357, 39:375–376
    puff induction, 39:336–358
    heterochromatin compaction, 37:11–13,
      37:281, 37:407–408
    protein synthesis and, 28:109–28:113
    puff activity effects, 39:258
    transposon mutation rate changes
      Antirrhinum majus, 28:78
      Drosophila, 28:91
Temperature effects
  homologous chromosome synapsis, 34:171
  plant chromosomes, 34:117
  polyteny level, 34:186
  pompon-like chromosomes, 34:154–157
  seasonal size differences, 34:277–278
Temperature-sensitive periods, for sex-
  controlling genes, C. elegans, 27:129,
    27:140, 27:150–27:151, 27:156, 27:176
Tem-R, mosquitoes and, 30:149
Tenascins, mouse gene encoding, 36:141–36:142
Teratocarcinomas, mouse
  HSP response to heat shock, differentiation
    and, 24:21–24:22
Teratogens
  defects induction
    in heart, 28:279–28:280
    in neural tube, 28:277–28:278

HSP induction, 28:278–28:279,
28:280–28:281
low-dose pretreatment effect, 28:280
Terminal repeats, telomeres and, 30:186–30:190
Terminal transferase
infusoria studies, 34:95–96
isolated chromosomes studies, 34:327–328
Testcrosses, *Mu* elements of *Zea mays* and,
30:97
Testis, *see* Gonads; Sex determination
Testis cells, mariner insect transposon-like
element in, 36:18, 36:19
Tetrahymena
HSP synthesis
heat-shock response and, 28:261, 28:262
thermotolerance and, 28:287
telomeres and
formation, 30:227
function, 30:202, 30:207, 30:209,
30:213–30:214
length, 30:217–30:218, 30:220–30:221
structure, 30:188–30:189, 30:193, 30:199
Tetrahymena thermophila, rRNA intron,
self-splicing, 25:224
Tetrasomes, *Gossypium* spp., 23:326
TF, *see* Transferrin
TF gene
chicken
expression in transgenic mouse
estrogen effect, 25:17–25:18
liver-specific, 25:17
X chromosome inactivation-
independent, 25:18
promoter, homology with human *TF*
promoter, 25:11–25:12
on chromosome 3, location and linkage
groups, 25:9–25:11
pseudogene and, 25:10
evolution
intragenic duplication during, 25:3–25:5
primitive in prochordate *Pyura*, 25:5–25:7,
25:8
homology with human TF cDNA,
25:6–25:7, 25:8
separation from linkage group in higher
primates, 25:11
expression sites
central nervous system, 25:14
during development, rat, 25:16–25:17
extinction in intertypic cell hybrids,
rodent, 25:28–25:29

liver, human, 25:13–25:14
mammary gland, rodents, 25:15
Sertoli cells, testis, 25:14–25:15
T cells, human, 25:15, 25:16
thymus gland, 25:15
promoter, human, homology with
chicken *TF* promoter, 25:11–25:12
metallothionein promoter, human,
25:25–25:26
TFR promoter, human, 25:11–25:12,
25:13
TFR, *see* Transferrin receptor
TFR gene, human
linkage to *TF* on chromosome, 25:3,
25:9–25:10
promoter region, homology with *TF*
promoter, 25:11–25:12, 25:13
TH, *see* Tyrosine-24:3-hydroxylase
α-Thalassemia
Jackson laboratory, 20:439–20:440
Oak Ridge, 20:438–20:439
telomeres and, 30:230
Thermotolerance
HSP role
Hydra attenuata, 28:258
mammalian cells, 28:255, 28:257–28:258,
28:280
plants, 28:259–28:260
impairment
with abnormal HSP, 28:244,
28:255–28:256
in *Hydra oligactis*, 28:258
induction by antibodies to HSP70,
28:257–28:258
in mutants, 28:253, 28:256–28:257
induction in *Drosophila*, 28:280, 28:284,
28:285
comparison with mammalian systems,
28:286
HSP synthesis and, 28:287–28:288
in mammals, 28:280
pretreatment with chemicals and, 28:280
Thermus thermophilus
manganese-containing SOD, 26:70, 26:71
superoxide dismutases and, 30:266–30:267
Thioacetamide, puff activity effects, 39:264
Thiobacillus ferooxidans, mercury resistance gene
of, 36:206
Thioflavine T, RNA synthesis inhibition, 39:75
Thionins, antifungal, barley, 28:201
Thiroxine, puff activity effects, 39:264

Threonine
dietary
ADH activity increase, Drosophila, 25:56
in pollen and styles, inverse correlation,
maize, 26:29
Thrifty gene hypotheses, 32:88
Thrombophilia, 33:135–170
overview, 33:135–138
antithrombin III, 33:135–136
coagulation inhibition, 33:135–136
coagulation regulation, 33:136–138
protein C system, 33:136–138
venous thrombosis, 33:138
protein C
activation, 33:142–143
anticoagulant properties, 33:138–140
deficiency effects, 33:147–148
overview, 33:136–138
resistance
discovery, 33:150–157
elucidation, 33:163–168
overview, 33:138
prevalence, 33:168–169
thromboembolic disease, 33:157–162
protein S
C4b-binding protein interactions,
33:144–147
deficiency effects, 33:148–150
protein C activation, 33:142–143
thromboembolism
activated protein C resistance,
33:157–162
protein C deficiency, 33:147–148
protein S deficiency, 33:148–150
thrombomodulin, 33:140–142
Thrombospondin gene, p53 transactivation of,
36:59
Thy-1 antigen, 20:300
Thymus gland, fetal, TF mRNA, 25:15
Tilapia, evolutionary genetics of fish and, 29:161
Ti-plasmids, genetic map of
conjugation mediated by, 22:232–22:234
isolation of Ti-plasmid transposon insertion
and deletion mutants, 22:234–22:237
octopine and nopaline utilization,
22:231–22:232
physical and genetic maps, 22:238–22:239
Tissue and cell culture
developmental morphogenesis, see Callus,
Gramineae

HSP induction, 24:20–24:22, see also Heat-
shock proteins
Tissue cultures
plants, genomic DNA variation,
28:81–28:83, 28:91
somaclonal variation and, 30:43, 30:48,
30:64–30:65
genetic consequences, 30:50–30:52,
30:54, 30:56–30:57, 30:59–30:61
Tissue development, see Neoplasia
Tissue specificity
carbonic anhydrases and, 30:329, 30:331,
30:349
mosquitoes and, 30:160, 30:170–30:171
Mu elements of Zea mays and, 30:108
Tissue-specific transacting factor (TTAF), in
sex-specific gene regulation by dsx,
Drosophila, 27:227–27:229
Tn3, Mu elements of Zea mays and, 30:106
Tn10, Mu elements of Zea mays and, 30:103,
30:106
Tnt-1
nitrate reductase and, 30:28
somaclonal variation and, 30:53
Tobacco
chitinase, structure and homologies, 28:199,
28:200
glucanase, structure and homologies,
28:199
nitrate reductase and
biochemistry, 30:7–30:8
gene expression, 30:9–30:12
genetics, 30:13, 30:19–30:20, 30:23,
30:27
somaclonal variation and, 30:44, 30:46,
30:51, 30:53, 30:58
transgenic, expression of
bean defense response genes, 28:207,
28:215–28:216
Drosophila HSP70 promoter, 28:249
soybean Gmhsp17.5E promoter,
28:265–28:266
tol gene, Neurospora crassa and, 29:44
Toluidine blue stain, RNA staining, 39:40–41
Tomaculous neuropathy, See also HNPP disease
in animal models, 36:27
in Déjerine-Sottas disease, 36:21
Tomato, see also Lycopersicon esculentum
nitrate reductase and, 30:14, 30:17, 30:28,
30:31

photosynthetic gene expression, fruit
development and, **28:**153
somaclonal variation and, **30:**43–**30:**44,
30:52, **30:**60
tom elements, *Drosophila* transposable elements
and, **29:**232, **29:**234–**29:**235,
29:248–**29:**249
Tooth anlage patterning, human malformation
genes
homeobox genes, **38:**23
tooth development, **38:**22–23
Topoisomerase, yeast ribosomes and, **29:**86,
29:88–**29:**89
Torpedo californica, evolutionary genetics of fish
and, **29:**178–**29:**179
TOR proteins, AT protein homology with,
36:90
Torulopsis glabrata, mitochondrial genome
genes
continuous and mosaic, **25:**198–**25:**199
vari, ribosomal protein-coding, **25:**214
introns, **25:**198
mutants and maps, **25:**204
size, comparison with *S. cerevisiae*, **25:**189
Toxic metals
for bacteria, **36:**205–**36:**226
inducible systems for removal of, **36:**189
Toxic substances, mosquitoes and, **30:**151
Tp(1) genes, puff development, **39:**291–294
TP53 tumor suppressor gene
characteristics of, **36:**47, **36:**56–**36:**61, **36:**71
implication in Li-Fraumeni syndrome, **36:**95
mutations in, **36:**58, **36:**77, **36:**98
Trace elements, uptake systems for,
36:188–**36:**189
Tradescantia, gametophytic-sporophytic genetic
overlap, **26:**26
tra-2 gene, X-chromosome replication, **39:**433
Trans-acting factors
carbonic anhydrases and, **30:**327
Drosophila transposable elements and,
29:257–**29:**260, **29:**276
Mu elements of *Zea mays* and, **30:**116
superoxide dismutases and, **30:**272, **30:**280,
30:284, **30:**286
Transaminase, in braconid wasps, **25:**139
Transcription
activation mechanisms, **39:**2–3
active chromosome region localization,
39:40–67

DNA–RNA hybrid antibodies, **39:**38,
39:47–52
ribonucleoprotein products, **39:**56–67
RNA specific histochemical staining,
39:40–41
transcription proteins, **39:**52–56
[^{3}H]uridine incorporation, **39:**39,
39:41–47
carbonic anhydrases and
chromosomal localization, **30:**334
genes, **30:**325–**30:**327, **30:**329–**30:**331,
30:333–**30:**334
genetic variation, **30:**345, **30:**347
dosage compensation, **39:**76–83
overview, **39:**76–79
sex chromosome activity, **39:**79–83
in *Drosophila hydei* primary spermatocytes,
23:192, **23:**194–**23:**199
Drosophila transposable elements and, **29:**230
cis-acting effects of retrotransposons,
29:240–**29:**241, **29:**243–**29:**256
foldback elements, **29:**288
P elements, **29:**265–**29:**266,
29:270–**29:**271, **29:**273–**29:**274
retrotransposons, **29:**231–**29:**237
trans-acting effects of retrotransposons,
29:258
evolutionary genetics of fish and, **29:**143,
29:161–**29:**162
inhibitor effects on functional organization,
39:67–76
mosquitoes and, **30:**127, **30:**150, **30:**152,
30:154, **30:**167–**30:**168
Neurospora crassa and
DNA transaction, **29:**20
metabolism, **29:**39–**29:**41
mitochondria, **29:**27, **29:**29–**29:**30
nitrate reductase and
function, **30:**3
gene expression, **30:**10–**30:**12
genetics, **30:**20, **30:**26–**30:**28
nontranscribed spacers, **39:**423
regulation, plant circadian clock pathways,
35:1–28
CAB gene characteristics, **35:**2–6
cis- and trans-acting element requirements,
35:20–25
cyanobacteria model, **35:**17–20
future research directions, **35:**25–28
overview, **35:**1–2

Transcription (continued)
  photoreceptors, 35:6–11
    blue-light receptors, 35:9–11
    phytochrome, 35:6–9
    phototransduction pathway analysis,
      35:15–17
    signal transduction intermediate
      identification, 35:11–14
  somaclonal variation and, 30:53
  superoxide dismutases and, 30:272
    molecular genetics, 30:273–30:274,
      30:276–30:277, 30:279–30:281,
      30:284–30:286
    physiology of mutants, 30:297,
      30:299–30:300, 30:306
  telomeres and, 30:199, 30:222–30:224,
    30:226
  yeast ribosomes and, 29:64, 29:103
    assembly, 29:95–29:96
    genetic analysis, 29:99, 29:101
    nucleolus, 29:86–29:87, 29:89–29:90
    ribosomal protein genes, 29:73,
      29:75–29:82, 29:84
    ribosomal RNA processing, 29:92–29:93
    synthesis changes, 29:84–29:85
  zeste in Drosophila melanogaster and, 29:302
    chromatin packaging, 29:338, 29:340
    DNA binding, 29:321–29:323,
      29:325–29:326
    function, 29:328
    molecular biology, 29:313,
      29:315–29:316
    protein, 29:332–29:333, 29:336–29:337
    transvection, 29:308–29:310
Transcription factors
  WT1 as possible, 36:70
  Xenopus laevis
    encoded by organizer, 31:41
    neural plate response to induction,
      31:59–65
  yeast ribosomes and, 29:95–29:96
Transcription initiation, Drosophila transposable
    elements and, 29:274
  cis-acting effects, 29:241, 29:245, 29:247,
    29:251
  retrotransposons, 29:233–29:234, 29:237,
    29:258
Transfection
  mosquitoes and, 30:163
  telomeres and, 30:205

Transferrin
  ancestry, common of human and chicken TF,
    25:4–25:5
  functions
    erythroid precursor differentiation and,
      25:22–25:23
    heme synthesis in reticulocytes and, 25:22
  properties, human, 25:2
  synthesis
    acute-phase reaction and, 25:27–25:28
    extinction in intertypic cell hybrids,
      rodent, 25:28–25:29
    in fetal tissues during development, mouse,
      25:18–25:19
    hormonal modulation, 25:26–25:27
    iron deficiency and, 25:25–25:26
    in proliferating T cells, human
      IL-2 autocrine cycle and, 25:20–25:21
      truncated 62-kDa species, 25:22
    in visceral yolk sac, human, 25:19
Transferrin receptor
  amino acid homology with TR, human,
    25:7–25:9
  in T cells, cytotoxicity and, 25:22
Transfer RNA
  genes, structure of, 21:134–21:140
    isoacceptors and development,
      21:140–21:147
    localization of genes by in situ hybridization,
      21:127–21:134
    mutants, 21:147–21:148
      lethal-meander, 1(2)me, 21:150–21:152
      minutes, 21:148–21:150
    number and diversity of genes for,
      21:126–21:127
    suppression and, 21:152–21:154
    search for nonsense suppressors in
      Drosophila, 21:154–21:155
    suppressor of sable, su(s),1–0,
      21:155–21:161
transfer (tra) gene
  alternative splicing
    Drosophila melanogaster, 31:247–249
Transformation
  Aspergillus nidulans
    applications, 23:153
    methods, 23:152–23:153
  Dictyostelium discoideum, 23:154
  fungal, 23:73–23:160
    ars significance for, 23:108–23:109

detection by
colony hybridization, 23:89,
23:94–23:95
complementation, 23:87–23:88,
23:90–23:93
donor DNA physical presence, 23:95
enzymatic assay, 23:88
immunoassay, 23:88–23:89
in different groups, 23:140–23:155
DNA uptake, biochemistry,
23:139–23:140
donor DNA effects, 23:101–23:103
frequency, dependence on
DNA nature and preparation,
23:96–23:97
spheroplast nature and preparation,
23:96–23:97
induction by
cell fusion, 23:79–23:80
cloned DNA, 23:79
total DNA, 23:79
mechanism, 23:155–23:160
with recombination, 23:98–23:101
without recombination, 23:98–23:99
in higher organisms, 23:77–23:79
Mucor racemosus, 23:154–23:155
Neurospora crassa
with cloned DNA, 23:145–23:147
with total DNA preparations,
23:140–23:143
transformant genetics, 23:143–23:144
Podospora anserina
with recombinant plasmids,
23:150–23:154
Schizosaccharomyces pombe
gene isolation for, 23:53–23:54
plasmid vectors for, 23:53–23:54
system for, 23:154
yeast
by plasmid carrying yeast and *E. coli* genes,
23:147, 23:152
transformer-2 (tra-2) gene
alternative splicing
Drosophila melanogaster, 31:249
Transgenic mouse
chicken *TF* gene expression, 25:17–25:18
models
apolipoprotein E analysis, 32:166–168
high-density lipoprotein metabolism
analysis, 32:178–180

low-density lipoprotein receptor protein
analysis, 32:152–153, 32:185
Transgenics
chromosomal aneuploidy study, 35:176–177
human disease models, mouse germ line
manipulation, 35:185–197
DNA sequence targeting, 35:191–194
future research directions, 35:195–197
gene targeting, 35:188–191
transgenic animals, 35:185–188
Translation
carbonic anhydrases and, 30:327, 30:343,
30:347
Drosophila transposable elements and, 29:235,
29:237, 29:266, 29:269, 29:284
evolutionary genetics of fish and,
29:161–29:162, 29:183
mosquitoes and, 30:152, 30:168
Neurospora crassa and, 29:2, 29:7, 29:11,
29:13, 29:27
superoxide dismutases and, 30:273, 30:281
yeast ribosomes and, 29:69, 29:103
ribosomal protein genes, 29:72, 29:75,
29:77, 29:80, 29:84
zeste in *Drosophila melanogaster* and, 29:328,
29:339
Translocation
Drosophila transposable elements and, 29:285,
29:287–29:288
evolutionary genetics of fish and, 29:135,
29:183
Gossypium hirsutum
homozygous lines, 23:300–23:301
Gossypium spp., 23:296–23:307
effect on
chromosome structure, 23:306–23:307
genome stability, 23:306–23:307
origin and identification, 23:296–23:303
use for analysis of
chromosome deficiency, 23:305–23:306
chromosome orientation, 23:306
gene location, 23:303–23:305
incipient genome differentiation, 23:305
mosquitoes and, 30:146
Neurospora crassa and, 29:7, 29:13–29:14
nitrate reductase and, 30:8, 30:11
somaclonal variation and, 30:49, 30:59
telomeres and, 30:223–30:224
yeast ribosomes and, 29:65, 29:70
Transportation, telomeres and, 30:214–30:216

Transposable-Element-Laden, Mu elements of
    Zea mays and, 30:79
Transposable elements, see also Transposons
    in Drosophila, see Drosophila, transposable
        elements
    mosquitoes and, 30:165, 30:172
    Mu elements of Zea mays and, 30:77, 30:79,
        30:81
    applications, 30:113
    future directions, 30:116
    gene expression, 30:108
    properties of transposition, 30:100, 30:103,
        30:105–30:108
    structure, 30:91, 30:96
    somaclonal variation and, 30:52–30:56,
        30:58, 30:61–30:62, 30:64
    telomeres and, 30:192–30:193, 30:214
Transposition bursts, Drosophila transposable
    elements and, 29:238
Transposon genes, position effect
    inactivation, 37:318–319
    P-element transformation, 37:308–309,
        37:311
Transposons
    activity changes, Drosophila, plants
    internal effects, 28:77–28:78
    temperature role, 28:78, 28:91
    in tissue culture, plants, 28:82–28:83,
        28:91
    cloning method, minute genes, protein
        synthesis theory, 38:92–116
    M(1)7C gene, 38:102–106
    M(1)15D gene, 38:101–102
    M(2)23B gene, 38:108–109
    M(2)30D/E gene, 38:93–95
    M(2)32A gene, 38:106–108
    M(2)32D gene, 38:109–110
    M(2)60E gene, 38:114–115
    M(3)66D gene, 38:110–114
    M(3)95A gene, 38:95–97
    M(3)95A^{prv11} gene, 38:97–101
    oho23B gene, 38:108–109
    RpL9 gene, 38:109–110
    RpL14 gene, 38:110–114
    RpL19 gene, 38:114–115
    RpS2 gene, 38:93–95
    RpS3 gene, 38:95–97
    RpS3^{prv11} gene, 38:97–98
    RpS3^{prv99} gene, 38:98–101
    RpS13 gene, 38:106–108

RpS5gene, 38:101–102
RpS6 gene, 38:102–106
string of pearls gene, 38:93–95
stubarista gene, 38:115–116
Drosophila transposable elements and,
    29:229–29:231
fungal
    nucleotide sequences, 23:122–23:124
    mapping, C. elegans, 27:73
    Neurospora crassa and, 29:46–29:48
    in oxygen defense mechanism assay,
        28:51–28:52
    population dynamics, 23:246–23:250
    in Drosophila melanogaster, 23:247–23:249
    in Escherichia coli, 23:248, 23:250
    tagging, Mu elements of Zea mays and,
        30:113–30:116
Transvection, zeste in Drosophila melanogaster and
    chromatin packaging, 29:340
    discovery, 29:302–29:303
    DNA binding, 29:319–29:320,
        29:322–29:323, 29:325–29:326
    function, 29:328
    interaction with white, 29:308–29:310
    mechanisms, 29:308–29:310
    molecular biology, 29:316
    mutations, 29:310–29:312
    polytene chromosomes, 29:318
    protein, 29:333–29:334
Transverse striation, see Bands
Tregalose, puff activity effects, 39:263
Trichodermin, yeast ribosomes and, 29:70,
    29:101
Trichogen cells
    bristle formation, 34:43–46
    long-term incubation, 34:299
Triethylamine, braconid wasp treatment during
    radiation exposure, 25:156
Trinactin, heat-shock puff induction, 39:351
Triosephosphate isomerase, mutations of genes
    encoding, 36:96
Triphenylstibine, puff activity effects, 39:264
Triplet repeat expansions
    autosomal dominant progressive ataxias,
        CAG repeat, 38:35–39
    Friedreich ataxia, GGA repeat, 38:55–57
Triplet repeat mutations, mouse models,
    35:181–183
Tripsacum dactyloides, Mu elements of Zea mays
    and, 30:96

Trisomes, *Gossypium* spp., **23**:326
Trisomy
 chromosome numerical abnormalities
  13, **33**:122–123
  14, **33**:122–123
  15, **33**:122–123
  16, **33**:121–122
  18, **33**:120–121
  21, **33**:115–120
  22, **33**:122–123
 etiology, **33**:105–106
 frequency, **33**:102–105
 mechanisms, **33**:123–125
Triticales
 aneuploidy in
  contribution of wheat and rye
   chromosomes, **21**:311–**21**:312
  frequency of, **21**:307–**21**:309
  general conclusions, **21**:312
  transmission of, **21**:310–**21**:311
 cytology of
  meiosis and, **21**:291–**21**:307
  mitosis and, **21**:287–**21**:291
 historical background, **21**:256–**21**:258
 improvement and assessment of hexaploid
   strains
  derivation of secondary hexaploids,
    21:272–**21**:273
  hybrid encrosis-a limiting factor,
    21:278–**21**:279
  possible bases for superiority of seondary
    hexaploids, **21**:279–**21**:281
  role of D genome in evolution of
    hexaploids, **21**:274–**21**:278
  role of triple hybrids, **21**:282
  use of male sterile wheat, **21**:282–**21**:283
 ploidy levels
  decaploid, **21**:265
  hexaploid, **21**:270–**21**:271
  octoploid, **21**:265–**21**:270
  tetraploid, **21**:271–**21**:272
 problems, progress and possibilities,
   21:312–**21**:313
 commercially released varieties,
   21:323–**21**:326
 diseases, **21**:319–**21**:320
 kernel shriveling, **21**:314–**21**:319
 meiotic instability, aneuploidy and sterility,
   21:313–**21**:314
 nutritive aspects, **21**:320–**21**:323

taxonomy, **21**:258–**21**:262
terminology, **21**:262–**21**:265
tetraploid
 chromosome analysis of, **21**:285–**21**:286
 development of secondary tetraploids,
   21:286
 production of tetraploids, **21**:283–**21**:285
 utility of tetraploids, **21**:286–**21**:287
Triticum durum, *mei* mutants, *asynaptic (as)*,
  26:159
tRNA
 genes, intercalary heterochromatin
   identification, **37**:207–208
 minute gene hypothesis, **38**:81–82
 mosquitoes and, **30**:130–**30**:131
 Neurospora crassa and, **29**:27–**29**:30
 yeast ribosomes and, **29**:65, **29**:68, **29**:89,
   29:95
Trophoblast cells, mammalian polytene
  chromosome occurrence, **34**:98–105
α-Tropomyosin, hypertrophic cardiomyopathy
  role, **35**:293–294, **35**:302–303
Troponin T, hypertrophic cardiomyopathy role,
  35:294–295, **35**:303–305
Trypanosoma brucei, HSP during development,
  24:15
Trypanosoma, telomeres and, **30**:199, **30**:225
Trypanosomes, telomeres and, **30**:217–**30**:218,
  30:224
Trypsin
 mosquitoes and, **30**:152–**30**:153
 puff activity effects, **39**:264
Tryptophan
 NUV absorption, **26**:108
 puff activity effects, **39**:253
Tryptophan oxidase, male/female activity,
  Drosophila
 X-chromosome fragment translocation to
   autosome and, **24**:406
TSP, *see* Temperature-sensitive periods
TTAF, *see* Tissue-specific trans-acting factor
Tuberous sclerosis
 chromosomal linkage of, **36**:94, **36**:95
 gene for, **36**:93, **36**:94, **36**:95
Tubulin gene family, *Drosophila melanogaster*,
  31:97–99
Tumor growth factor
 Mad role in transduction pathway of, **36**:91
 p21 induction by, **36**:62
 p27 induction by, **36**:63

Tumor growth factor (continued)
  as possible tumor suppressor, 36:93
  receptor for, 36:77
Tumorigenic mechanisms, loss of genetic
    material in, 36:46
Tumors, see also Cancer
  in Drosophila
    malignant, brain, in 1(2)37Cf mutations,
      24:182
    melanotic, Ddc gene cluster and, 24:180
  evolutionary genetics of fish and,
      29:170–29:173
  telomeres and, 30:208
  in transgenic mouse, induction by
    human papovaviruses, 24:306–24:307
    myc-MMTV constructs, 24:307–24:308
    SV40 early region, 24:305–24:306
Tumor suppressor genes
  and, 30:208
  antisense transcripts of, 36:103
  characteristics of, 36:47–36:50
  complex organization of, 36:67
  criteria for, 36:46–36:47
  disruption mechanisms of, 36:94–36:105
  dominant-negative effects of, 36:102
  human cancer and, 36:45–36:136
  hypermethylation effects on, 36:102
  modifier effects on, 36:100–36:104
  mutations of, 36:51, 36:95–36:99
  position effect varigation in, 36:100
  products of, 36:53–36:94
  RNA editing in, 36:100
Tumor suppressor proteins
  aberrant subcellular localization of,
      36:104–36:105
  regulation of, 36:105–36:106
Tunis, CMT4 disease in, 36:6
Turnera ulmifolia, heterostylous
  incompatible pollen inhibition, 26:28
  MGS, excess pollination and, 26:16
tu(1)Sz^{ts} gene, band organization, 39:147
twine gene
  Drosophila melanogaster
    effects in female meiosis, 31:92–93
    effects in male meiosis, 31:91–92
Two-hit requirement, for tumorigenesis, 36:52,
      36:53, 36:54, 36:69, 36:81, 36:87
Tyamphenicol, heat-shock puff induction,
      39:352
Types, 34:127–130
Typha latifolia, pollen ontogeny, 26:4

Tyramine β-hydroxylase, Drosophila, in wild-
    type and mutant brain, 24:140–24:141
Tyrosinase, Drosophila, PPF effect during
    development, 24:195–24:196
Tyrosine
  conversion from phenylalanine, 32:200
  conversion to sclerotin and melanin, insects,
      24:147
  heat-shock puff induction, 39:352
  puff activity effects, 39:253
Tyrosine decarboxylase, Drosophila brain
  in Ddc mutations, 24:165
  in per^{O} allele, 24:166
Tyrosine-3-hydroxylase, Drosophila
  gene coding for, 24:139–24:140
  reactions connected with, 24:138–24:139
Tyrosine kinase, characteristics, 33:197
Tyrosine-O-hydroxylase, Drosophila
  accumulation in lethal translucida mutation,
      24:156–24:157
  detection in hemolymph, 24:142–24:143
  during development, 24:154–24:155
  in vitro substrate for acid phosphatase, 24:155
  in vivo hydrolysis by alkaline phosphatase-1,
      24:154–24:155
Tyrosine-O-sulfate, transport and utilization by
    Neurospora crassa, 31:192–194

U2 auxiliary factor, 31:221–222
Ubiquitin
  amino acid analog-induced, animals, 28:254
  in heat-shock response
    abnormal protein degradation and,
      24:62–24:63
    HSP gene activation, 24:62–24:63
  synthesis in
    yeast and chicken cells, 24:61
    young rodents, 24:12
  impaired function in mouse mammary cells
    ts85, 28:253, 28:258–28:259
  stress-inducible, yeast, 28:253
  yeast ribosomes and, 29:71
UB11, yeast ribosomes and, 29:71
UB12, yeast ribosomes and, 29:71
UB13, yeast ribosomes and, 29:71
UDPglucose : flavonol 3-O-glycosyltransferase,
    maize
  developmental control by regulatory genes,
      24:105–24:108

Ultrabithorax
  Drosophila transposable elements and,
    29:247
  gene, homeotic, trunk-specifying, *Drosophila*,
    27:310, 27:349, 27:373, 27:374
  protein product, homeodomain sequences,
    27:370, 27:371
  regulation by other genes, 27:267
  zeste in *Drosophila melanogaster* and
    DNA binding, 29:318, 29:320–29:323,
      29:325
    function, 29:327
    protein, 29:332–29:333
    transvection, 29:305–29:306,
      29:308–29:310, 29:312
Ultraviolet irradiation, evolutionary genetics of
    fish and, 29:175
Ultraviolet light
  braconid wasp damage
    egg nucleus and, 25:163
    embryo during development and,
      25:163–25:164
  Drosophila transposable elements and,
    29:265
  induction of chromosome breakage in fungi
    by, 36:247
  Neurospora crassa and, 29:19–29:22, 29:24
  Schizosaccharomyces pombe sensitive mutant
    injuries, 23:22–23:26
    dark repair pathways, 23:26–23:35, *see also*
      Dark repair
    recovery after, 23:35–23:40, *see also*
      DNA
Ulysses, *Drosophila* transposable elements and,
    29:239
up1, *Mu* elements of *Zea mays* and, 30:109,
    30:113
Upstream activating sequences
  binding to PRTF, yeast
    in α-specific genes, 27:42–27:46
    in a-specific genes, 27:46–27:48
  yeast ribosomes and
    ribosomal protein genes, 29:73,
      29:75–29:76, 29:78–29:79
    synthesis changes, 29:84–29:85
Urate oxidase, in *ry* and *mal* mutants, *Drosophila*,
    28:59
Urates, in braconid wasp fat body
  oocyte growth and, 25:143
  species-specific, diet effects, 25:136, 25:142
  X-ray effects, 25:148

Uric acid
  Drosophila
    absence in *ry* and *mol* mutants, 28:58,
      28:59
    antioxidant role, 28:58, 28:59
    puff activity effects, 39:264
[³H]Uridine
  active chromosome region labeling, 39:39,
    39:41–47, 39:426–430
  interband detection, 39:87
Uridine, heat-shock puff induction, 39:352
Urotensin, evolutionary genetics of fish and,
    29:198
usp gene, puff development, 39:317
Ustilago maydis
  avirulence genes, 28:171
  chromosome rearrangements in, 36:264,
    36:285
  DNA recombinational repair, 24:338
Ustilago maydis, *Neurospora crassa* and, 29:22
Utrophin/DRP, characteristics, 33:195–196

Vaccines, influenza virus, production of,
    20:26–20:27
Vacuoles, yeast ribosomes and, 29:82
Valinomycin, heat-shock puff induction,
    39:352
Vanadate, *Neurospora crassa* and, 29:40
van⁺ gene, *Neurospora crassa* and, 29:40
Variable–diversity–joining recombination, DNA
    break repair mechanisms
  break formation, 38:186–188
  nonhomologous end-joining, 38:204–205
Variable number tandem repeat polymorphisms
  diabetes-susceptibility gene identification,
    32:58
  phenylalanine hydroxylase gene haplotype
    identification, 32:209–211
Vasopressin, evolutionary genetics of fish and,
    29:196–29:197, 29:200
Vasotocin, evolutionary genetics of fish and,
    29:196–29:197
Vectors
  in molecular cloning, 23:80–23:86
    bacteriophages, 23:84
    cosmids, 23:84–23:85
    plasmids, 23:81–23:84
    versatile for fungi, construction,
      23:138–23:139

Vegetative incompatibility, *Neurospora crassa* and, **29:**44, **29:**48
Vegetative reproduction
cost of shifting from outcrossing to, **24:**350–**24:**351
survivorship, **24:**348
VEGF gene, p53 protein mutant effects on, **36:**61
Ventralizing genes, effects on *zen* expression, *Drosophila*
maternal gene, *cactus*, **27:**279, **27:**283, **27:**284, **27:**288, **27:**294, **27:**297
zygotic genes
decapentaplegic (dpp), **27:**295, **27:**297–**27:**300
short gastrulation (sog), **27:**300–**27:**301
tolloid (tld), **27:**297, **27:**299
twisted gastrulation (tsg), **27:**300–**27:**301
Ventral uterine precursor cells, *C. elegans*, **27:**66, **27:**81
Vermilion gene
Drosophila transposable elements and, **29:**251–**29:**252
oligogene bands, **39:**129–131, **39:**134
recombination size estimation, **39:**96
Vertebrates, HSP gene induction by heat
CCAAT box and, **24:**44–**24:**45
HSE long-range effect, **24:**44–**24:**45
HSTF and, **24:**45–**24:**47
Very low-density lipoproteins, *see* Lipoprotein metabolism
VHL protein
aberrant subcellular locallization of, **36:**104, **36:**105
function of, **36:**85
tumor-suppressor gene effect on, **36:**46
as tumor suppressor gene product, **36:**49
VHL tumor suppressor gene
characteristics of, **36:**49, **36:**84–**36:**85
hypermethylation of, **36:**102
implication in von Hippel-Lindau disease, **36:**95
mutations of, **36:**84
Vibrio anguillarum, iron-regulated gene in, **36:**191, **36:**192, **36:**195, **36:**196, **36:**197
Vibrio cholerae
HlyU protein from, **36:**220
iron-regulated gene in, **36:**190, **36:**191, **36:**196
Vibrio vulnificus, iron-regulated gene in, **36:**191

Vicia faba, telomeres and, **30:**225
Vinblastin, heat-shock puff induction, **39:**350
Viral vectors
gene transfer
in Gaucher disease, **32:**35–36
in phenylketonuria
adenoviral, **32:**248–251
retroviral, **32:**246–248
risk of use, **32:**4–5
Virulence functions, of *Agrobacterium* plasmids, **22:**244–**22:**246
Viruses
Drosophila transposable elements and, **29:**235, **29:**238
evolutionary genetics of fish and, **29:**171, **29:**188
morphology change induction, **34:**286–289
Vision, evolutionary genetics of fish and, **29:**177–**29:**178
Visual pigment genes, evolutionary genetics of fish and, **29:**177–**29:**178
Visual rhythms, *Drosophila* chronogenetics, **38:**157–158
Visual system
Drosophila melanogaster
optomotor-blind (omb) mutant, **31:**141–142
sevenless (sev) mutant, **31:**140–141
small-optic-lobes (sol) mutant, **31:**142–143
Vital genes, gene expression inactivation, position effect, **37:**316–318
Vitamin B$_6$, heat-shock puff induction, **39:**352
Vitamin E, dietary, effect on longevity, *Drosophila*, **28:**57
Vitellogenic carboxypeptidase, mosquitoes and, **30:**154
Vitellogenin, mosquitoes and, **30:**153–**30:**154, **30:**169
Vocal cord weakness, in CMT2 disease, **36:**6
Volvox carteri, heat-shock-induced sexuality, **24:**14
adaptation to temperature changes and, **24:**15
Von Hippel-Lindau disease
chromosomal linkage of, **36:**49, **36:**84–**36:**85, **36:**95
tumor suppressor gene role in, **36:**49, **36:**84–**36:**85, **36:**95
Von Recklinghausen neurofibromatosis, *See* Neurofibromatosis type 1

Vp1, Mu elements of *Zea mays* and, 30:93
VPC, *see* Vulval precursor cells
Vulva, development, C. *elegans*
   AC generation, 27:79, 27:81
   cell lineages of VPC, *see* Vulval precursor
      cells
   morphogenesis, 27:87–27:88
   mutant phenotypes, 27:78, 27:81
   pathway model, 27:78, 27:80
   VPC-AC interactions, 27:75–27:78
Vulval precursor cells, C. *elegans*
   anchor cell effects, 27:75–27:78
   cell lineages
      execution, gene control, 27:84–27:87
      primary, 27:85
      secondary, 27:85–27:87
   generation, gene control, 27:79
   genes controlling cell type, *see* Cell-type-
      controlling genes, C. *elegans*
   specification, gene control, 27:81–27:84
   regulatory circuitry, 27:95–27:98

WAF1 tumor suppressor gene
   characteristics of, 36:47
   isolation of, 36:61
WAGR syndrome
   mutation implicated in, 36:70
   Wilms' tumor with, 36:69
waxy, somaclonal variation and, 30:57
Wheat
   meiosis, genetic control, 26:184
   aneuploid gamete production and,
      26:186
   somaclonal variation and, 30:56, 30:63
   (*Triticum aestivum*), frost hardiness
      invertase isozymes and, 28:109
      multiple genes, 28:105–28:107
whirlgig (wrl) mutant
   Drosophila melanogaster, 31:100
white gene
   band organization, 39:145–147
   chromosomal rearrangements, 39:95
   dosage compensation, 39:77–78
   telomeres and, 30:203
   zeste in *Drosophila melanogaster* and
      chromatin packaging, 29:339–29:340,
      29:342–29:343
   discovery, 29:303–29:305

   DNA binding, 29:318, 29:320–29:325
   function, 29:327–29:328
   molecular biology, 29:313
   polytene chromosomes, 29:316
   protein, 29:332, 29:334, 29:337
   transvection, 29:305, 29:309–29:312
white locus, *Drosophila* transposable elements
   and
   foldback elements, 29:286–29:288
   mariner, 29:278–29:281
   P elements, 29:270, 29:272
   retrotransposons, 29:251, 29:253–29:257
Wilm's tumor
   chromosomal linkages of, 36:95
   mutations implicated in, 36:70, 36:71,
      36:99
   paired-box gene expression, 33:263–264
   similarity to retinoblastoma, 36:69
   telomeres and, 30:206, 30:208
   tumor suppressor gene role in, 36:47, 36:48,
      36:50, 36:64, 36:69–36:72, 36:92,
      36:95
Wilson disease, 33:233–248
   clinical findings, 33:235, 33:237–238
   copper homeostasis, 33:233–235
   future research directions, 33:247–248
   Long-Evans Cinnamin rat model,
      33:246–247
   molecular genetics, 33:242–245
Wineries, as habitats for *Drosophila* spp.,
   25:69–25:70
Wiskott–Aldrich syndrome
   characteristics, 35:78–81
   cloning studies, 35:81–84
      animal models, 35:83–84
      gene map, 35:81–82
      mutation analysis, 35:82–83
   future research directions, 35:89–90
   historical perspective, 35:61–63
   overview, 35:57–58
Wit-1 tumor suppressor gene, transcripts of,
   36:72, 36:92, 36:103
World Wide Web sites, mouse genomics,
   35:165–168
WT1 gene, gonad determination, 33:294–296
WT1 protein
   function of, 36:98
   implication in Wilms' tumorigenesis, 36:71,
      36:72, 36:81
   zinc-finger motif in, 36:69, 36:70

WT1 tumor suppressor gene
 antisense transcripts of, **36**:103
 characteristics of, **36**:48, **36**:52, **36**:92,
  36:106
 on chromosome, **36**:11, **36**:48, **36**:52, **36**:69,
  36:95
 complex structure of, **36**:67, **36**:74
 implication in Wilms' tumor, **36**:48, **36**:52,
  36:69, **36**:95
 mutations of, **36**:70, **36**:71, **36**:81, **36**:99
 posttrascriptional regulation of, **36**:71–**36**:72
Wuchereria, mosquitoes and, **30**:123
Wx, *Mu* elements of *Zea mays* and, **30**:94
wx, *Mu* elements of *Zea mays* and, **30**:88
Wyllie, Andrew, apoptosis concept
  development, **35**:35–53
 acceptance, **35**:49–53
 applications, **35**:50–52
 definition, **35**:40–41
 morphology, **35**:41–46
 overview, **35**:35–36
 shrinkage necrosis, **35**:36–40
 studies, **35**:46–49

Xanthine dehydrogenase
 in braconid wasps
  after orbital flight, **25**:141–**25**:142
  interspecies differences, **25**:142
 Drosophila
  male/female activity, **24**:407–**24**:408
  cloned *ry*[+] relocation to X chromosome
   and, **24**:407–**24**:410
 nitrate reductase and, **30**:17–**30**:19
 uric acid production, *Drosophila*, **28**:59
Xanthine oxidase
 Drosophila
  developmental control by regulatory genes,
   24:95–**24**:96
  nitrate reductase and, **30**:7
Xanthurenic acid, in braconid wasp eye color
  mutants, **25**:139
X/A ratio
 denominator elements, **31**:6–7
 numerator elements, **31**:5–6
 in sex determination
  Caenorhabditis elegans, **27**:122–**27**:125
   DNA microinjection, feminizing effects,
    27:169–**27**:170

  dosage compensation and,
   27:152–**27**:154
  dpy, mutations, feminizing effects in
   2X/3A animals, **27**:166–**27**:169
   suppression of *her-1* masculinization
    phenotype, **27**:167
  sdc-1
   mosaic analysis, **27**:176–**27**:177
   mutations, **27**:166, **27**:176
   xol-1 mutations and, **27**:166
  Drosophila melanogaster, **27**:122,
   27:189–**27**:191
   autosomal component, **27**:215–**27**:216
   change at blastoderm stage,
    27:195–**27**:196
   Sxl gene response to, **27**:190–**27**:192,
    27:195, **27**:200, **27**:201, **27**:205
   model, **27**:210–**27**:211
   X-chromosomal component,
    27:211–**27**:215
   X-linked numerators (*sisterless a and b*),
    27:166, **27**:212–**27**:215
   numerator elements, genetic properties,
    27:165–**27**:166
  and *Sxl* activity, **31**:4
XASH-1 gene
 Xenopus laevis, **31**:59–64
XASH-3 gene
 Xenopus laevis, **31**:59–64
Xcaudal-1 gene
 Xenopus laevis, **31**:35, **31**:37
Xcaudal-2 gene
 Xenopus laevis, **31**:35, **31**:37
X chromosome
 -autosome ratio, *see* X/A ratio
 centromeric heterochromatin DNA structure,
  37:102–104
 chromatid synapsis variation, **34**:154–156
 CMTX diseases linked to, **36**:7, **36**:20,
  36:21, **36**:29, **36**:34
 diptera morphology, **34**:132–133
 dosage compensation, *see* Dosage
  compensation
 (*Drosophila*)
  effect on hybrid viability, **36**:174–**36**:175
  in hybrids, **36**:163, **36**:164, **36**:165,
   36:171
  mutations of, **36**:144, **36**:169
 gene number calculation, **39**:94–96
 α-heterochromatin cytogenetics, **37**:127–128

β-heterochromatin cytogenetics,
37:124–126
heterochromatin gene expression
modification, 37:339–341
hsp protein regulation, 39:380
intercalary heterochromatin identification,
tandem repeats, 37:222
long-term incubation, 34:297
mitotic heterochromatin characteristics,
37:57–60
mutation effects, 34:307–308
pompon-like chromosomes, 34:140–150
replication characteristics, 39:430–434
subdivision 1B, see Subdivision 1B of X
chromosome, Drosophila
XDH, see Xanthine dehydrogenase
X elements, telomeres and, 30:190–30:193,
30:200, 30:221, 30:224
Xenopus
evolutionary genetics of fish and, 29:161
yeast ribosomes and, 29:96
Xenopus brachyury (Xbra) gene
Xenopus laevis, 31:34, 31:39–40
Xenopus laevis
HSE in oocytes
CCAAT box and, 24:44, 24:55–24:56
HSP gene induction by heat and,
24:44–24:45
HSP70 synthesis
during development, 24:11
heat-shock-induced in oocytes,
24:54–24:56
HSTF and, 24:55–24:56
neurogenesis
anterior–posterior axis formation
Hox gene role, 31:56–57
pattern
induction, 31:54–55
lability, 31:53–54
posterior dominance, 31:55–56
prepattern, 31:53–54
retinoic acid role, 31:56–57
competence
protein kinase C function, 31:51
spatial, 31:49–50
temporal, 31:48–49
Xotch function, 31:51–53
neural plate response
structural and physiological proteins,
31:66–68

transcription factors, 31:59–65
Xwnt genes, 31:65–66
organizer
characterization, 31:33–36
secreted proteins, 31:41–43
transcription factors, 31:36–40
signaling
combined, 31:45–47
homeogenetic induction, 31:47–48
planar, 31:45
vertical, 31:44–45
tetraploidization in, 36:149
yeast ribosomes and, 29:83, 29:95
Xforhead gene, Xenopus laevis, 31:34, 31:38–39
XIF6 gene
Xenopus laevis, 31:62, 31:67
XIF3 gene, Xenopus laevis, 31:62, 31:67
Xiphophorus, evolutionary genetics of fish and,
29:144, 29:171, 29:173–29:174
Xkrox-20 gene, Xenopus laevis, 31:60, 31:65
Xlabial-2 gene
Xenopus laevis, 31:35, 31:37
Xlabial-1 gene, Xenopus laevis, 31:35, 31:37
Xlim-1 gene, Xenopus laevis, 31:34, 31:38–39
X-linked disorders, see Dilated cardiomyopathy;
Duchenne muscular dystrophy; X-linked
immunodeficiency disorders
X-linked genes, Drosophila
activities in heteroploids
metafemales, 24:385–24:386
metamales, 24:384–24:385
triploid females, 24:382
triploid intersexes, 24:382–24:384
aneuploidy for large X-chromosome segments
and, 24:386–24:388
dosage compensation
control by specific genes, 24:391–24:397,
see also Genes, Drosophila melanogaster
discovery, 24:371–24:373
mRNA level and, 24:380–24:381
perspectives, 24:421
regulatory hierarchy, 24:418–24:419
RNA synthesis, 24:378–24:380
sex differentiation and, 24:390–24:391
tRNA level and, 24:380
wild-type alleles and, 24:373–24:376
X chromosome/autosome ratio and,
24:381–24:389, 24:418–24:421
sex differentiation and, 24:389–24:391
Y chromosome and, 24:391

X-linked immunodeficiency disorders
future research directions, 35:89–90
gene therapy, 35:87–89
hyper-immunoglobulin M syndrome
characteristics, 35:84–85
cloning studies, 35:85–87
animal studies, 35:86–87
gene map, 35:85–86
mutation analysis, 35:86
historical perspective, 35:63–65
overview, 35:57–58
severe combined immunodeficiency
cloning studies, 35:74–78
animal models, 35:77–78
cytokine receptor signaling, 35:76–77
gene map, 35:74–76
γ_c-chain gene organization, 35:77
mutation analysis, 35:77
historical perspective, 35:59–61
phenotype, 35:73–74
Wiskott–Aldrich syndrome
characteristics, 35:78–81
cloning studies, 35:81–84
animal models, 35:83–84
gene map, 35:81–82
mutation analysis, 35:82–83
historical perspective, 35:61–63
x-linked agammaglobulinemia
cloning studies, 35:67–73
animal models, 35:73
Bruton's agammaglobulinemia tyrosine
kinase role, 35:69–71
gene map, 35:67–69
mutation analysis, 35:71–72
historical perspective, 35:58–59
phenotypes, 35:65–67, 35:72–73
XLPOU-2 gene
Xenopus laevis, 31:61, 31:65
XLPOU-1 gene, Xenopus laevis, 31:61, 31:65
X mental retardation syndrome, mutation role
in, 36:99
Xnot gene
Xenopus laevis, 31:35, 31:37
Xotch gene, in neural competence, Xenopus
laevis, 31:51–53
X protein, binding of p53 by, 36:57
X rays
ADH mutant induction, Drosophila, 25:48
effects on braconid wasps
egg hatchability decline, 25:151–25:153
infecundity induction, 25:153–25:155

life-span decrease, 25:146–25:149
protection by
aminothiol compounds, 25:156–25:157
chelating agents, 25:157
dietary cysteine and glutathione, 25:157
nitrogen, 25:156
oxygen, 25:155
sperm damage, 25:150
Neurospora crassa and, 29:20–29:21, 29:25
XRCC4, DNA break repair mechanisms,
nonhomologous end-joining, 38:194,
38:200
XSha-2 gene
Xenopus laevis, 31:62, 31:67–68
Xtwist gene
Xenopus laevis, 31:35, 31:400
Xwnt genes
Xenopus laevis, 31:63, 31:65–66
XY pseudohermaphroditism, Wilms' tumor
with, 36:69

Y chromosome
centromeric heterochromatin DNA structure,
37:102
(Drosophila)
effect on hybrid viability, 36:172–36:173
mutations of, 36:144
heterochromatin gene expression
modification, 37:335–339
mitotic heterochromatin characteristics,
37:65–74
Drosophila hydei, 37:68–72
Drosophila melanogaster, 37:65–68
protein accumulation, 37:73–74
in situ hybridization, 37:66–72
Ste gene, 37:66–68
Yeast
artificial chromosomes
libraries, 35:166, 168
Neurospora crassa and, 29:12, 29:16
telomeres and, 30:198
transgenesis, 35:176–177
cell types, genetic control
α cells
mating competence, 27:34, 27:41
MATα1 role, 27:37–27:38,
27:42–27:46
α/α cells, 27:40–27:41, 27:48
sporulation, 27:34, 27:42

a cells
  mating competence, 27:34, 27:41
  MATα2 role, 27:40, 27:46–27:49
  haploid-specific genes and, 27:38–27:41,
    27:51–27:53
chromosomes
  mapping by new methods,
    23:120–23:121
DNA
  break repair studies, nonhomologous end-
    joining, 38:193–196, 38:201–203,
    38:205
  insertion sequences, 23:122–23:124
gene expression
  of E. coli, 23:127–23:132
  higher eukaryotic, 23:134–23:136
  human interferon, 23:137
  of Neurospora crassa, 23:132–23:134
  nif from Klebsiella pneumoniae, 23:130,
    23:132
gene molecular cloning, 23:90–23:93
genome complexity, 23:76
heat-shock response
  HSP70 as molecular chaperone, 28:261
  HSP classes, role in mutants,
    28:256–28:257
  at normal temperature
    in mutants, 28:254
    paromomycin-induced, 28:254
    ubiquitin role, 28:253
HSP, starvation-induced, 24:15–24:16
  sporulation and, 24:15–24:16
HSP-encoding genes
  HSE, binding to HSF, 28:245
  HSP70
    organization, 28:237–28:238
    self-regulation, 28:251
  HSP90, organization, 28:239–28:240
mating, pheromone-receptor binding and,
  27:34–27:37, 27:41
maturase functions, 24:270–24:271
meiosis model, chromosome segregation
  fidelity, 35:261–265
mitochondrial genes, split organization,
  24:246–24:247
Neurospora crassa and, 29:17–29:19, 29:22,
  29:39, 29:44, 29:49
plasmid combined with those from E. coli
  characteristics, 23:148–23:150
  replication in yeast and bacteria,
    23:138–23:139

PRTF, gene expression regulation,
  27:53–27:56
  MATα1 and, 27:42–27:46
  MATα2 and, 27:46–27:48
  MCM1-encoded, 27:49–27:50
ribosomes, 29:63–29:64, 29:103–29:104
  assembly, 29:93–29:98
  biosynthesis changes, 29:84–29:85
  nucleolus, 29:85–29:87
  proteins, 29:87–29:90
  small nucleolar RNAs, 29:90–29:91
  rDNA mutations, 29:98–29:99
  ribosomal protein genes, 29:71–29:74
  coordinate expression, 29:75–29:84
  ribosomal proteins, 29:64–29:71
  ribosomal RNA processing, 29:91–29:93
  mutations, 29:99–29:103
Saccharomyces cerevisiae
  DNA recombinational repair
    cross-link, 24:337
    in excision repair mutants, 24:338
    against heterogenous chemicals,
      24:337–24:338
  genetic crosses with S. douglasii,
    24:270–24:271
  maturase coded by intron b14, 24:271
Schizosaccharomyces pombe, DNA
  recombinational repair, 24:338
structural diversity of mtDNA, in
  Saccharomyces cerevisiae, 22:32–22:38
  in Schizosaccharomyces pombe, 22:38–22:39
  variation in size and organization,
    22:29–22:32
superoxide dismutases and, 30:252
  molecular genetics, 30:275–30:277,
    30:283–30:288
  physiology, 30:257, 30:259–30:261,
    30:263
  physiology of mutants, 30:288–30:289,
    30:293, 30:296–30:297,
    30:301–30:308
  structure, 30:264, 30:266,
    30:268–30:269, 30:272
telomeres and
  elongation, 30:208–30:209, 30:211,
    30:213–30:214
  formation, 30:228
  gene expression, 30:222, 30:224
  length, 30:217–30:218, 30:220–30:221
  replication, 30:204–30:205, 30:221
  structure, 30:190–30:193, 30:200–30:201

Yeast (continued)
transformants
donor DNA effect on, 23:101–23:103
methods for detection, 23:88–23:89,
23:94–23:95
transformation
biotechnology and, 23:125
frequency, 23:96
minichromosomes during, 23:101–23:102,
23:113–23:114
by plasmid carrying yeast and E. coli genes,
23:147, 23:152
recombination and, 23:124–23:125
Y elements, telomeres and, 30:190–30:193,
30:221, 30:224
yellow gene
oligogene bands, 39:137
telomeres and, 30:204
yellow loci
Drosophila transposable elements and, 29:281
P elements, 29:270–29:271,
29:273–29:274
retrotransposons, 29:241, 29:243–29:247,
29:257–29:258, 29:260
zeste in Drosophila melanogaster and,
29:305, 29:325–29:326
Yersinia enterocolitica, iron-regulated gene in,
36:190, 36:191
Yersinia pestis, iron-regulated gene in, 36:190,
36:191
Yolk protein, sex-specific gene expression
in fat body, Drosophila
regulation by dsx, 27:221–27:223
yp1-yp2 gene pair and, 27:225–27:227
in hermaphrodite intestine, C. elegans,
27:174, 27:178–27:179
regulation in various animals, 27:181
Yolk sac, visceral, human, TF and other protein
synthesis, 25:19

z¹, zeste in Drosophila melanogaster and,
29:311–29:312, 29:336–29:337
Zea mays, Mu elements of, see Mu elements of
Zea mays
Zebrafish, evolutionary genetics of fish and,
29:176
Zein, maize, developmental control by
regulatory genes, 24:108–24:110

Zerknüllt gene
Drosophila
expression pattern
cis-regulatory elements and,
27:302–27:303
dorsal-mediated repression,
27:295–27:297
initiation in wild-type and mutant
embryos, 27:293–27:294
in null mutations of zygotic ventralizing
genes
dpp_ mutants, 27:297–27:300
tsg_ and sog_ mutants,
27:300–27:301
regulation by maternal factors in
embryo, 27:287–27:297, see also
Dorsal-group genes
identification, 27:281, 27:317
mutant (zen_) phenotype, 27:281–27:285
cuticle preparation of embryo, 27:283,
27:284
during gastrulation, 27:282–27:283
during germ band elongation, 27:282,
27:283
protein product distribution,
27:285–27:287, 27:319
required for normal head development,
27:280
target genes, 27:303–27:304
amnioserosa and optic lobe
differentiation, 27:303
transcripts during embryogenesis, 27:285,
27:317–27:319
zen2 gene, structure, 27:316, 27:320
zeste in Drosophila melanogaster, 29:302, 29:343
chromatin packaging, 29:337–29:343
discovery, 29:303–29:305
DNA binding, 29:318–29:326
function, 29:326–29:330
molecular biology, 29:313–29:316
polytene chromosomes, 29:316–29:318
protein, 29:330–29:337
transposable elements and, 29:258, 29:260
transvection, 29:305–29:312
zhr mutation (Drosophila), chromosome linkage
of, 36:171–36:172
Zinc
bacterial resistance to, 36:221,
36:223–36:226
carbonic anhydrases and, 30:337

metallothionein gene transcription and,
25:25, 25:26
in proteins, 36:188
superoxide dismutases and, see Superoxide
dismutases
tolerance, expression in pollen, 26:15
MGS and, 26:19–26:20
Zinc-65, braconid wasp feeding effects,
25:161–25:162
Zinc-finger motif

in BRCA1 protein, 36:88
in WT1 protein, 36:69, 36:70
Zinc-finger transcription factors
during neural plate induction
Xenopus laevis, 31:65
zipper gene, 31:110
Ziti gene, protein synthesis theory, 38:118–119
Zone of polarizing activity, limb development
role, 38:16–18
z^{op}, *zeste* in *Drosophila melanogaster* and, 29:312

Contributor Index

Abbott, Ursula K., 20:217
Adrian, Gwendolyn S., 25:1
Ahuja, Mulkh R., 20:127
Amrein, Hubert, 27:189

Baum, James A., 21:347
Bell, C., 36:1
Bergson, Clare, 27:363
Bernstein, H., 24:323
Bieberich, Charles, 24:285
Bienz, Mariann, 24:31
Bond, Ursula, 24:1
Bowman, Barbara H., 25:1
Brookfield, John F.Y., 36:137
Brown, Melissa A., 36:46
Bryan, Ruth, 27:1

Campos-Ortega, Jose a., 27:403
Chadwick, Robin, 27:363
Chambers, Geoffrey K., 25:40
Chandlee, Joel M., 24:73
Chellym Jamel, 33:233
Clegg, Michael T., 23:235
Cullis, Christopher A., 28:73

Dahlback, Bjorn, 33:135
Danchin, Antoine, 24:223
Del Giudice, Luigi, 25:186
Dixon, Richard A., 28:165

Eisen, Howard J., 21:2
Eisenstark, A., 26:100
Endrizzi, J.E., 23:272
Epperson, Bryan K., 23:235

Gaul, Ulrike, 27:239
Glaser, David, 27:1
Golubovskaya, Inna N., 26:149
Grosch, Daniel S., 25:110

Gruss, Peter, 33:255
Guerinot, Mary Lou, 36:187
Gupta, P.K., 21:256

Haites, N., 36:1
Harrison, Maria J., 28:165
Hassan, Hosni, 26:65
Hassold, Terry J., 33:101
Hennig, Wolfgang, 23:179
Herrera-Estrella, Luis, 28:133
Hilliker, Arthur J., 28:43
Hjelmeland, Leonard M., 21:2
Hooykaas, P.J.J., 22:210
Hopf, F.A., 24:323
Hutter, Pierre, 36:157

Jack, Thomas, 27:363
Jackle, Herbert, 27:239
Jacobs, Patricia A., 33:101

Kafatos, F.C., 24:223
Kaufman, Thomas C., 27:309
Key, Joe L., 28:235
Kimpel, Janice A., 28:235
Kohel, R.J., 23:272
Kubli, Eric, 21:123
Kuziora, Michael A., 27:363

Lang, Matti A., 21:2
Lawrence, Christopher W., 21:173
Leach, Robin J., 33:63
Lecanidou, R., 24:223
Levine, Michael, 27:277
Lindahl, Lasse, 21:53
Lingappa, J.R., 24:223
Lucchesi, John C., 24:371

Malik, Vedpal Singh, 20:38
Manning, Jerry E., 24:371

Mariani, B.D., 24:223
McCarrey, John R., 20:217
McGinnis, Nadine, 27:363
McGinnis, William, 27:363
Meyer, Barbara J., 27:118
Michod, R.E., 24:323
Miller, D.R., 23:1
Mishra, N.C., 23:74
Mitsialis, S.A., 24:223
Monaco, Anthony P., 33:233
Morrish, Fionnuala, 24:431
Mulcahy, David, 26:1

Nagao, Ronald T., 28:235
Nebert, Daniel W., 21:2
Negishi, Masahiko, 21:2
Nguyen, H.T., 24:223
Nothiger, Rolf, 27:189

O'Connell, Peter, 33:63
Olsen, Gary, 27:209
Otaviano, Ercole, 26:1

Pelham, Hugh R., 24:31
Perkins, David D., 36:239
Petersen, Nancy S., 28:275
Petes, Thomas D., 33:1
Phillips, John P., 28:43
Phipps, J., 23:1
Priyadarshan, P.M., 21:256
Pukkila, Patricia J., 33:4

Regulski, Michael, 27:363
Roberts, Roland G., 33:177
Rodakis, G.C., 24:223
Romano, C., 24:223
Rushlow, Christine, 27:277
Russell, Elizabeth S., 20:358

Scandalios, John G., 21:347
Scandolios, John G., 28:2

Scandolis, John G., 24:73
Scangos, George, 24:285
Schafer, Alan J., 33:275
Schilperoort, R.A., 22:210
Schlesinger, Milton J., 24:1
Scholtissek, Christoph, 20:1
Sederoff, Ronald R., 22:2
Seeger, Mark A., 27:309
Sorenson, John C., 22:109
Shapiro, Lucille, 27:1
Simpson, June, 28:133
Snell, George D., 20:2916:149
Spiker, Steven, 22:145
Spoerel, N., 24:223
Sprague, Jr., George F., 27:33
Steinman-Zwicky, Monica, 27:189
Sternberg, Paul W., 27:63
Stuart, Edward T., 33:255

Thomashow, Michael F., 28:99
Triman, Kathleen L., 33:1
Tsitilou, S.G., 24:223
Turcotte, E.L., 23:272

Vasil, Indra K., 20:127, 24:431
Vasil, Vimla, 20:127, 24:431
Villeneuve, Anne W., 27:118

Westenberg, David J., 36:187
Wolf, Klaus, 25:186
Wright, Theodore R.F., 24:127

Yang, Funmei, 25:1
Yokota, Yoshifumi, 33:255

Zengel, Janice M., 21:53
Zhimulev, I.F., 37:1, 39:1